PRIVATE ACCESS
Private Art Collections in Germany, Austria and Switzerland

Skadi Heckmüller

Germany

Austria

Carinthia

Upper Austria

Vorarlberg

Switzerland

Aargau

Appenzell Innerrhoden

Basel-Landschaft

Basel-Stadt

Grisons

Lucerne

St. Gallen

Ticino

Valais

Zurich

Introduction

My books are the result of personal passion. As an enthusiastic backpacker, for several decades now, I've explored unusual sites of contemporary art. My travel fever has led me to the remotest corners of the world. But after many exploratory trips, I became aware of the treasures currently hidden in German-speaking countries. Here, countless passionate art lovers seek to show their collections to the public rather than keep them behind closed doors. This transpires either in private collection presentations or in public institutions that have been created in cooperation with private collectors. In addition to the classic museum landscape with its public, cultural, and educational mission, it is these unique places—with the various biographies and motivations of the collectors—that add impressive aspects to a visitor's encounter with art.

Due to my enthusiasm for unique collections, not mentioned in this book are corporate collections without a specific person of reference, purely monographic-oriented private museums, as well as exhibition rooms that are privately run but do not show their collections. Although I have tried to be comprehensive with my compilation, I could not cover all twentieth- and twenty-first-century art collections in Germany, Austria, and Switzerland. These will be the destinations of my next trips.

Apart from the collections in Berlin, the museums are often located outside urban centers. It was therefore important to me to make this museum guide as practical as possible: Navigation aids and additional tips should make the journey easier. I have only mentioned parking if the individual situation so requires. Information on how to get there by public transport was more important to me. Should some practical information no longer be up to date, I request your understanding, as some details often change at very short notice due to the private nature of the collections. For this reason, a quick look at the corresponding website before visiting is advisable.

I would like to thank all the collectors presented here. Without their commitment to individual artists but also to art and culture in general, the art scene in Germany, Austria, and Switzerland would not be as multifaceted and innovative as it is today. I greatly admire the art collectors for the courageous steps they have taken in making their collections accessible to the public. They enable deep insight into their innermost beings because this is reflected—in my opinion—in a collection that has been carefully compiled over several decades. They reap admiration for it, but must also face bureaucratic obstacles with patience and perseverance. I would also like to take this opportunity to thank the many employees who have often assisted me with good ideas.

I would also like to thank my parents, who have always encouraged my desire to travel and my interest in art, as well as my numerous friends who have also supported this project with heartfelt tips and assistance. Last but not least, I would like to thank Anna Kessel, Matthias Kliefoth, Charlotte Riggert, and Rebecca Wilton from DISTANZ Verlag as well as Uta Grosenick and Mathias Beyer. Without their outstanding commitment, such an extensive project could not have been realized.

I very much hope discovering and getting to know these unique places will bring you as much pleasure as it did to me. Enjoy diving into a beautiful and inspiring world of art!

Skadi Heckmüller

Germany

242
238
166
162
154
168
176
98–144
148
182
172
212
204
180, 208
230
216, 220
224
186, 190
194, 202
234
198
158
228
160
66
68
64
38
62
8
20
56
14
52
28, 40
34
94
16, 60
92
30
42
70, 82–90
78
26
12, 44
74
24
48

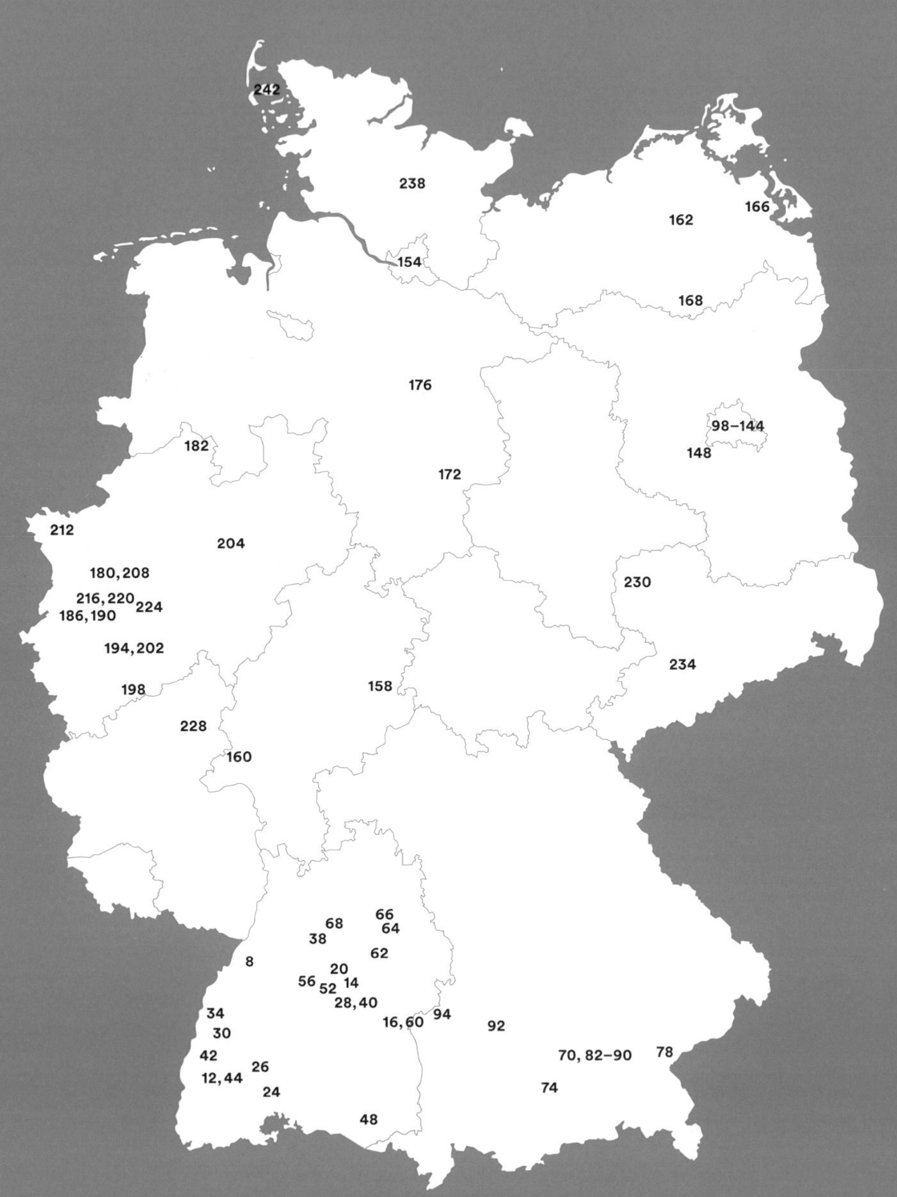

8
Museum Frieder Burda

One of the most internationally known private museums in Germany is located directly on the Lichtentaler Allee promenade, not far from Baden-Baden's old town. The original location for the private museum was the holiday resort of Mougins on the Côte d'Azur, loved by both Frieder Burda (1936–2019) and Picasso. Fortunately, French bureaucracy and an attractive offer from the city of Baden-Baden to provide a suitable piece of land led the collector to build the museum in his hometown.

New York architect Richard Meier rightly describes the white, twenty-million-euro building he designed as a "jewel in the park." Opened in 2004, the proportions of the Frieder Burda Museum respond to the adjacent neoclassical building, the Staatliche Kunsthalle Baden-Baden built by Hermann Billing—a glass bridge connects the buildings. The museum, flooded with daylight, is characterized by its light and openness. Visitors inside literally "float" through the floors and rooms, which can be flexibly designed in terms of size. The building, made of steel, concrete, and glass with countless views over the surrounding green areas, has already won several architectural awards.

The Frieder Burda Collection concentrates on classical modern and contemporary art. Today it comprises around one thousand works by selected artists. From the very beginning, the collector's interest in art has focused on his fascination with color and its emotional expression. He only bought what fascinated him and felt a close connection to every work of art in the collection. Frieder Burda's passion for collecting began in 1968 during his first visit to documenta with the purchase of a red slit painting by Lucio Fontana. In retrospect, Frieder Burda saw the purchase as a kind of protest against his father, the publisher Franz Burda, who, at the time, collected German Expressionists. In the course of his collecting career, however, Frieder Burda returned to the Expressionists himself because of his love of color. The collection contains numerous works by Max Beckmann, Ernst Ludwig Kirchner, Alexej von Jawlensky, Wilhelm Lehmbruck, and August Macke. Pablo Picasso's late work, highly esteemed by Burda, is also represented with an extensive

Museum Frieder Burda
Baden-Baden, Baden-Württemberg

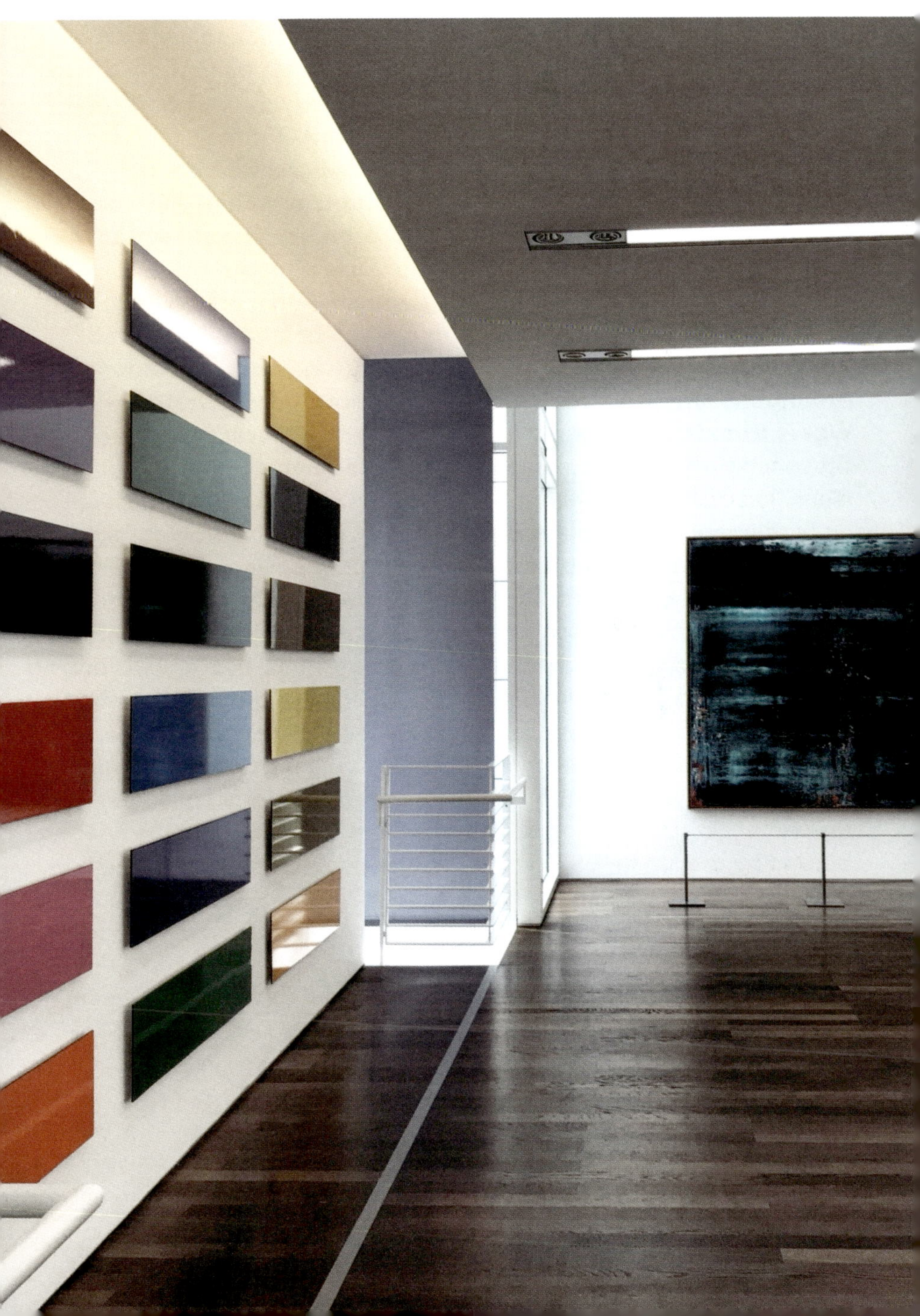

collection. The collection clearly focuses on the second half of the twentieth century and the latest developments in painting. American Abstract Expressionism is represented impressively with works by Jackson Pollock, Willem de Kooning, and Mark Rothko.

The contemporary German artists Georg Baselitz, Markus Lüpertz, Sigmar Polke, and Gerhard Richter, as well as Austrian Arnulf Rainer, are particularly well represented. The collection's interests of the last years were directed are directed towards the latest successful generation of painters, such as Neo Rauch, Matthias Weischer, and the 2019 deceased Eberhard Havekost. Across an area of approximately 1,040 m², three to four temporary exhibitions are organized annually by various guest curators. Works from the Frieder Burda Collection often form the core of the exhibitions and are supplemented by important international loans. In small cabinet exhibitions, masterpieces from the museum's collection are also displayed in a separate section, commenting on the themes of the major temporary exhibitions. Since 2018, James Turrell's room-light installation *Accretion Disk*, specially conceived for the museum, has been permanently shown in the basement.

Frieder Burda was a collector with passion, expertise, and vision. After the death of their father in 1986, he and his older brother Franz retired from the Burda publishing house and demonstrated their entrepreneurial skills in the further development of various company investments. To secure the long-term existence of the collection and make it accessible to the public permanently, he founded the Frieder Burda Foundation in 1998. The foundation financed the construction of the museum and also bears the costs of running the museum. Also an exhibition space and a forum for international contemporary art were opened in Berlin-Mitte at the end of 2016 under the direction of Frieder Burda's step-daughter Patricia Kamp with the name Museum Frieder Burda / Salon Berlin (see p. 106).

Museum Frieder Burda
Baden-Baden, Baden-Württemberg

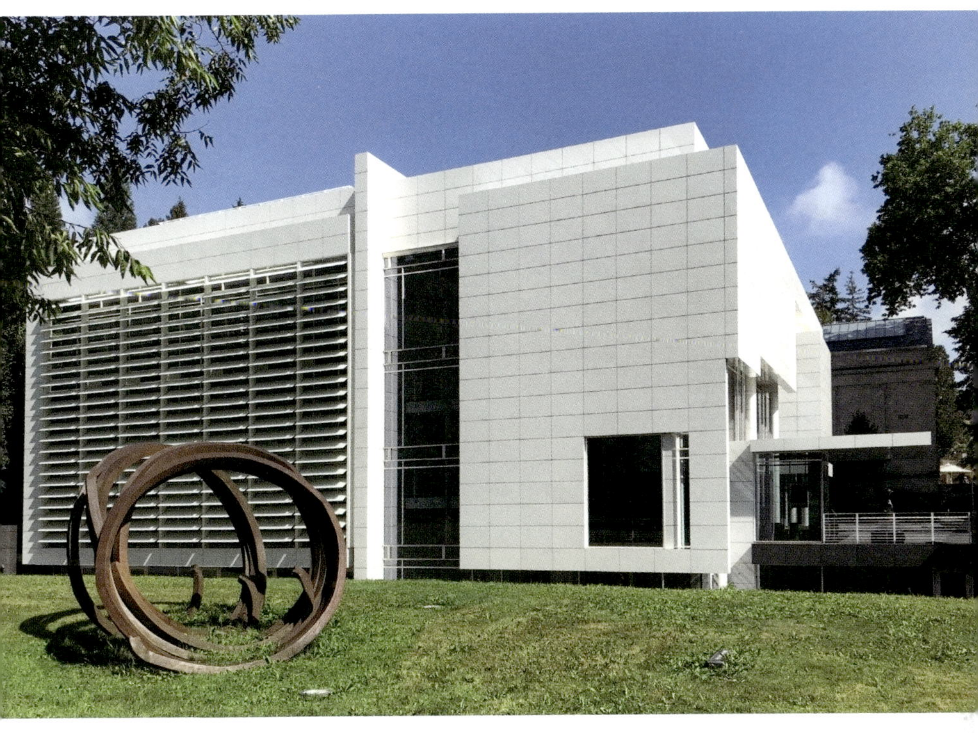

Museum Frieder Burda
Lichtentaler Allee 8b
D-76530 Baden-Baden
Phone: +49 7221 398980
office@museum-frieder-burda.de
museum-frieder-burda.de

Opening hours
Tue–Sun, 10 a.m.–6 p.m.
Public tours take place on Saturdays, Sundays, and public holidays at 11 a.m. and 3 p.m. (€4 plus admission).
There are numerous special lectures, film screenings, workshops, and concerts. The inviting Café Kunsthalle, whose interior is redesigned every few years to reflect important exhibitions, is located over the glass bridge.
The café and the museum's attractive concept store are open during exhibition hours.

Entrance fees
Adults / Reduced / Family / Students from age 9:
€14 / €11 / €27 / €5
Combined ticket with Staatliche Kunsthalle Baden-Baden:
€18 / €14
The Museum-PASS-Musées offers free admission.

Arrival by public transportation
The train station is located approx. 5 km outside the city center of Baden-Baden. Direct bus connections from the station to the Museum Frieder Burda stop are offered by lines 201 and 216.

Restaurant tips
On the opposite side of Lichtentaler Allee, you will find Rizzi – WineBistro & Restaurant with a lovely terrace in the sun (rizzi-baden-baden.de; Augustaplatz 1). At Rive Gauche, Middle Eastern and Mediterranean delicacies are served in a modern ambiance (rive-gauche.restaurant; Lichtentaler Allee 8). Gourmets can enjoy "cuisine du coeur" at Jardin de France. The star chef Stéphan Bernhard's French kitchen achieves the most unusual creations (lejardindefrance.de; Lichtentalerstr. 13; closed Sundays and Mondays).

Extra tip
The neighboring Staatliche Kunsthalle Baden-Baden shows mostly contemporary and Conceptual art. The Kunsthalle has beautiful premises and a nice café (kunsthalle-badenbaden.de).

12 Kunstraum Alexander Bürkle

In the middle of the industrial area Freiburg-Nord, the Kunstraum Alexander Bürkle is open to visitors. Opened in 2004 as a culturally sponsored project from the Alexander Bürkle Elektrogroßhandelsgruppe at the company's headquarters, the rooms have been operated by the Ege Art and Culture Foundation since 2015. The foundation's collection of contemporary art is presented in two to three internationally oriented exhibitions each year.

For thirty years, the focus of the collection has been on conceptual and self-reflexive painting. With more than 600 works from various creative periods, including by Marcia Hafif, Günter Umberg, and Dieter Villinger, it provides a representative overview of radical monochrome painting. In recent years, the collection's horizon has been extended to include works that open up to space; Adrian Schiess and Reto Boller incorporate the movement of the viewer into their work concepts. The same applies to the sculptures and installations of the most famous artists in this collection: Donald Judd and Dan Flavin, two leading representatives of Minimalism, and Richard Long, who strongly influenced Land Art.

In nine white cubes, group exhibitions generated from the collection and supplemented by loans are shown across almost 1,000 m^2. In addition to the presentation, mediation, and conservation of the collection, younger representatives of contemporary art are also regularly invited to develop projects related to the collection. Since 2007, the Alexander Bürkle Group has awarded the Alexander Bürkle Art Prize, endowed with 10,000 euros, to young artists every three years.

Kunstraum Alexander Bürkle
Freiburg, Baden-Württemberg

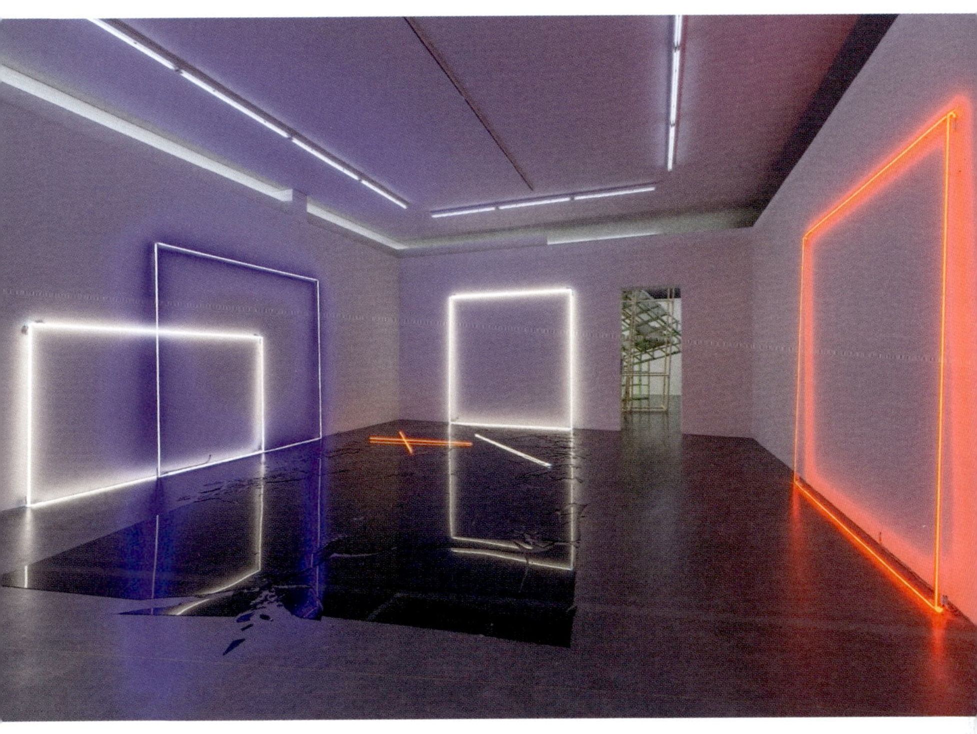

Kunstraum Alexander Bürkle
Robert-Bunsen-Str. 5
D-79108 Freiburg
Phone: +49 761 5106606
kunstraum@alexander-buerkle.de
kunstraum-alexander-buerkle.de

Opening hours

Tue–Fri as well as Sundays and holidays 11 a.m.–5 p.m. The Kunstraum remains closed during the Christmas holidays and installation periods. Free guided tours are regularly offered. There are lectures and discussions on current art topics, as well as specific observations of works.

Entrance fees

Free admission

Arrival by public transportation

From the bus stop at the main station, take bus 7200 in the direction of Emmendingen to the Stübeweg stop. The collection is located behind the Alexander Bürkle headquarters in a two-story building with corrugated iron cladding.

Restaurant tips

Unfortunately, there are no restaurants or cafés in the surrounding industrial area. For dinner, head towards the old town. In the simple Yepa Yepa, there are Mexican snacks (yepayepa.de; Merianstr. 30; closed on Sundays) and the Hotel & Restaurant Kreuzblume serves regional delicacies (kreuzblume-freiburg.de; Konviktstr. 31; closed on Mondays and Tuesdays). On the same street is the starred restaurant Wolfshöhle (wolfshoehle-freiburg.de; Konviktstr. 17W; closed on Sundays and Mondays).

Extra tips

A visit to Freiburg (you can also visit the Morat Institute for Art and Art Studies here on Saturdays, see p. 44) can be easily combined with a visit to the Frieder Burda Museum in Baden-Baden or a trip to the Black Forest to the KUNSTRAUM GRÄSSLIN in St. Georgen and the Villa Haiss Museum in Zell am Harmersbach (see pp. 8, 26, and 30).

14 Domnick Collection

On a hill at the edge of the Swabian Alb, nature, architecture, and art are united into a Gesamtkunstwerk. In the approximately 1,000 m² square buildings, designed in 1967 by the Stuttgart architect Paul Stohrer, the simple Bauhaus-style rooms are wholly subordinated to art. From the very beginning, this location served as a museum, event, residential, and living space at the same time.

The subtle individualist Ottomar Domnick (1907–1989) was a specialist in neurology and psychiatry, author, cellist, patron, filmmaker, and passionate art collector. Greta Domnick, who was an equal partner to her husband, managed the clinic with him as a specialist in neurology and psychiatry and shared his enthusiasm for art and culture. Encouraged and supported by their friendships with art historian Hans Hildebrandt and painter Willi Baumeister, the couple began building their collection in 1946. This is characterized by a focus on abstraction, with works by Willi Baumeister, Hans Hartung, and Fritz Winter forming a significant group. The purchase of the adjacent property in 1977 made it possible to create a sculpture park in which 32 works in bronze, iron, and steel—including sculptures by Joannis Avramidis, Alf Lechner, and Bernar Venet—can be seen today. After the death of Greta Domnick in 1991, the state of Baden-Württemberg received the 8,000 m² property, including all works of art and assets, on the condition that a charitable foundation be established. This is how a dependent foundation came to be created, owned, and sponsored by the state of Baden-Württemberg. Since 2017, the State Palaces and Gardens of Baden-Württemberg have managed the collection. In 1982, the property as a whole was placed under monument protection.

Both the house and the surrounding park were renovated in 2005. The new hanging brings the early painting to the fore more strongly than before, accompanied by African and New Guinean masks, which are part of the collection. However, due to the more museum-like hanging and some of the structural changes, part of the original charisma of this special place was lost. And so the new guardians of the collection are planning to restore the Domnick hanging in the not so distant future.

Domnick Collection
Nürtingen, Baden-Württemberg

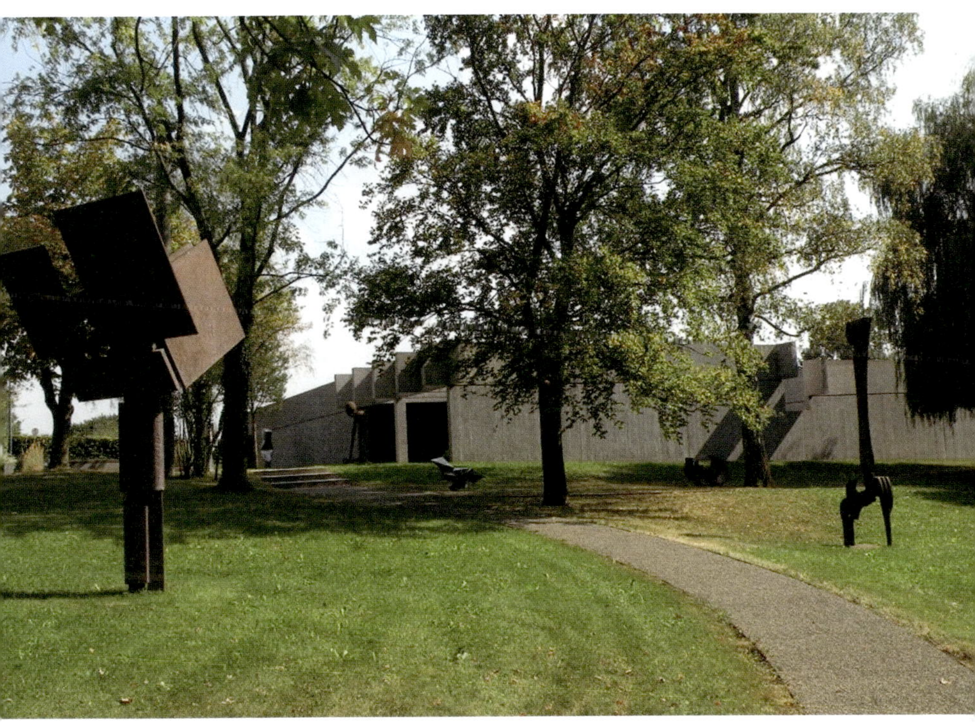

Domnick Collection
Domnick Foundation
Oberensinger Höhe 4
D-72622 Nürtingen
Phone: +49 7022 51414
stiftung@domnick.de
domnick.de

Opening hours
May to October, Sat, Sun, and public holidays, 2–6 p.m.; November to April, Sun, 2–5 p.m. Public tours take place every Sunday and during summer holidays at 2:30 p.m. and 4 p.m. Other dates can be organized by appointment. Special tours, concerts, and readings are held infrequently.

Entrance fees
Adults / Reduced:
€8 / €4

Arrival by public transportation
Take bus line 74 from Nürtingen ZOB (near the train station Nürtingen) or Stuttgart-Degerloch to the Hardt stop (see bwegt.de).

Parking
The car park is just behind the foundation building on the right-hand side.

Restaurant tips
In the old town of Nürtingen, around the Schloßberg, there are some interesting shops, bars, and the attractive Café Schümli (schuem.li; Schloßberg 3). At the Marktplatz, Belsers restaurant serves innovative award-winning cuisine (belsers.com; Brunnsteige 15).

Extra tips
Near the foundation, there are several organic farms and, in the summer, fields with flowers you can pick yourself. A short walk behind the car park offers a wonderful view of large parts of the Swabian Alb. A visit to the relatively nearby Museum Ritter in Waldenbuch in the morning is advised (see p. 52).

16 Sammlung FER Collection

Dr. rer. nat. Friedrich Erwin Rentschler (1932–2018), whose initials give the collection its name, passionately collected contemporary art for more than fifty years. Growing up in a family home interested in art and culture, as a teenager he laid the foundation for his future collecting activity. His father promised him a gift of his choice in recognition of his graduation. Swaying between a saintly Gothic figure and a motorcycle, he chose the statue of Saint Barbara. After the early death of his father, the pharmacist took over the family pharmaceutical factory in Laupheim and made it one of the world's leading pharmaceutical and biotechnology service companies. Unbridled curiosity and the desire to discover, as well as excellent analytical skills, were the recipe for success for Rentschler's entrepreneurial activities and also for the development of his collection. He died in 2018. During the early decades of his career, he concentrated on postwar Constructive Art, new trends of the 1960s such as Minimal Art, Concept Art, and Arte Povera, and the so-called young or wild painting of the 1980s. In principle, Friedrich E. Rentschler regarded art as visualized ideas, and so he was primarily interested in works that forced new perspectives and critically examined the art system. Friedrich E. Rentschler and his wife, Maria Schlumberger-Rentschler, who continues to actively supervise the collection, acted as founding partners of the ZKM | Zentrum für Kunst und Medien in Karlsruhe and as generous lenders worldwide. However, the idea of a semipublic presentation of their collection in rooms of their own was only born with the restructuring of the company in Laupheim and the loss of storage space for art. On the fourth floor of the Ulmer Stadtregal, a complex of buildings developed from the now-unused Iveco Magirus fire-brigade props factory, built in the 1950s, the collectors found ideal spaces for their depot and exhibition visions. In 2004, the city's own project development company PEG, together with Braunger Wörtz Architekten and Rapp Architekten, gutted the building down to its supporting structure and then filled it—like a

Sammlung FER Collection
Ulm, Baden-Württemberg

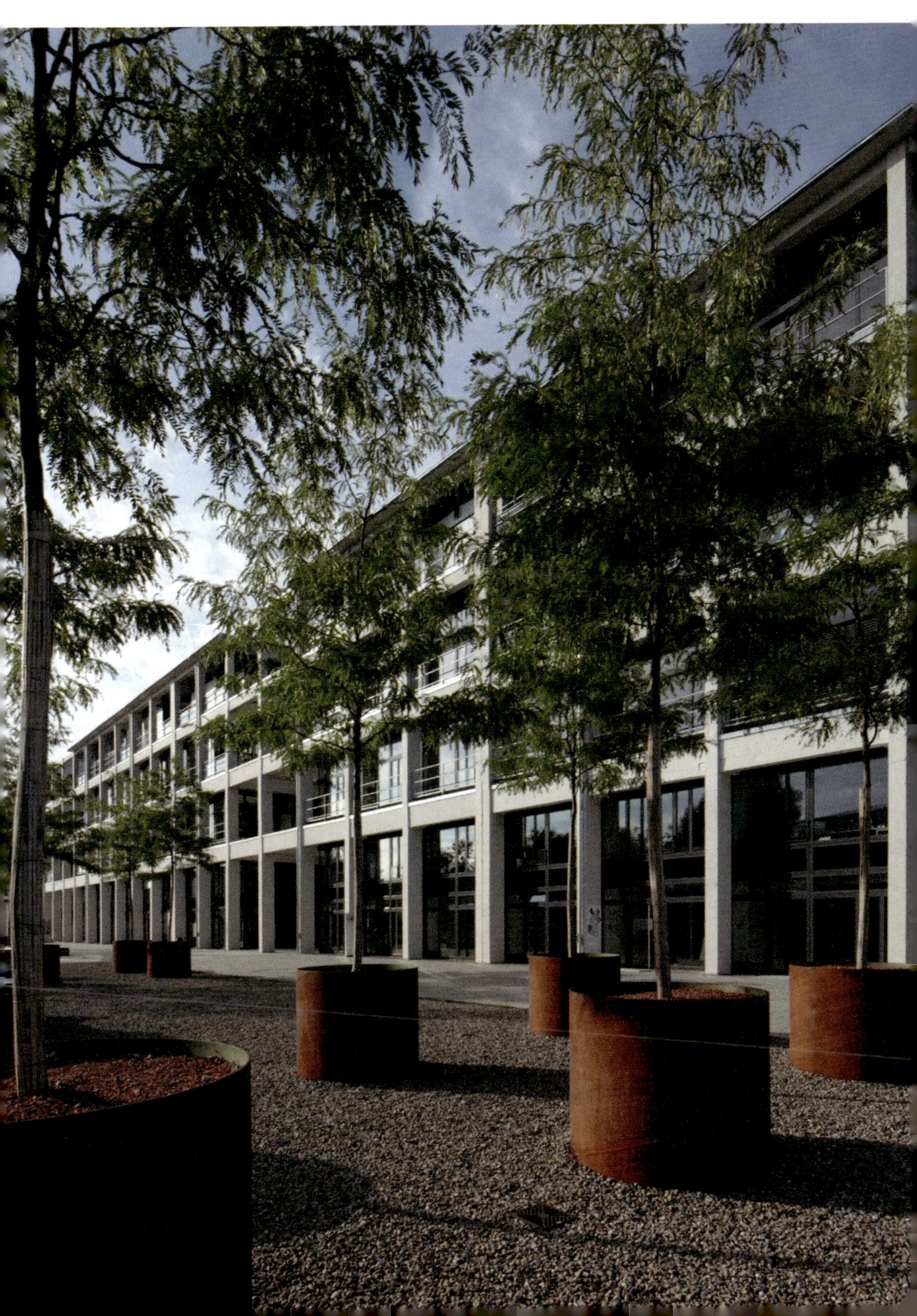

shelf—with new uses and new users. The mixture of life, living, and working, which received several awards during the construction phase, received the German Architecture Prize in 2011. The official opening of the Sammlung FER Collection took place in 2009. With its large areas and high windows, the building offers ideal conditions for the more expansive individual works and work complexes. The exhibition rooms with an area of approximately 700 m² are grouped around the art depot. Starting in the first room, one is led past an early key work by Joseph Kosuth, *One And Three Doors* (1965), several works by Elaine Sturtevant and Giovane che guarda Lorenzo Lotto, a work originally painted by Lorenzo Lotto in 1505 and photographically reproduced by Giulio Paolini in 1967. In the following rooms, there are works by Dan Flavin, Keith Haring, Carl Andre, Donald Judd, and Robert Barry as well as the first modular sculpture by Sol LeWitt. It continues with a room presenting the Fibonacci turtle by Mario Merz, a sculpture by Guiseppe Penone, and the *Letto con fuoco* (1968) by Jannis Kounellis. Furthermore, there are works on display by Sylvie Fleury, Liam Gillick, Isabell Heimerdinger, Mathieu Mercier, and Hans-Peter Feldmann.

Sammlung FER Collection
Ulm, Baden-Württemberg

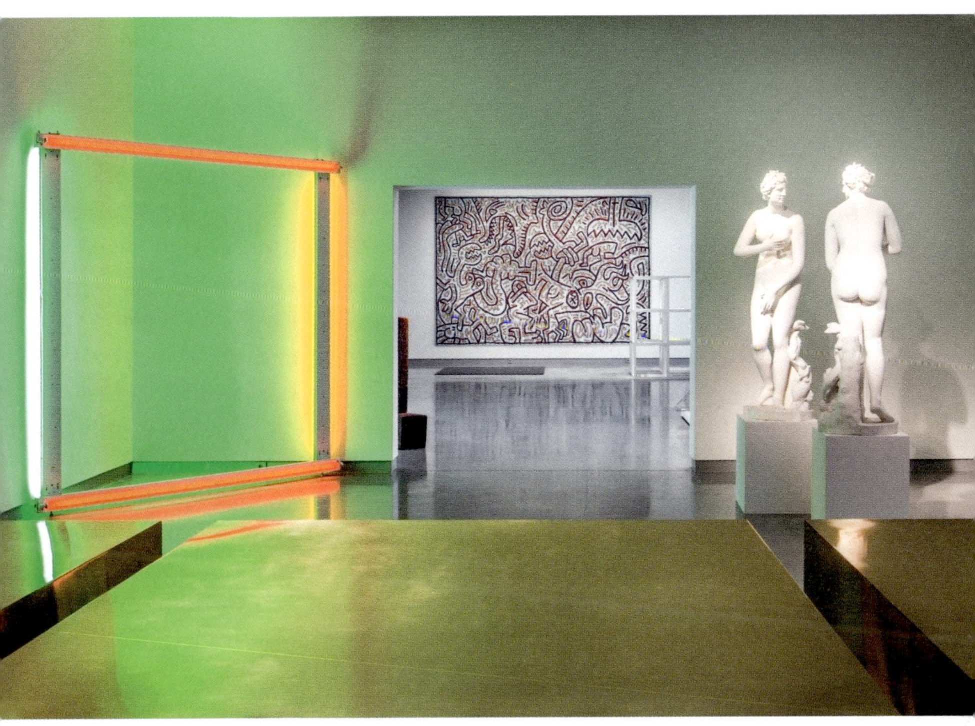

Sammlung FER Collection
Im Stadtregal
Magirus-Deutz-Str. 16
D-89077 Ulm
Phone: +49 731 3885478
maria.schlumberger@fer-collection.de
fer-collection.de

Opening hours
A visit, including a guided tour, is only possible after registration on the website.

Entrance fees
Adults: €15

Arrival by public transportation
From the main station take tram line 1 (direction Söflingen) to the Sonnenstraße stop. Walk about ten minutes through several small streets in northern direction to the collection. At entrance C (16/18) take the elevator in the atrium to the third floor.

Parking
A few parking spaces are available in front of the building. Drivers should enter "Einsteinstr. 60" as the navigation destination.

Restaurant tip
The Italian restaurant Boccaccio is located 3 km from the collection. (ristorante-boccaccio.de; Michelsbergstr. 8).

Extra tips
The Museum Villa Rot presents temporary exhibitions of contemporary art (villa-rot.de; Schlossweg 2, 88483 Burgrieden-Rot). Kunsthalle Weishaupt (see p. 60) and The Walther Collection in Neu-Ulm (see p. 94) can be visited at the same time.

20 Froehlich Collection

Many museum visitors have become familiar with the Froehlich Collection over the last few decades: the renowned works in the collection are often lent out for blockbuster exhibitions. Less well known, however, is the fact that art lovers in Leinfelden near Stuttgart at the headquarters of JW Froehlich Maschinenfabrik GmbH have been able to take part in guided tours and art talks in the middle of the collection's exhibition depot since 2009. Josef Wolfgang Froehlich and his wife Anna have been among the most important internationally active German art collectors since the 1980s. Having grown up in Bad Ischl, Austria, Josef Wolfgang Froehlich only became acquainted with art at a late age—as a young man, his interest was more in social and political topics. He studied automotive engineering and, as part of the Marshall Plan, went to the United States, where he also earned a degree in business administration. He then held various positions with North American companies. Based in Stuttgart since 1962, he founded a factory there that manufactures assembly and testing equipment as well as leak test equipment, especially for the automotive industry. Anna Froehlich, who had fled Hungary to Germany as a young woman, invested her first earnings in art but was likewise more interested in social issues. The couple developed their shared enthusiasm for art rather casually, initially by buying works to embellish their own four walls. But an encounter with Joseph Beuys in 1982 turned Anna and Josef Froehlich into veritable collectors and patrons of contemporary art virtually overnight. In a spectacular performance at documenta 7, Beuys melted a replica of Ivan the Terrible's golden tsar's crown into a rabbit. Fascinated by the transformation of the symbol of power into a sign of peace, Josef Froehlich acquired the *Friedenshase* (Peace Rabbit, 1982) and also donated to the financially endangered project *7000 Oaks* (1982). At the artist's request, the *Friedenshase* was installed as a permanent loan in a safe at the opening of James Stirling's new building for the Staatsgalerie in Stuttgart in 1984. In 1992, Josef Froehlich donated the work to the Staatsgalerie. The Beuys and Froehlich families friendship lasted until Beuys' death in 1986. In addition to other works by Joseph Beuys, artists such as

Froehlich Collection
Leinfelden-Echterdingen, Baden-Württemberg

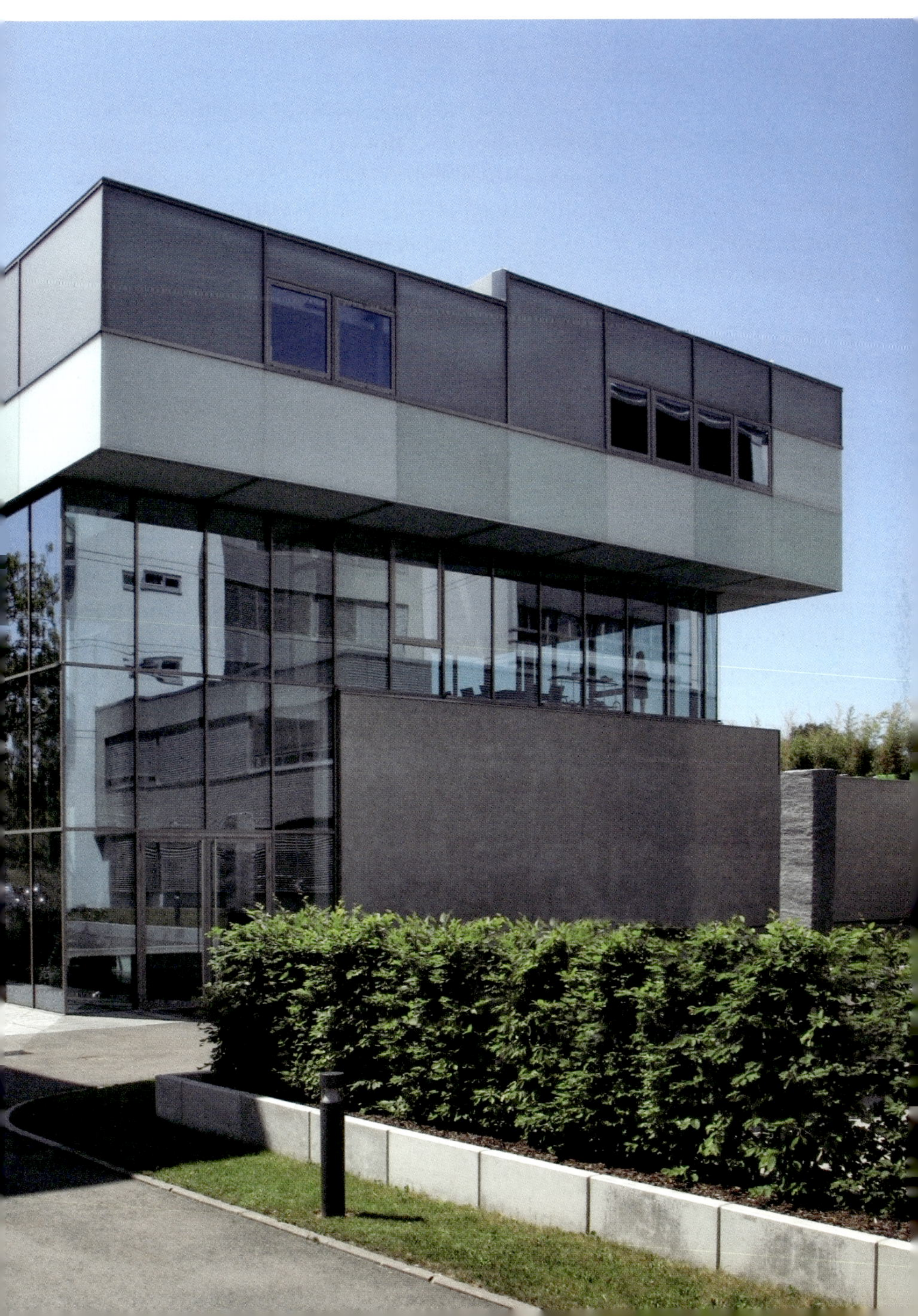

Georg Baselitz, Gerhard Richter, Anselm Kiefer, and others from the collector's generation are included, especially American minimalists such as Donald Judd, Dan Flavin, and Frank Stella, as well as Andy Warhol and Bruce Nauman. Following his friendship with Beuys, Josef Froehlich became interested in personally getting to know other artists and meeting them in their studios. He visited Georg Baselitz in Derneburg; Imi Knoebel in Düsseldorf; Walter De Maria, Jeff Koons, On Kawara, and Brice Marden in New York; Donald Judd in Texas; and Damien Hirst in England. He was also a familiar face at Andy Warhol's Factory. The collection, which has been supported by the Froehlich Foundation since 1995, comprises around three hundred works by about thirty artists. Jenny Holzer, Agnes Martin, Sigmar Polke, Brice Marden, and Zhan Wang must be added to the names already mentioned, and last but not least, twelve copper engravings by Albrecht Dürer belong to the collection, which is based on the collector couple's penchant for the medium of drawing. They are also interested in consistently depicting the work phases of individual artists. With the support of their daughter Anita Froehlich, the works are generously loaned to museums. In the exhibition space of the minimalist glass cube designed by Stuttgart architect Gabriele Glöckler, individual positions of the collection are presented in annual rotation. There are also permanently installed works such as a sled by Joseph Beuys under the stairs; above the entrance door, already prominently visible from the outside, a neon work by Bruce Nauman; and on the first floor in the conference room a man-sized, gilded bronze sculpture by Elmgreen & Dragset. In order to be able to show the complete collection, an extension onto south-bordering property will open in 2020.

Froehlich Collection
Leinfelden-Echterdingen, Baden-Württemberg

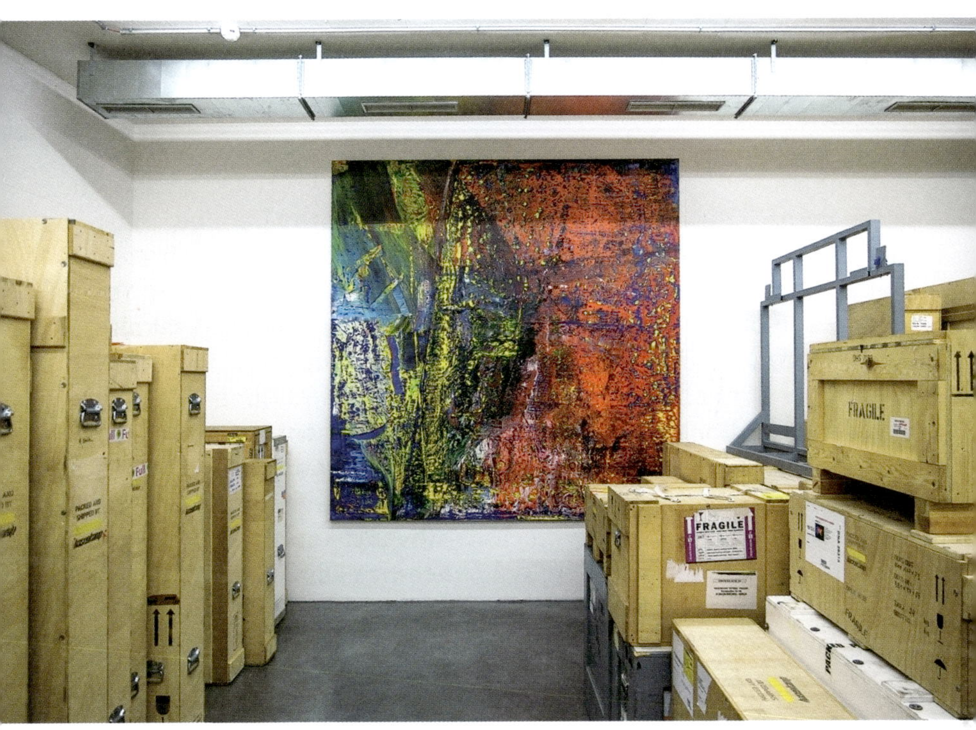

Froehlich Collection
Kohlhammerstr. 20
D-70771 Leinfelden-Echterdingen
Phone: +49 711 753944
info@sammlung-froehlich.de
sammlung-froehlich.de

Opening hours
Visits and participation in guided tours and other events are possible after registering in advance at info@sammlung-froehlich.de. Guided tours take place every second Monday of the month from 5:30–6:45 p.m., art talks with different guests every third Wednesday of the month at 7:30 p.m. There are occasional workshops on selected artists from the collection.

Entrance fees
Free admission

Arrival by public transportation
From Stuttgart's main station you can reach Leinfelden by taking the S3 (direction Flughafen/Messe), the S2 (direction Filderstadt), or the U5 in approx. 25 minutes. From there, it is less than a ten-minute walk to the collection.

Restaurant tips
For those traveling by car and in the mood for upscale cuisine, it is possible to enjoy French dishes from Germany's youngest star chef Erik Metzger in the nearby Waldenbuch restaurant at Gasthof Krone (krone-waldenbuch.de; Nürtinger Str. 14, 71111 Waldenbuch). French gourmet cuisine is also served in the Fässle restaurant in Degerloch. The lunch menu offered Tuesdays to Fridays is particularly worth recommending (restaurant-faessle.de; Löwenstr. 51, 70597 Stuttgart (Degerloch); easily accessible with the U5).

Extra tip
Contemporary art exhibitions are presented in the elaborately restored former factory villa of the Merkel family, situated picturesquely in a park (Villa Merkel, Galerien der Stadt Esslingen am Neckar; villa-merkel.de; Pulverwiesen 25, 73726 Esslingen am Neckar).

24 Fürstenberg Contemporary

In the immediate vicinity of the origin spring of the Danube, the Fürstlich Fürstenbergische Sammlungen show exhibits such as uniforms, miniatures, photographs, weapons, and trophies on the history and culture of the House of Fürstenberg as well as curiosities such as Napoleon's travel urinal and his silver dinner plate, and the forerunner of the bicycle across approximately 2,500 m². There are also art collections and natural history departments with stuffed animals from all over the world. The presentation dates back to 1868 when Prince Karl Egon III established the museum. With Fürstenberg Contemporary, Modernism made its way into the collections in 2011 as well. The project, founded by heirs Prince Christian and Princess Jeannette zu Fürstenberg, consists of a scholarship program at Heiligenberg Castle in Linzgau, annual temporary exhibitions, and the establishment of a collection. This can be seen in ten rooms on the top floor of the museum and—supplemented by a few older positions—is made up of works by the young artists of the funding program, including among others, Michael Sailstorfer, Kai Althoff, Gregor Schneider, Dirk Bell, Petrit Halilaj, Gusmão & Paiva, Andreas Slominski, and Juliette Blightman. On the same floor, in addition to rooms with paintings and sculptures from the sixteenth century in the reconstructed skylight hall and framed by plaster casts of Greek and Roman statues, there is the installation *This Room is my Castle of Quiet* by Julian Göthe from 2004. On the third floor, changing exhibitions of contemporary art are shown twice a year on approximately 150 m². The first exhibition is always dedicated to the presentation of the scholarship holders from the previous year, while the second exhibition shows artists of more considerable renown such as Paloma Varga Weisz or Victor Man.

Fürstenberg Contemporary
Donaueschingen, Baden-Württemberg

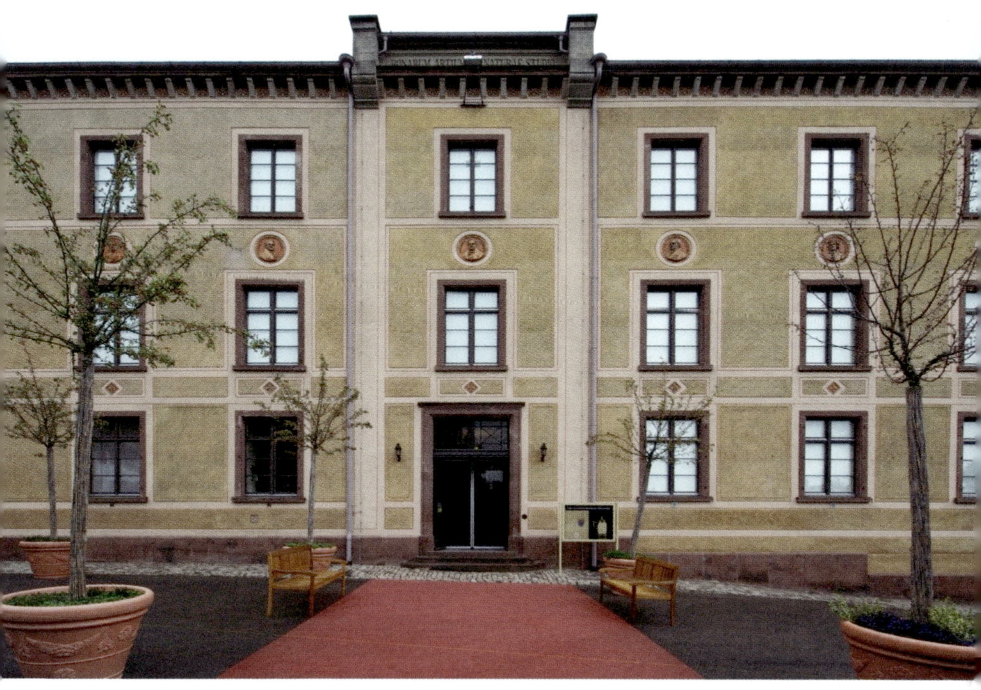

Fürstenberg Contemporary
Am Karlsplatz 7
D-78166 Donaueschingen
Phone: +49 771 229677563
info@fuerstenberg-zeitgenoessisch.com
fuerstenberg-zeitgenoessisch.com

Opening hours
April–November
Tue–Sat 10 a.m.–1 p.m./2–5 p.m.,
Sun/Holidays 10 a.m.–5 p.m.

Entrance fees
Adults / Reduced / Family ticket:
€5 / €4 / €10

Arrival by public transportation
The Fürstlich Fürstenbergische Sammlungen building can be reached in about ten minutes from the railway station via Josefstraße into the city center.

Parking
There are temporary but free parking spaces available in the city center.

Restaurant tips
Not far from the collections, typical Baden dishes are served in the Baaders Schützen Inn (schuetzen-donaueschingen.de; Josefstr. 2; closed Tuesday evenings and Wednesdays). Foodies can indulge themselves in the Die Burg restaurant (burg-aasen.de; Burgring 6, 78166 Donaueschingen-Aasen; closed on Mondays and Tuesdays), which has been awarded a Bib Gourmand in the Michelin Guide. The Flair Hotel Grüner Baum restaurant serves Black Forest cuisine (flairhotel-gruenerbaum.de/Restaurant; Friedrich-Ebert-Str. 59).

Extra tip
The former estate of sculptor Erich Hauser is an ensemble of art and architecture in a spacious park. A visit to the Erich Hauser Art Foundation is worthwhile, particularly with a tour through the sculpture park, workshop, housing pyramid, and the home, which includes an art collection (erichhauser.de; Saline 36, 78628 Rottweil; usually open on the last Sunday of the month during the summer months).
Donaueschingen is also home to the Museum Art.Plus (museum-art-plus.com; Museumsweg 1).
It is a good idea to visit the KUNSTRAUM GRÄSSLIN in St. Georgen after registering (see p. 26).

26 KUNSTRAUM GRÄSSLIN

Since the opening of the KUNSTRAUM GRÄSSLIN, a trip to St. Georgen in the Black Forest has been worthwhile: The Grässlin family has been personally committed to contemporary art here for many years. As early as the 1970s, the parents began to collect works of German Informel. Their four children have been collecting contemporary art since the early 1980s. Among others, groups of works by friend and artist Martin Kippenberger, Albert Oehlen, Günther Förg, Isa Genzken, Reinhard Mucha, Franz West, Cosima von Bonin, and Heimo Zobernig have been purchased.

The project “Räume für Kunst” (Spaces for Art) has existed since 1995, which uses up to twenty empty shops, factories, administrative buildings, but also the plenary hall of the town hall, the city garden, and the private houses of the family members as exhibition venues.

In the summer of 2006, the KUNSTRAUM GRÄSSLIN opened with an exhibition area of approximately 200 m². Built according to a design by Cologne architect Lukas Baumewerd, the elegant and functional ensemble consists of three independent structures: the exhibition hall, the art depot, and Kippys Restaurant. The opening was preceded in 2004 by the establishment of the Grässlin Foundation, which is responsible for exhibition operations.

Every two years, exhibitions of works from the collection are presented in the KUNSTRAUM GRÄSSLIN and the external rooms. Individual presentations alternate with thematic group exhibitions.

In 2010, the Grässlin family received the ART COLOGNE prize for their outstanding services in the field of art education.

KUNSTRAUM GRÄSSLIN
St. Georgen, Baden-Württemberg

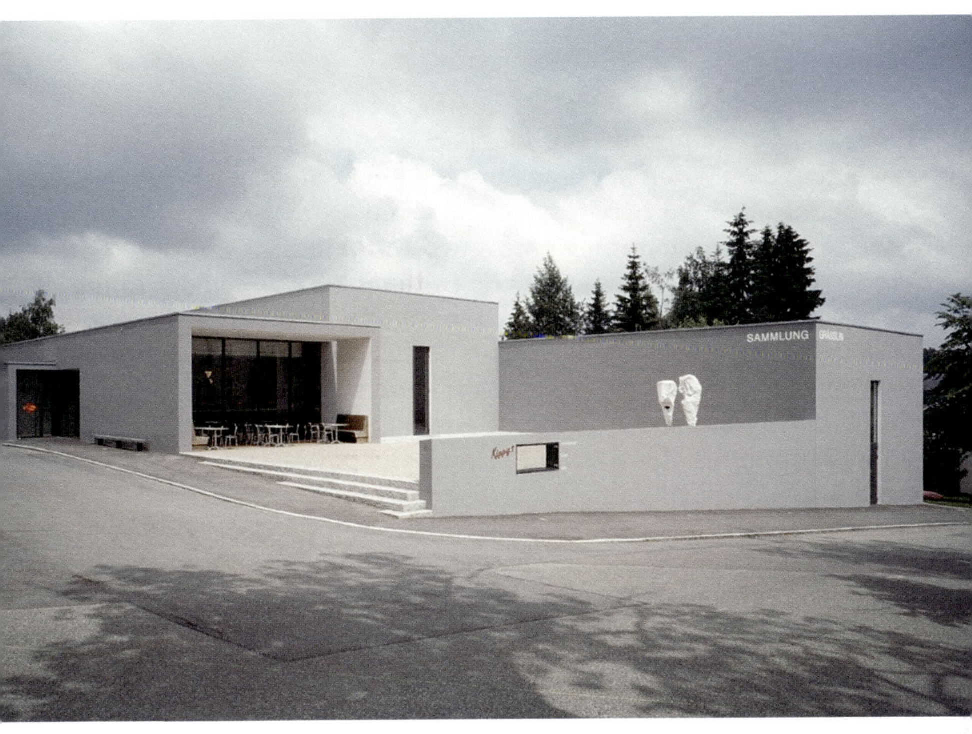

KUNSTRAUM GRÄSSLIN
Museumstr. 2
D-78112 St. Georgen
Phone: +49 7724 9161805
info@sammlung-graesslin.eu
sammlung-graesslin.eu

Opening hours
The Grässlin Collection has no regular opening hours. A detailed three- to four-hour guided tour through the art rooms and the KUNSTRAUM GRÄSSLIN must be arranged by telephone or email. Some of the external rooms for art can also be visited without a guided tour. A tour plan can be found on the website. Several times a year, "Kultursonntage" (Cultural Sundays) offer a combined breakfast in Kippys Restaurant followed by a guided tour (€18). The dates can be found on the website.

Entrance fees including tour
Adults / Reduced / Children up to 12 years and holders of the museum pass: €10 / €8 / free

Arrival by public transportation
St. Georgen is easily accessible with Deutsche Bahn RE and IC trains. KUNSTRAUM GRÄSSLIN is a good ten minutes walk from the train station.
It is also possible to take the bus lines 50, 51, and 7265 to Schwarzes Tor.

Restaurant tips
Part of the collection complex is the versatile, modern Kippys Restaurant. The region has several top hotels with excellent restaurants. The exclusive fine-dining restaurant Oscars in the Parkhotel Adler, which opened in 2018, is worth mentioning (parkhoteladler.de; Adlerplatz 3, 79856 Hinterzarten). Nearby, you will find the best ice cream in the region in the simple ice cream café Rino (rino-eiscafe.de; Oberndorferstr.18, 78713 Schramberg).

Extra tips
The Froschmuseum (Frog Museum) by Sabine Grässlin in an empty shop in St. Georgen is home to a collection of more than 3,000 works that will make you smile (sammlung-graesslin.eu/sammlung-graesslin/informationen/froschmuseum; Am Markt 3; visit by appointment). You can also take a detour to visit the Museum Villa Haiss in Zell am Harmersbach (see p. 30).

28 Gratianusstiftung

At the edge of Reutlingen's city center, art lovers will find a special gem. The Gratianusstiftung, founded in 2001, is based on years of collecting by painter Gabriele Straub and her husband, industrial engineer Hanns-Gerhard Rösch.

Since 2004, in a carefully renovated Werkbund villa from 1909, works from the collection ranging from the Paleolithic era to the present day have been presented on two floors.

The idea of showing and traversing a history of development is deliberately avoided in this small World Art museum. The collection is not based on chronological order or on the clarification of a specific cultural reference but offers a dialogue of content across time and cultural boundaries. Leading aspects of the collection include color as a substance of painting and seeing, as well as the sense for the quality of the material in the works of art. The quite different artifacts are shown together in such a way that relationships are made visible. Works of Classical Modernism by Alexej von Jawlensky, Pierre Bonnard, and Henri Matisse; and works by Giorgio Morandi, Josef Albers, and Antonio Calderara can be found in the collection as well as, for example, a Khmer goddess (twelfth to thirteenth century) or a bi-disk from China (fourth to third century BC). In particular, contemporary art is represented by an extensive collection of works dedicated to color by Raimer Jochims and Gabriele Straub. In addition, there are works by contemporary artists on the subject of color by Ingrid Floss, Erwin Gross, José Heerkens, Günther Holder, Michael Kolod, Rainer Nepita, Thomas Schlereth, Jerry Zeniuk, and others. Every six years a new hanging with works from the collection takes place.

Gratianusstiftung
Reutlingen, Baden-Württemberg

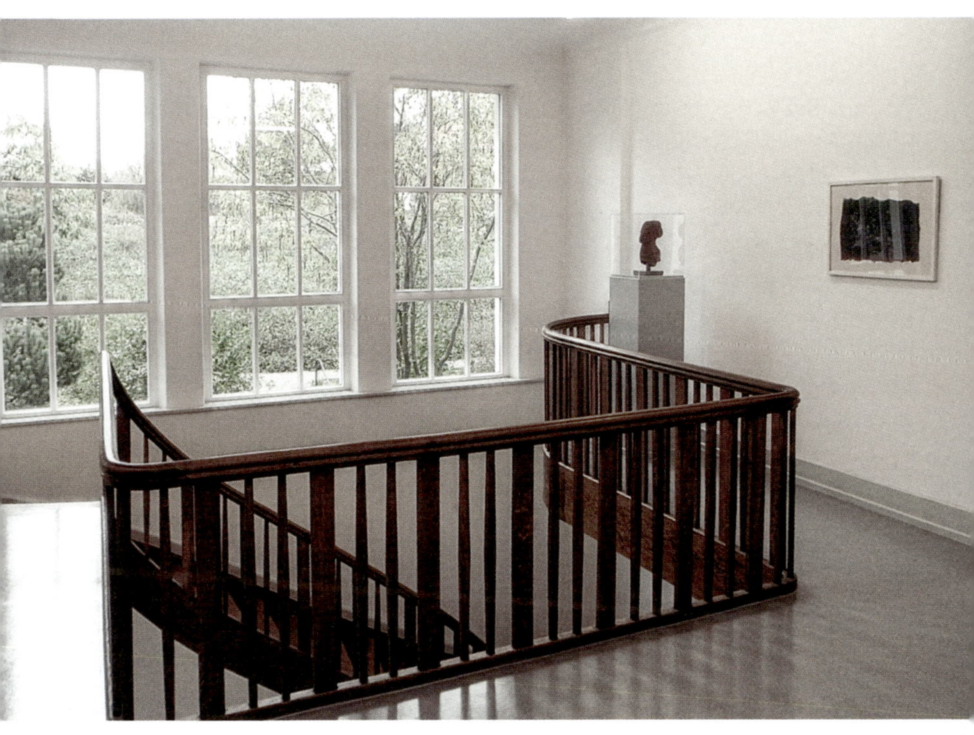

Gratianusstiftung
Gratianusstr. 11
D-72766 Reutlingen
Phone: +49 7121 490177
info@gratianusstiftung.de
gratianusstiftung.de

Opening hours
Mon 2–6 p.m., every first Thursday of the month 6–8 p.m. (except on public holidays), and by appointment.

Entrance fees
Free admission

By public transportation
The foundation can be reached on foot in approx. fifteen minutes from the railway station.

Parking
It is possible to park at the corner of Panoramastraße/Gratianusstraße and walk up Gratianusstraße on the right.

Restaurant tips
There are nice cafés all around the Marienkirche. The modern Waldcafé Restaurant, which offers a beautiful landscape view, is just 7 km away. (waldcafe-pfullingen.de; Vor dem Urselberg 1, 72793 Pfullingen).

Extra tip
If you register, you may be able to visit the Stiftung für konkrete Kunst on the same day (see p. 40).

30 Museum Villa Haiss

The idyllic little town of Zell am Harmersbach at the foot of the Black Forest is known not only for its tradition but, since 1997, also for its modern and contemporary art. This is thanks to gallery owner Walter Bischoff and his wife, Dr. Uta Klein-Bischoff, former co-owner of the Zeller natural-medicine company Dr. Gustav Klein. Raised in Stuttgart, Walter Bischoff studied architecture there and then founded his own office, which he ran for over twenty years. He moved to Zell am Harmersbach in the early 1980s for his second wife. Active as a collector and painter since the 1950s, he became a gallery owner in Chicago in 1983. From this time in the United States, a former apricot farm in San José has remained with him, which has been used as an artist's studio since 1987 as part of the Bischoff scholarship. In 1988, he returned to Germany and opened a gallery in Stuttgart in 1989, later another one in Berlin. He gave up both in 2010 and has since concentrated on the location in the Black Forest. Parallel to their gallery activities, in the mid-1990s the Bischoff couple acquired the former factory villa built in the first half of the nineteenth century by the family and owners of the Zell-based ceramic firm Haiss. The extensive reconstruction of the historically listed ruin—the entrance door, the staircase, and the old floorboards were preserved—took almost two years before the building could be opened in 1997 as a museum for the collection and as a gallery for temporary exhibitions. On the ground floor, three to four special exhibitions are presented as part of a commercial gallery operation. On the two upper floors, approximately 120 works from the collection of circa one thousand works are permanently shown on about 500 m². A few of the works are on loan from other collectors. All in all, this results in a representative cross section of international painting, photography, and sculpture from 1945 onwards. Bischoff's primary interest is in Informel art and early GDR artists, which Bischoff collected and supported long before the Wall fell. The museum exhibits works by artists such as ARMAN, Stephan Balkenhol, Emil Schuhmacher, Joseph Beuys, Georg Baselitz, Jürgen Brodwolf, Christo and Jeanne-Claude, Jim Dine, Hans Hartung, Damien Hirst, Yves Klein, Heinz Mack, A.R. Penck, Otto

Museum Villa Haiss
Zell am Harmersbach, Baden-Württemberg

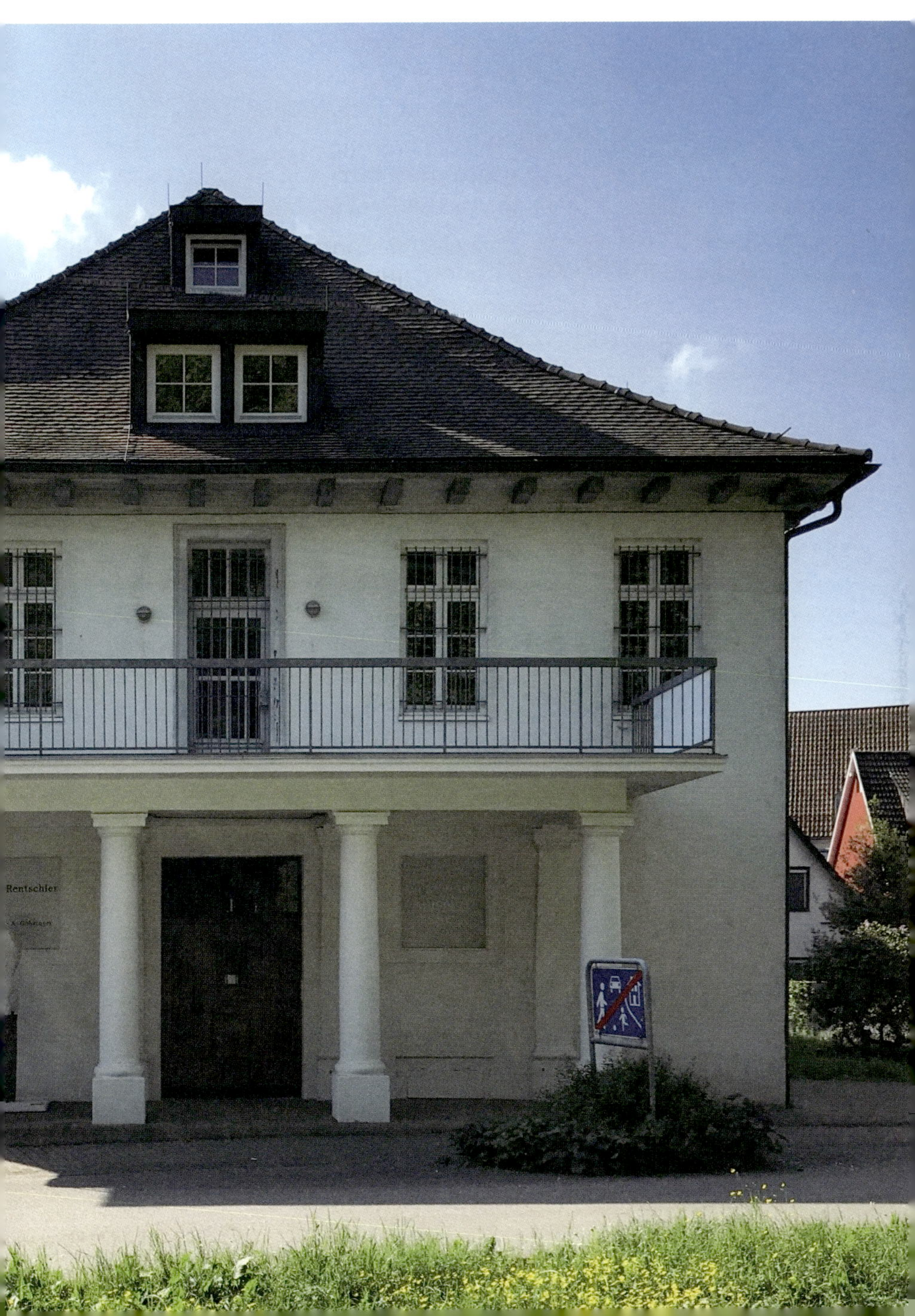

Piene, Mel Ramos, Gerhard Richter, Thomas Ruff, Cindy Sherman, K.R.H. Sonderborg, Daniel Spoerri, Fred Thieler, Günther Uecker, Andy Warhol, Fritz Winter, HP Zimmer, Olaf Nicolai, and Tadashi Kawamata.

Since 1999, in a small sculpture park opposite the museum entrance, five original sections of the Berlin Wall with colorful graffiti have been standing next to a bronze sculpture by the artist Lluís Cera. These are the only five connected parts of the Berlin Wall outside Berlin. Half of this extraordinary piece of contemporary history was financed by Bischoff and the other half by local entrepreneurs and private individuals.

Museum Villa Haiss
Am Park 1
D-77736 Zell am Harmersbach
Phone: +49 7835 549987
museum-villa-haiss@artbischoff.com
artbischoff.com/museum-villa-haiss

Opening hours
Thu–Sun 2–6 p.m.

Entrance fees
Adults / Reduced / Adolescents up to age 18: €5 / €3 / €2
Free admission for Museum-Pass-Musée holders

Arrival by public transportation
Via Biberach (Baden) you can reach Zell am Harmersbach with the Südwestdeutsche Verkehrs-AG trains. From the train station, it is a five-minute walk to the museum.

Parking
Parking is available next to the building.

Restaurant tips
Cake and breakfast are available at Café Alt-Zell (Hauptstr. 9). Cake fans will get their money's worth at the StadtCafé am Storchengraben (Grabenstr. / Kanzleiplatz). Close to the museum, the Bräukeller Restaurant serves local and international dishes (braeukeller-zell.de; Fabrikstr. 8). In the Hotel-Gasthof Kleebad guests are spoiled with Baden cuisine (kleebad.de; Jahnstr. 8).

Extra tips
Walter Bischoff is a founding member of the Zeller Kunstwege project, in which sculptures are presented from May to October at various locations throughout the town every even-numbered year (zeller-kunstwege.de). The main street is home to the ASAS Art Center, a 480 m² exhibition space for Chinese art. The project is a result of the cooperation between the Museum Villa Haiss and the Chinese art institute ASAS – Asian Scene Art Space, in Beijing (artbischoff.com/ausstellungen/asas/; Hauptstr. 40; usually open by appointment only).

Museum Villa Haiss
Zell am Harmersbach, Baden-Württemberg

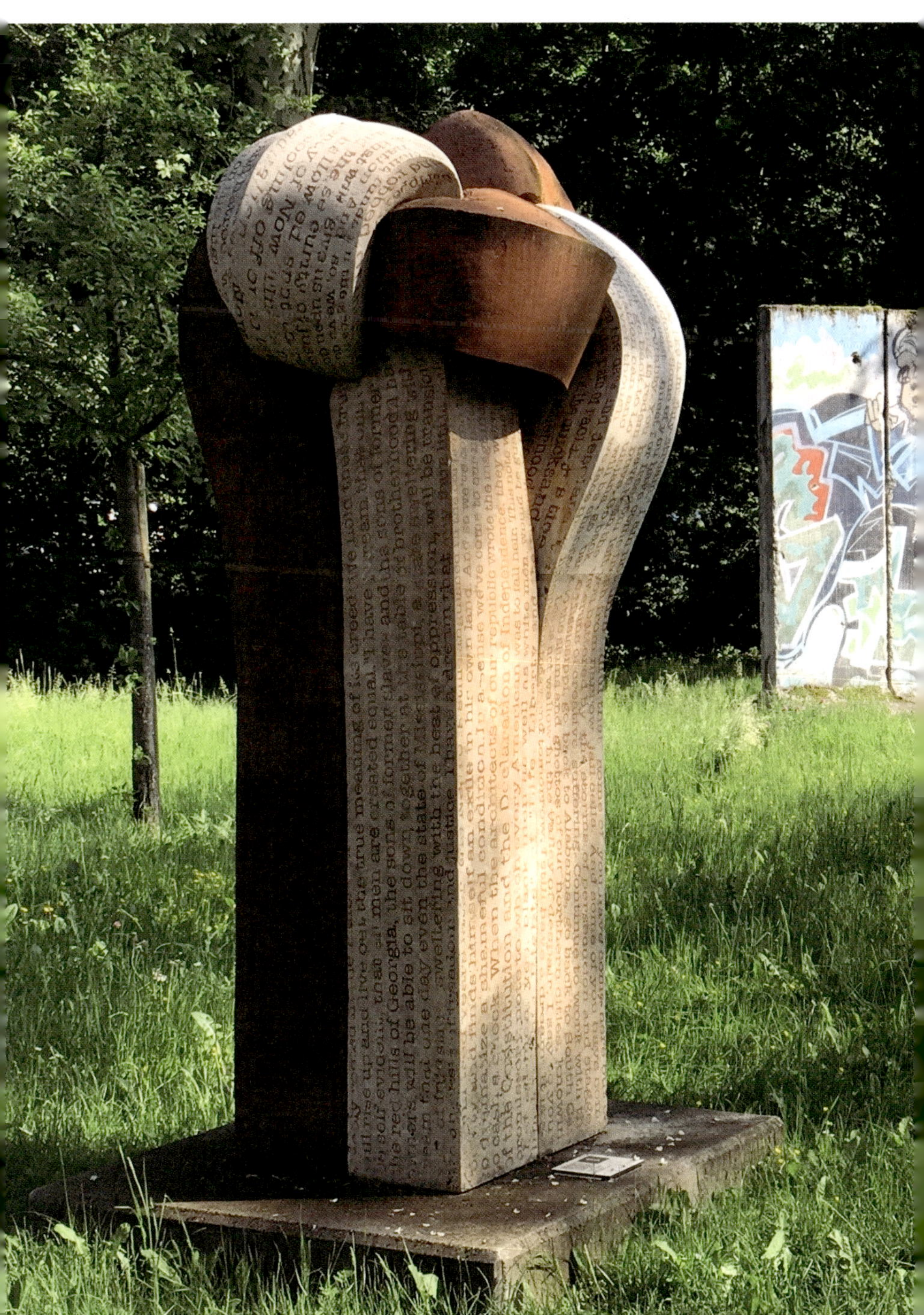

34 Museum für Aktuelle Kunst / Sammlung Hurrle Durbach

In 2010, the Museum für aktuelle Kunst I Sammlung Hurrle Durbach was opened by the entrepreneur, art, and sports patron Rüdiger Hurrle in the well-known wine village on the top floor of a former mother-child clinic, which now houses the Hotel Vier Jahreszeiten. His passion for collecting began in the 1960s and was mainly directed towards German art after 1945 and its predecessors at the beginning of the 1920s, as well as art from the Upper Rhine region, including Switzerland and Alsace. With significant works of the 1950s and 1960s German Informel, by artists from the groups Quadriga (Karl Otto Götz), ZEN 49 (Rupprecht Geiger), and the Salon des Réalités Nouvelles, which was created at the same time in France, Lyrical Abstraction forms a focal point of his collection. Hurrle also paid great attention to the figuration of the 1920s and after the Second World War by artists such as Paul Kleinschmidt, Karl Hubbuch, Otto Laible, and Karl Hofer. In addition, the beginnings of a New Figuration are illustrated not only by works by Willi Baumeister and HAP Grieshaber, but also by the next younger generation such as Horst Antes, Herbert Kitzel, and Heinz Schanz. The collector is also interested in relationships between artists, friendships, conflicts, teacher-pupil relationships, and groupings. The Hurrle Durbach collection, which comprises over 2000 works, includes numerous works by the CoBrA group (Asger Jorn), Munich's SPUR group (HP Zimmer), and the outstanding Gruppe Kriegfried (Harald Häuser), which emerged from Per Kirkeby's class at the Karlsruhe Academy. The collection also includes many artists from the former GDR, Leipzig, and New Leipzig schools, such as Werner Tübke, Arno Rink, Michael Triegel, and A. R. Penck. Until the 1990s, the collection concentrated on traditional mediums, including painting,

Museum für Aktuelle Kunst / Sammlung Hurrle Durbach
Durbach, Baden-Württemberg

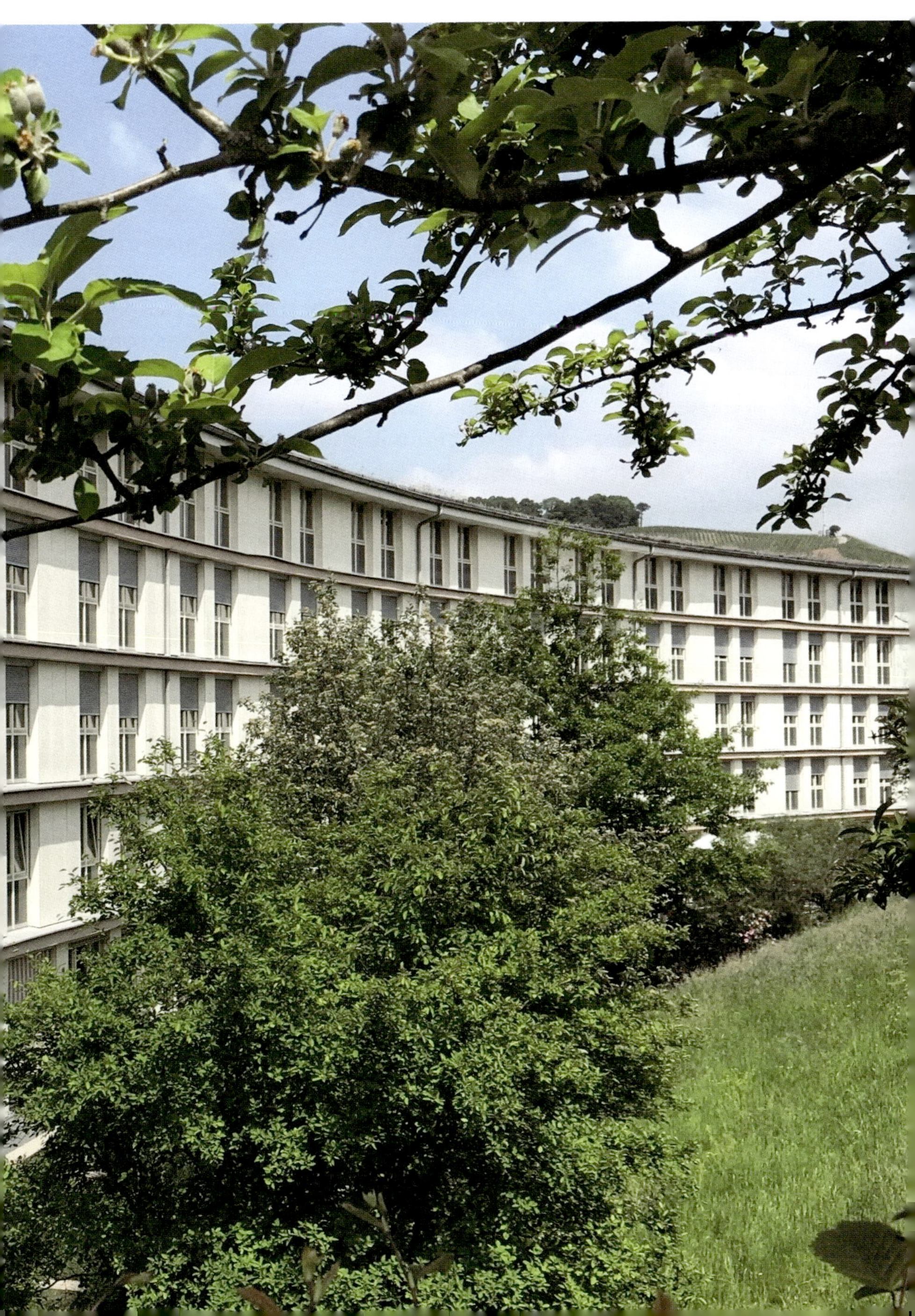

sculpture, and graphic art, but the spectrum in contemporary art has also expanded to include photography and new media. The diverse networks of relationships are illustrated in the extensive permanent exhibition of the collection, in which individual positions and areas are only sporadically changed. One room permanently presents a timeline of the development of abstract art from 1913 to 1960 with a focus on southwest German art. Large special exhibitions, which change three times a year, are curated according to the collection, and whose works come primarily from the collection, present individual art movements or positions. More contemporary works are shown in the smaller exhibition series *Profile* in der Kunst am Oberrhein. These exhibitions, which also change three times a year, take place in the last four rooms of the approximately 1,700 m^2 exhibition space and are usually on loan from two artists.

Rüdiger Hurrle has been professionally and privately committed to the region for decades. In 1973, he founded Hurrle GmbH, the first clinic in Blieskastel and Durbach. In the 1990s, he had the mother-child clinic built, which now houses the museum. In 1998, the Hurrle Group was one of the largest private hospital companies in Germany and was taken over by MediClin AG at the end of the 1990s. However, the building in Durbach, in which the museum was first opened and shortly afterward the hotel, remained the property of Rüdiger Hurrle.

Museum für Aktuelle Kunst / Sammlung Hurrle Durbach
Durbach, Baden-Württemberg

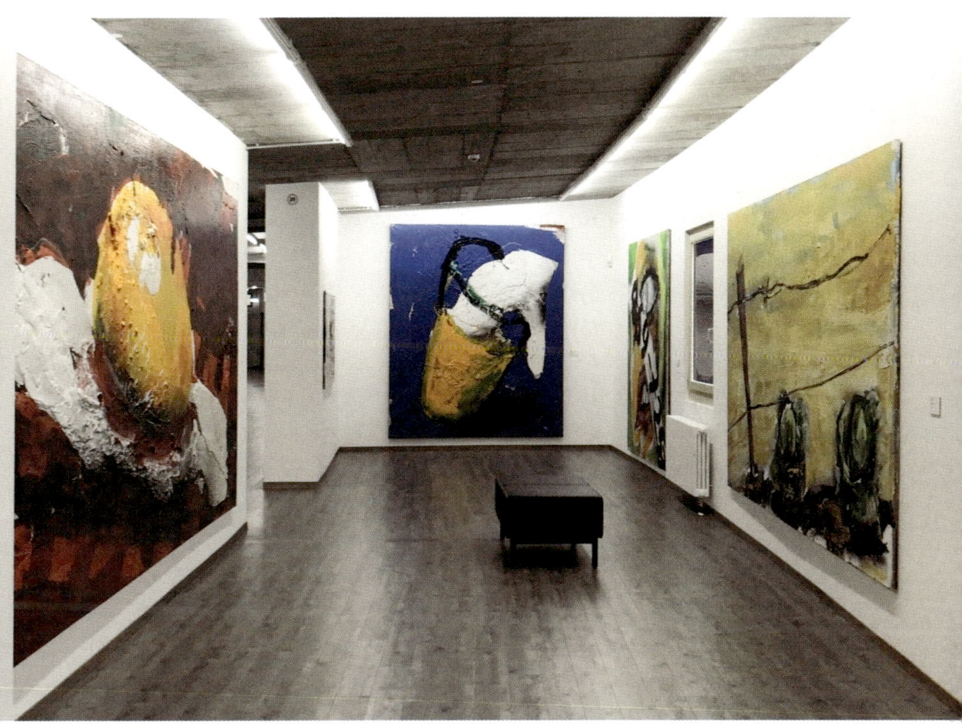

Museum für aktuelle Kunst / Sammlung Hurrle Durbach
Vier Jahreszeiten Durbach GmbH & Co. KG
Almstr. 49
D-77770 Durbach
Phone: +49 781 93201402
mail@museum-hurrle.de
museum-hurrle.de

Opening hours
Wed–Fri 2–6 p.m., Sat/Sun and holidays 11 a.m.–6 p.m.; except on December 24 and 31 and during brief installation phases
There are public guided tours (usually on the fourth Sunday of the month at 3 p.m.; €4 plus admission). There is also a small café and shop in the museum.

Entrance fees
Collection and current exhibition: Adults / Reduced / Family ticket / Youth (ages 10–18) / Museum-Pass-Musées holders: €7 / €5 / €15 / €3 / free

Arrival by public transportation
From the Offenburg railway station, take bus line 7142 to the Haus Vier Jahreszeiten stop.

Parking
There is a free underground parking garage in the building.

Restaurant tips
Gourmets will be delighted by the unusual menus of star chef André Tienelt in the restaurant Wilder Ritter (ritter-durbach.de; Tal 1). Alsatian cuisine is offered at Micheliwitsch (Lindenplatz 4; +49 781 42118; reservations required). In the wine shops of the Graf Wolff Metternich winery (weingut-metternich.de; Grol 4; closed Sundays) and the Durbacher Winzergenossenschaft (durbacher.de/durbacher/winzergenossenschaft) it is possible to degust the region's wines.

Extra tips
The Durbach sculpture park, founded by Rüdiger Hurrle, is just a few meters from Vier Jahreszeiten. If the weather is fine, a short hike through the vineyards to Staufenberg Castle is worthwhile (schloss-staufenberg.de; Schloss Staufenberg). The tri-national region on the Upper Rhine has a high density of private and state art museums. The Art Valley website (art-valley.eu) offers a good overview. For drivers, it is a good idea to combine a visit to the Museum für Aktuelle Kunst with a detour to the Museum Villa Haiss (see p. 30).

38 KUNSTWERK / Sammlung Klein

The KUNSTWERK museum, designed by Pforzheimer architect Folker Rockel, was opened in 2007 across a factory complex in the industrial area of the rural Eberdingen-Nussdorf. He created a light-filled exhibition hall of approximately 1,000 m², achieving dynamic and generous spaces through its open construction while offering refined presentation possibilities.

For over thirty years, entrepreneur Peter W. Klein and his wife, Alison, have have been collecting contemporary art from all over the world. What began with the purchase of artworks for the offices of the Rectus company led, many years later, to his own museum, which presents parts of the collection in the form of two temporary exhibitions per year, now consisting of around 2,100 works. The focus of their ongoing collecting is on painting (Alex Katz, Anselm Kiefer, Karin Kneffel, Sean Scully, and Corinne Wasmuht, for example), photography (by Gregory Crewdson, Elger Esser, Rosemary Laing, Tracey Moffatt, and Shirin Neshat, among others) and contemporary indigenous art. In addition to the well-known names, the collection also features artists who are not yet established. In their purchases, Alison and Peter W. Klein do not follow the trends of the art market, but rely on their intuition.

The couple is also committed to the children and young people of the region and organize educational programs. By establishing the Alison und Peter W. Klein Stiftung, the aim is not only to secure the long-term future of the exhibition forum, but also to promote the cultural, social, educational, and sporting interests of the community.

KUNSTWERK / Sammlung Klein
Eberdingen-Nussdorf, Baden-Württemberg

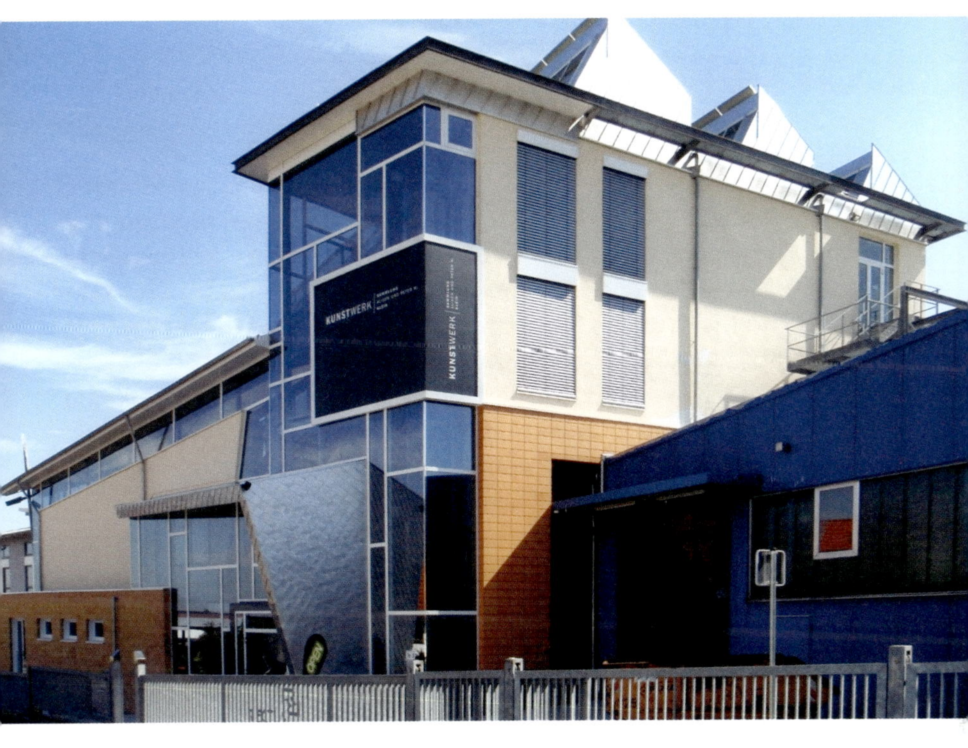

KUNSTWERK / Sammlung Klein
Siemensstr. 40
D-71735 Eberdingen-Nussdorf
Phone: +49 7042 3769566
kunstwerk@sammlung-klein.de
sammlung-klein.de

Opening hours
Wed–Fri, Sun 11 a.m.–5 p.m.
For new hangings, the museum is closed twice a year for about two weeks.
Public guided tours take place with the head of the collection every first Wednesday of the month at 3 p.m. and every first and third Sunday at 11:30 a.m. and 3 p.m. (€5). Workshops for children can be organized on request. The CafeK is located in the adjacent building.

Entrance fees
Free admission

Arrival by public transportation
Starting in Stuttgart, you reach Nussdorf by bus 592 (direction Eberdingen) from Vaihingen or by bus 502 (direction Riet) from Feuerbach.
From the bus stop Nussdorf-Martinstraße it is a five-minute walk to the museum.

Restaurant tips
You can enjoy local Swabian cuisine in the friendly Ratsstüble Nussdorf (ratsstueble-nussdorf.de; Martinstr. 14). Gourmets should stop at Herrenküferei, which offers regional and classic dishes with the changing seasons (herrenkueferei.de; Marktplatz 2, 71706 Markgröningen; closed Sundays and Mondays) or try the ambitious star cuisine of Steffen Ruggaber in the Hotel Restaurant Lamm Rosswag (lamm-rosswag.de; Rathausstr. 4, 71665 Vaihingen / Enz-Rosswag; closed Sun–Tue).

Extra tip
A few kilometers away you will find the Celtic Museum Hochdorf / Enz, which, in addition to a permanent exhibition and an opportunity to explore Celtic burial mounds, also regularly offers special exhibitions on technologies of archaeological research (keltenmuseum.de; Keltenstr. 2, 71735 Eberdingen-Hochdorf).

40 Stiftung für konkrete Kunst

Since 1989, the Stiftung für konkrete Kunst has been located in a building designed by Philipp Jakob Manz for the former Christian Wandel metal sheet and machine factory, which is now owned by the city. The tasks of the foundation, headed by Manfred Wandel and Dr. Gabriele Kübler, include collecting, archiving, and exhibiting Concrete, Constructive, and Conceptual art. In addition to the art collection, whose spectrum ranges from Russian Constructivism to Bauhaus and De Stijl to contemporary positions, the foundation's holdings also include several artists' archives. The Wandel Collection also continues to be available as working material and for research purposes. Through loans, the foundation is in constant contact with museums and art institutions in Germany and abroad.

To ensure that the "Wandel-Halls" remain a long-term top-class center for concrete art, the collection of the renowned Stiftung für konkrete Kunst was donated to the city of Reutlingen on July 1, 2017. It is continuing the foundation's exhibition work with a new department at the Kunstmuseum Reutlingen in the approximately 1,000 m² third floor of former foundation. The collection comprises 99 works with a total of around 1,100 individual parts of prominent artists (such as Bernard Aubertin, François Morellet, Aurelie Nemours, and Anton Stankowski). Manfred Wandel generously supplemented the new municipal collection with a donation of additional works from his private collection. Visitors can look forward to highly considered exhibitions in rooms that were reopened in 2018 and are now administered by the city.

But the Stiftung für konkrete Kunst is also continuing a reduced version of its work in its rooms in the attic and ground floor on approximately 2,000 m². Its ongoing exhibition activities are based on the private collections in the care of the foundation, above all the Collection Manfred Wandel and numerous artists' depots. The foundation also retains the four large archives (Archiv Stiftung für konkrete Kunst, Archiv Manfred Wandel, Archiv Max Bense [since

1988], and Archiv Bernard Aubertin [since 1997]). Furthermore, three to four exhibitions are presented annually in the beautiful rooms. Within the framework of thematic shows, the foundation does not present the works in isolation, but in a comprehensive cultural, scientific, and social context. At monographic exhibitions, too, visitors have an opportunity to discover modern works of art in combination with Russian icons or Bauhaus furniture from a new perspective. Through intensive mediation work—each visitor is accompanied personally—connections are developed and perceptions sensitized. In addition to retrospectives of Jesús Rafael Soto, François Morellet, Gottfried Honegger, and Bernard Aubertin, the foundation also presents young artists who are not yet established, thus offering them an important forum. And so Reutlingen is an unexpected mecca for Concrete art.

Stiftung für konkrete Kunst
Eberhardstr. 14
D-72764 Reutlingen
Phone: +49 7121 370328
skk.kuebler@t-online.de
gk@stiftungkonkretekunst.de
stiftungkonkretekunst.de

Opening hours
By appointment; closed in August. All visitors will be accompanied individually through the exhibition. Free admission

Kunstmuseum Reutlingen / Konkret
Eberhardstr. 14
D-72764 Reutlingen
Phone: +49 7121 3032322
kunstmusem@reutlingen.de/konkret
reutlingen.de/konkret

Opening hours
Tue–Sat 11 a.m.–5 p.m., Thu 11 a.m.–7 p.m., Sun/holidays, 11 a.m.–6 p.m.
Free admission

Arrival by public transportation
The foundation and the museum are located almost next to Reutlingen main station. Walk along platform 1 and follow the red brick Deutsche Post building. Cross the parking lot in front of this building, to arrive at Eberhardstraße, turn right here. After approx. 50 m, you reach the five-story "Wandel-Halls." The foundation can be reached via a white glass door, on which the bell is also located. Take the elevator to the top floor.

Parking
The foundation has a private car park. From here, it is possible to access the entrance in the white glass wall of the building.

Extra tips
The Kunstmuseum Reutlingen / Galerie (a branch of the Kunstmuseum Reutlingen, which is dedicated entirely to contemporary art; reutlingen.de/galerie) and the very active Kunstverein Reutlingen (kunstverein-reutlingen.de) are in the same building as the Stiftung für konkrete Kunst and the Kunstmuseum Reutlingen / Konkret. A visit to the Stiftung für konkrete Kunst and the Kunstmuseum can be combined with a visit to the nearby Gratianusstiftung (see p. 28).

42
messmer foundation / kunsthalle messmer

Jürgen A. Messmer discovered his love of art in the 1970s while studying industrial engineering in Munich. In 1978, he succeeded in acquiring large parts of the estate of André Evard (1876–1972), a pioneering painter of Swiss Modernism and a university friend of Le Corbusier's. Through André Evard, Messmer found his way to Concrete Constructive art, which today forms the core of his collection, which focuses on Representational and Abstract works of Classical Modernism and Contemporary art. In 2005, in memory of his deceased daughter, Jürgen A. Messmer founded the messmer foundation. The kunsthalle messmer opened in 2009 with the foundation as the sponsor in the front part of the historic brewery building in Riegel am Kaiserstuhl. The Riegeler brewery used the listed brewery castle directly on the banks of the Elz River from 1876 until its closure in 2003. The conversion into residential and work rooms as well as service and commercial areas took place after the acquisition by the Freiburg's Gisinger Group in 2006.

Up to three temporary exhibitions of Classical Modern and Contemporary art are held annually in the large museum room. The collection includes works by Bernard Aubertin, Günter Fruhtrunk, Heinz Mack, Max Bill, Sonia Delaunay, Raoul Dufy, Otto Freundlich, François Morellet, Bridget Riley, Günther Uecker, Victor Vasarely, and Carlos Cruz-Diez. A sculpture garden also contains numerous sculptures from the collection by Gottfried Honegger, Gerhard Frömel, Gerald Baschek, and since 2018, Otmar Alt. In keeping with the foundation's purpose, the kunsthalle messmer invites entries for the André Evard Prize for Concrete Constructive art, endowed with 10,000 euros, approximately every three years.

messmer foundation / kunsthalle messmer
Riegel am Kaiserstuhl, Baden-Württemberg

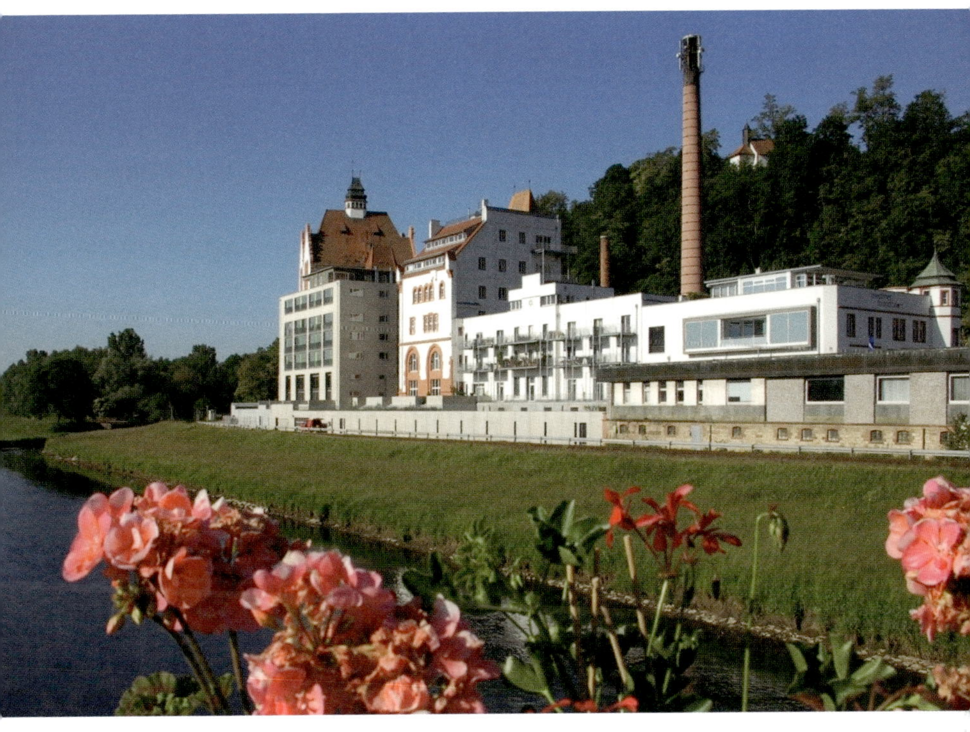

messmer foundation/ kunsthalle messmer
Grossherzog-Leopold-Platz 1
D-79359 Riegel am Kaiserstuhl
Phone: +49 7642 9201620
info@kunsthallemessmer.de
kunsthallemessmer.de

Opening hours
Tue–Sun 10 a.m.–5 p.m. as well as most holidays, except during brief exhibition installation periods. Public guided tours take place on Sundays at 2:30 p.m. (€5 plus admission) and every second Wednesday of the month at 5 p.m. (included in admission price). Registration by telephone or email is requested.
Café Evard is located in the Kunsthalle and is open during exhibition hours.

Entrance fees
Adults / Reduced / Students over age 9 / Family ticket: €12.50 / €10.50 / €5 / €25

Free admission for holders of the Museum-Pass-Musée

Arrival by public transportation
From Offenburg and Freiburg, take the Deutsche Bahn to the Riegel-Malterdingen station. From there, walk 1.2 km to the Kunsthalle or take the hourly SWEG bus lines 102/103 to Rathaus Riegel or the Kaiserstuhlbahn (SWEG) via Gottenheim to the Riegel Ort stop.

Parking
Free parking is available in front of the building at Grossherzog-Leopold-Platz.

Restaurant tips
On Fridays between 6 and 8 p.m. locals meet at the Römerbräu Riegel private brewery not far from kunsthalle messmer (roemerbraeu.de). In the neighboring town of Endingen is Merkles Restaurant, Pfarrwirtschaft & Garten (merkles-restaurant.de; Hauptstr. 2, 79346 Endingen am Kaiserstuhl), and the Restaurant zum Alten Wagenmann (Hauptstr. 38).

Extra tip
Both Colmar and Freiburg can be reached from here by car in less than an hour.

44 Morat-Institut für Kunst und Kunstwissenschaft

Standing in Freiburg's industrial area in front of the Morat-Institut's commerce complex, one wouldn't suspect what art treasures are hidden behind the walls. The Morats are personally committed to the preservation and promotion of art and, in addition to the collection, maintain a comprehensive specialist library with more than 100,000 books.

The patron and author Franz Armin Morat's interest in art began in his youth and he started collecting in 1953. He came from an industrial family in the Black Forest and initially financed his passion with his father's fortune. Later, he ensured the survival of the foundation by skillfully rearranging the collection, although it was difficult for him to part with his works.

Founded in 1983, the Institut is a foundation under civil law with the purpose of building up, maintaining, and presenting art collections, as well as promoting research in the arts. The Morat family had previously been active for fifteen years with the Heine-Stiftung für Philosophie und Kritische Wissenschaft. This foundation's assets were transferred to the Morat-Institut in 1984, with the focus shifting from literature to fine arts. At the same time, Franz Armin Morat transferred substantial parts of the collection to the Institut.

Today, the Morat-Institut's collections consist of approximately 20,000 works. Many of them are works on paper, but there are also some five hundred large-format paintings in the collection. The collection of prints includes engravings and etchings by Albrecht Dürer, Martin Schongauer, and Rembrandt. Classical Modernism is represented with works by Max Beckmann, James Ensor, Alberto Giacometti, and Giorgio Morandi. The main focus, however, is clearly on Francisco de Goya, whose complete oeuvre is present with 260 sheets in first editions and early prints. There is also a collection of Renaissance medals, including all of Pisanello's major

Morat-Institut für Kunst und Kunstwissenschaft
Freiburg, Baden-Württemberg

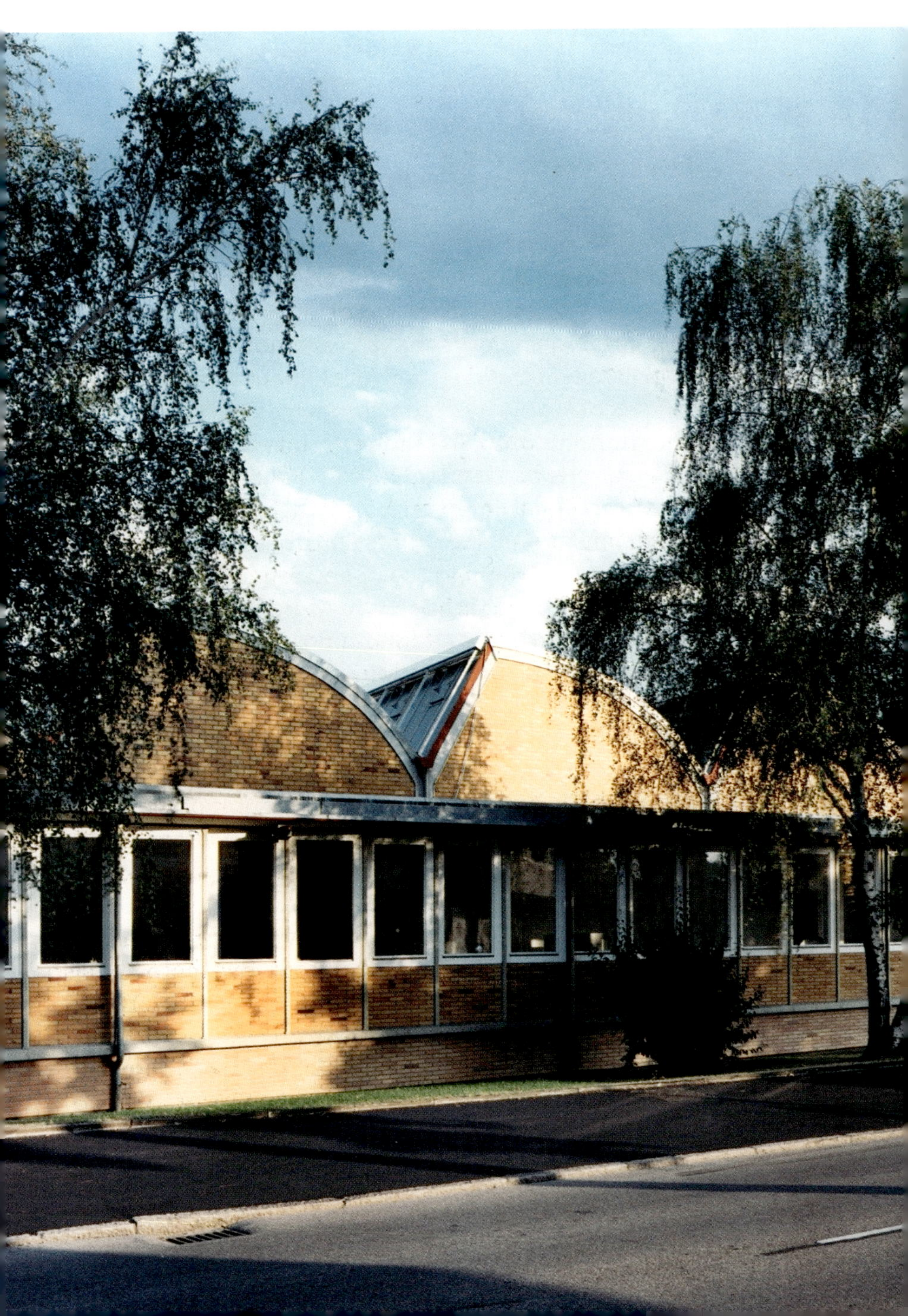

works and a self-portrait from Leon Battista Alberti. The selection of works by Carl Schuch, an important painter from the second half of the nineteenth century who emerged from the Leibl circle, is also impressive. However, contemporary art is by far the most extensive collection of the Morat-Institut. It deliberately concentrates on a relatively small group of artists with whom a personal relationship existed or still exists. More than twenty artists from Germany and abroad have been supported by the foundation through acquisitions or scholarships, and often with publications as well. This part of the collection grows continuously thanks to donations from artists and their heirs. The collection includes extensive overviews of works by Franz Bernhard, Ernst Hermanns, Kurt Kocherscheidt, Artur Stoll, Ian McKeever, and Herbert Maier, among others. Numerous objects by Dietrich Schön can be found in the 1,200 m^2 sculpture garden. Another focus of the collection is on African art with masks and sculptures by tribes from the Upper Volta region (Lobi, Gurunsi, Bobo, Mossi, and Bwa). Irrespective of the art movement, zeitgeist, or medium, Morat prefers to buy entire work complexes.

The various parts of the collections are shown alternately in the 1,500 m^2 Morat halls. The industrial halls, built in the industrial architecture style of the late 1950s, were initially used for the manufacture of blinds. Due to the natural light and a ceiling height of up to eight meters, they are ideal for the presentation and storage of various works. The first exhibitions were held in one section of the building in 1987. Step by step, the entire halls were adapted to the new requirements of a deliberately unadorned exhibition venue.

Morat-Institut für Kunst und Kunstwissenschaft
Freiburg, Baden-Württemberg

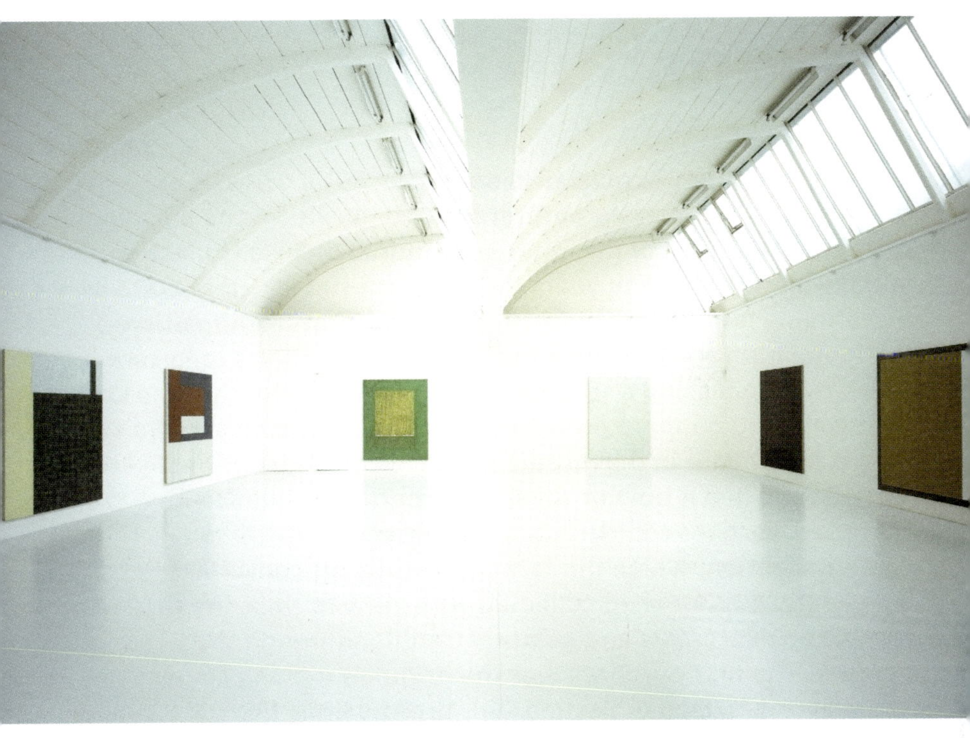

Morat-Institut für Kunst und Kunstwissenschaft
Lörracher Str. 31
D-79115 Freiburg
Phone: +49 761 4765916
info@morat-institut.de
morat-institut.de

Opening hours
Sat 11 a.m.–6 p.m. and by appointment. If you register in advance, you may have the good fortune of a personally guided tour by Franz Armin Morat. The soloists of ensemble recherche regularly organizes contemporary chamber concerts in the Institut's rooms (ensemble-recherche.de).

Entrance fees
Free admission

Arrival by public transportation
From the main train station walk a few meters to the bus station and take bus 11 in the direction of Munzinger Straße, get off at Lörracher Straße (see Google Maps and rvf.de for timetable information).

Restaurant tips
Close to the Institut, at 5 Senses Coffee, there is fantastic coffee and a wide range of breakfasts, cakes, and other healthy snacks (5sensescoffee.de; Wiesentalstr. 22). Excellent food is available at the cozy Hirschen Inn in Freiburg-Lehen (hirschen-freiburg.de; Breisgauer Str. 47). The kitchen offers both international and original Baden dishes and was honored with fifteen points in Gault & Millau. There are numerous cafés and restaurants in the attractive old town of Freiburg.

Extra tips
During a visit to the Morat-Institut, a visit to the Kunstraum Alexander Bürkle (see p. 12) is also worthwhile, as is a detour to the Museum Frieder Burda in Baden-Baden (p. 8), to the KUNSTRAUM GRÄSSLIN (p. 26) in St. Georgen in the Black Forest, and the Museum Villa Haiss in Zell am Harmersbach (p. 30).

48 Kunstmuseum Ravensburg

The Kunstmuseum Ravensburg, opened in 2013, owes its existence to a public-private partnership. The basis for the museum is a permanent loan of the Peter and Gudrun Selinka Collection, initially limited to thirty years, which was established in 2003 as a charitable foundation. In 2009, the City of Ravensburg offered the foundation an opportunity to give the collection a long-term home by establishing a suitable museum. To achieve this, the City of Ravensburg cooperated with building contractor Georg Reisch, who is an investor in the museum, from Georg Reisch GmbH & Co. KG, and had it built on an area in need of renovation near the Humpis-Quartier and Ravensburger museums.

The collection, which the former advertising consultant Peter Selinka (1924–2006) had collected with his wife since the 1950s, follows an expressive and gestural tradition through the twentieth century. The first purchase was the drypoint etching *Liegender Mädchenkopf* (Head of Resting Girl, 1917) by Ernst Ludwig Kirchner, which he purchased from a Berlin gallery in 1952. About two-thirds of the 230 works in the foundation's collection consist of Expressionist works with a focus on the artists of the Die Brücke group such as Ernst Ludwig Kirchner, Erich Heckel, or Otto Mueller. It was above all paintings, drawings, and prints from 1910 and 1911 in which the artists spent time together on the Moritzburg Lakes and the North Sea and in which the characteristic expressive style developed. The collection also includes works by Gabriele Münter, Alexej von Jawlensky, and Wassily Kandinsky from the circle of the Munich artist movement Der Blaue Reiter. A highlight of the collection and the absolute darling of the public is Alexej von Jawlensky's *Spanische Mädchen* (Spanish Girl, 1912), which Peter Selinka bought from the banker and later vice president of the United States, Nelson Rockefeller, in the 1970s. At the end of the 1970s, Selinka extended his collecting activities to Paris after visiting a Pierre Alechinsky exhibition and meeting the member of the CoBrA artists' group. The works represented in the collection

Kunstmuseum Ravensburg
Ravensburg, Baden-Württemberg

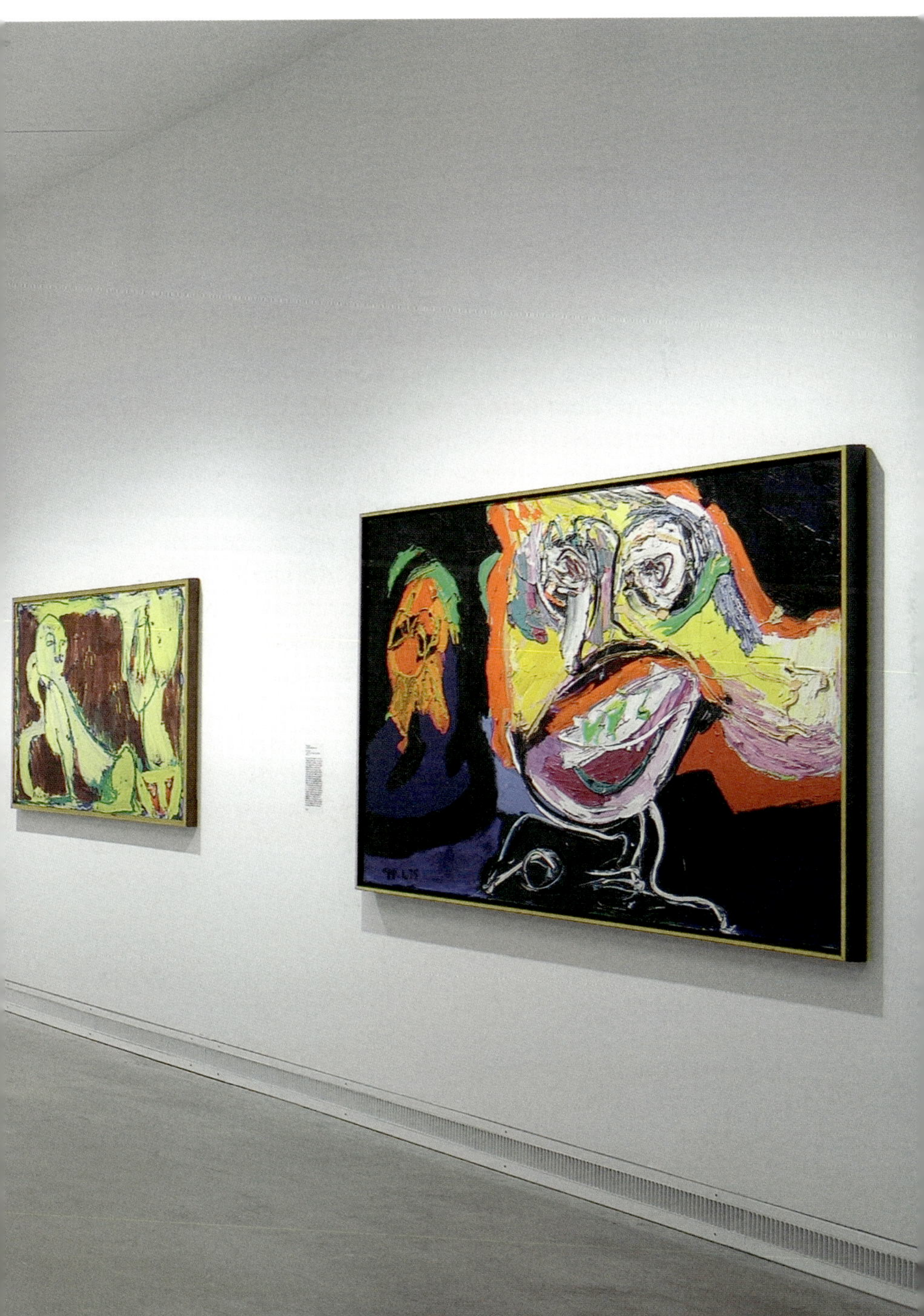

by CoBrA artists such as Asger Jorn, Carl-Henning Pedersen, Pierre Alechinsky, Christian Dotremont, Karel Appel, and Corneille provide a sound basis for tracing the development of this international movement after its dissolution. Through Asger Jorn, young graduates of the Munich Art Academy came into contact with the ideas of CoBrA. Lothar Fischer, Heimrad Prem, Helmut Sturm, and Hans-Peter Zimmer then joined forces from 1958 to 1966 to form the group SPUR, which has over thirty works in its collection.

The architectural office Lederer + Ragnarsdóttir + Oei won the 2009 architectural competition for the Kunstmuseum. The Stuttgart architects oriented the Kunstmuseum in historic Ravensburg following the motto "First comes the city, then the house." Characteristic for this is the use of used bricks as material for the façade. The quite purist interior of the building is the world's first certified museum in passive house construction. The modern vaulted ceiling on the top floor is particularly impressive. In 2013, the architectural office received the German Architecture Prize and the DAM Prize for Architecture in Germany for its museum construction. In 2014, the Kunstmuseum Ravensburg was nominated for the European Museum Award (EMYA). The German section of the international art critic association AICA awarded it the Museum of the Year 2015 prize.

Three main exhibitions and three smaller exhibitions of twentieth- and twenty-first-century art are presented annually on three floors of the museum's 700 m² of exhibition space.

Kunstmuseum Ravensburg
Ravensburg, Baden-Württemberg

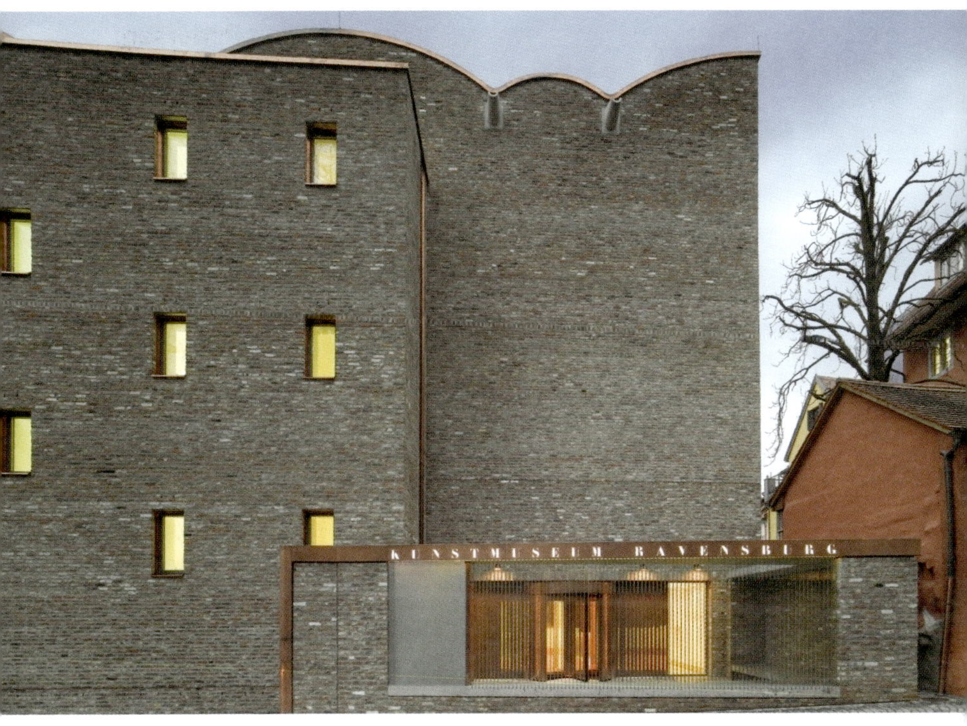

Kunstmuseum Ravensburg
Burgstr. 9
D-88212 Ravensburg
Phone: +49 751 82810
kunstmuseum@ravensburg.de
kunstmuseum-ravensburg.de

Opening hours
Tue–Sun 11 a.m.–6 p.m., Thu 11 a.m.–7 p.m., closed on Mondays, except public holidays
Numerous guided tours, lectures, and workshops for children and adults are offered. Public guided tours of the special exhibitions take place every Sunday at 3 p.m.; no registration is required (€5 plus admission).

Entrance fees
Adults / Reduced / Children under age 18: €7 / €4 / free
Ravensburger Museum Ticket (four Ravensburger museums): €17

Arrival by public transportation
From the Ravensburg railway station, it is a fifteen-minute walk through the old town to the museum.

Parking
Parking at the Obertor (Marktstraße) car park is recommended.

Restaurant tips
The café and restaurant Stippe serves cakes and just about everything from home-style German to Asian cuisine (Gespinstmarkt 19). German and international dishes, as well as the famous Humpis beer, are available at Gaststätte Humpis (Marktstr. 47). Authentic African cuisine is served for lunch in the African Queen shop (Herrenstr. 28; closed Sundays). The Ravensburger cult pub Räuberhöhle (Burgstr. 14) is only a few meters away from the art museum.

Extra tips
With the medieval Museum Humpis-Quartier (museum-humpis-quartier.de; Marktstr. 45) and the museum Ravensburger (ravensburger.net/museum-ravensburger-english/home/index; Marktstr. 26), the museum forms an attractive museum district in the Ravensburger upper town. In the city, there are still many buildings from the thirteenth century and a concert hall to be admired. The viewing platform on the Veitsburg offers a panoramic view of the city and the surrounding countryside to the Alps.

52 Museum Ritter / Sammlung Marli Hoppe-Ritter

In 1985, lawyer Marli Hoppe-Ritter began supporting young artists and, together with her husband, acquiring modern works of art. Inspired by the exhibition *Von zwei Quadraten* in the Wilhelm-Hack-Museum (1986), the granddaughter of the chocolate manufacturer and co-owner of Ritter Sport built up the collection based on the theme of squares starting in 1994. The diversity of painterly and sculptural concepts of the square, its continuing topicality as a form, and the exciting connections that emerge across the art of the twentieth and twenty-first centuries result in a convincing collection concept. Beginning with Kasimir Malevich, the square has become a paradigm of Modernism. Countless artists, mostly in Abstract and Concrete art, have dealt with the square in form and content.

The wish for a permanent location for the collection was fulfilled in 2005 with the opening of the Museum Ritter, which is financially supported by the Marli Hoppe-Ritter-Stiftung zur Förderung der Kunst. The commissioned Swiss architect, Max Dudler, is known for his austere buildings in the tradition of modern Rationalism. With the striking limestone cube, he has succeeded in creating an architectural contrast between open and closed forms. The austerity of the building, erected on a floor plan of 44 × 44 m, is playfully interrupted by a trapezoidal passage flooded with light. Inside the building, an inviting, bright, and exciting spatial structure was created on two floors.

Every year, three to four exhibitions are held here on an area of approximately 700 m². In most cases, a representative cross section of the collection consisting of circa one thousand works is shown. There are also regular solo exhibitions, which are supplemented by loans from the artists or other collections. The collection's spectrum of tension ranges from historical positions such as Russian Constructivism (Kasimir Malevich), the Dutch group De Stijl

Museum Ritter / Sammlung Marli Hoppe-Ritter
Waldenbuch, Baden-Württemberg

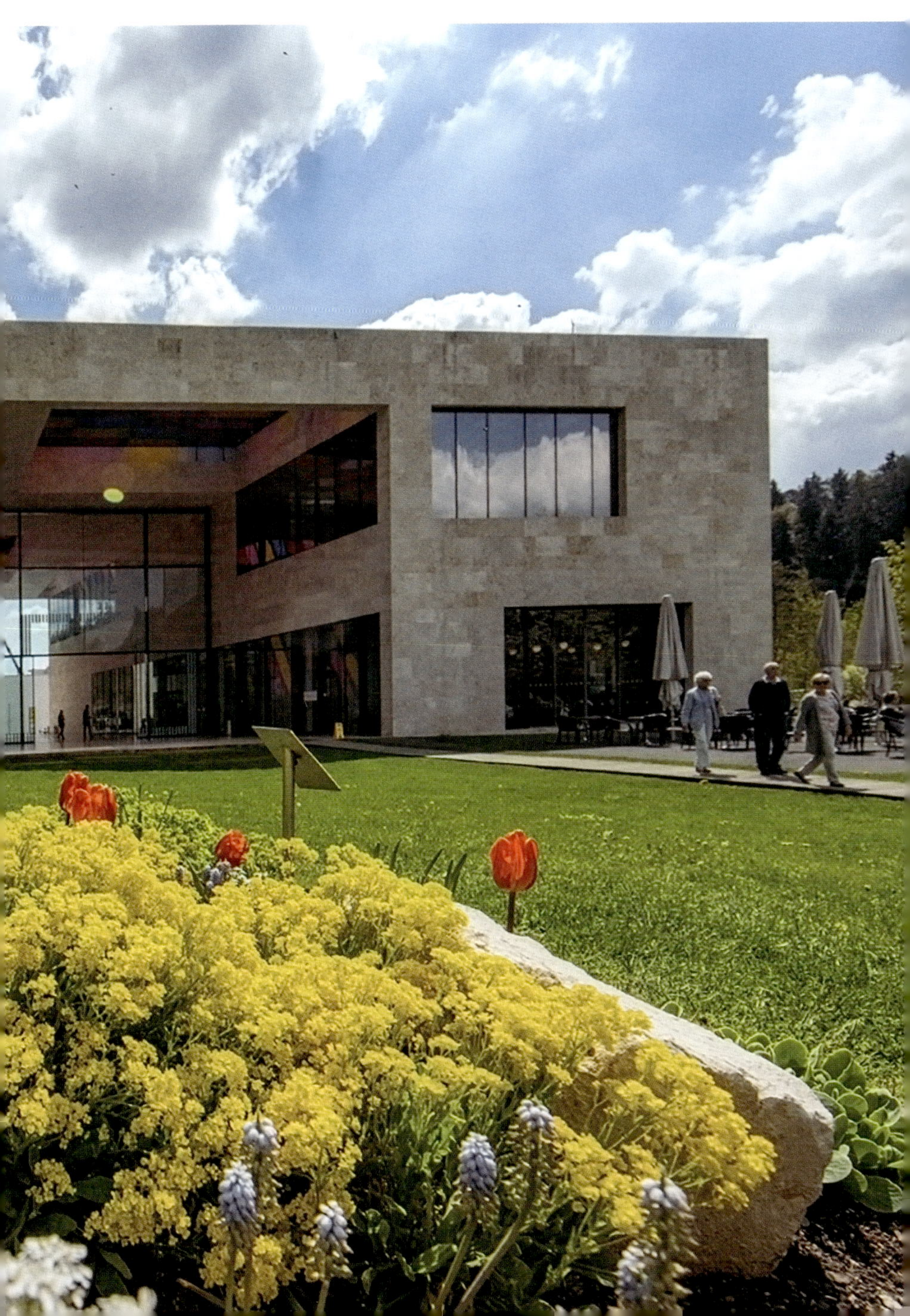

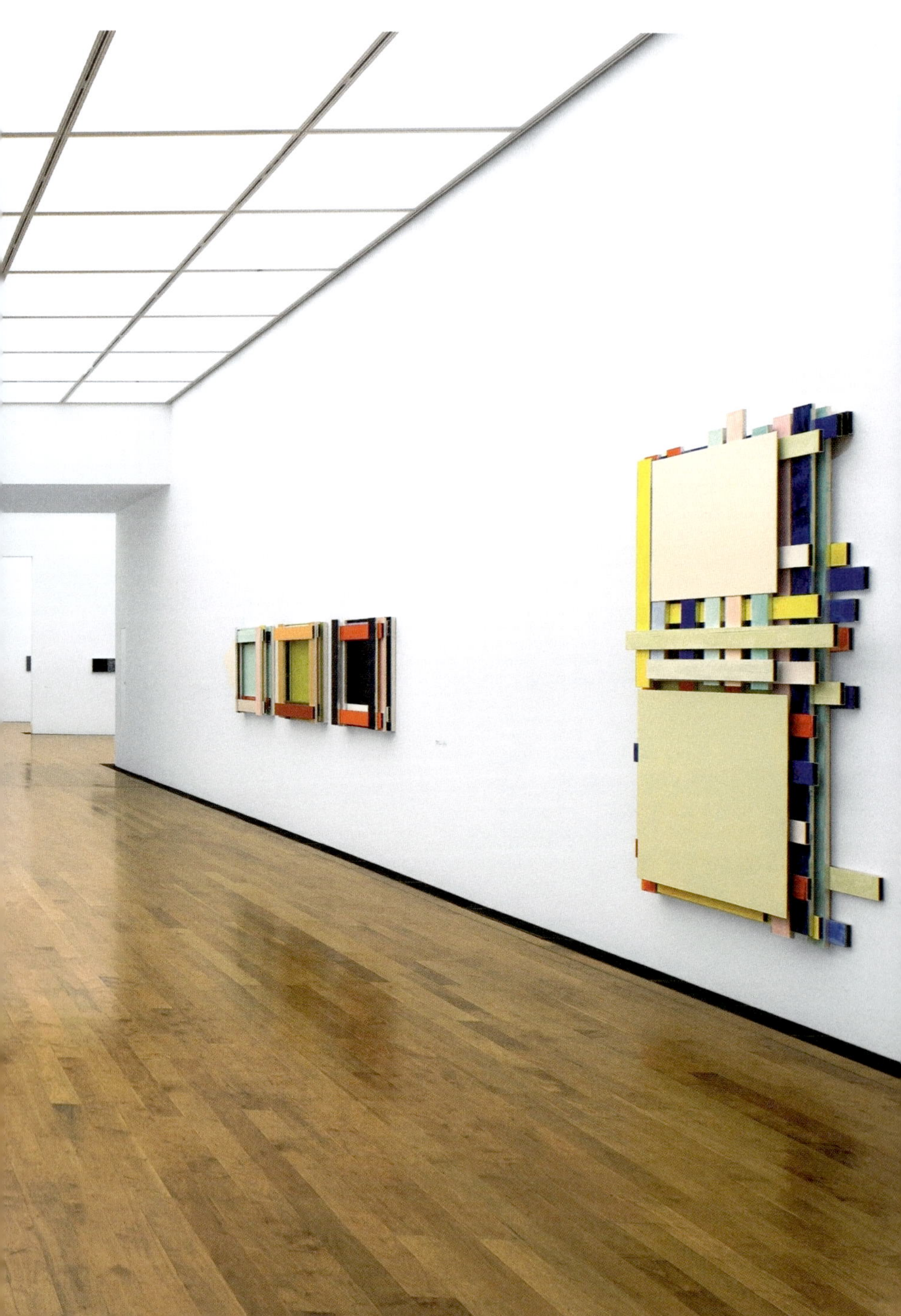

(Theo van Doesburg), and the Bauhaus (Josef Albers) to the School of Zurich Concretists (Richard Paul Lohse), Op Art (Victor Vasarely), and Minimalism (Imi Knoebel) to the present (Gerold Miller, Esther Stocker, and Jacob Dahlgren).

The varied program of events and the particularly visitor and child-friendly atmosphere allow an intensive examination of the geometric-abstract art of the twentieth and twenty-first centuries.

Museum Ritter
Alfred-Ritter-Str. 27
D-71111 Waldenbuch
Phone: +49 7157 535110
besucherservice@museumritter.de
museum-ritter.de

Opening hours
Tue–Sun, 11 a.m.–6 p.m.
Public tours of the exhibition take place on Sundays and public holidays at 3 p.m. During the school holidays, the "Kunstatelier" holiday program is offered for children ages 7 and over. The museum shop contains multiples from the fields of art and design for purchase, as well as more traditional offerings. The museum café with a magnificent terrace is open daily from 9 a.m. to 6 p.m.

Entrance fees
Adults / Reduced / Children and youths up to age 18: €6 / €4 / free
An audio guide is available free of charge at the ticketing counter.

Arrival by public transportation
You can get to the museum from Stuttgart with the S2/S3 by changing trains in Leinfelden or Echterdingen and taking buses 826, 828 or 815 to Waldenbuch Postamt (see Google Maps and vvs.de). You can also take the Airport Sprinter (Bus 828) from Stuttgart Airport to Waldenbuch.

Restaurant tips
The cozy, family-run Osteria da Maria serves homemade pasta dishes, delicious pizzas, and Italian wines (osteria-da-maria.de; Marktstr. 9; closed Tuesdays). Gourmets will be impressed by the award-winning cuisine at Gasthof Krone. An excellent lunch is served from Wednesday to Friday. As part of the Kultur Gourmet program, the museum and Gasthof Krone offer a combination of a guided tour of the museum and a 4-course menu once a month on Sunday afternoons (krone-waldenbuch.de; Nürtinger Str. 14; closed Mondays and Tuesdays).

Extra tips
In the building opposite the museum, you will find the Ritter Sport chocolate shop, the chocolate exhibition, and the chocolate workshop. Children from age 7 up can make their own chocolate in workshops. Registration is required via the Ritter Sport website (schokowerkstatt.ritter-sport.de).
Located on the outskirts of the town and directly on site, with picturesque half-timbered buildings and the Ritter Museum, is Schönbuch Nature Reserve, which welcomes visitors for hiking and cycle tours (naturpark-schoenbuch.de). The Museum Ritter is also located directly on the Museum Cycle Path, which stretches from Weil der Stadt to Nürtingen.
An approx. 30 km long route, the so-called Sculptoura takes cyclists from Grafenau-Dätzingen to Waldenbuch, passing over eighty sculptures. In individual sections, the Sculptoura can also be explored on foot. A small circuit with numerous sculptures around the Museum Ritter gives a little taste of the big route (sculptoura.de).
Non-local visitors should consider a visit to the Domnick Collection in Nürtingen after visiting the Museum Ritter (see p. 14).

56 SCHAUWERK Sindelfingen

The Stuttgart region was enriched in 2010 with a large private museum. Even though the surroundings of the SCHAUWERK Sindelfingen do not seem very attractive, a side trip to the collection of Christiane Schaufler-Münch and Senator Peter Schaufler, who died in 2015, is indispensable for art lovers.

Shortly after Peter Schaufler took over the management of Bitzer Kühlmaschinenbau GmbH in Sindelfingen after the sudden death of his father in 1979, he and his wife discovered contemporary art as a source of inspiration. The initial spark came from their first encounters with the artistic work of the ZERO Group (Günther Uecker, Heinz Mack, and Otto Piene) and the movement's pioneers, such as Lucio Fontana. The purist aesthetics of their works, which were among the first purchases at the beginning of the 1980s, had a long-term influence on the course of the collection. The clarity of the pure color and the absence of all figurative elements were decisive criteria for the couple for decades and still are to this day for Christiane Schaufler-Münch. The versatile collection also focuses on Minimal Art (Donald Judd, Dan Flavin, Imi Knoebel, and John McCracken), Conceptual Art (Joseph Kosuth) and Concrete Art (Hanne Darboven and François Morellet). The collection also focuses on German contemporary photography (Andreas Gursky, Thomas Ruff, Thomas Struth, Thomas Demand, Candida Höfer, and Wolfgang Tillmans). Historical positions are just as present as representatives of recent art movements.

Until the opening of his collector's museum, the entrepreneur from Sindelfingen was rather reserved and quiet. His art treasures were only accessible to employees of the Bitzer branches. With the relocation of production from Sindelfingen to Rottenburg, the production hall and a high-bay warehouse on the premises of the company's headquarters were suddenly empty. Thus, the idea of converting these rooms into a public exhibition space for the collection came about. The Stuttgart-based planning office BFK Architekten was commissioned with the conversion into a

SCHAUWERK Sindelfingen
Sindelfingen, Baden-Württemberg

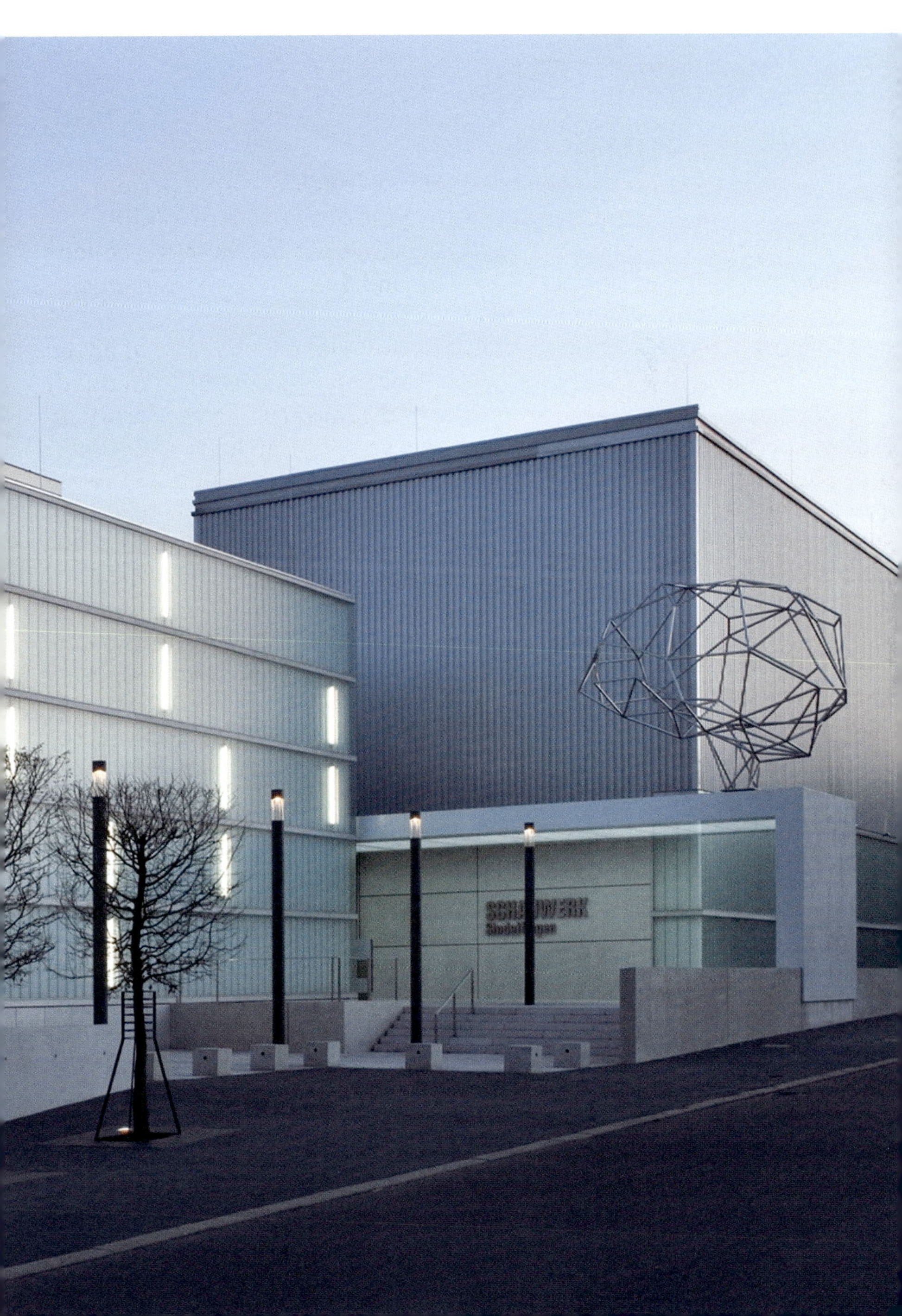

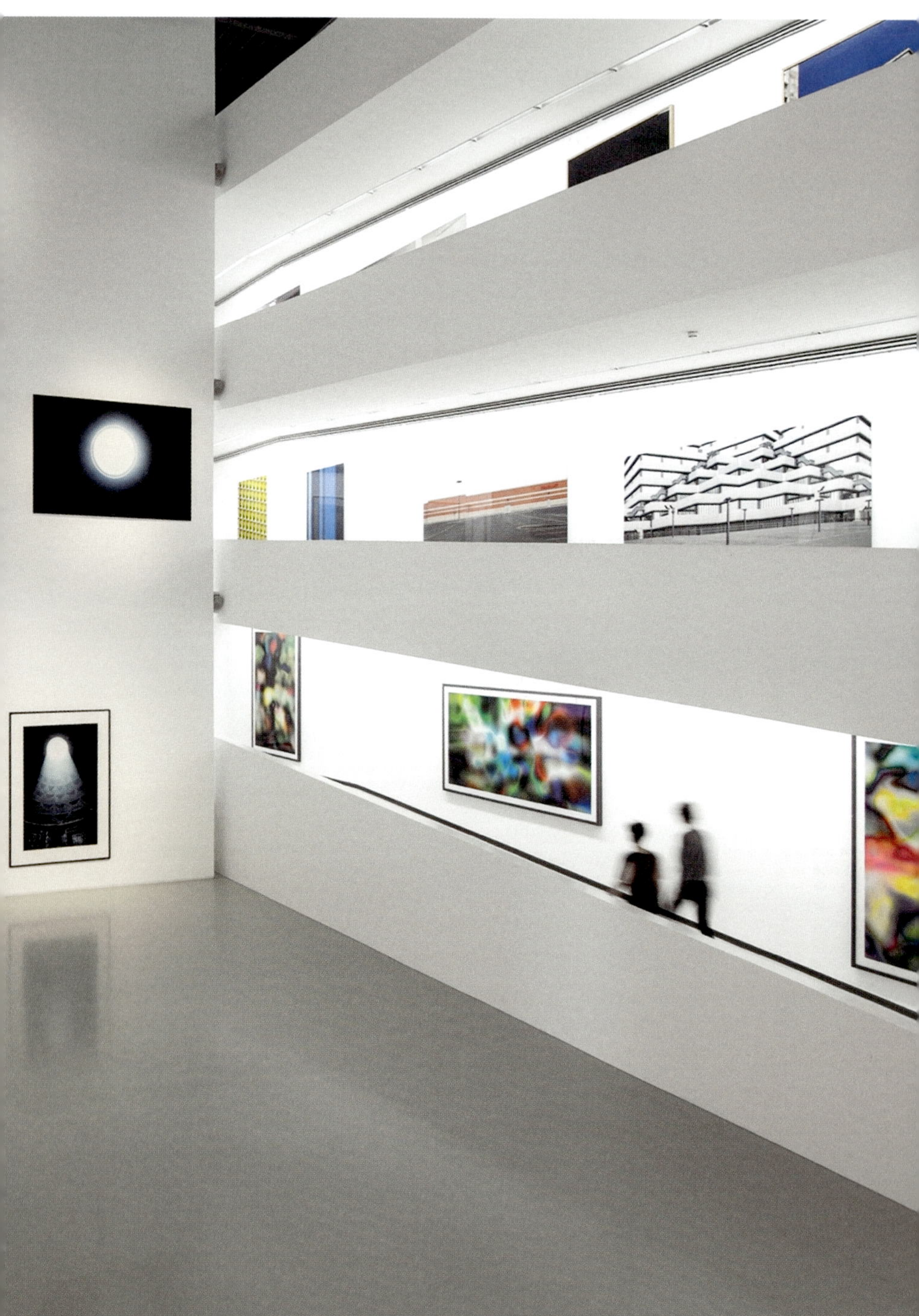

bright and spacious museum complex. Today, visitors are given insights into the approximately 3,500 works in the collection on an exhibition area of approximately 6,500 m². Painterly positions, sculptures, light works, and room installations are on view, as well as contemporary photographs, which are shown separately in the high-bay warehouse. The various levels, views, and exciting lines of sight make it possible to view the exhibited works in a variety of ways. The clear and austere architecture offers a harmonious framework, while at the same time, pays tribute to its industrial history.

The Schaufler Foundation, a non-profit foundation set up in 2005 by the collector couple to promote science, research, and art, is the owner and operator of the museum as well as the owner of part of the collection. The name SCHAUWERK (exhibition factory) is intended to create a link between the former use of the buildings and art. In the future, the changing presentation of the collection will continue to be complemented by targeted projects with individual artists and other accompanying events.

SCHAUWERK Sindelfingen
Eschenbrünnlestr. 15/1
D-71065 Sindelfingen
Phone: +49 7031 9324900
contact@schauwerk-sindelfingen.de
schauwerk-sindelfingen.de

Opening hours
Sat/Sun, 11 a.m.–5 p.m.
90-minute public guided tours take place on Tuesdays and Thursdays at 3 p.m. (on these two weekdays, a visit is only possible within the framework of the tour), Saturdays at 3 p.m. and Sundays at 11 a.m. Thematic tours are offered on Sundays at 3 p.m. Registration is not necessary.

Entrance fees
Adults / Reduced / Children up to age 18, students, and museum pass holders: €8 / €5 / free
The guided tours are included in the entrance fee.

Arrival by public transportation
From the Stuttgart main station, take the S1 towards Herrenberg to the Goldberg stop.

Parking
The museum offers its own parking facilities.

Restaurant tips
Near SCHAUWERK, the simple Gaststätte Goldbachsee serves traditional Swabian dishes. In summer, a seat on the terrace with a view of the lake is recommended (goldbachsee.de; Schwertstr. 16). Excellent Italian food is served in the evening at the upscale Ratskeller Da Vittorio (ratskeller-davittorio.de; Rathausplatz 1; closed Sundays). Modern versions of Swabian cuisine are served in the cozy Kramers Stüble (erikson.de/kramers-stueble; Hanns-Martin-Schleyer-Str. 8, Hotel Erikson).

Extra tips
Both the Museum Ritter (see p. 52) and the Domnick Collection (p. 14) are located near SCHAUWERK.

60 Kunsthalle Weishaupt

Since 2007, it has been possible to admire the private Weishaupt collection next to the Museum Ulm near the town hall. The elegant restraint and lightness of the building by Wolfgang Wöhr, a former collaborator of the well-known New York architect Richard Meier, is a work of art in its own right. The property on which the building stands was provided by the city of Ulm. After sixty-six years, the Kunsthalle Weishaupt will become fully owned by the city.

On two floors with an area of almost 1,300 m^2, there are on average two temporary exhibitions per year that can be seen here. They are, for the most part, generated from the collection and supplemented by external loans for individual exhibitions.

The managing partner of the internationally active Max Weishaupt GmbH, Siegfried Weishaupt, has been collecting art together with his wife for over fifty years. Important starting points of the collection were a preference for the geometric compositions of Max Bill, one of the founding directors of the Hochschule für Gestaltung Ulm, and an enthusiasm for the works of Josef Albers. Over the years, the couple turned increasingly to Abstract Expressionism. In addition to works by Mark Rothko and Yves Klein, for example, works by ZERO group artists were also purchased. Representatives of American Pop Art—Andy Warhol, Roy Lichtenstein, Robert Indiana, and the graffiti painter Keith Haring—are represented, as are the contemporary artists Liam Gillick, Robert Longo, and Markus Oehlen. Today, the collection comprises over 400 paintings and sculptures as well as numerous works on paper. It is looked after by director and art historian Kathrin Weishaupt-Theopold, who, as the daughter of the collector couple, has been connected to art since her childhood.

Kunsthalle Weishaupt
Ulm, Baden-Württemberg

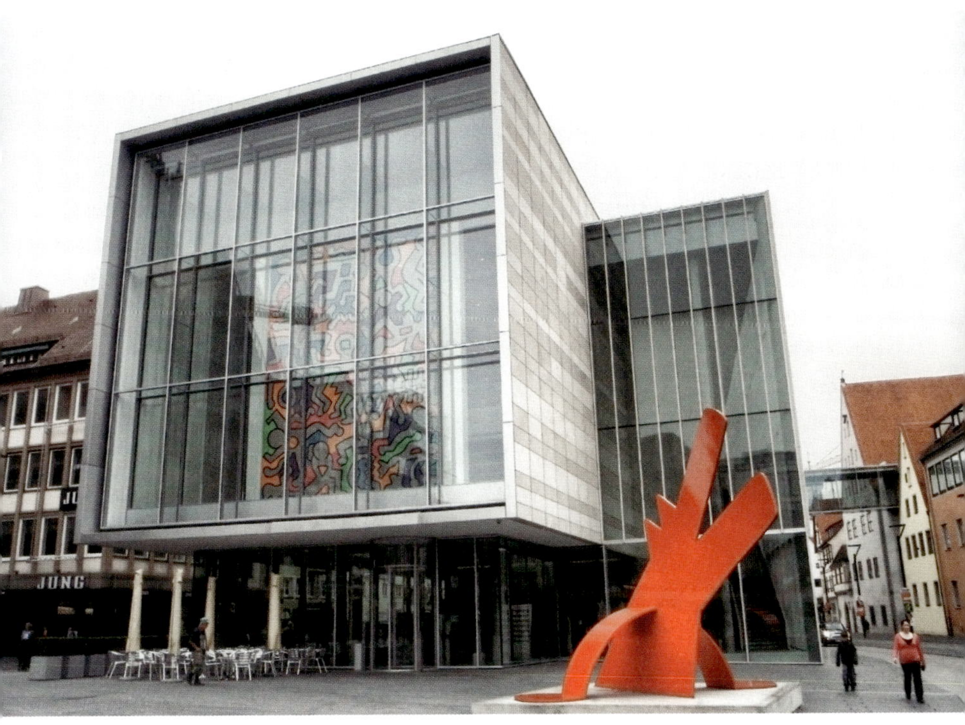

Kunsthalle Weishaupt
Hans-und-Sophie-Scholl-Platz 1
D-89073 Ulm
Phone: +49 731 1614360
info@kunsthalle-weishaupt.de
kunsthalle-weishaupt.de

Opening hours
Tue–Sun 11 a.m.–5 p.m.;
Thu 11 a.m.–8 p.m.
Public tours take place on Thursdays at 6 p.m. (except on public holidays) and Saturdays at 2 p.m. (€2 plus admission).
On one Sunday a month at 3 p.m. there are guided tours for children (€2).
The café-restaurant billbar is located on the ground floor of the Kunsthalle Weishaupt. It also has a wine bar.

Entrance fees
Adults / Reduced / Children and teenagers up to age 18:
€6 / €4 / free
Combined ticket with the Museum Ulm: €12 / €10
Free entry on the first Friday of the month.

Arrival by public transportation:
From the central train station you can either take bus line 5 in the direction of Hasenweg / Washingtonallee to Rathaus Ulm. In less than fifteen minutes you can walk to the Kunsthalle.

Parking
Parking is available directly under the Kunsthalle Weishaupt in the multistory car park at the town hall (access via Neue Straße).

Restaurant tip
The rustic restaurant Zur Forelle is located in the middle of the historic fishermen's quarter. Excellent Swabian and Mediterranean dishes are served here. (ulmer-forelle.de; Fischergasse 25).

Extra tips
A visit of the Museum Ulm is recommended and possible with a combined ticket (the permanent exhibition can be visited free of charge on the first Friday of the month). Since 1999, the Foundation Collection Kurt Fried has been presented on three floors in a specially constructed new building. The publisher and art critic collected works of art from Europe and the USA after 1945, including Gerhard Richter, Günther Uecker, and Daniel Spoerri. The buildings are connected by a bridge (museumulm.de; Marketplace 9). It is also possible to combine a visit to the Sammlung FER Collection (see p. 16) and The Walther Collection in Neu-Ulm (p. 94).

62
Würth Collection

In the 1960s Reinhold Würth laid the foundation for the Würth Collection, which today comprises almost 18,000 works of art by around 2,800 artists. Its focus is on sculpture, painting, and graphics from the end of the Middle Ages to the present. In addition to Classical Modernism, which is impressively represented by artists such as Edvard Munch, Ernst Ludwig Kirchner, Emil Nolde, Max Beckmann, and Pablo Picasso, it is above all statuary and sculpture that increase in importance. Among others, renowned artists such as Eduardo Chillida, Tony Cragg, Antony Gormley, Anish Kapoor, Henry Moore, Bernar Venet, and Katsura Funakoshi are represented in the collection. Extensive work complexes by Hans Arp, Anselm Kiefer, Horst Antes, Christo and Jeanne-Claude, Georg Baselitz, and Max Bill can also be seen. The destruction of an extensive Max Ernst collection, which had been released for sale by its previous owner, was prevented thanks to its purchase by Reinhold Würth. In 2003, he also made every effort to ensure that the late medieval Fürstlich Fürstenberg Collection of Paintings was preserved for the public in Baden-Württemberg. The collection process continues to develop through new acquisitions made by Reinhold Würth in consultation with his art advisory board. In November 2017, for example, the Würth Collection received a significant number of top-class postmodern and contemporary works from the liquidated Austrian Essl Collection. The strong presence of art and the diverse activities around art topics are a part and consequence of the corporate culture lived in the Würth company. The exhibitions and the hangings in offices and cafeterias provide an exemplary basis for an inspiring coexistence of art and everyday business.

Adolf Würth GmbH & Co.KG operates the four exhibition halls in Baden-Württemberg. In addition, since 1999, ten art galleries have successively operated in various foreign companies of the Würth Group. This is also the case in Austria in the Art Room Würth Austria in Böheimkirchen and Switzerland in the Forum Würth Arlesheim, the Forum Würth Rorschach, and the Forum Würth Chur.

Würth Collection Baden-Württemberg

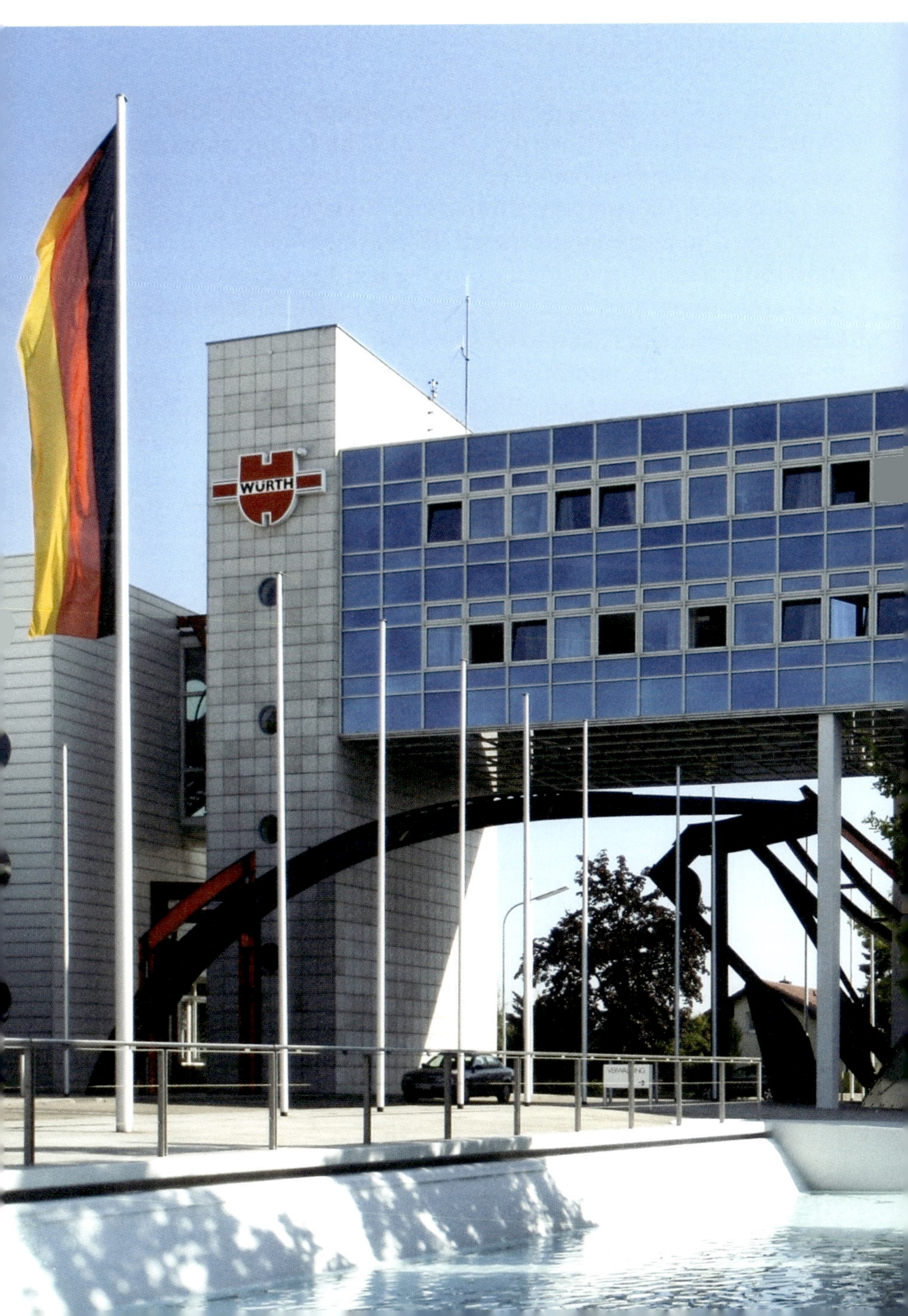

64 Kunsthalle Würth

Opened in 2001, the Kunsthalle is located in the middle of the Schwäbisch Hall old town on the site of the former Hall Löwenbrauerei. Danish architect Henning Larsen succeeded with an exemplary integration of this modern three-story building into a historic environment. The harmonious use of different building materials, the generous, almost free-floating staircases, the views of the medieval city, and the cleverly arranged exhibition rooms are sure to impress architecture lovers. The exhibition area originally covered approximately 2,000 m², and after the renovation of the brewhouse and the joining of the two buildings, an additional circa 650 m² were added. The two exhibition floors are used for two to three temporary exhibitions per year. The program is based on the current focus of the Würth Collection. In addition to its own holdings, the Würth Collection regularly presents high-caliber loans.

Kunsthalle Würth
Lange Str. 35
D-74523 Schwäbisch Hall
Phone: +49 791 946720
kunsthalle@wuerth.com
kunst.wuerth.com

Opening hours
Daily 10 a.m.–6 p.m.
The Kunsthalle is closed for a few weeks during the installation of exhibitions. During the Freilichtspiele Schwäbisch Hall events in June and August, the Kunsthalle is open every day until 7 p.m. Public tours are offered for €6 on Sundays at 11:30 a.m. and 2 p.m. There is an exhibition-specific program for themed and children's tours as well as lectures (registration is required at kunsthalle@wuerth.com). In the museum, there is a small museum shop and a cafeteria.

Entrance fees
Apart from special exhibitions, a visit to the museum is free of charge.

Arrival by public transportation
From Schwäbisch Hall railway station, follow the signs to the Kunsthalle. It takes about five minutes to get to the museum, which can be recognized from afar by the high tower of the former brewery.

Parking
Parking is available in the P3 Alte Brauerei / Kunsthalle Würth or at P4 Im Ritter. To get to Museum Würth from Kunsthalle Würth, drive approx. 20 km north on the B19 to Gaisbach / Künzelsau.

Restaurant tips
Right next to the Kunsthalle is the former brewery of the Haller Löwenbrauerei, renovated by Stuttgart architect Erich H. Fritz. A versatile range of food, frequently accompanied by background music, is offered across several floors in the brewhouse. The view from the terrace is magnificent (sudhaus-sha.de; Lange Str. 35/1; closed Mondays).
Somewhat outside the city, connoisseurs will be spoiled with Swabian cuisine in the modern star restaurant Reber's Pflug (rebers-pflug.de; Weckriedener Str. 2; closed Sunday).
Delicious, innovative dishes are served in the simple but fun Osho Restaurant (ohso-restaurant.de; Zollhüttengasse 1; only open in the evenings Wed–Sat).

Extra tip
A few minutes walk to the west is the Johanniterhalle, a secularized twelfth-century church building which has been historically restored. As a branch of the Kunsthalle Würth, the Johanniterhalle is the ideal location for the Würth Collection of Old Masters.
The core of the collection is the former Fürstlich Fürstenberg Collection of Paintings at Donaueschingen, acquired in 2003 (kunst.wuerth.com; Im Weiler 1).

Kunsthalle Würth
Schwäbisch Hall, Baden-Württemberg

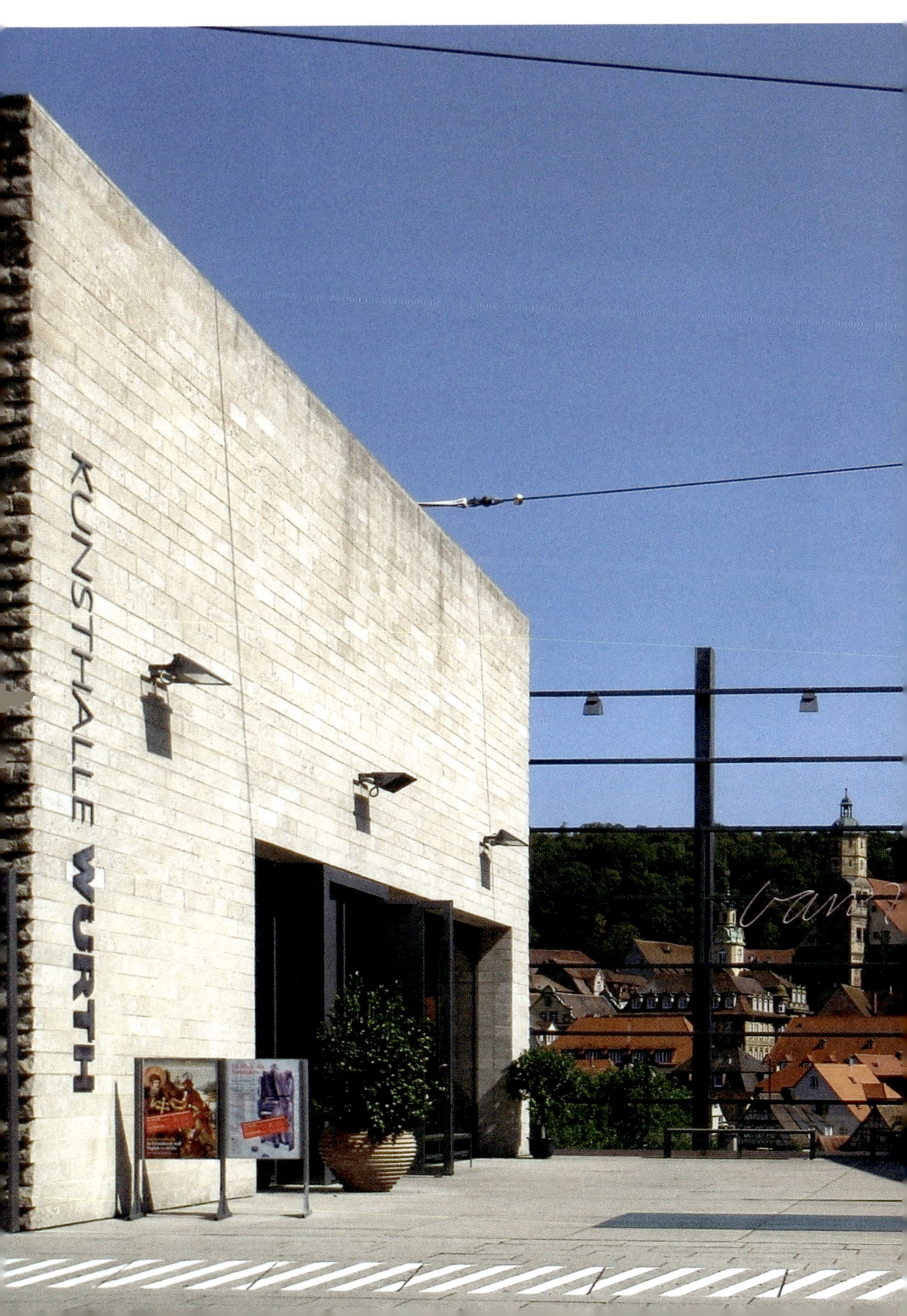

66
Museum Würth

Integrated into the company's administration building, two independent museum areas were created in 1991: the Museum for Modern and Contemporary Art and the Screw and Thread Collection. Influenced by postmodern views of the 1980s, the Stuttgart architectural office Müller-Djordjevic created an open meeting place for the world of work and culture. Upon arrival, the generous building forecourt immediately impresses with a multitude of sculptures by international artists.

In the museum, mostly annually changing exhibitions are shown, most of which relate to the new collection purchases. Sometimes thematically oriented or special monographic exhibitions with shorter durations are also presented.

Museum Würth
Adolf Würth GmbH & Co. KG
Reinhold-Würth-Str. 15
D-74653 Künzelsau
Phone: +49 7940 152200
museum@wuerth.com
kunst.wuerth.com

Opening hours
Daily 11 a.m.–6 p.m.
Public tours are offered irregularly on Sundays at 11 a.m. and cost €6 (registration is necessary at museum@wuerth.com).
There is a small museum shop in front of the exhibition hall.
The cafeteria is open until 5 p.m.

Entrance fees
Apart from special exhibitions, a visit to the museum is free of charge.

Arrival by public transportation
From the Schwäbisch Hall-Hessental train station, take bus number 28 via Schwäbisch Hall train station to the Gaisbach Museum Würth stop (efa-bw.de).

Parking
Parking is available in the Würth company parking lot.
To get to Kunsthalle Würth from Museum Würth, drive approx. 20 km south on the B19 to Schwäbisch Hall.

Restaurant tip
The Hotel-Restaurant Anne-Sophie, opened by Carmen Würth in 2003, shows how successfully people with and without disabilities can work together. The kitchen of the gourmet restaurant handicap (Hauptstr. 22–28, closed Mondays and Tuesdays) and the Restaurant Anne-Sophie (Schlossplatz 9) serve seasonal and regional dishes (hotel-anne-sophie.de).

Extra tips
In Künzelsau, in the private atmosphere of Hirschwirtscheuer, it is possible to view the Sommer artists' family permanent exhibition as well as changing exhibitions of modern and contemporary art from the Würth Collection (kunst.wuerth.com; Scharfengasse 12).
On his 80th birthday, Reinhold Würth dedicated a congress and cultural center to his wife Carmen with a chamber music hall as the crown jewel, which is the home of the newly founded Würth Philharmonic Orchestra. The center, designed by David Chipperfield, is connected to a sculpture garden with installations by Anthony Caro, Niki de Saint Phalle, Jaume Plensa, and Georg Baselitz (carmen-wuerth-forum.de; Am Forumsplatz 1).

Museum Würth
Künzelsau, Baden-Württemberg

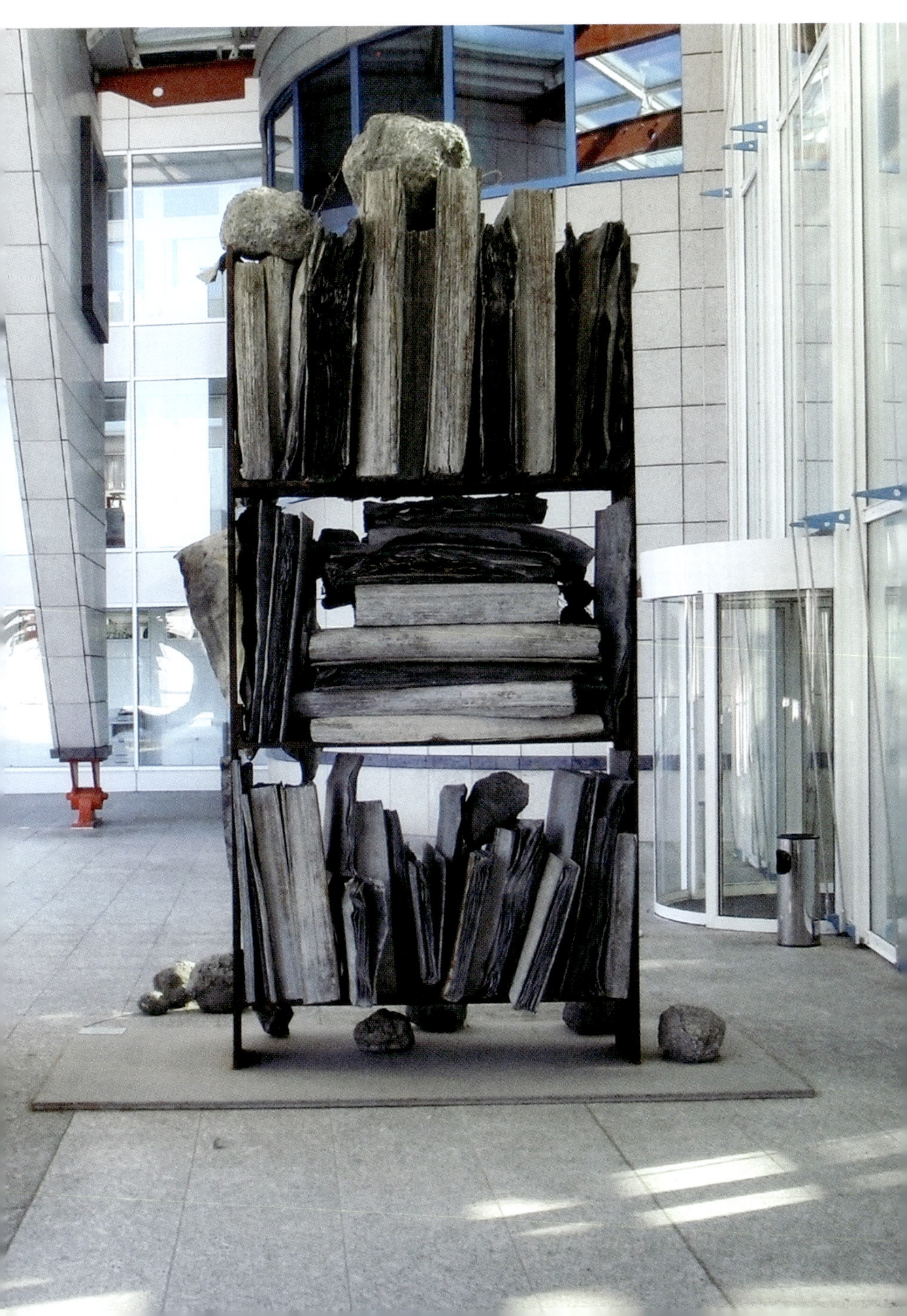

68
Zander Collection

Since 1996, the listed Stadionsche Castle in Bönnigheim has housed the Zander Collection, one of the most important international collections of Naïve Art and Art Brut. Over sixty years, gallery owner and collector Charlotte Zander (1930–2014) collected numerous masterpieces of unique art historical value. Initially, she focused on artists such as Joseph Beuys and Gerhard Richter, yet after visiting several avant-garde galleries in the 1950s, her interest shifted to the works of Naïve artists, initially, and in particular, André Bauchant's paintings. The artists of Western modernism were in search of counterworlds. Non-European works of art, paintings by children or the mentally ill, and the art of autodidacts became a spiritual fountain of youth beyond academic norms for them. Like these artists, Charlotte Zander also recognized the quality and significance of the works of the highly diverse personalities of the classical Naïve which corresponded to a longing for originality. Thus, unique groups of works by Henri Rousseau, Séraphine Louis, André Bauchant, Camille Bombois, and Louis Vivin are represented in the Zander Collection, which includes over 4,500 art pieces. None of them ever studied at an art academy, and all had other professions.

The fact that the art of autodidacts never completely fell into oblivion is also thanks to Charlotte Zander, who founded Galerie Charlotte in Munich in 1971 alongside her work as a collector. It was one of the few institutions in Germany that represented Naïve Art and made it internationally known. When she left the gallery in 1995, Zander sought a suitable location for her monumental collection. The town of Bönnigheim bought the property of Bönnigheim Castle, which was built by master builder Anton Haaf for Friedrich Graf Stadion in 1756 as a summer palace, as part of a constructive interest group.

Zander Collection
Bönnigheim, Baden-Württemberg

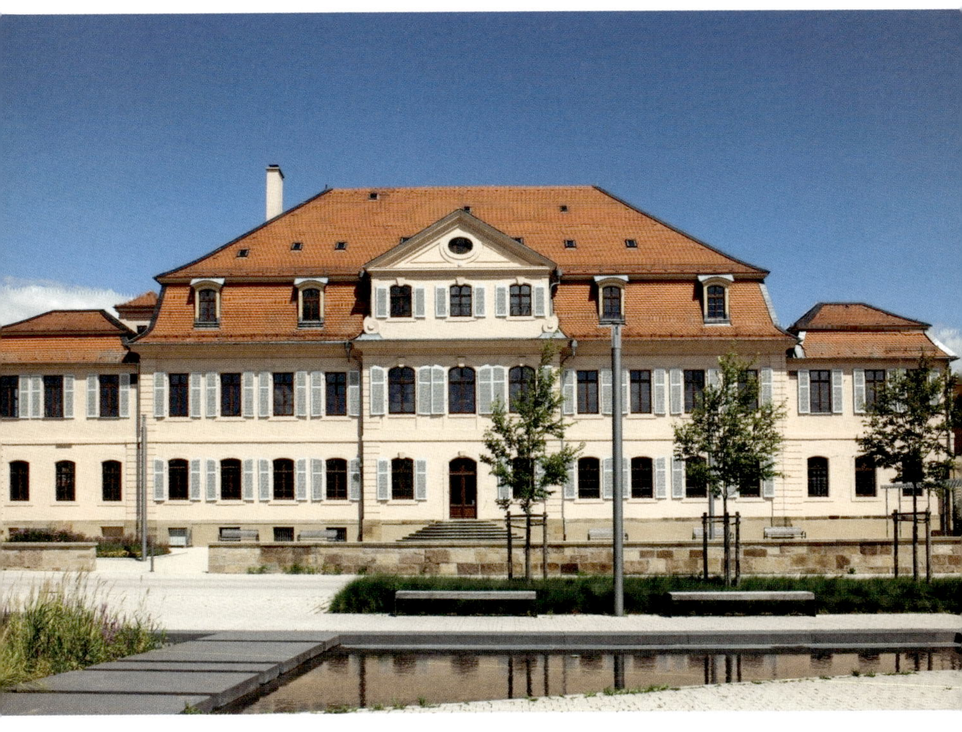

Sammlung Zander
Schloss Bönnigheim
Hauptstr. 15
D-74357 Bönnigheim
Phone: +49 7143 4226
info@sammlung-zander.de
sammlung-zander.de

Opening hours
Thu–Sun 10 a.m.–5 p.m. as well as most holidays
One-hour public tours are offered on the first Sunday of the month at 2 p.m. (€8.50 including admission).

Entrance fees
Adults / Reduced / Children ages 6–16: €6 / €4 / €3

Arrival by public transportation
The bus stop Am Schloss in Bönnigheim can be reached from ZOB Bietigheim-Bissingen (at the station) by bus 554 and from Kirchheim am Neckar by bus 574.

Parking
There is plenty of parking in the old city parking lot behind the castle (navigation address: Bleichwiese).

Restaurant tips
Ratsstüble Bönnigheim in a historical half-timbered house offers Swabian delicacies (ratsstueble-boennigheim.de; Hauptstr. 35). At Café Hüftgold you can live up to its name ("hip's gold"): here breakfast and delicious cakes can be enjoyed (cafe-hueftgold.com; Am Schlosspark 4/1).

Extra tips
Wine lovers will be delighted by the award-winning wine and the traditional company of young winegrower Christian Dautel (weingut-dautel.de; Lauerweg 55; closed in the afternoon on Sundays and weekdays). If there is not enough time for a side trip to the winery, a visit to the small vinotheque, which can be found right next to the castle, is a good idea (Schlossstr. 35).
Drivers can combine a visit to the Zander Collection with a visit to the Kunsthalle Würth in Schwäbisch Hall (see p. 64).

70 Museum Brandhorst

In 2009, the Kunstareal in Munich made a colorful gain with the opening of the Museum Brandhorst. On the site of the former Turkish barracks, Berlin architects Sauerbruch Hutton created an aesthetic contrast to the neighboring concrete building of the Pinakothek der Moderne.

The façade, which has more than 36,000 colored, approximately one-meter ceramic rods, and simultaneously fulfills the function of a sound-absorbing wall, almost looks like an abstract painting. The outer skin of the box-shaped, energy-saving building, bathed in twenty-three different colors, optically changes with the movement of the viewers. Inside, visitors are surprised with rational architecture. The bright and high interiors, mostly illuminated by daylight and fitted with plank floors, exude an airy and warm atmosphere.

The initial interest of Henkel's heir Udo Brandhorst and his wife, Anette Brandhorst, was not only in fine arts but especially in collaborations between painters and poets. This preference is reflected impressively in a collection of original edition books illustrated by Pablo Picasso, which are presented in special exhibitions in the museum. Drawings and collages by, among others, Kasimir Malevich, Kurt Schwitters, and Joan Miró, complement the complex.

In the course of the collector's activities, the focus shifted more to contemporary art. The Brandhorst couple was particularly enthusiastic about the works of American artist Cy Twombly. With over 170 paintings, drawings, and sculptures, today, the collection offers the most extensive overview of his artistic development worldwide. Twombly's monumental work *Lepanto* (2001), consists of twelve paintings originally created for the Venice Biennale and tells the story of the bloody naval battle in the Gulf of Corinth in 1571, is permanently on view in one of the museum's central rooms. In contrast to the historical background of the work, the room, which has a calming effect, was specially designed according to the artist's wishes. Andy Warhol is also present in the collection with more than one hundred works from all phases of his career,

Museum Brandhorst
Munich, Bavaria

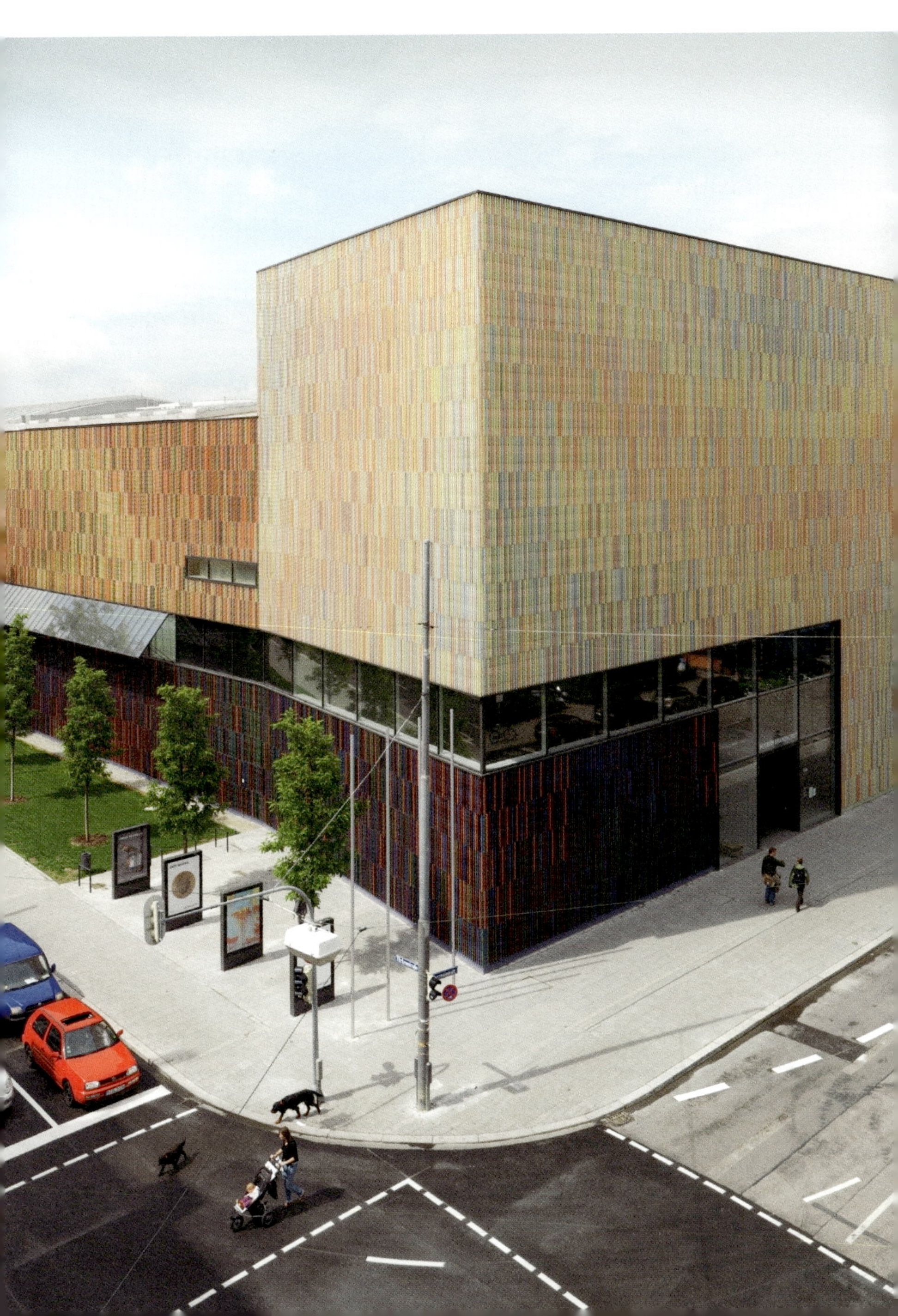

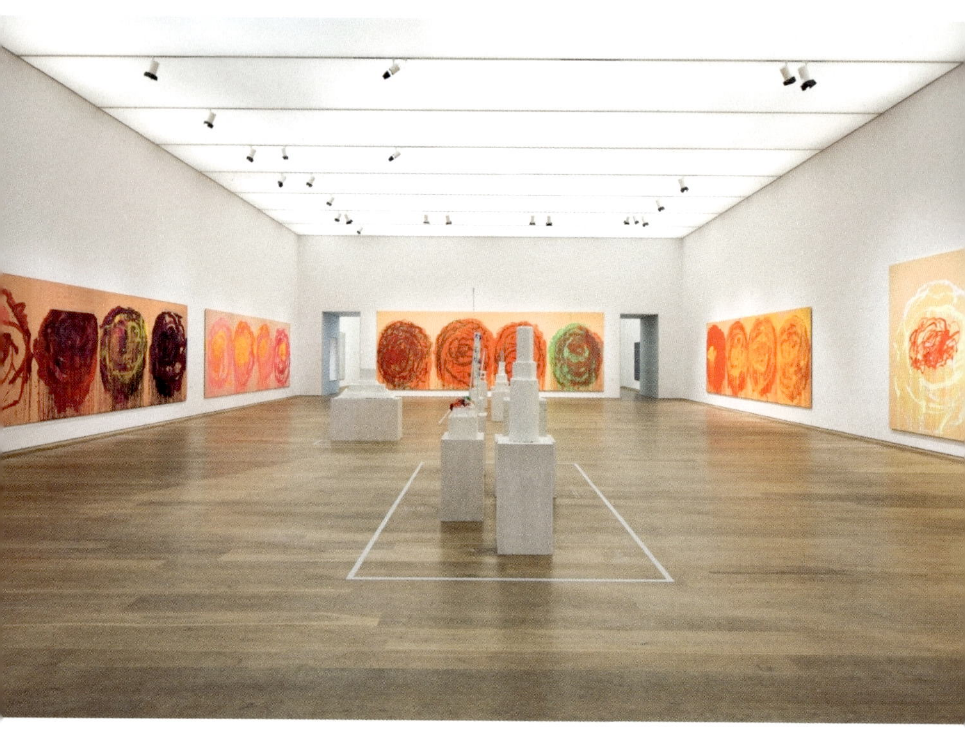

Museum Brandhorst

Kunstareal München
Theresienstr. 35 a
D-80333 München
Phone: +49 89 238052286
info@pinakothek.de
museum-brandhorst.de

Opening hours

Tue–Sun 10 a.m.–6 p.m.,
Thu 10 a.m.–8 p.m.
Public guided tours, which are included in the entrance fee, take place on Tuesdays at 3 p.m. and Saturdays at 4 p.m.
The dates for themed and special tours, as well as concerts and workshops held within the framework of the Kunstareal events, can be found on the exhibition page or the program page of the Pinakothek museums (only in German: pinakothek.de/programm).
The museum also houses a café and the Walther König bookshop. Since 2019, the foyer has also served as a venue for performances, film screenings, and other events. The curtain is a work of artist duo Guyton\Walker.

Entrance fees

Adults / Reduced: €7 / €5
Sundays: €1
Children and youths up to age 18 are admitted free of charge.
Day ticket for the Museum Brandhorst, the three Pinakotheken, and the Sammlung Schack without special exhibitions: €12
5-visit-pass for the Museum Brandhorst, the three Pinakotheken, and the Sammlung Schack without special exhibitions: €29.

Arrival by public transportation

From the main station take bus 100 in the direction of Ostbahnhof Munich get off at the Pinakotheken stop. The Universität (U3, U6) underground station is located nearby.

Restaurant tips

There are numerous restaurants and snack bars in the immediate vicinity. Opposite the museum entrance, at Ballabeni Icecream, you will find a large number of delicious ice cream varieties (ballabeni.de; Theresienstr. 46). The upscale Japanese restaurant Tokami serves excellent sushi in an authentic ambiance (tokami.de; Theresienstr. 54, closed Sundays). Good coffee and tasty French pastries can be found at Boulangerie Dompierre (dompierre.de; Türkenstr. 21). At the noble Italian Limoni, the guest is king, only open in the evenings (limoni-ristorante.com; Amalienstr. 38; closed Sundays). Innovative vegan cuisine is served in the modern Gratitude restaurant (gratitude-restaurant.de; Türkenstr. 55).

which is probably unique in Europe. The collection also includes artists such as Sigmar Polke, Georg Baselitz, Gerhard Richter, Alex Katz, Jean-Michel Basquiat, Ed Ruscha, Mike Kelley, and Damien Hirst. Additionally, there are objects, installations, and video works by Mario Merz, Bruce Nauman, Jannis Kounellis, Franz West, Katharina Fritsch, Christopher Wool, Robert Gober, Isaac Julien, Anri Sala, Wade Guyton, Wolfgang Tillmans, David Claerbout, Kerstin Brätsch, and others.

The founding of the museum was made possible by an exemplary partnership between the Udo and Anette Brandhorst Foundation, established in 1993, and the Bavarian State Painting Collections. With the proceeds of the foundation's capital, it is possible to continuously expand the collections of twentieth- and twenty-first-century art in exchange and consultation with the Pinakothek der Moderne to an extent that is unimaginable today with public funds.

Extra tips

You can also visit the Pinakotheken and the Sammlung Schack (pinakothek.de). If you would like to visit several museums, a day ticket is worthwhile. Adjacent to the Museum Brandhorst and the Pinakothek der Moderne, since 2010, the immense sculpture *Large Red Sphere* (2002) by American artist Walter De Maria invites contemplation. The original main entrance to the Turkish barracks, built in 1826, was transformed into an unusual art project due to a cooperation between the Bavarian State Painting Collections, the Pinakothek der Moderne Foundation, and the Udo and Anette Brandhorst Foundation. A donation from the Pinakothek der Moderne foundation made the conversion possible by Sauerbruch Hutton architectural office. The plastic core of the walk-in installation was acquired by the Udo and Anette Brandhorst Foundation (entrance at Türkenstr. 17; viewing times, excluding Mondays, April to October 11 a.m.–7 p.m., and November to March, noon–3 p.m.).
World-class exhibitions are often shown at the nearby Espace Louis Vuitton (eu.louisvuitton.com/eng-e1/art/espaces-louis-vuitton#munchen; Maximilianstr. 2a).
A visit to the Museum Brandhorst is worth combining with a visit to the Goetz Collection (see p. 82), the Alexander Tutsek-Stiftung (p. 90), as well as the Metropol Kunstraum—which requires a reservation (p. 86).

74
Buchheim Museum

The Buchheim Museum, situated on the shores of Lake Starnberg in the middle of the Höhenried Park landscape, was opened in 2001. Lothar-Günther Buchheim (1918–2007) attached great importance to versatility and openness—qualities that are also reflected in his collection. The painter, photographer, publisher, and author (among others, he wrote the book *Das Boot*, 1973) grew up in Chemnitz. He never felt like an art collector, but instead saw himself as a "collector and mediator," as an "art demonstrator with a missionary touch." After several museums sought to include his renowned Expressionist collection in their holdings, but thankfully rejected his numerous "secondary collections," the idea of creating his own museum arose.

From the outset, Buchheim envisioned a varied and lively museum for his "conglomeration." The original location was the Villa Maffei site in Feldafing, but a citizens' petition in 1997 prevented its realization. The neighboring community of Bernried then made the Hirschwiese available for the construction of the museum on the grounds of the Höhenried Clinic of the Upper Bavarian State Insurance Institution, the park of which had been built by the founder Wilhelmina Busch-Woods (from the US Anheuser-Busch brewery dynasty) in the 1930s. To adapt the building to the terrain, architect Günter Behnisch had to rotate the building ninety degrees and modify the design. The multiunit open structure, whose entrance level ends in a spectacular footbridge floating twelve meters above the lake, incorporates nature and landscape. Each art movement has its own area in the building with an exhibition area of circa 3,200 m², so that one could speak of "four museums under one roof." At the center is the Expressionist collection, with selected paintings, watercolors, drawings, and prints by Ernst Ludwig Kirchner, Erich Heckel, Karl Schmidt-Rottluff, Max Pechstein, Emil Nolde, and Otto Mueller. When Buchheim began to take an interest in works of art by Die Brücke painters in the 1950s, the German art market concentrated primarily on Abstract art, which prompted Buchheim to make his first purchases and to compose and publish several books on the Expressionists.

Buchheim Museum
Bernried, Bavaria

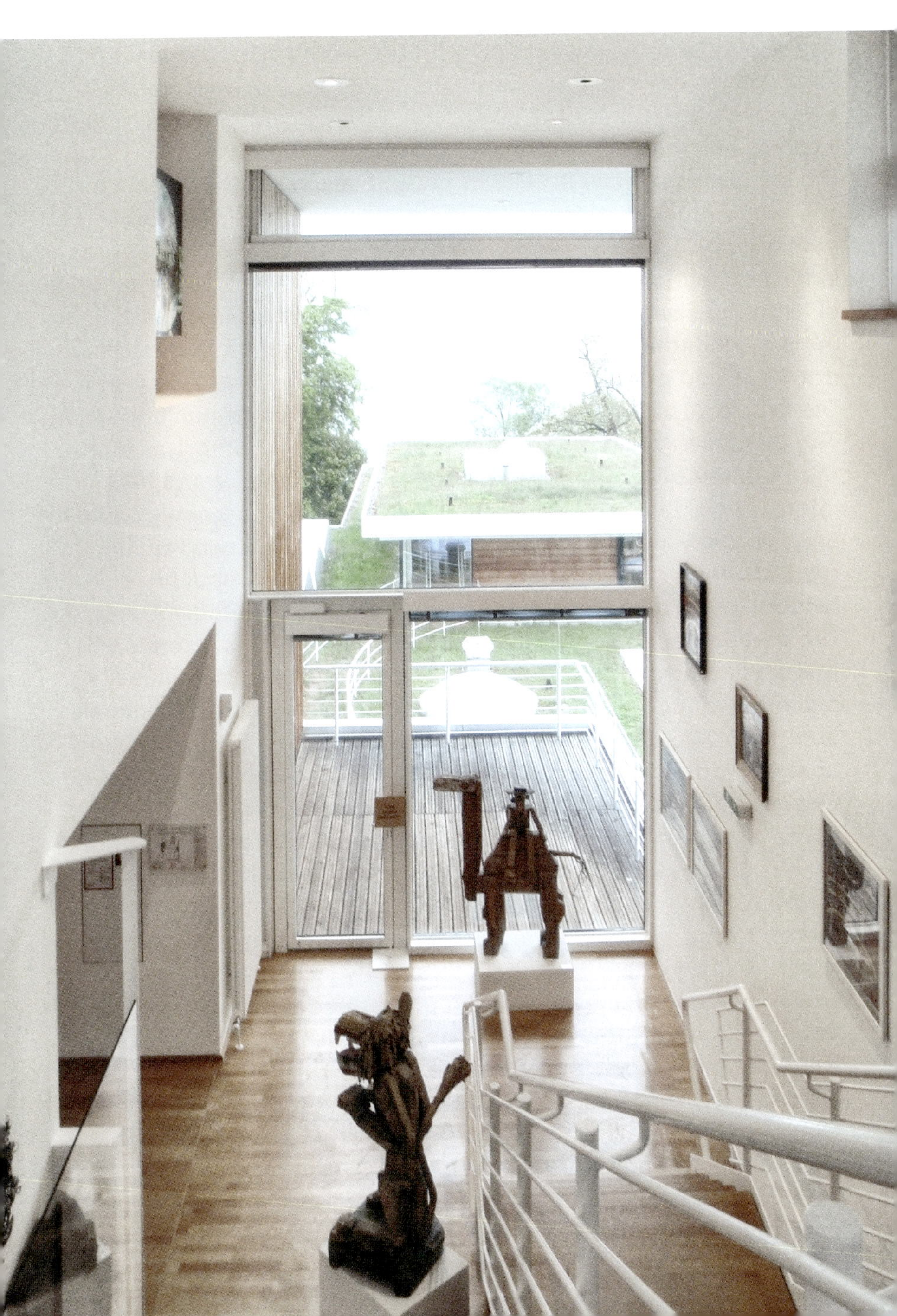

The desire to surround himself with the works of art he described every day and his instinct for the hunt were the driving forces behind the creation of the collection. Since Buchheim understood Expressionism as a broad-based movement that did not end with the dissolution of Die Brücke in 1913, he also acquired works by subsequent generations of artists in the form of Expressionist paintings by Max Kaus and Otto Dix. In 2017, Buchheim's Expressionist collection was supplemented by a loan from the collection of Würzburg engineer and entrepreneur Prof. Hermann Gerlinger, initially limited to ten years. In addition to paintings, watercolors, drawings and prints, documents, sculptures, and handicrafts by Die Brücke artists also found their way into the museum collection. The Gerlinger Collection, which is still growing, comprises more than 1,030 works. Thanks to his focus on Die Brücke and his intensive contact with Karl Schmidt-Rottluff, Gerlinger was able to acquire many significant works. By combining the two holdings, the Buchheim Museum became—alongside the Lenbachhaus—the leading institution of German Expressionism in Southern Germany.

In addition to Expressionism, Buchheim turned his attention to folk art and ethnology. The kaleidoscope, entitled "secondary collections," comprises reverse glass paintings, carousel animals, about 4,000 glass paperweights, popular prints, farmer's cupboards, porcelain, ceramics, glass, textiles, jewelry, sculptures, masks, and cult objects from Africa, Oceania, and Asia.

A further part of the collection consists of the collector's photographs and pictures and those of his wife, Diethild Buchheim, who died in 2014. In addition to submarine photographs and drawings from his time as a naval war correspondent, his fretsaw figures from the giant circus Buffi are particularly striking. Furthermore, works by autodidacts such as the one-armed Bavarian wood sculptor Hans Schmitt, the ventriloquist Josef Muskat, or the Parisian Naïve artist Hector Trotin are exhibited.

Lothar-Günther Buchheim was not looking for art; he found it. Classifications such as "valuable" or "worthless" and categories such as "high" and "low" art were irrelevant to him.

The Buchheim Museum is supported by the Buchheim Foundation, founded in 1995.

Buchheim Museum
Museum of Phantasy / Buchheim Collection
Am Hirschgarten 1
D-82347 Bernried am Starnberger See
Phone: +49 8158 99700
info@buchheimmuseum.de
buchheimmuseum.de

Opening hours
April to October Tue–Sun/Holidays 10 a.m.–6 p.m.; November to March Tue–Sun/Holidays 10 a.m.–5 p.m.
At 2:30 p.m., on Sundays and public holidays, there are public tours of the collections and current special exhibitions (€3.50 plus admission to the museum). The current program of events, as well as the dates for the children's tours and workshops, can be found on the website under the heading "News/Calendar." The museum also has a small shop and the Café Buffi.

Entrance fees
Adults / Reduced / Family ticket: €9,50 / €5 / €21
If you present a train ticket or a taxi receipt, you will receive a small discount on the entrance fee. Museum Buchheim is a partner of the MuSeenKarte (museen-landschaft-expressionismus.de).

Arrival by public transportation
From Munich, you can take the S6 to Tutzing and then a taxi to the museum. Alternatively, you can take the regional train to Bernried station and reach the museum on foot in about half an hour. During the summer months, you can travel from Starnberg to Bernried on the Starnberger See liner ships of the Bayerische Seenschifffahrt (combined ticket with admission €23.50; seenschifffahrt.de).

Parking
The museum has a parking place on the museum grounds.

Restaurant tips
In the Bernried Hofladen with adjoining café, there is ice cream, cakes, and homemade pasta (bernrieder-hofladen.de; Tutzinger Str. 12D). Praline lovers will be in heaven at Clement Chococult, right next to the railway station (clement-chococult.de; Bahnhofstr. 25). At Restaurant Pfaffenwinkel at the Hohenpähl golf course, guests as well golfers are served regional and international dishes. Particularly noteworthy are the cheese fondue and inexpensive lunch menu (restaurant-pfaffenwinkel.de; Am Hochschloß, 82396 Pahl; closed for winter in January and February). In Tutzing, you will find Café Käthe with a colorful vintage living room (cafe-kaethe.com; Hallberger Allee 14, 82327 Tutzing; closed on Sundays and Mondays).

Extra tip
It is worth making a detour to the Franz Marc Museum in Kochel. In a modern building extension, works by Franz Marc are juxtaposed with the works of Die Brücke artists (franz-marc-museum.de; Franz Marc Park 8–10, 82431 Kochel am See).

78 DASMAXIMUM KunstGegenwart

Since 2011, Traunreut has been home to a museum that would also attract attention in a major art metropolis. In 2010, Heiner Friedrich, son of Alzmetall founder Harald Friedrich, founded the Stiftung DASMAXIMUM, which exhibits works of art collected by him. Away from the surrounding tourist sites, the former gallery owner and collector has realized a permanent "art setting" and a place of intense reflection. Heiner Friedrich grew up in Berlin, then in Upper Bavaria's Kirchberg, and studied philosophy in Munich. In 1962, through his first wife, he met Six Friedrich and Franz Dahlem, who inspired his interest for contemporary art. The following year, the three opened the Galerie Friedrich & Dahlem in Munich together. With a combination of a flair for trend-setting art and unshakeable courage, Friedrich made a selection that included highlights of American and European art. As one of the very first gallery owners to do so, in Munich and later also in Cologne, he supported the Minimal, Land Art, and Conceptual artists Joseph Beuys, Sigmar Polke, Gerhard Richter, Donald Judd, Cy Twombly, Walter De Maria, Blinky Palermo, Carl Andre, John Chamberlain, Dan Flavin, and Andy Warhol, all of whom were unknown at the time. Even when Heiner Friedrich moved his gallery to New York in 1971, without Franz Dahlem since 1966, he remained true to his artists. In 1974, Friedrich founded the Dia Art Foundation in New York with art historian Helen Winkler and his later wife, Philippa de Menil. It was an outstanding project with which he secured the long-term opportunity to support "his" artists with patronage for large-scale projects that could hardly be financed otherwise. The support of Walter De Maria's *Lightning Field* (1977), Donald Judd's Chinati Foundation in Marfa, James Turrell's light project *Roden Crater* (1974) in Flagstaff, and Joseph Beuys's *7000 Oaks* (1982) contributed to Friedrich's legendary reputation.

This background explains the unusual exhibition concept and the quality of the works seen in the museum. The location also has to do with Friedrich's biography: The city of Traunreut only

DASMAXIMUM KunstGegenwart
Traunreut, Bavaria

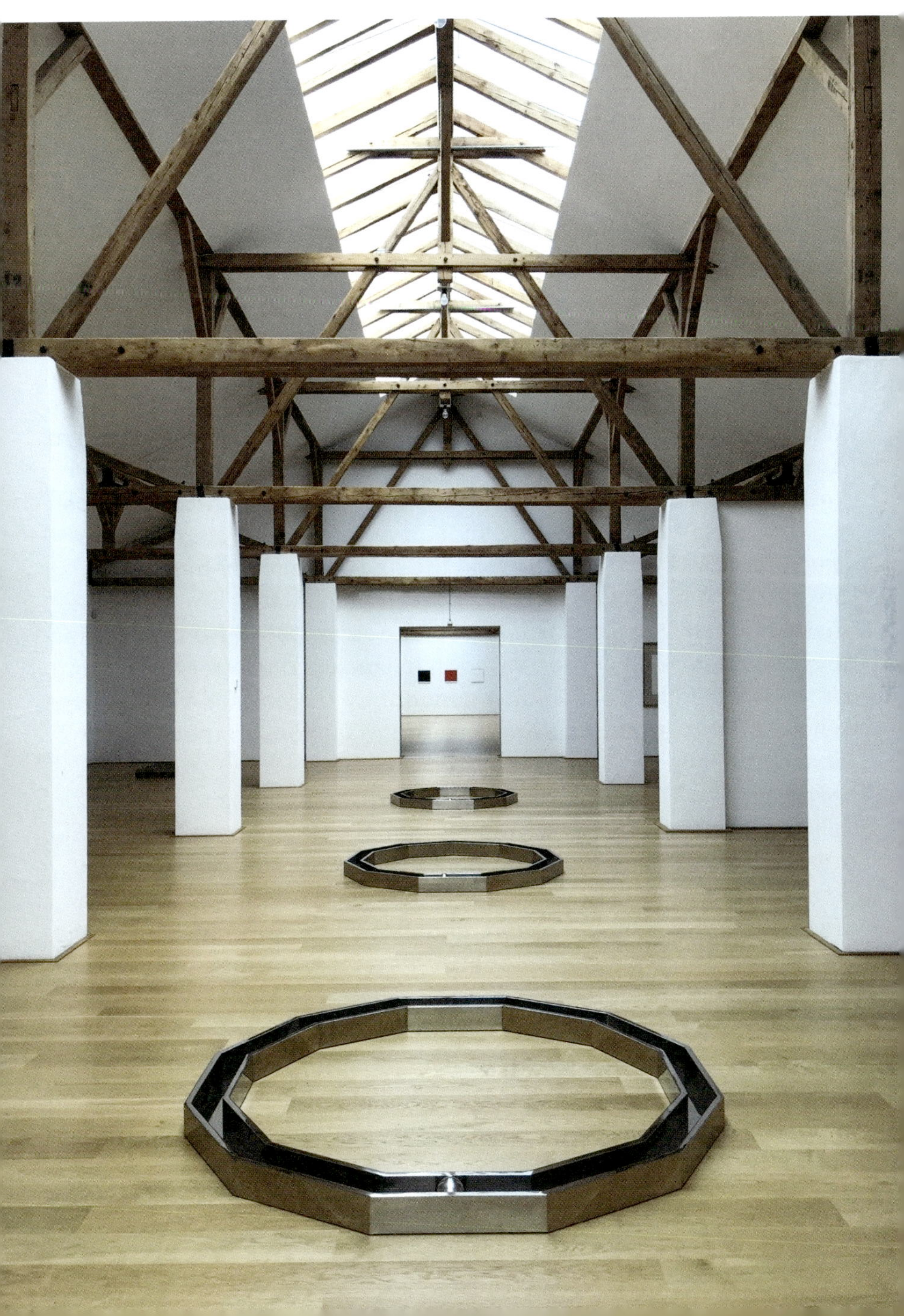

developed in 1945 on the grounds of an army ammunition depot founded by the National Socialists in 1938, after smaller companies settled in the numerous depot and factory halls after the Second World War. Harald Friedrich acquired the part of the site on which DASMAXIMUM stands today at the end of the 1940s. As heir to his parents' business, Heiner Friedrich had the factory, which was still in industrial use until the end of the 1990s, rebuilt. Since its opening, the "daylight" museum has been expanded several times and now permanently displays around 200 works by ten artists in five halls on 4,300 m^2. Friedrich's credo, "One artist, one room, permanently," has been consistently implemented. The American artists John Chamberlain, Dan Flavin, Walter De Maria, and Andy Warhol, and German artists Georg Baselitz, Uwe Lausen, and Imi Knoebel, as well as Austrian artist Arnulf Rainer, are represented with extensive groups of works. In a hall opened in 2016, the most extensive continuous presentation of artist Blinky Palermo, who died young, is "juxtaposed" with the mathematically precise works of Conceptual and Land Art artist Walter De Maria. The complete installation of Dan Flavin's *European Couples* (1966–1971) is located in an inconspicuous green wooden barracks. The exterior coloring of the large halls is based on a concept by the painter Maria Zerres, who used the primary color chord of the façades to thematize the conscious rededication of the site.

Friedrich, who lives in the United States, continues to support his artists, as can be seen from his numerous collaborations with other institutions. His commitment to the work of Joseph Beuys is particularly intense. The action 7000 Oaks – City Forestation Instead of City Administration, initiated by Beuys for documenta 7, was one of the most significant art projects of all time. A million-year-old basalt stone was placed as a stable guardian next to each of the young trees. With the help of the Stiftung DASMAXIMUM Foundation, the last exposed basalt columns from the quarry near Kassel were brought to Traunreut and the oak plantations in honor of Joseph Beuys have been continued at prominent locations in Traunreut since 2015 as a sign of a new future.

DASMAXIMUM KunstGegenwart Traunreut, Bavaria

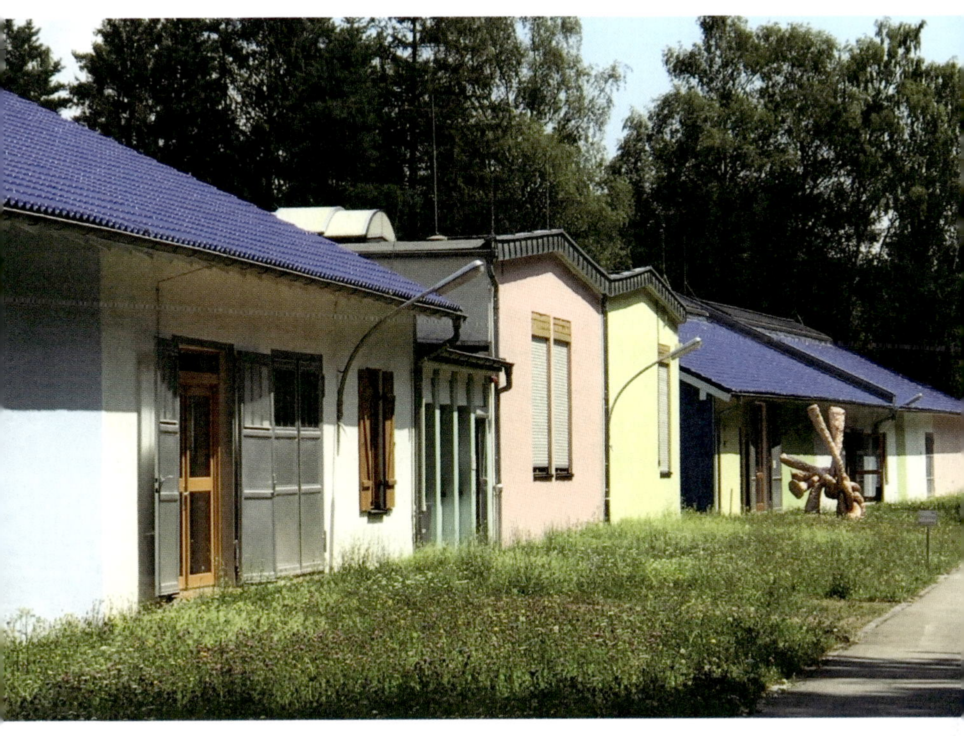

DASMAXIMUM KunstGegenwart
Fridtjof-Nansen-Str. 16
D-83301 Traunreut
Phone: +49 8669 1203713
mail@dasmaximum.com
dasmaximum.com

Opening hours
April to September Sat/Sun noon–6 p.m.
October to March Sat/Sun 11 a.m.–4 p.m.
Winter break in December
Individual theme tours, workshops for school classes and adults, as well as separate lectures, are held. The events are communicated on Facebook and via newsletter.

Entrance fees
Adults / Reduced / Children (school classes) / Family ticket: €8 / €5 / €2 / €12

Arrival by public transportation
Coming from Traunreut station, keep left, turn left into Kantstraße, then right into Werner-von-Siemens-Straße and then right into Fridtjof-Nansen-Straße (about a ten-minute walk).

Parking
There is a marked parking lot to the right of the museum entrance.

Restaurant tips
In Palling, Bavarian cuisine is served at the Dorfgasthof Michlwirt (michlwirt.net; Steinerstr. 2, 83349 Palling; closed Sundays).

Extra tips
If the weather is fine, a visit to the Fraueninsel and the Herreninsel on Lake Chiemsee is recommended. The unfinished New Palace Herrenchiemsee leaves no doubt about the absolutist delusions of Bavarian fairytale king Ludwig II. As part of the "Königsklasse" program, contemporary works of art of the highest quality from the Pinakothek der Moderne's collection can be admired in summer. (herrenchiemsee.de; 83209 Herrenchiemsee). In the historic fishing village of Polling, 50 km southwest of Munich, it is possible to visit a monumental light artwork by the American artist Dan Flavin, presented in cooperation with the museum DASMAXIMUM (fischerbaukunst.de; Weilheimer Str. 12–14, 82398 Polling). The fascinating Dream House can be "experienced" in the Pollinger Regenbogenstadl—a space with reciprocal interpenetration of light and sound, visual art, and music (regenbogenstadl.de; Georg Rueckert Str. 1, 92398 Polling; open in summer on Saturday afternoons and Sundays, in winter only on Saturday afternoons).

82 Sammlung Goetz

The former private museum of Ingvild Goetz in Munich-Oberföhring, situated in a park-like garden, is a place of pilgrimage for architecture fans and art lovers alike. Designed by Swiss architects Herzog & de Meuron and completed in 1993, the minimalist cube with a façade of wood, glass, and aluminum has truly made architectural history. The building consists of a wooden construction resting on an open reinforced concrete tub, sunken into the ground to its upper edge. Circumferential window bands frame the structure. Diffused daylight penetrates through the matt glass into the interior of the rooms. The large exhibition hall and the BASE 103 extension, specially designed in 2004 for the presentation of media works, are located in the basement. Three smaller exhibition rooms are located on the upper floor. Due to the sophisticated architecture and the different heights of the walls, plastered in white, it is almost impossible to tell on which level one is standing at any given time. The building could be said to have mystical qualities. Helmut Federle, who is also represented in the collection with artworks, advised the architects on the design of the exhibition rooms with their modular spatial structure.

Ingvild Goetz collected more than 5,000 works of art, mostly from the 1960s to the present day. The collection is based on artists of the Arte Povera movement, such as Jannis Kounellis and Mario Merz, whom she exhibited in the 1970s in her galleries in Munich and Düsseldorf. At the time, they were not well-known. She also presents works by Cy Twombly, Andy Warhol, and Bruce Nauman. In 1984, Ingvild Goetz gave up her gallery activities to devote herself to the systematic development of her collection and the discovery and promotion of mostly young and, as of yet, unknown artists. Many American artists from the 1980s such as Robert Gober, Roni Horn, Richard Prince, and Mike Kelley are represented in the collection, as are the Young British Artists Tracey Emin and Sarah Lucas. In addition to drawings, graphics, paintings, photographs, and sculptures, the collection also focuses on video and film works and spatial installations. Ingvild Goetz's predilection

Sammlung Goetz
Munich, Bavaria

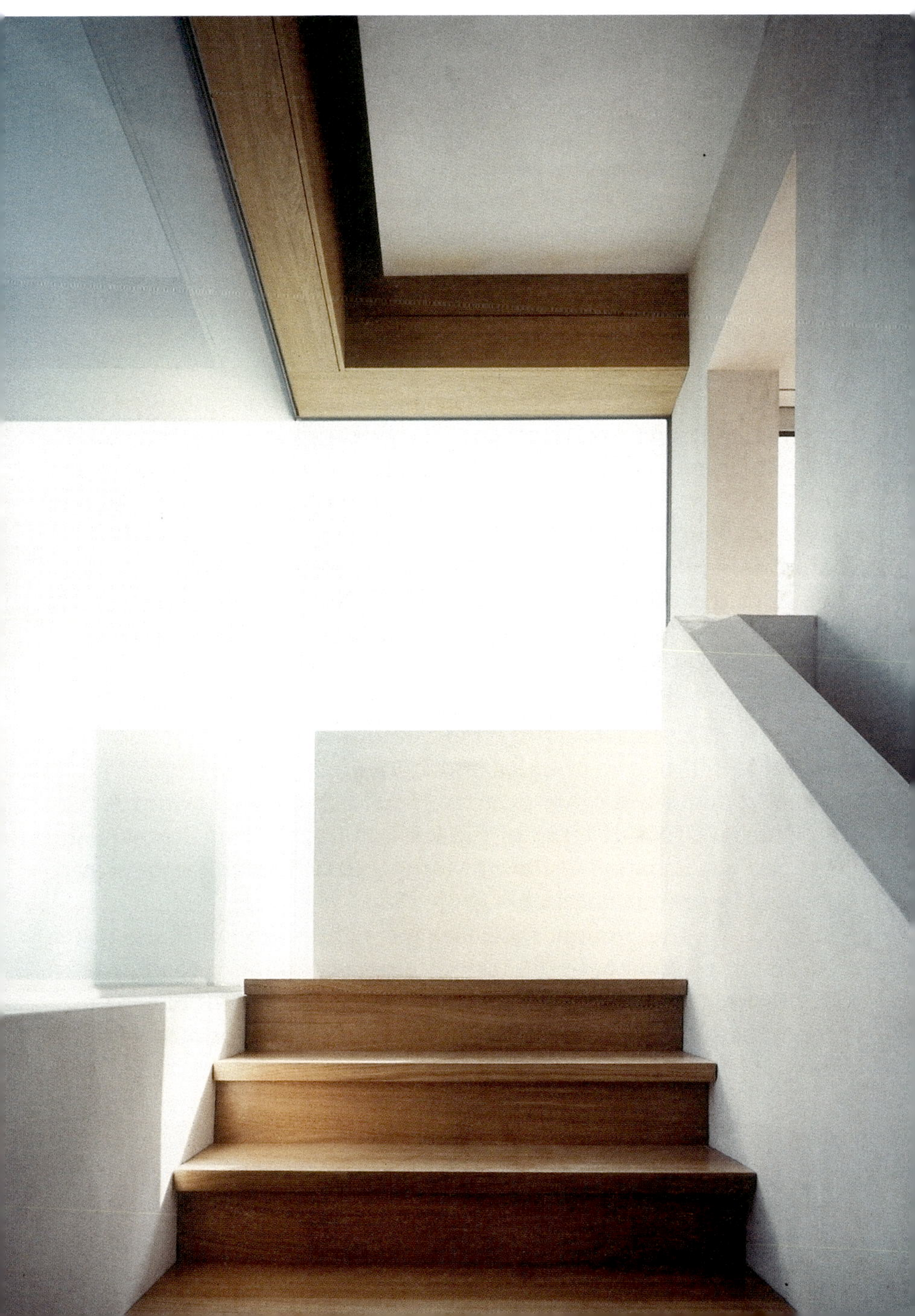

for “difficult” art, which is intended to challenge the perception of the viewers, runs through all decades of collecting.

On January 1, 2014, Ingvild Goetz donated 375 works of media art and the Munich exhibition building to the Free State of Bavaria. She made the remaining works available to selected museums in Bavaria on permanent loan for an initial period of ten years. As an honorary director, she will, however, remain associated with the museum, which is now officially part of the Staatliche Museen und Sammlungen Bayern (Bavarian State Museums and Collections). In curated temporary exhibitions, prominent works from the Sammlung Goetz will continue to be shown in a space almost 600 m². As before, the temporary exhibitions are conceived by Ingvild Goetz and her employees in collaboration with the artists. The exhibitions will be designed and presented in such a way that the artworks show the world to the visitors in a way they had never previously imagined. The aim is to promote openness of perception and constant reflection on thinking and views.

Besides the wall piece *Blaues Dreieck* (1969) by Blinky Palermo on the upper floor, only *Untitled – Portrait of Ingvild Goetz* (1993) by Félix González-Torres can still be seen in the basement as a permanent work of art. The typeface on the window band reflects a mixture of events in world history and the collector’s personal moments in the form of dates and keywords.

Among numerous other awards, Ingvild Goetz was awarded the Federal Cross of Merit of the Federal Republic of Germany in 2011 and the Bavarian Order of Merit in 2013. The collector is also involved in various charitable projects.

Since 2011, the Sammlung Goetz has cooperated with the Haus der Kunst in Munich. In the former air-raid shelter of the museum, adapted for the presentation of film and video, temporary exhibitions with media works from the collection are shown twice a year.

Sammlung Goetz
Munich, Bavaria

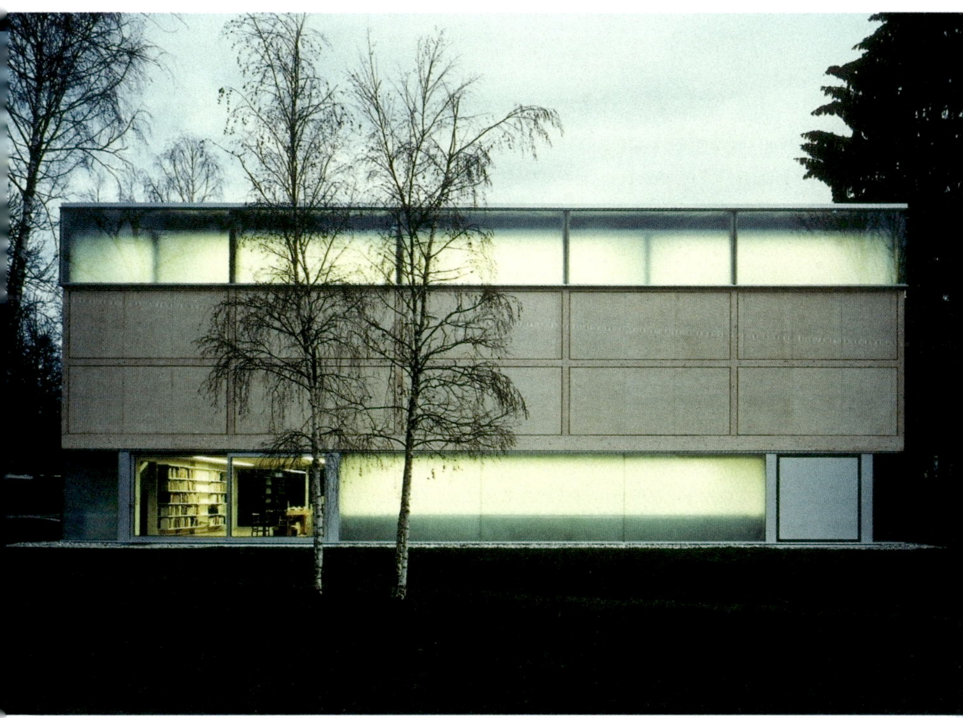

Sammlung Goetz
Oberföhringer Str. 103
D-81925 München
Tel. +49 89 95939690
info@sammlung-goetz.de
sammlung-goetz.de

Opening hours
Thu/Fri 2–6 p.m., Sat 11 a.m.–4 p.m. Visits are only possible during opening hours after registering on the website or by telePhone: Current offers for art education can be found on the website.
In the nearby office, curators and students have access to a comprehensive reference library with approx. 7,000 volumes relating to art from the last sixty years.
The museum building is not suitable for wheelchairs or strollers.

Entrance fees
Free admission

Arrival by public transportation
At the main station take the U4 in the direction of Arabellapark to the stop Richard-Strauss-Straße. From here, take the city bus lines 188 or 189 in the direction of Unterföhring-Fichtenstraße and get off at Bürgerpark Oberföhring. The entrance is directly opposite. At the entrance gate, ring the "Sammlung Goetz" bell; after entry, you'll find the glass entrance door on the left of the building.

Parking
Unfortunately, there are no parking spaces in front of the Sammlung Goetz. However, it is possible to park your car in the Bürgerpark Oberföhring car park, located opposite.

Restaurant tips
Near the collection are the upscale restaurant and hotel Freisinger Hof (freisinger-hof.de; Oberföhringer Str. 189–191). There one can enjoy Southern German and Austrian cuisine. Not far away is the Bavarian Gasthof Sankt Emmeramsmühle with a beer garden that is popular with chic Munich residents (emmeramsmuehle.de; St. Emmeram 41).

Extra tips
Drivers can take an excursion to the south of Munich to the colorful Archiv Geiger after making an appointment (archiv-geiger.de; Muttenthalerstr. 26).
It is an excellent idea to combine a visit to the Sammlung Goetz with an appointment at Metropol Kunstraum (see p. 86), a detour to the Alexander Tutsek-Stiftung (p. 90), as well as the Museum Brandhorst (p. 70).

86
Metropol Kunstraum

In the middle of Schwabing, small exhibitions are regularly shown in a former gas station. Metropol Kunstraum was created in 2007, initiated by entrepreneur and collector Markus Michalke, who, apart from a few exceptions, presents positions from his collection on approximately 40 m². The focus of the collection, and thereby the exhibitions, is on paper works and sculptures. American Minimalism of the 1960s and 1970s and the following generation of artists characterize the program. Michalke began collecting this art movement at the end of the 1990s. He sees his art space primarily as a place of shared art experience, but also as a place of experimentation for himself. The possibility of exhibiting an artist's entire series or having several individual works enter into dialogue makes it clear to him whether the depth of the collection is sufficient to be able to grasp and understand the respective artist's work in its entirety. And so, there are numerous drawing series in the collection of several hundred works. In three annual, mostly monographic exhibitions, Michalke presents selected artists with several works. In the past, these were Günther Förg, Donald Judd, Robert Ryman, Gabriel Orozco, Fred Sandback, Sol LeWitt, Gordon Matta-Clark, and Jill Baroff. A small catalog always accompanies the respective exhibitions.

The Metropol Kunstraum is an unusual exhibition venue, the architecture and charm of the old Metropol Garage have been preserved with a love for detail. The well-known gas station and garage were built in 1955 as the base of an apartment building. The projecting canopy, with its trumpet-shaped supports, and the oval, glazed salesroom, which is now used for the exhibitions, were typical of the gas station architecture during the years of economic boom. The color contrasts on the columns and the edge of the roof hint at what fuel brand was sold here over many decades.

Metropol Kunstraum
Munich, Bavaria

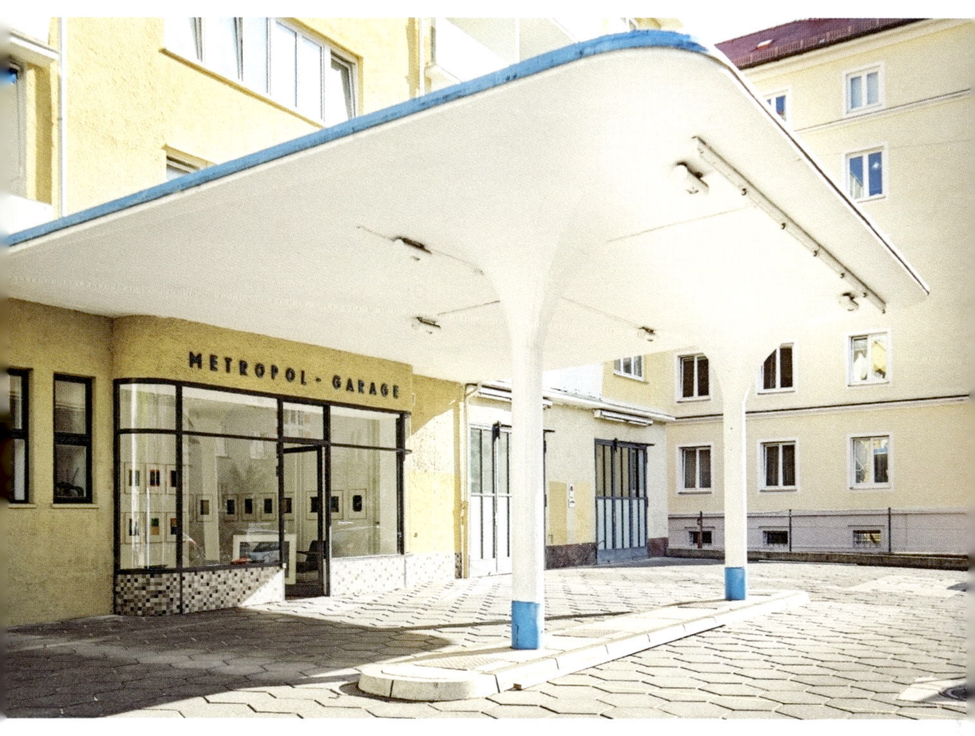

Metropol Kunstraum
Georgenstr. 42
D-80799 München
info@metropolkunstraum.de
metropolkunstraum.de

Opening hours
Wed 4:30–6:30 p.m. or by appointment

Entrance fees
Free admission

Arrival by public transportation
From Karlsplatz (Stachus) you can reach Nordendstraße in a few minutes with tram 27 (direction Petuelring).

Restaurant tips
KANSHA restaurant, inspired by Japan's Buddhist temple kitchen, serves "plant-based food" at its best (kansha-restaurant.de; Occamstr. 6; open evenings only). The cafe serves breakfast and homemade cakes (Georgenstr. 35).

Extra tips
A visit to the late Baroque Asam Church (officially St.-Johann-Nepomuk Church) is also a good idea (Sendlinger Str. 32). Museum Brandhorst (see p. 70) and the Alexander Tutsek-Stiftung (p. 90) are very close to the Kunstraum.

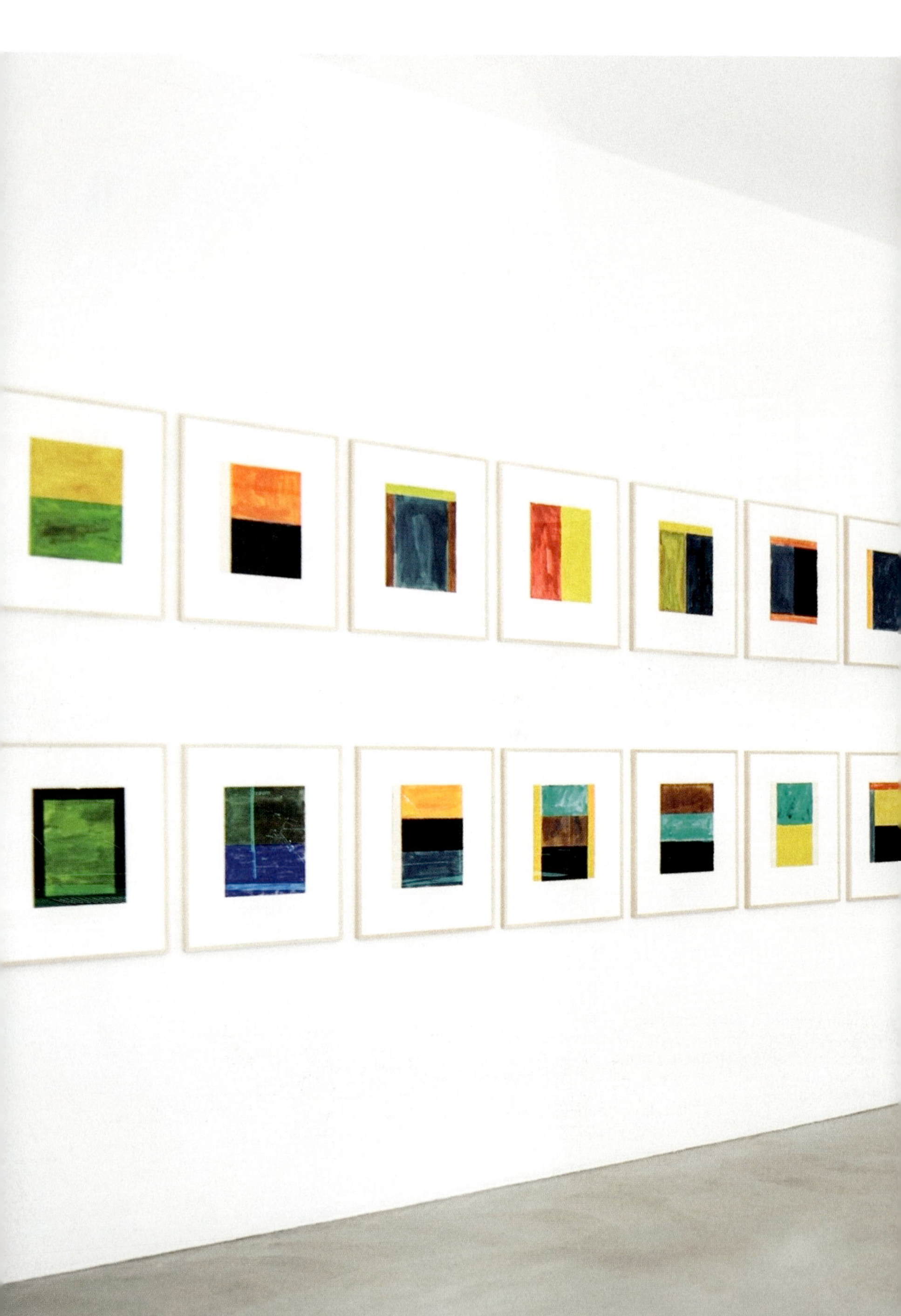

Metropol Kunstraum
Munich, Bavaria

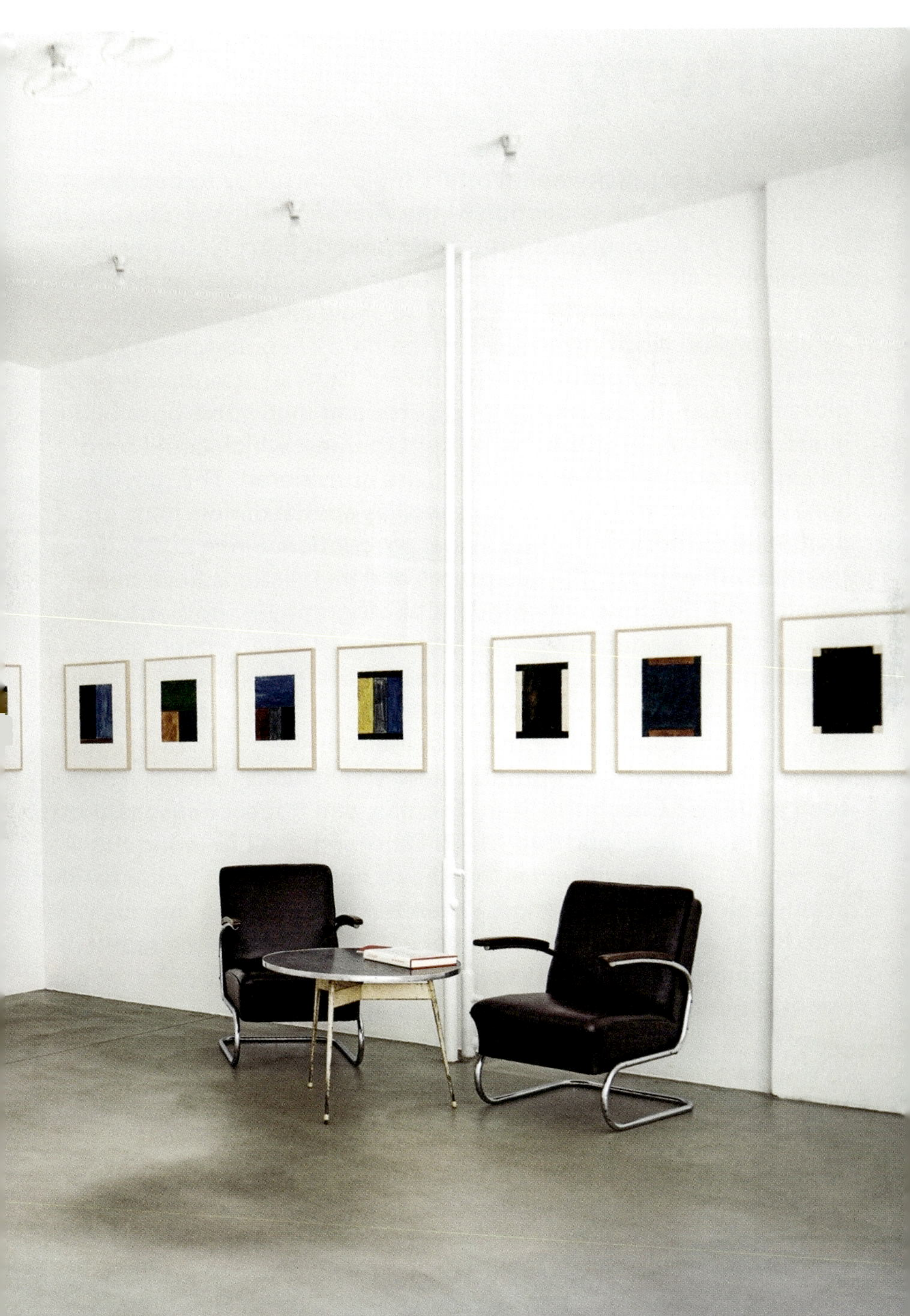

90 Alexander Tutsek-Stiftung

A visit to Munich-Schwabing offers the opportunity to become acquainted with the collection of the Alexander Tutsek-Stiftung in the rooms of a lavishly restored and converted Art Nouveau villa. Originally built in 1911 for sculptor Georg Albertshofer as a studio house, it has been used since 2004 to show annually changing exhibitions on innovative topics in the field of contemporary glass across an area of approximately 250 m². Special attention is paid to glass as a material as well as its diverse and innovative possibilities in art. Here, subtle and transcendent themes, which could hardly be expressed with other materials, are considered. The play of light with color and structure, as well as spatial dimensions, are a challenge to more than one's visual perception. Since 2008, using the medium of glass, the sculptures and installations have been curated in a dialogue with modern photography—another focal point of the foundation's collection. The collection encompasses a broad spectrum of the latest trends in these two art media. Young and internationally renowned artists such as Tony Cragg, Mona Hatoum, Kiki Smith, and Pae White are represented in the collection. In the field of photography, new acquisitions include artists such as James Casebere, Stan Douglas, and Robert Rauschenberg.

Alexander Tutsek and Eva-Maria Fahrner-Tutsek founded the Alexander Tutsek-Stiftung in 2000 as a nonprofit institution for the promotion of art and science. When the entrepreneur and his wife, who holds a doctorate in psychology, began to build their collection of contemporary glass art, they realized that this material had not yet found its place in the German art world. Contemporary glass art was still mostly unknown to the local public—in contrast to the art scene in the United States and some European countries. In addition to the idea of giving the young art form a forum and actively supporting it, the desire to promote the latest in science as well as innovative projects and research work in engineering, especially in the fields of glass, ceramics, stone, and rare-earth elements, came from personal professional experience.

Alexander Tutsek-Stiftung
Munich, Bavaria

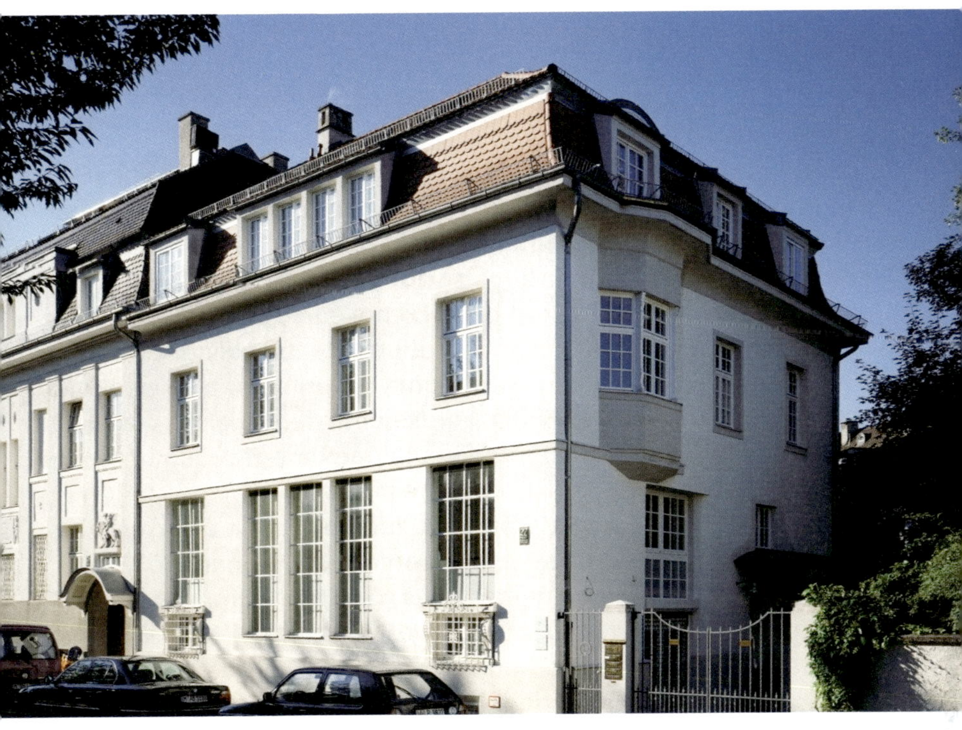

Alexander Tutsek-Stiftung
Karl-Theodor-Str. 27
D-80803 München
Phone: +49 89 55273060
info@atstiftung.de
atstiftung.de

Opening hours
Tue–Fri 2–6 p.m., closed holidays and during installation periods. Public guided tours are offered regularly (register at event@atstiftung.de or +49 89 552730611).

Entrance fees
Free admission

Arrival by public transportation
The closest stop is Bonner Platz (U3).

Restaurant tips
Only a few minutes walk away is Gasthaus Weinbauer (weinbauer-muenchen.de; Fendstr. 5), where guests can dive into Fleischpflanzerl (meatballs) and Backhendl (fried chicken). Fans of authentic Thai cuisine will be inspired by Longgrain (longgrain.de; Belgradstr. 45). In the same neighborhood, the simple Nabo's restaurant prepares tasty Eastern and Lebanese meals (Belgradstr. 47). The beautiful concept store galore# offers good coffee, smoothies, and healthy, delicious snacks (storegalore.de; Belgradstr. 47).

Extra tips
Your visit to the Alexander Tutsek-Stiftung can easily be combined with a visit to the Goetz Collection (see p. 82), a trip to the Kunstareal München, the Pinakothek museums, and the Museum Brandhorst (p. 70). A visit to the nearby Metropol Kunstraum is also possible by appointment (p. 86).

92 KUNSTMUSEUM WALTER

Opened in 2002, in the imposing Glaspalast, the private Kunstmuseum Walter comprises modern and contemporary art as well as some works of Classical Modern art. The collection focuses on West and East German paintings and sculptures from 1945 to the present day. The collection has been compiled by Prof. Dr. h. c. Ignaz Walter since the early 1970. About thousand of the collection's works are permanently exhibited on two floors covering an area of about 6,000 m^2. There are a thousand works in the depot, and a further nine hundred works are presented in the permanent collection in the Staatsgalerie Stuttgart.

Mainly international art is presented on the first floor. In addition, there are numerous works from different creative phases of West German artists, including Sigmar Polke, Günther Förg, Gerhard Richter, Georg Baselitz, Elvira Bach, and Anselm Kiefer. A spiral staircase leads to the second floor, where art from the former GDR, in particular, the Leipzig School by Bernhard Heisig, Werner Tübke, and Wolfgang Mattheuer and the New Leipzig School by Neo Rauch and Rosa Loy, is shown.

The eventful history of the former industrial building is exciting. The massive factory of iron, concrete, and glass was planned in 1908/09 by Stuttgart architect Philipp J. Manz on behalf of the Mechanische Baumwoll-Spinnerei und Weberei Augsburg (SWA) and built on a site of almost half a hectare. After only a short time, the Augsburgers christened the building "Glaspalast" because during the night shift the light shone through the large windows far into the surrounding dark. When the factory started production in 1910, 26,000 spindles and 492 looms went into operation, and 2,935 people were employed here. With the decline of the Augsburg textile industry, production ended with the bankruptcy of the SWA company in 1988. The building stood empty for over ten years until entrepreneur Ignaz Walter, partner, chairman of the board and later the supervisory board of the Walter Bau AG, bought the completely dilapidated building in 1999.

KUNSTMUSEUM WALTER
Augsburg, Bavaria

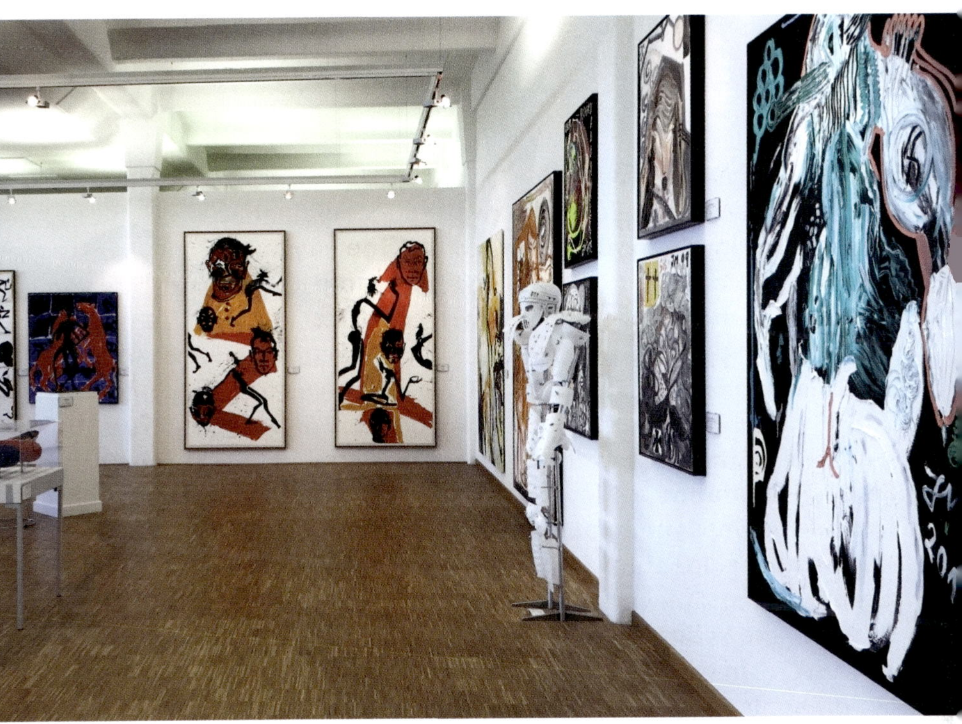

KUNSTMUSEUM WALTER
Beim Glaspalast 1
D-86153 Augsburg
Phone: +49 821 8151163
office@kunstmuseumwalter.com
kunstmuseumwalter.com

Opening hours
Fri–Sun and holidays 11 a.m.–6 p.m. and upon request (individuals and groups)
Individual guided tours and museum educational activities for children, adolescents, and school classes are offered.

Entrance fees
Adults / Reduced / Students / Family ticket: €6 / €5 / €2.50 / €14
Combination ticket (includes admission to the H2 – Zentrum für Gegenwartskunst and the Staatsgalerie für Moderne Kunst): €9

Arrival by public transportation
From the train station, walk to Königsplatz, then take tram line 1 (direction Lechhausen / Neuer Ostfriedhof) to the Jakobertor stop and from there, take bus 33 to the Glaspalast stop.

Restaurant tips
Restaurant Magnolia offers modern crossover cuisine (magnolia-restaurant.de; closed Saturday afternoons). Vegan dishes and cakes are served in the Kresslesmühle in the Dreizehn (muehle-dreizehn.de; Barfüßerstr. 4). Christian Grünwald serves innovative cuisine of the highest level in the award-winning restaurant August (0821 35279; Johannes-Haag-Str. 14; reservations required). Creative cuisine is also offered in the Restaurant Lustküche (restaurant-lustkueche.de; Mittlerer Lech 23; closed Sundays).

Extra tips
The Glaspalast also houses the H2 – Zentrum für Gegenwartskunst, which alternates between its own collection and special exhibitions (kunstsammlungen-museen.augsburg.de/h2-zentrum-fuer-gegenwartskunst-im-glaspalast), and the Staatsgalerie für Moderne Kunst, a branch gallery of the Pinakothek der Moderne in Munich that presents highlights from the holdings of the Bavarian State Painting Collections after 1950 (pinakothek.de/node/236). But the absolute highlight is a visit to the St. Moritz Church. The London architect and designer John Pawson, who was commissioned with the redesign, created a highly impressive "church space of the future." The niche with the puristic basin on the left side of the entrance has a very special atmosphere (moritzkirche.de; Moritzplatz 3).

94
The Walther Collection

The Walther Collection, located in the rural Burlafingen district of Neu-Ulm, concentrates on the exploration, collection, exhibition, and publication of modern and contemporary photography and video art. Opened in 2010, the complex consists of several adjacent buildings with a total exhibition area of 1,000 m^2. The Walther Collection Project Space, a branch of the collection with 160 m^2 of exhibition space, is located in the West Chelsea Building in New York. The exhibitions there change quarterly and complement the longer-term program of the museum in Burlafingen. The Walther Family Foundation, a New York registered charitable foundation, finances the collection and the exhibition.

The unusual location for this unique private collection stems from the biography of collector Artur Walther. Originally from Burlafingen, Walther has lived in New York for decades. With an MBA from Harvard Business School, he became a partner at Goldman Sachs and one of the founders of the International Swaps and Derivates Association (ISDA). In 1994, at the age of 45, Walther stepped away from his stressful life as an investment banker and enthusiastically threw himself into the art scene. From then on, architecture, design, and photography have been of particular interest to him, and he began his studies at the renowned International Center of Photography in Manhattan, which, around two decades later, awarded him the Infinity Award 2016 for his commitment and his collection. More than twenty years ago, the collection was founded on works by German New Objectivity photographers, such as August Sander and Karl Blossfeldt. Walther later expanded the collection beyond European and American photography when he discovered Chinese and African photography—today, these are the focus of the collection. David Goldblatt, Jo Ractliffe, Mikhael Subotzky, Guy Tillim, Ai Weiwei, Zhang Dali, Song Dong, Zhang Huan, Samuel Fosso, Rotimi Fani-Kayode, and Santu Mofokeng are represented. That Artur Walther likely has the most extensive collection of African photographs today is due

The Walther Collection
Neu-Ulm, Bavaria

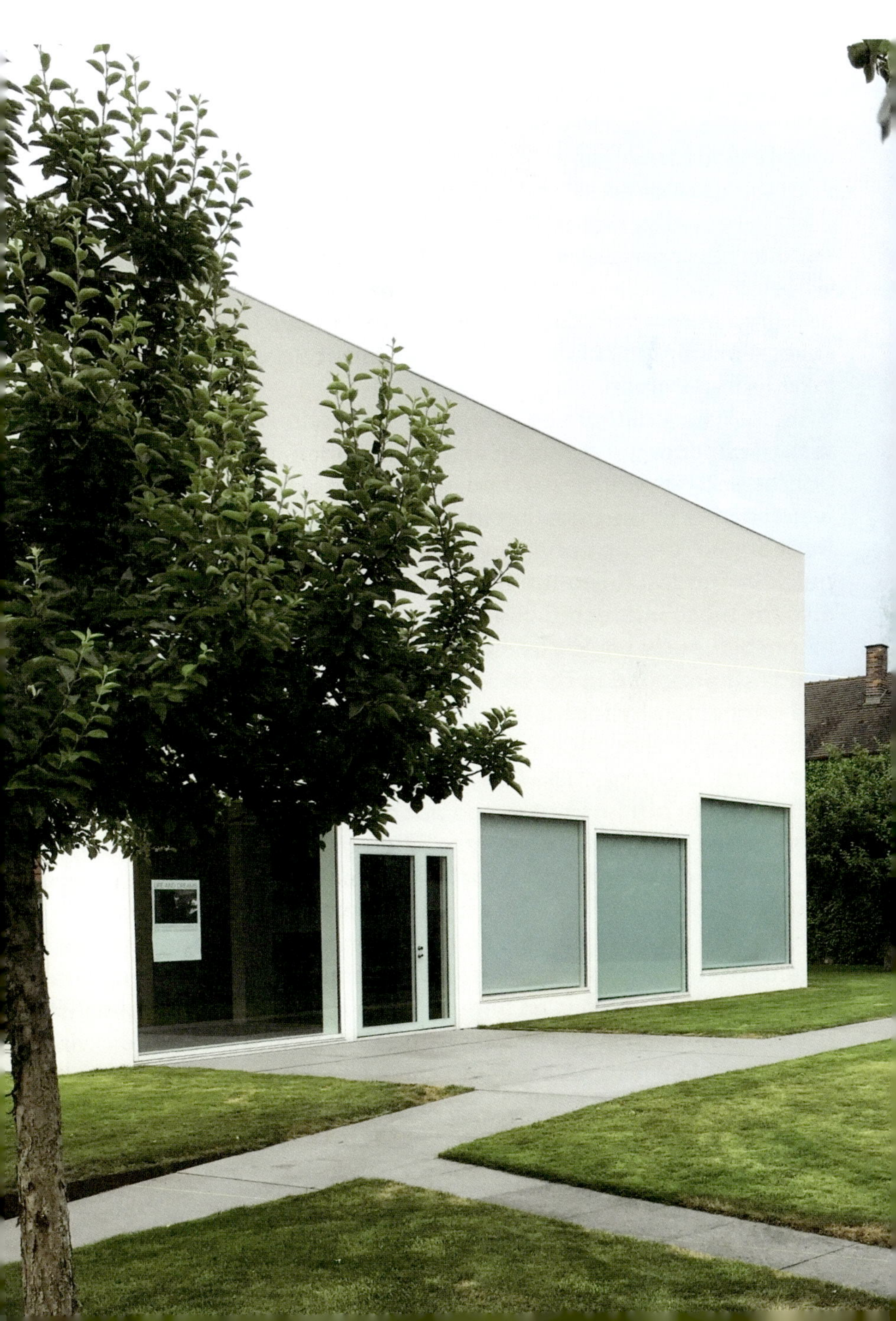

in part to his bond with Nigeria-born curator Okwui Enwezor, with whom he traveled to Africa. Only a few of the artists he collects have a Western gallery representative because Walther buys mainly while traveling. Once he has selected an artist, he collects with the gaze of an exhibition maker—conceptually and broadly.

More recently, Walther has been particularly interested in vernacular photography, a term that has established itself for works whose authors are unknown. In recent years, the collection has acquired numerous of these series, which have been presented in several exhibitions in the New York Project Space and somewhat later in Burlafingen.

Since Artur Walther sees the art of mediation as the central task of collecting, he was an early member of important museum boards and committees. When, after the death of his mother, he was faced with the question of what should happen to her house in Burlafingen, the idea of his own museum in his home country arose quickly. The result is not only exciting for photography lovers, but also for those interested in architecture. The entire complex, which inconspicuously blends into the neighborhood, consists of four buildings arranged in the form of a quarter circle on a lawn of grass and connected by footpaths. Three buildings each allow for a specific exhibition program within the framework of the central theme. The fourth building, "The Grey House," is a three-story residential building with office, library, and apartment. The only new building of the three exhibition buildings, "The White Cube" designed by the Ulm office of Braunger Wörtz Architekten, consists of exposed concrete and in-situ concrete in the basement. The monolithic three-story building creates an open atmosphere through its different, partly large-scale windows and square wall openings. The main exhibition room is an underground basement, the minimalist upper floor resembles a lounge. "The Green House," covered with ivy, is a typical local two-family house from the 1950s, which was also purchased by Artur Walther. The rooms inside were gutted, and their cabinet-like size makes them suitable for the presentation of small-format photography and video works. "The Black House" is Walther's former parental home and now offers a private area as well as rooms for the presentation of serial works and video art.

International curators reorganize the collection and the acquisitions annually with different thematic emphasis.

The Walther Collection
Reichenauer Str. 21
D-89233 Neu-Ulm
Phone: +49 731 1769143
info@walthercollection.com
walthercollection.com

Opening hours
May to November Thu–Sun 2–5 p.m. as well as International Museum Day (May 18) and the Ulmer Kulturnacht Ulm/Neu-Ulm (September 14). Private guided tours are also possible outside the official exhibition months by appointment.
Public guided tours take place every Friday at 5 p.m. and every first Sunday of the month at 3 p.m. during the exhibition period (free of charge).

Entrance fees
Free admission

Arrival by public transportation
Take bus 84 or 88 from Ulm's main station to the Burlafingen Dorfplatz bus stop.

Restaurant tip
Home-brewed beer and Swabian cuisine are served in the rustic Schlössle brewery-restaurant parlor with its beautiful beer garden with chestnut trees (schloessle.com; Schlössleweg 3, 89231, Neu-Ulm).

Extra tips
In the Neu-Ulm Sculpture Park, objects from Werner Schneider's collection by Tony Cragg, Stephan Balkenhol, and Bernar Venet can be discovered around the gallery in the Venet House (galerie-im-venet-haus.de; Bahnhofstr. 41).
A simultaneous visit to the Weishaupt Kunsthalle (see p. 60) and the Sammlung FER Collection (p. 16) in Ulm is also possible.

98
Museum Berggruen

Since 1996, the Museum Berggruen has been located near Charlottenburg Palace and is affiliated with the Nationalgalerie. Journalist, author, and art dealer Heinz Berggruen (1914–2007) was considered one of the most important collectors of Classical Modern art worldwide. In 2000, he sold his collection of 165 works to the Stiftung Preussischer Kulturbesitz (Prussian Cultural Heritage), originally intended as a permanent loan, for a patronage price. Today, the collection in the Museum Berggruen—supplemented by other substantial loans from the family—is one of the most important locations of Classical Modernism. At the center of the permanent exhibition is Picasso's multifaceted oeuvre, with more than 120 works, from which his various creative periods are clearly identifiable. On view are central works such as Picasso's famous motif of the sitting harlequin from the Rose Period and numerous portraits of the Dora Maar. Other focal points include over sixty works by Paul Klee as well as works by Henri Matisse, Georges Braque, and Alberto Giacometti.

After studying literature and art history and briefly working as a journalist, Berggruen, who was of Jewish heritage, emigrated to the United States via Copenhagen in 1936. In 1939, he became a staff member at the San Francisco Museum of Modern Art, for which he prepared an exhibition by Mexican painter Diego Rivera. It was through him that Berggruen met Frida Kahlo, with whom he had a brief affair. As early as 1940, he bought his first painting in Chicago for one hundred dollars, the now famous watercolor *Perspective-Spuk* (1920) by Paul Klee, which accompanied him for forty years as a talisman, but is unfortunately no longer in the collection. In 1947, he settled on the Left Bank of the Seine in Paris as an art dealer. Equipped exclusively with enthusiasm as seed capital, he relied on his intuition and his confident instinct for quality. He soon won Picasso's friendship and trust and traded his works. It was not until 1980 that Berggruen gave up his gallery activities to be able to devote himself entirely to the expansion of his collection. In 1973, he returned his US citizenship in favor of German citizenship. On the occasion of the opening of the

Museum Berggruen
Berlin

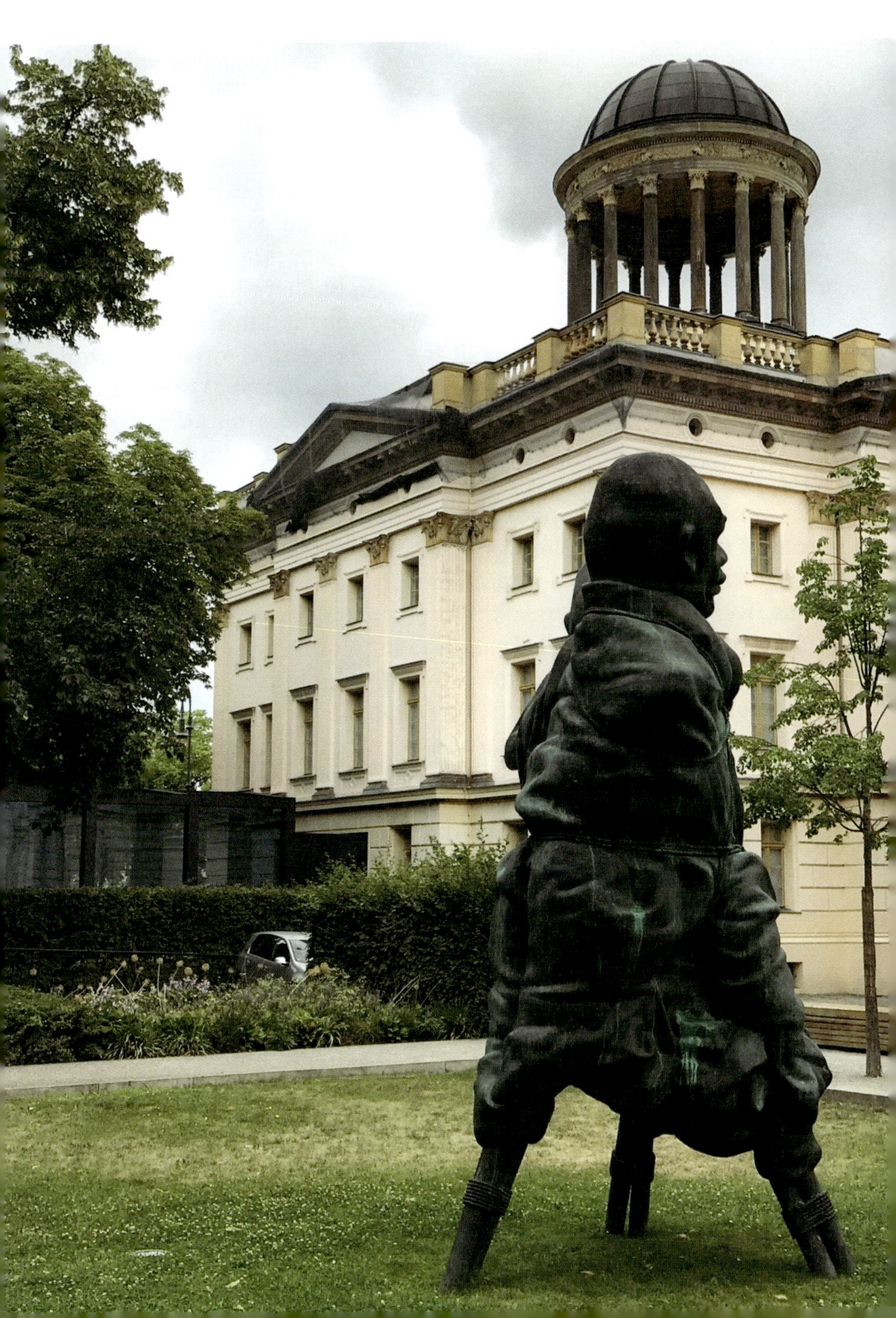

five-year Berggruen Collection exhibition at the British National Gallery in 1991, Wolf-Dieter Dube, then General Director of the Staatliche Museen zu Berlin, and Heinz Berggruen met in London. Berggruen's subsequent visit to Berlin was followed by the decision to house the collection here in a separate museum.

The western Stüler building, originally designed by Friedrich August Stüler for the Gardes du Corps, the mounted bodyguard of the King, was used for the Collection of Classical Antiquities until 1993 and subsequently converted for the Berggruen collection according to the designs of the architectural office of Hilmer Sattler. To create the necessary space for additional family loans, the State of Berlin donated the Alte Kommandantur adjacent to the Stüler building to the Stiftung Preußischer Kulturbesitz. In 2012, the two buildings were connected with a glass pergola as part of an elaborate conversion by the Kuehn Malvezzi architectural office. The collection has since shone in a new light on an exhibition area of approximately 1,200 m², spread over three floors each. Special exhibitions regularly take place on the ground floor of the Stüler building, supplementing and deepening the central themes of the collection and its artists. In the small documentation room, which is also on the ground floor, a worthwhile film about Heinz Berggruen is permanently played. As part of the expansion of the museum, a small sculpture garden was created on the courtyard side, which was given the name Bettina Berggruen Garten in honor of Heinz Berggruen's wife. As a contemporary homage to the art of Classical Modernism, a sculpture ensemble by Düsseldorf artist Thomas Schütte has been installed there today.

Museum Berggruen Berlin

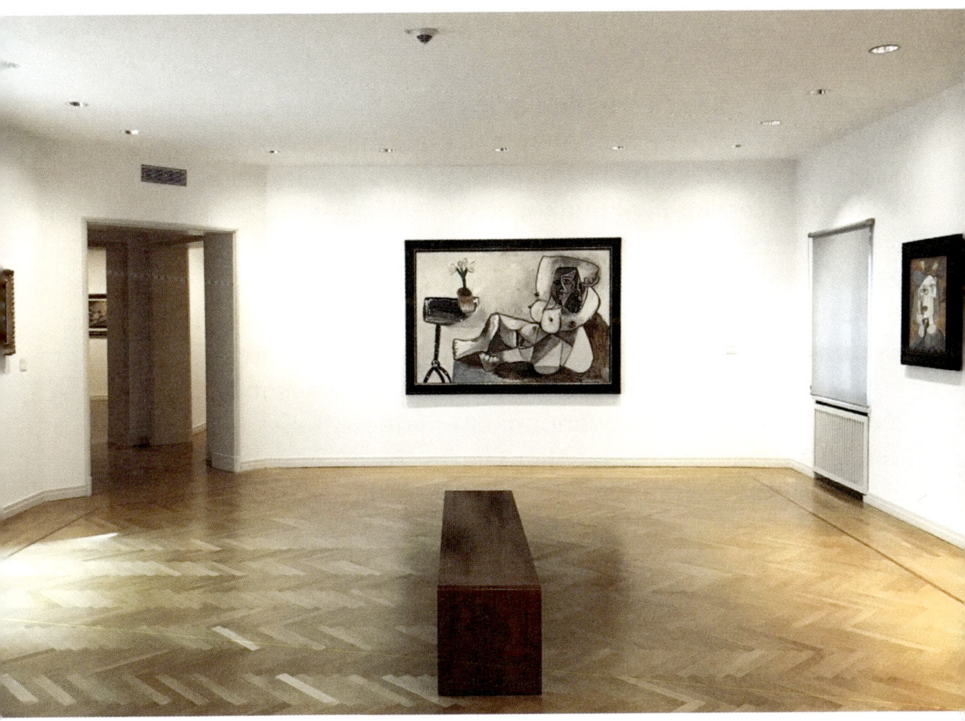

Museum Berggruen
Staatliche Museen zu Berlin
Schloßstr. 1
D-14059 Berlin
Phone: +49 30 266424242
smb.museum/mb

Opening hours
Tue–Fri 10 a.m.–6 p.m., Sat/Sun 11 a.m.–6 p.m.
Public guided tours take place on Sundays at 3 p.m. (€4 plus admission).

Entrance fees
Museum Berggruen and Scharf-Gerstenberg: Adults / Reduced / Children and Adolescents up to the age of 18 as well as museum pass Berlin holders: €10 / €5 / free

Arrival by public transportation
Relatively nearby S- and U-Bahn stops are Westend (S41, S42, S46), Sophie Charlotte Platz (U2) and Richard Wagner Platz (U7).

Extra tips
The neighboring Bröhan Museum is a unique, epochal museum for Art Nouveau, Art Deco, and Functionalism. Exhibits from the Arts and Crafts and Fine Arts disciplines are presented here in interesting room ensembles. The museum bears the name of its founder founder, Karl H. Bröhan, who bequeathed his private collection to the state of Berlin on the occasion of his sixtieth birthday (broehan-museum.de; Schloßstr. 1a).
Architecture fans could consider a detour to the Jesuit Church of St. Canisius. A visit to the church is worthwhile, it was built according to the plans of the Berlin architects Heike Büttner, Claus Neumann, and George Braun and received an award at the Architecture Prize Berlin 2003. It can be visited on weekdays from 11 a.m. to 4 p.m. (st.canisius-berlin.de; Witzlebenstr. 30). It is a good idea to visit the Scharf-Gerstenberg Collection across the way on the same day, as the admission ticket is also valid here (see p. 136).

102
Boros Collection

No other city like Berlin has such a wide range of private museums. Specialized collection concepts are combined with historical sites, such as the remarkable exhibition spaces of Karen and Christian Boros in a former civil bunker.

Pursuant to an “immediate Führer directive” issued by Adolf Hitler, Albert Speer was commissioned to draw up an extensive construction program to improve the safety of the civilian population. Based on Speer’s plans, his subordinates, including the architect Karl Bonatz, started building the so-called “type bunkers.” The “Reichsbahnbunker Friedrichstraße” is an example of the M1200 model; the label indicates the number of people it was designed to hold, though up to 4,000 individuals sought refuge in it on many occasions. Styled to look like a Renaissance fortress, the bomb shelter was meant to remain in place after the end of the Second World War as a so-called “war memorial.” After the capitulation in 1945, the Red Army occupied the bunker instead and used it as a military prison. In the 1950s, it was popularly known as the “banana bunker” because the “Volkseigene Betrieb Obst Gemüse Speisekartoffeln” stored Cuban dried and tropical fruits here. After the fall of communism fetish and SM orgies, as well as trance and techno parties, took place in the black-painted and graffiti-sprayed, sound-and-light-insulated rooms. Until 1996, one of the most famous German techno clubs was located here.

In 2003, Christian and Karen Boros acquired the by then abandoned building and commissioned Jens Casper from the Berlin office Realarchitektur to carry out the extensive conversion work. Taking into account monument protection requirements, the number of rooms was reduced from 120 to eighty by breaking through ceilings and walls with diamond saws and laboriously crushing huge pieces of concrete. The 3.5-m thick concrete-steel cover was opened and today serves as the foundation for a glass bungalow with a floating roof and a spacious terrace.

The building was converted for its present used in five years of renovations. The architects created spaces of various sizes, with ceiling heights ranging from 7.5 to 43 feet, to accommodate

Boros Collection
Berlin

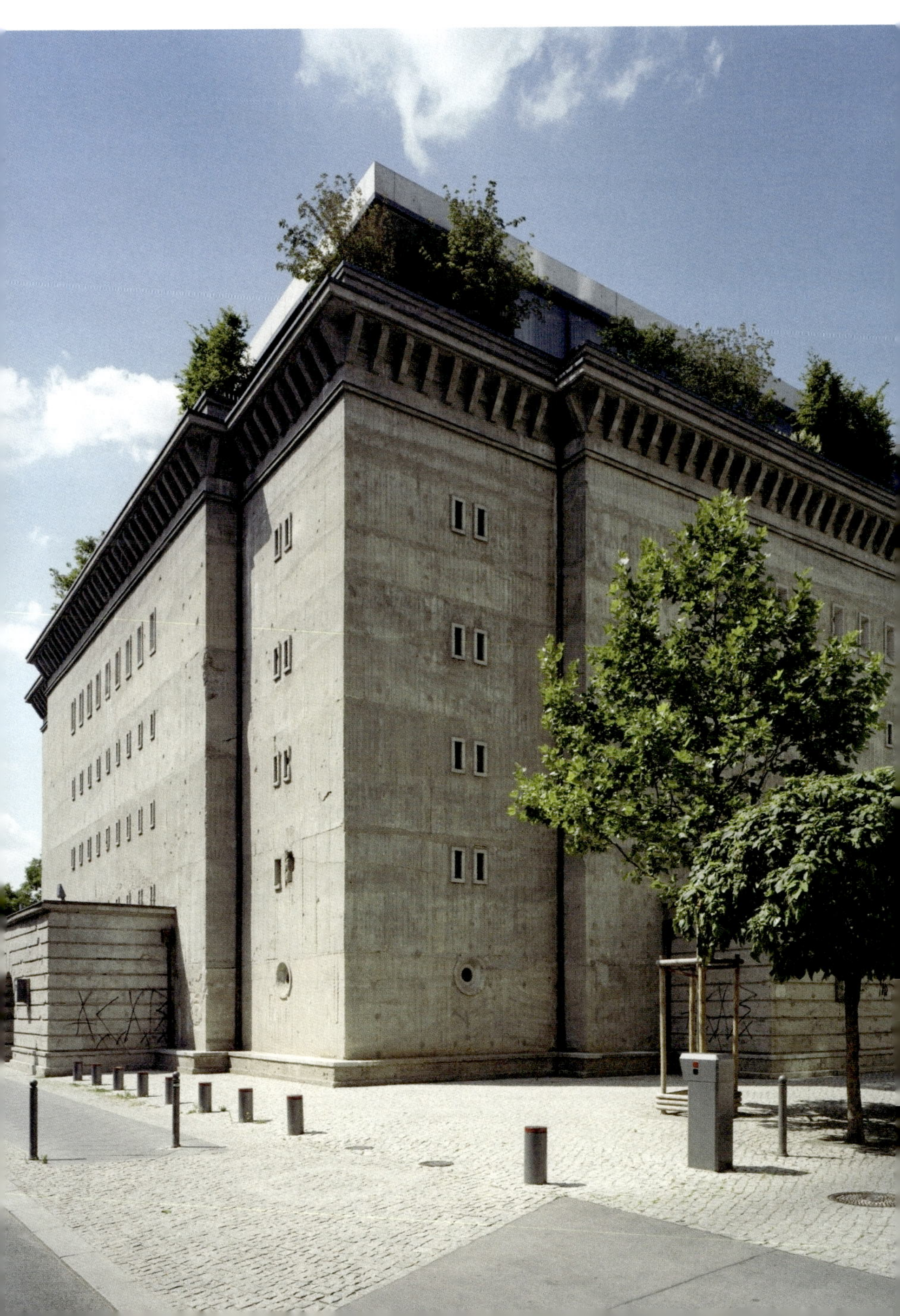

presentations of contemporary art in diverse media including sculpture, painting, photography, and video. Despite the considerable structural alterations, visible traces of the building's former uses remain. War damage to the landmarked exterior reminds visitors and passersby of the site's history. The art, often in large formats, fits organically into the interior spaces, some of which have been left unfinished, with bare concrete floors, wall, and ceilings, while others have been fitted out as white cubes. The temporary exhibitions are produced in close collaboration with the artists, who sometimes create works specifically for the galleries. Karen and Christian Boros have consistently sought to showcase the output of cutting-edge artists, and each new presentation features rising stars of the art world in dialogue with ensembles by mainstays of the collection such as Olafur Eliasson, Wolfgang Tillmans, or the Young British Artists.

To ensure the experience, the collection is shown only to small groups of preregistered guests. A team of young art educators introduces visitors to the history of the building and the ideas behind the art on view.

The third presentation of the collection has been on view since 2017. It is quieter and more personal than its predecessors. With works of art by the so called digital natives generation including artists such as Avery Singer and Katja Novitskova, the exhibition reflects on the ideal and social added value of art. Artists who, like He Xiangyu and Sergej Jensen, bring classical media of artistic production into the contemporary context are also shown.

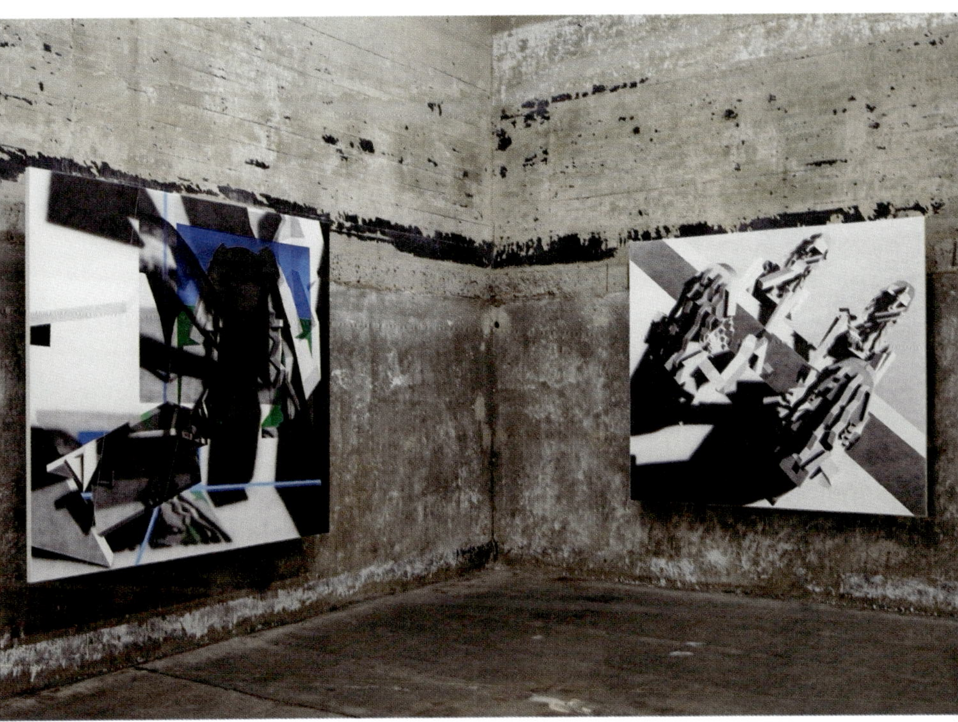

Boros Collection
Bunker, Reinhardtstr. 20
D-10117 Berlin
info@sammlung-boros.de
sammlung-boros.de

Opening hours
Thu 3–8 p.m. and Fri–Sun 10 a.m.–8 p.m.
A tour of the collection is only possible by registration via the website and as part of a 1.5-hour guided tour. Early registration is recommended, as the dates are often fully booked a few weeks in advance.

Entrance fees
Adults / Reduced:
€15 / €9

Arrival by public transportation
From Hauptbahnhof, take bus 147 (direction Ostbahnhof) to the corner Friedrichstraße / Reinhardtstraße or bus TXL (direction Alexanderplatz) to Karlplatz on Reinhardtstraße. The subway station Oranienburger Tor (U6) as well as the S- and U-Bahn station Friedrichstraße are close to the collection.

Restaurant tips
Cakes and small, simple dishes can be enjoyed in the Böse Buben Bar in a cozy atmosphere and between densely filled bookshelves (boesebubenbar.de; Marienstr. 18). The Grill Royal which is internationally renowned for its steaks and illustrious guests (grillroyal.com; Friedrichstr. 105b, daily from 6 p.m.) is also within walking distance.

Extra tips
There are numerous museums and exhibition spaces in the vicinity, such as Hamburger Bahnhof – Museum für Gegenwart (hamburgerbahnhof.de; Invalidenstr. 50–51) and the exhibition space of Wolfgang Tillmans' Between Bridges Foundation, founded in 2017 (betweenbridges.net; Keithstr. 15). Also worth seeing is the former studio of the artist Michel Majerus. The eponymous Estate regularly organizes exhibitions (michelmajerus.com; Knaackstr. 12). A chapel with an installation by James Turrell is located in the Dorotheenstadt Cemetery (the dates are on the website evfbs.de/index.php?id=602; Chausseestr. 126). The me Collectors Room (see p. 130), Museum Frieder Burda / Salon Berlin (p. 106), Collection Regard (p. 134), and Sammlung Hoffmann (p. 124) are also very close by.

106
Museum Frieder Burda / Salon Berlin

Since the end of 2016, the worthwhile Museum Frieder Burda Museum in Baden-Baden (see p. 8) has gained a young annex in Berlin. Located on the third floor of the Former Jewish Girls' School, the Salon Berlin is an exhibition space and forum for international contemporary art. Under the curatorial direction of Patricia Kamp, Frieder Burda's stepdaughter, who has accompanied the collector's museum activities for many years, the Salon Berlin is both a showcase and a field of experimentation. Patricia Kamp, an art historian, has personally taken over the special design of the rooms with an exhibition area of 150 m². Her goal is to continue to lead the collection into the future and to keep it alive. Therefore, Salon Berlin sees itself as a place of exchange and inspiration—both between historical, artistic positions and the present, as well as between museum and artists, and not least between Baden-Baden and Berlin. In three to four thematic exhibitions each year, an extraordinary correspondence is initiated in which aspects of the extensive Frieder Burda Collection enter a dialogue with a younger generation of artists reflecting the Berlin scene. Most of the contemporary works are on loan from artists and galleries. In the past, works belonging to the collection by William N. Copley were juxtaposed with works by Candice Breitz and works by Georg Baselitz with Flavio de Marc. Time and again, visitors can also enjoy highlights of German Expressionism—after all, this art movement is a focal point of the Frieder Burda Collection.

The former Jewish Girls' School, which is located in the middle of the Auguststraße art district, was built in 1927/28 in the style of New Objectivity according to plans by the community architect Alexander Beer and opened in 1930. After the National Socialists closed it, a temporary military hospital was set up here in 1942. From 1950 to 1996, the school was used by various high schools in Berlin. After being left to decay for ten years, it was made temporarily accessible for the 4th Berlin Biennale as well as for an exhibition on Hannah Arendt's 100th birthday in 2006. With the help of

Museum Frieder Burda / Salon Berlin
Berlin

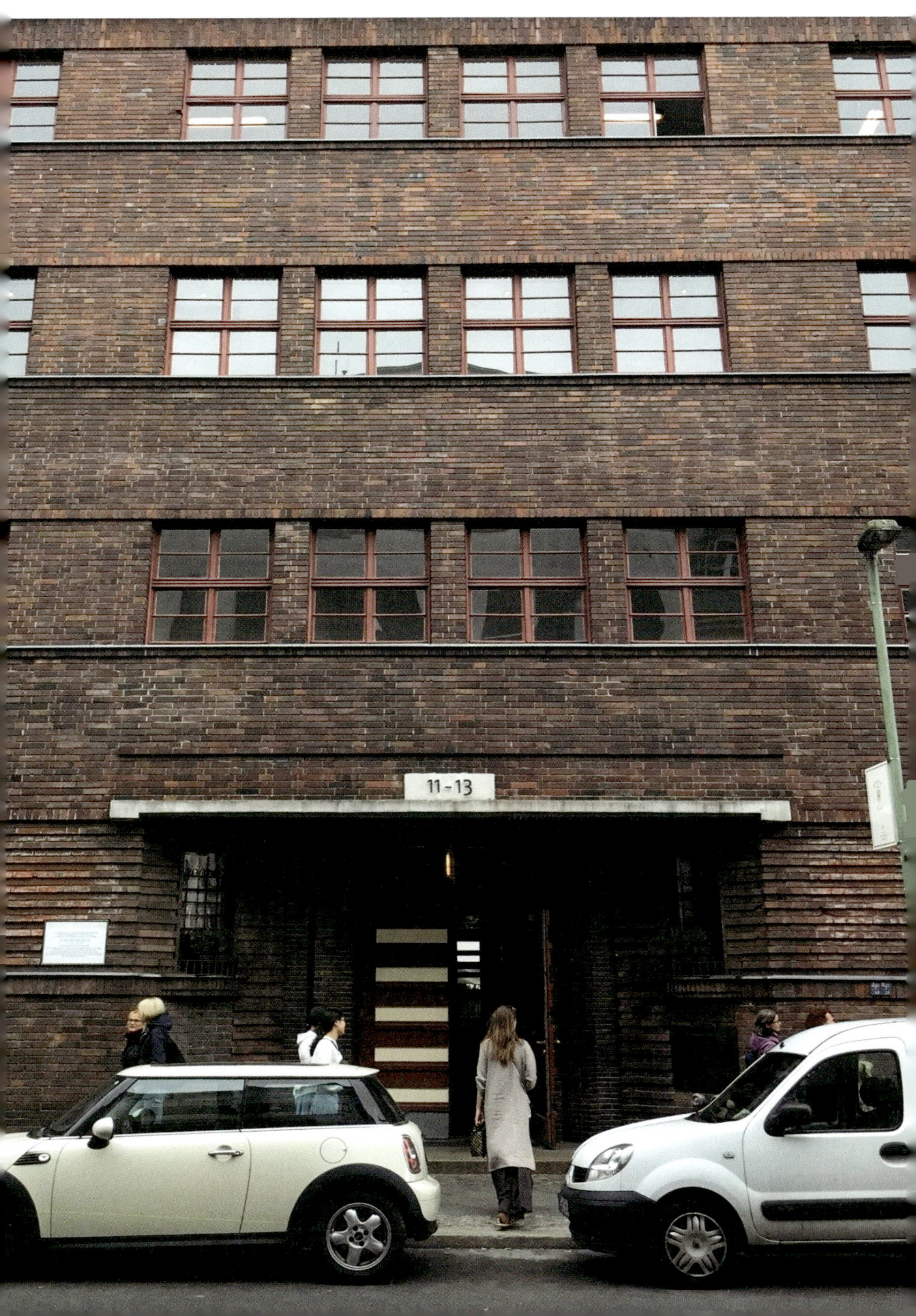

the Conference on Jewish Material Claims Against Germany, the school was officially handed over to the Jewish community in 2009. To preserve the unique aura of the building with its eventful history, gallery owner Michael Fuchs rented the building on a long-term basis and had it minimally repaired by Grüntuch Ernst Architekten in cooperation with the office for the protection of cultural heritage. The reopening took place in 2012.

Museum Frieder Burda / Salon Berlin
Auguststr. 11–13
D-10117 Berlin
Phone: +49 30 24047404
salon@museum-frieder-burda.de
museum-frieder-burda.de

Opening hours
Thu–Sat noon–6 p.m.
During Gallery Weekend and Berlin Art Week, the opening hours are different. Closed for several weeks between Christmas and New Year's and during installation phases.
Exhibition tours are offered during opening hours.

Entrance fees
Free admission

Arrival by public transportation
The Oranienburger Straße S-Bahn station (S1, S2, S25, S26) is around the corner.

Restaurant tips
Pauly Saal (paulysaal.com), a star restaurant curated with contemporary art, is located in the same building, as well as the American Deli Mogg (moggmogg.com), which is famous for its pastrami and pulled pork sandwiches. Another favorite is Café Bravo, designed by Dan Graham in 1999, in the courtyard of the KW Institute for Contemporary Art across the street (see below).

Extra tips
The Michael Fuchs Gallery, also located on the third floor, has been using the roof terrace since 2018 as a kind of artist's playground. Unfortunately, the the Rooftop Playground is rarely accessible (maedchenschule.org/de/kunst). The KW Institute for Contemporary Art presents exhibitions of contemporary art. The area is the main exhibition venue of the Berlin Biennale, which takes place during the summer months of even years (kw-berlin.de; Auguststr. 69).
It is advisable to combine a visit to the Salon with visits to the me Collectors Room Berlin (see p. 130) and the Collection Regard (p. 134).

Museum Frieder Burda / Salon Berlin
Berlin

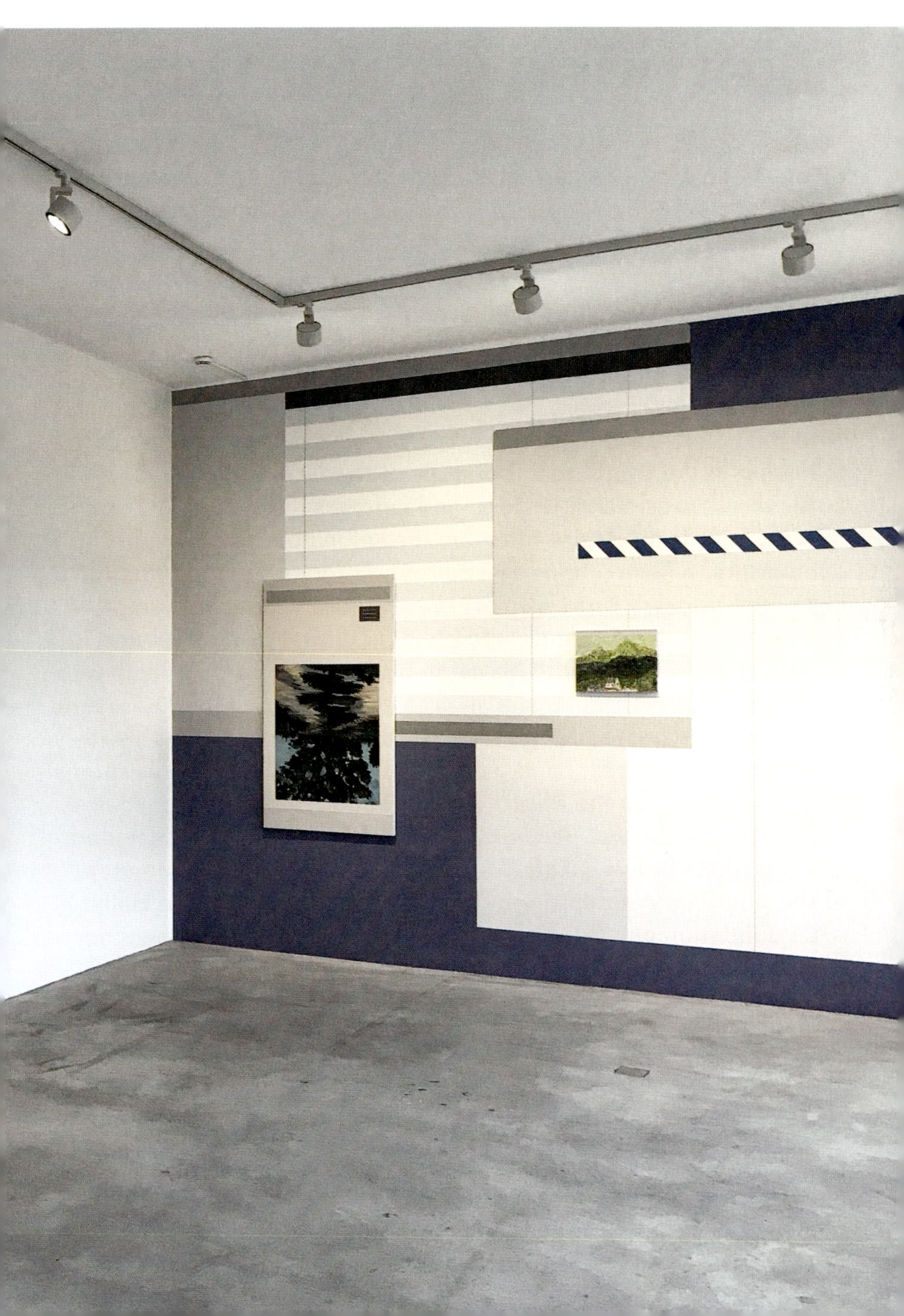

110
Salon Dahlmann / Miettinen Collection

Salon Dahlmann—named after the last owner of the house in which it is located, Hildegard Dahlmann—is home to part of the Miettinen Collection. In 2010, the Miettinen family acquired the Berlin Gründerzeit house in the middle of Charlottenburg. Timo Miettinen, owner and chairman of the industrial company Em Group Oy, which his father founded in the 1950s, is one of Finland's most important private collectors. He has worked in Germany for many years and has remained closely associated with the country. As a perfect host, Timo Miettinen has been following in the traditional footsteps of the Berlin salon since 2012, where musicians, writers, and painters meet in light-flooded old rooms. It is his desire to revive the salon concept of open encounters, whose origins can be found around Kurfürstendamm, in a contemporary form with art presentations, concerts, and performances. He also wants to build a cultural bridge between Germany and Finland with his salon project. The salon, which was renovated in 2019 and covers an area of approximately 300 m^2 and has previously hosted temporary exhibitions in cooperation with other private collectors and gallery owners, now comprises rooms designed solely for the Miettinen Collection, which are partially accessible to visitors. Berlin-based artist Björn Dahlem designed the light installation *Lokale Gruppe* (2010) for the entrance area of the building. A sculpture by Hans Arp, on loan from the Hans Arp Foundation and Sophie Taeuber-Arp e. V., stands in the inner courtyard.

Timo Miettinen developed his enthusiasm for collecting stamps and coins at an early age. Together with his art-loving mother, he began collecting Finnish landscape painting from the end of the nineteenth and early twentieth centuries as a fifteen year old. Today, the collection, which has grown to over 1,000 works, focuses on international contemporary art, with Finnish artists being a critical component.

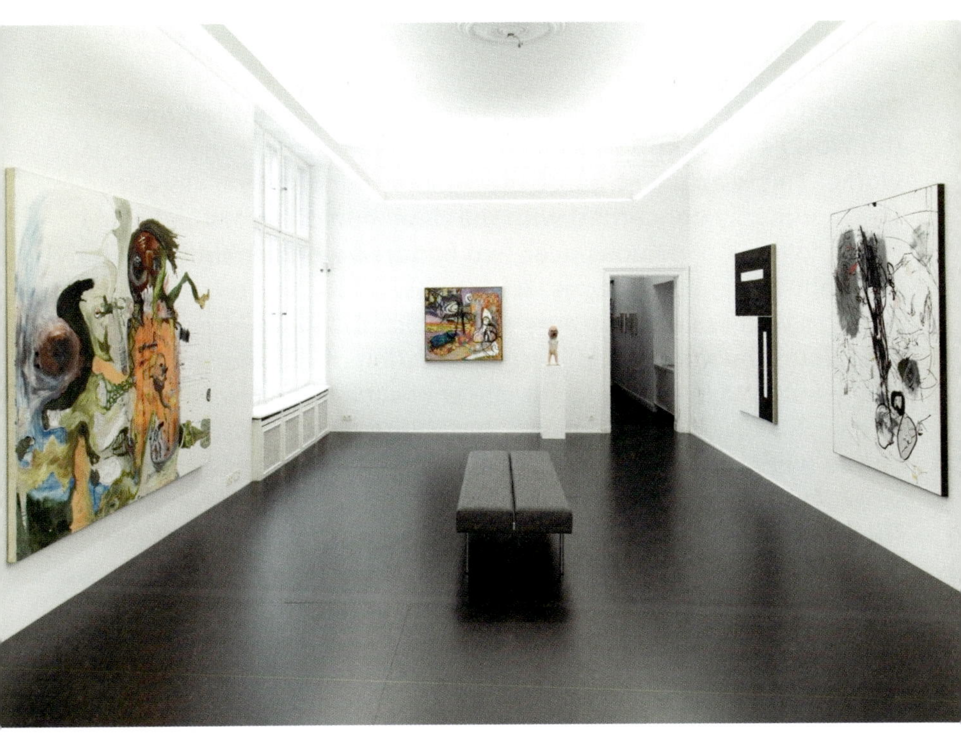

Salon Dahlmann / Miettinen Collection
Marburger Str. 3
D-10789 Berlin
Phone: +49 30 88725683
info@salon-dahlmann.de
salon-dahlmann.de

Opening hours
From September 2019, Sat noon–6 p.m.
Various public events take place regularly.
The gallery Robert Grunenberg (robertgrunenberg.com) and the Hildegard Bar (hildegardbar-berlin.de) are located in the same building.

Entrance fees
Free admission

Arrival by public transportation
The collection is located between U-Bahn stations Kurfürstendamm (U1/U9), Augsburger Straße (U2/U3), and Wittenbergplatz (U1/U2/U3), as well as near the DB, RB, and S-Bahn station at Zoologischer Garten.

Restaurant tips
The specialties on the sixth floor of the well-known KaDeWe department store have been seducing hungry shoppers for decades. Following a conversion by Rem Koolhaas' architectural office OMA, a visit to the fine foods department has certainly become even more attractive (kadewe.de; Tauentzienstr. 21–24). The "Kantini" food market in Bikini Berlin offers a direct view of the zoo (bikiniberlin.de/de/kantini; Budapester Str. 38–50).

Extra tips
For art and architecture lovers, a detour to the Kindl Centre for Contemporary Art in Neukölln is recommended. Exhibitions are presented in different rooms in the former brewery. A look at the café and the cube-shaped boiler house are worthwhile (kindl-berlin.de; Am Sudhaus 3). In the rooms of the private institution KUNSTSAELE Berlin, independent curators develop thematic group exhibitions of contemporary art (kunstsaele.de; Bülowstr. 90). A visit to Salon Dahlmann can easily be combined with visits to the EAM Collection (see p. 112) and the Kienzle Art Foundation (p. 128).

112
EAM Collection

Starting in the 1960s, Elke and Arno Morenz assembled one of the world's most important private collections of French Lettrism works. This is an avant-garde movement founded by Isidore Isou in 1945, primarily concerned with the depiction of letters and signs.

The collection includes over two hundred works (paintings, drawings, photographs, collages, sculptures, prints, and experimental films) as well as Lettrist tracts and books. Extensive documentation chronicles the multidisciplinary orientation of this movement, which has developed in parallel with currents such as concrete and visual poetry, Fluxus, Conceptual art, and ZERO. The collection focuses on the works of Maurice Lemaître and Isidore Isou. In addition, works by François Dufrêne, Roland Sabatier, Gabriel Pomerand, Gil J Wolman, and Jean-Pierre Gillard, among others are shown. The collectors themselves are often found among the works in the collection—a tribute to those who were among the first to believe in Lettrist art and poetry and who actively promoted it over many decades.

The cornerstone of the EAM Collection (an abbreviation for Elke and Arno Morenz Collection) was laid in 1962 when the young Elke Ploss met Maurice Lemaître in the garden of the Musée Rodin during her training as a bookseller in Paris. He introduced her, and later her husband, Dr. Arno Morenz, to the Lettrist circles. Enthusiastic about the innovative and aesthetic ideas, the couple began to acquire works directly from the studios of Lettrist artists because only a few galleries wanted to represent the nonconformists.

After the death of his wife in 2009, Arno Morenz moved from Paris to the Spree with the collection in 2011 to be able to present the ideas of the movement, which is underestimated by the art world to this day, to a broader audience. Since 2013, he has been exhibiting key works from the collection in his 450 m^2 apartment on the fifth and sixth floors of an old Charlottenburg building.

EAM Collection Berlin

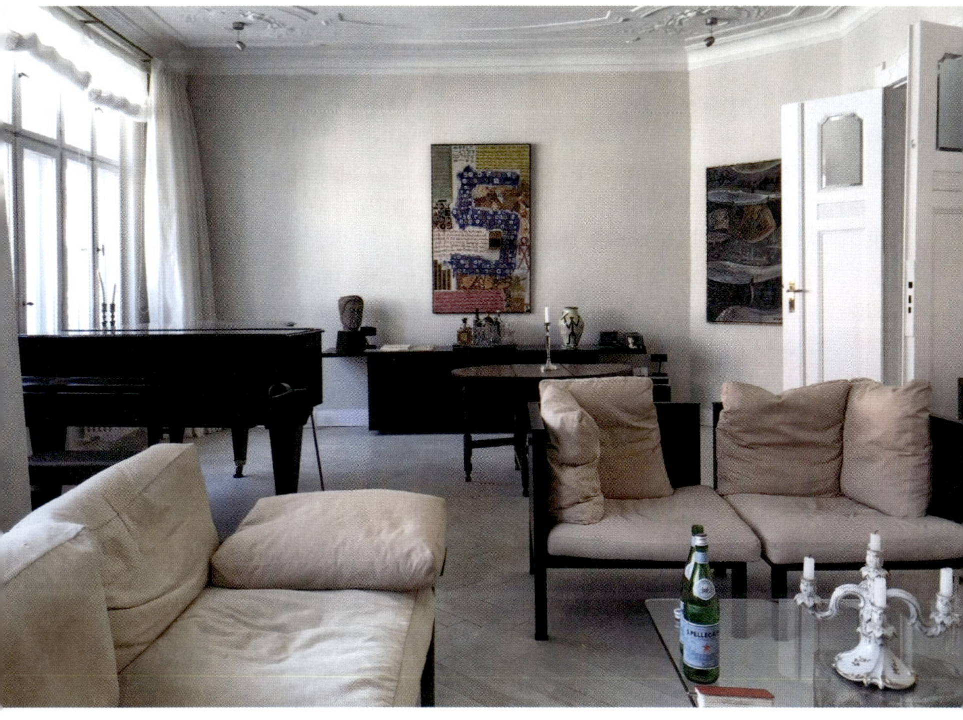

EAM Collection
Sybelstr. 62
D-10629 Berlin
Phone: +49 30 88720913
eam-collection.de
info@eam-collection.de

Opening hours
Visits to the collection can be arranged at short notice by appointment (contact info@eam-collection.de, +49 30 88720913 or +49 172 8684953).
Each year, four to six interesting theme-related events take place, for which registration is necessary.

Entrance fees
Adults / Reduced:
€8 / €4

Arrival by public transportation
The nearest train stations are Adenauerplatz (U7) and Berlin-Charlottenburg (S-Bahn and regional trains).

Restaurant tips
Around the corner, at Café Early Bean, it is possible to get coffee and tasty snacks during the day (Clausewitzstr. 9). The Restaurant Louis Laurent serves French cuisine in a charming atmosphere. The lunch menus are particularly recommendable in terms of price (louis-laurent.de; Giesebrechtstr. 16). In the same building is the Café Maître Münch, where one can enjoy cakes and tarts (cafe-maitre-muench.de).

Extra tips
The non-profit foundation C/O Berlin presents up to twenty top-class individual and group exhibitions of internationally renowned photographers every year (co-berlin.com; Hardenbergstr. 22–24).
A visit to the EAM Collection can easily be combined with visits to the Salon Dahlmann (see p. 110) and the Kienzle Art Foundation (p. 128).

114
The Feuerle Collection

Since 2016, architecture and art lovers have been able to experience an extraordinary, almost sensual experience in Kreuzberg. Not far from Gleisdreieck, Désiré Feuerle shows works from his collection on 7,350 m^2 by bringing together international contemporary artists, imperial Chinese furniture, and early Khmer sculptures in a unique way. As with the Boros Collection, a former bunker from the Second World War was repurposed for the Feuerle Collection. Unlike the air-raid shelters for citizens, which strikingly stand out in German cityscapes, this former telecommunications bunker is a flat building, constructed for the protection of the Deutsche Reichsbahn's telecommunications network. Therefore, instead of small rooms, the ground floor and basement contain large, connected areas with massive pillars. Between 1959 and 1962, the so-called BASA bunker was used for the Senate Reserve (a legally prescribed provisioning of the Berlin Senate in the event of a second blockade of West Berlin) and later as a general storage facility. Acquired by Désiré Feuerle and Sara Puig in 2011, it was renovated from 2012 to 2015 by British architect and designer John Pawson in close collaboration with the collector himself and with the support of the Berlin architectural firm Realarchitektur. Apart from a few breakthroughs, discreet fixtures, and the dust-binding floor covering, the original atmosphere was retained.

The generosity of the rooms and their aura offer an ideal prerequisite for the permanent, quite stringent concept of the exhibition and experience. After visitors have locked their telephones and bags (but not their jackets—these are indispensable due to the constant room temperature of eighteen degrees) in the entrance area, the tour begins in the basement. After a brief introduction, the group enters a narrow room. In the completely darkened Sound Room, the two-and-a-half-minute piece *Music for Piano 20* by John Cage, composed in 1953 for the dancer and choreographer Merce Cunningham, calms the senses. Through this experience, visitors should be able to concentrate fully on seeing and experiencing the artworks. The first steps into the sparsely lit exhibition hall are a kind of revelation. Khmer sculptures from the seventh to thirteenth

The Feuerle Collection
Berlin

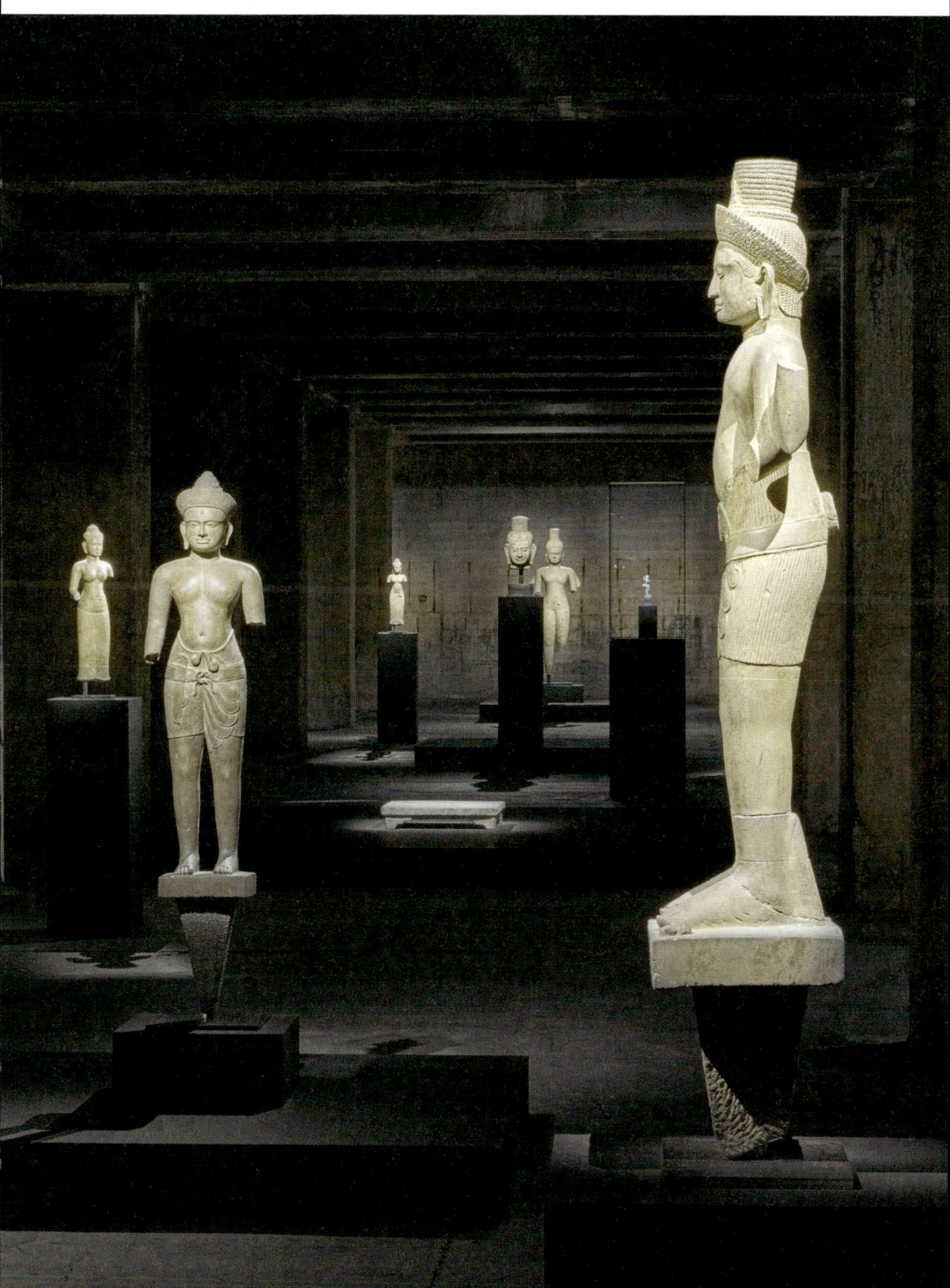

centuries made of stone and bronze, imperial Chinese stone and scholarly furniture, ranging from the Han Dynasty to the Qing Dynasty, from 200 BC to the eighteenth century, correspond with contemporary works. Small, erotic black-and-white photographs by Nobuyoshi Araki as well as silvery iridescent works by British photographer Adam Fuss are positioned between the pieces of furniture, *Torus* (2002) a round, mirrored object by Anish Kapoor, is presented on the back wall. The lighting sets a dramatic stage for the exhibits. The lighting system was personally curated down to the smallest detail by Désiré Feuerle, who regards light as part of the architecture and a form of language. The most impressive oeuvre, however, was created by the architects in collaboration with the collector. Behind four-meter glass panes on the left of the exhibition hall is the mystical Lake Room with a water surface of 2,200 m^2. Due to the reflection, the asymmetrical room appears almost twice as high. In addition, the Lake Room represents a sustainable energy supply, because the entire bunker is heated from here using a geothermal heat pump.

On this level, there is also the Incense Room, which visitors can only enter during a booked Incense Ceremony. The semi-mirrored glazing of the built-in, dark glass box throws various perspectives of the basement back into the room and thus becomes practically invisible itself.

Désiré Feuerle's passion for collecting began in childhood. He was initially interested in special keys, and later on, silver tea and coffee pots. At the age of twenty-five, he dreamed of his own museum. Since then, he worked as a consultant for renowned collections of modern, contemporary, and Asian art, but in the 1990s, he pioneered work in his gallery in Cologne by bringing contemporary and old art into correspondence with each other and stimulating visitors to see and experience them anew.

The Feuerle Collection
Berlin

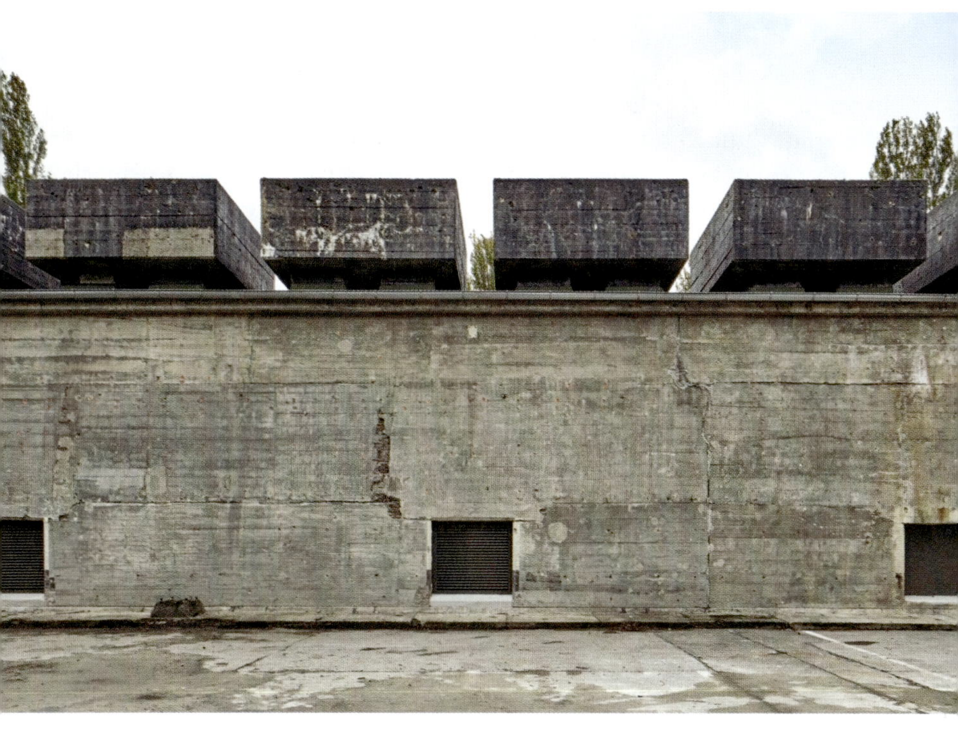

The Feuerle Collection
Hallesches Ufer 70
D-10963 Berlin
Phone: +49 30 25792320
info@thefeuerlecollection.org
thefeuerlecollection.org

Opening hours
Fri 2–7 p.m. (last tour at 6 p.m., Sat/Sun 11 a.m.–7 p.m. (last tour at 6 p.m.) with online ticket purchase.
Visits are only possible for adults and adolescents over age 16.

Entrance fees
Adults / Reduced: €18 / €11
The regular ticket for the Feuerle Collection does not allow access to the Incense Room and participation in an Incense Ceremony. The visit is only possible after prior registration (€1,000 for up to four persons).

Parking
A few parking spaces are available if arranged in advance.

Restaurant tips
Brasserie Le Bon Mori serves French cuisine. The cost is reasonable for the dishes that are served (lebonmori.de; Stresemannstr. 21). Craft beer fans will be thrilled by the trendy restaurant and beer garden BRLO Brwhouse. Guided tours of the brewery are also offered in the building constructed by the GRAFT architectural office using overseas shipping containers (brlo-brwhouse.de; Schöneberger Str. 16).

Extra tips
The Feuerle Collection is about 20 minutes' walk from Potsdamer Platz. A visit to Daimler Contemporary at the same time is recommended. On the fifth floor of the historic Haus Huth villa, temporary exhibitions show a selection from the Daimler Art Collection as well as loans (art.daimler.com; Alte Potsdamer Str. 5). It is also possible to visit the exhibitions in the nearby Martin-Gropius-Bau (berlinerfestspiele.de/en/gropiusbau/programm/start; Niederkirchnerstr. 7). From 2020/21, the New National Gallery by Ludwig Mies van der Rohe, renovated by Chipperfield Architects, will also be reopened (smb.museum/en/museums-institutions/neue-nationalgalerie/home; Potsdamer Str. 50).

118 Fluentum

In spring 2019, a private art venue in a historic setting opened west of Berlin. Founded by the Berlin software entrepreneur and collector Markus Hannebauer, Fluentum is a platform for the production, collection, and presentation of contemporary art with a focus on film and video. Fluentum organizes exhibitions that change twice a year in its unusual rooms. These not only show works from its own collection and coproductions but also curated individual positions by selected artists.

Inspired by a visit to the video art fair Loop in Barcelona, Hannebauer began collecting time-based art in 2010 and frequently acquires stirring and complex works. His collection includes works by around fifty artists including Omer Fast, Hito Steyerl, William Kentridge, Andreas Gursky, Hiwa K, Ming Wong, Guido van der Werve, and Lynne March. Markus Hannebauer is often involved in the production process of the works. This allows him closer contact with the artists and a better understanding of their ideas and techniques.

Fluentum is fascinating in its many facets: the entire complex in Dahlem was initially planned and realized by Fritz Fuß in 1936–1938 as the seat of the Luftgaukommando of the National Socialist government. After a brief occupation by Soviet troops, the US Army confiscated the buildings in 1945 and used them as the headquarters of the American military governor. Eckart Muthesius repaired them for the Americans, all Nazi symbols were removed, and for decades the marble-clad foyer and Kennedy Hall were popular venues for the receptions of various US presidents. General Lucius D. Clay controlled the airlift from here in 1948/49 during the blockade of West Berlin. In 1994, US units left the area. The northern building alone continues to be used as the consular section of the American embassy. During its vacancy, the area was used as film set for several Hollywood movies, including *Operation Valkyrie* and *Inglourious Basterds*. Starting in 2011, a group of investors gradually acquired the vacant buildings from the Bundesanstalt für Immobilienaufgaben (Institute for Federal Real Estate) and converted them into condominiums. After Hannebauer bought the 1,000 m²

Fluentum
Berlin

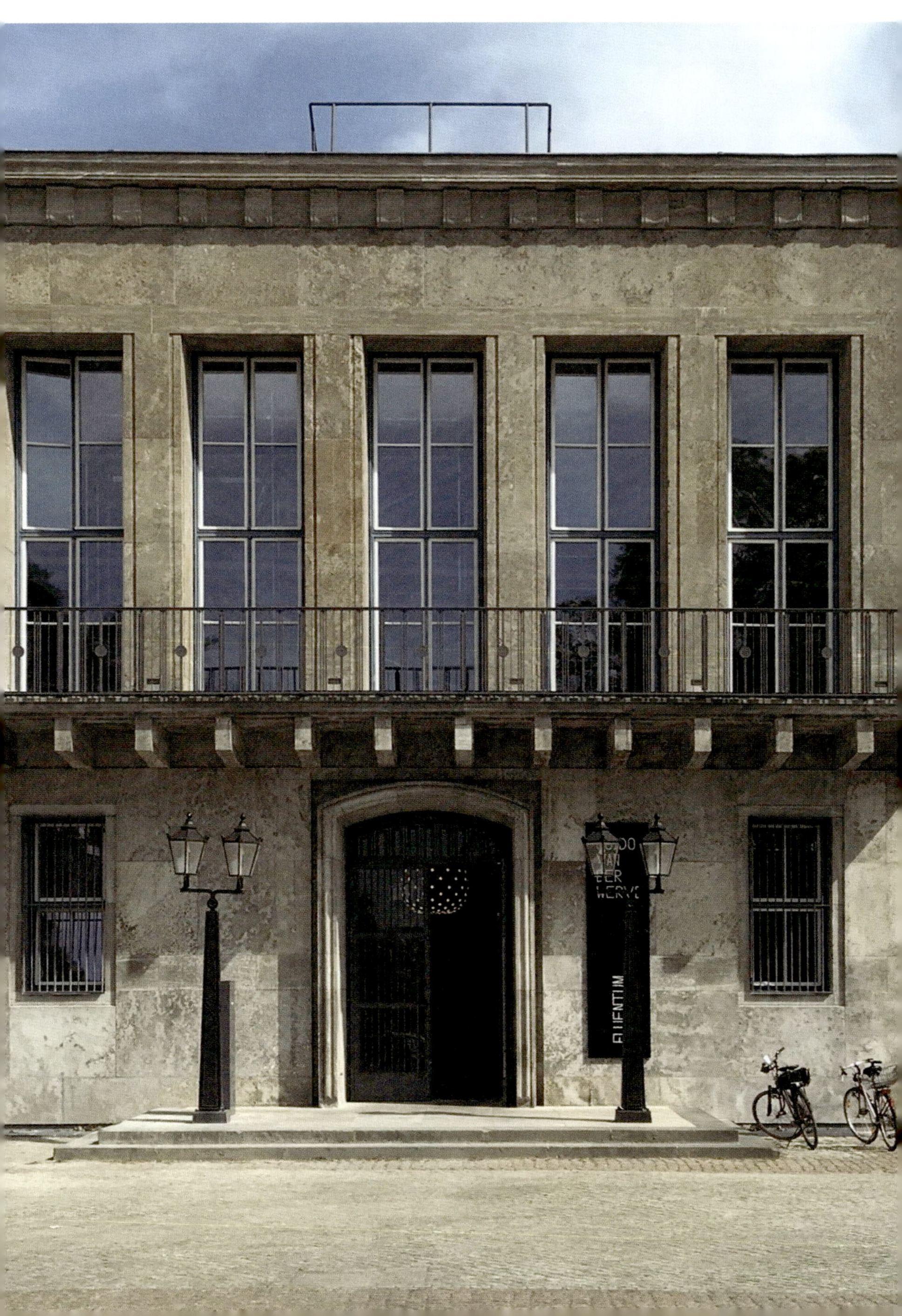

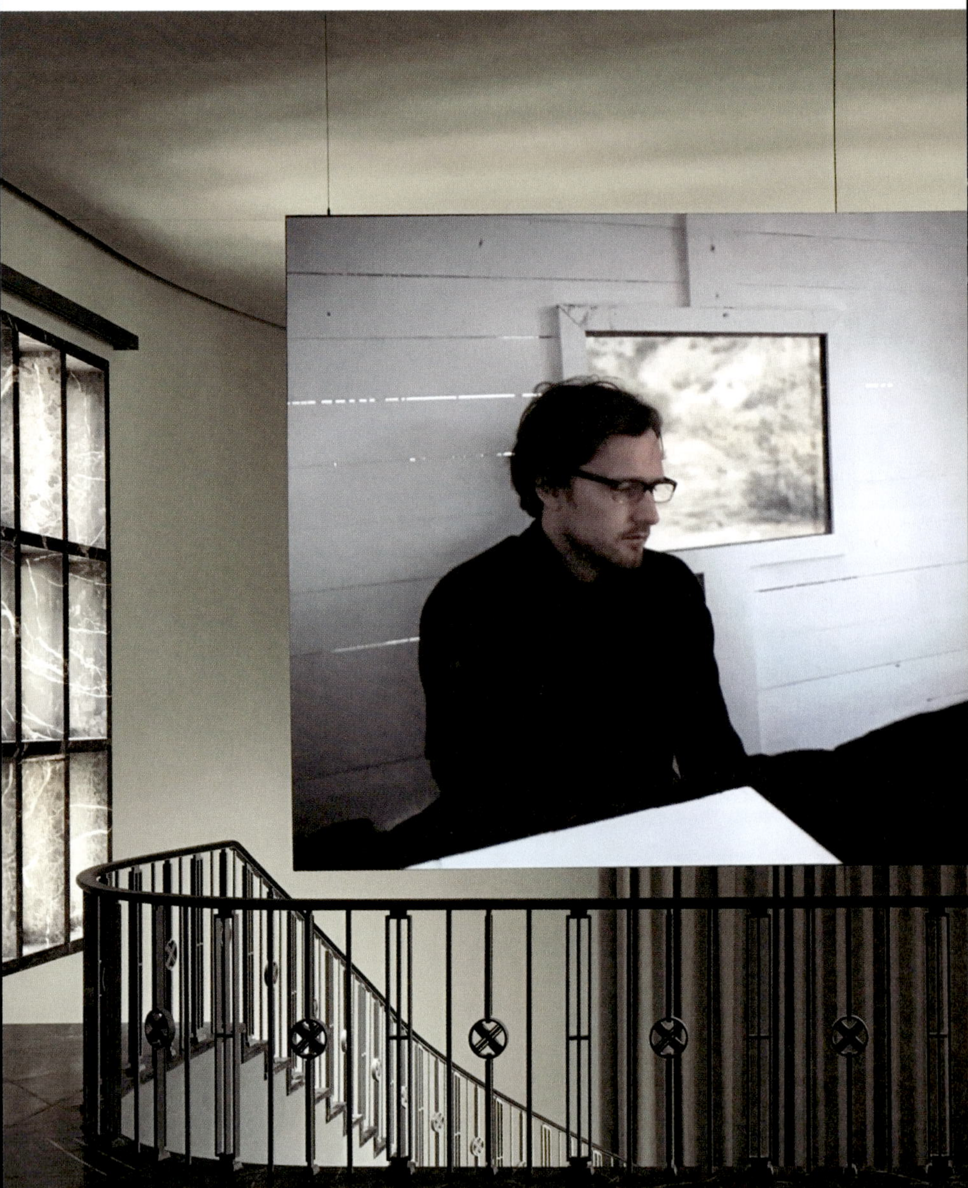

historically-listed middle section of the property in 2016, he had the interior converted by architects Sauerbruch Hutton into a residential section and an exhibition area of approximately 600 m^2. Since 2019, the foyer, clad in dark marble with several side niches in the same style, the impressive two-story staircase rotunda, and a gallery have been open to the public. All floors, walls, and ceilings were stripped, technically equipped, and then restored to their original condition. The contemporary reinforced concrete ceiling was allowed to remain uncovered. The sacred marble, however, offers historical resistance to the contemporary works.

Fluentum
Clayallee 174
D-14195 Berlin
info@fluentum.org
fluentum.org

Opening hours
During exhibitions, Sat 11 a.m.–2 p.m. Occasionally, events with artists are held.

Entrance fees
Free admission

Arrival by public transportation
The stop Oskar-Helene-Heim (U3) is only a few meters away from Fluentum. After crossing Argentinische Allee and Clayallee at the intersection, turn right into a large driveway before the American consulate building and walk straight towards the exhibition building.

Restaurant tips
The Châlet Suisse serves typical Swiss dishes (chalet-suisse.de; Im Jagen 5 / Clayallee 99). A little further away, a hunting lodge's simple garden café is located directly on Lake Grunewald (cafe-im-jagdschloss.de/das-cafe; Hüttenweg 100).

Extra tips
The nearby Brücke Museum shows the works of German Expressionists (bruecke-museum.de; Bussardsteig 9). Only two underground stations away is Haus am Waldsee, where a range of changing contemporary exhibitions take place (hausamwaldsee.de; Argentinische Allee 30).

122 Sammlung Haupt

At the Märkische Ufer, visitors have a rare opportunity to gain insights into a thematically focused private collection within a "normal" law firm. For over twenty years, Dr. Stefan Haupt, a Berlin lawyer for copyright, media, and publishing law, has been collecting works of art that deal with the subject of money. The continually growing collection comprises almost three hundred works in a wide variety of techniques and offers a range of insights into how artists reflect the social and individual value and significance of money. In addition to unique pieces, ready-mades, photographs, or collages with real money, there is a broad spectrum of artist's money in the form of prints and paintings. Numerous artist books, posters, and video works round off the collection. The focus of the collection has changed slightly in recent years. In addition to numerous works by artists such as Julia Herfuhrt, Digital Art and documentaries of public performances financed by the collector have increasingly found their way into the collection. Among the highlights are numerous works by Joseph Beuys, assemblages by Barton Lidice Beneš, as well as the light object *$* (2000) by French artist Mathieu Mercier, photographs by Jerry Berndt, and works by Timm Ulrichs, Lawrence Weiner, and Stephan Balkenhol. Dr. Stefan Haupt's favorite piece, however, remains the work that laid the foundation for the collection in 1997: *Money for Art*, also from 1997, by Taiwanese artist Lee Mingwei, who lives in New York and Paris. The work consists of five photographs and an origami sculpture. It is the documentation of an action in which the artist handed over folded ten-dollar bills to a total of nine people and documented their individual use at intervals of six and twelve months. The excerpts from the collection are shown on the fourth floor in four small rooms and the corridor on a total of approximately 150 m^2 of office space. The collection is also shown in external exhibitions such as in 2016/17 at the Bode-Museum or in 2018 at the Reinbeckhallen, both in Berlin.

Sammlung Haupt
Berlin

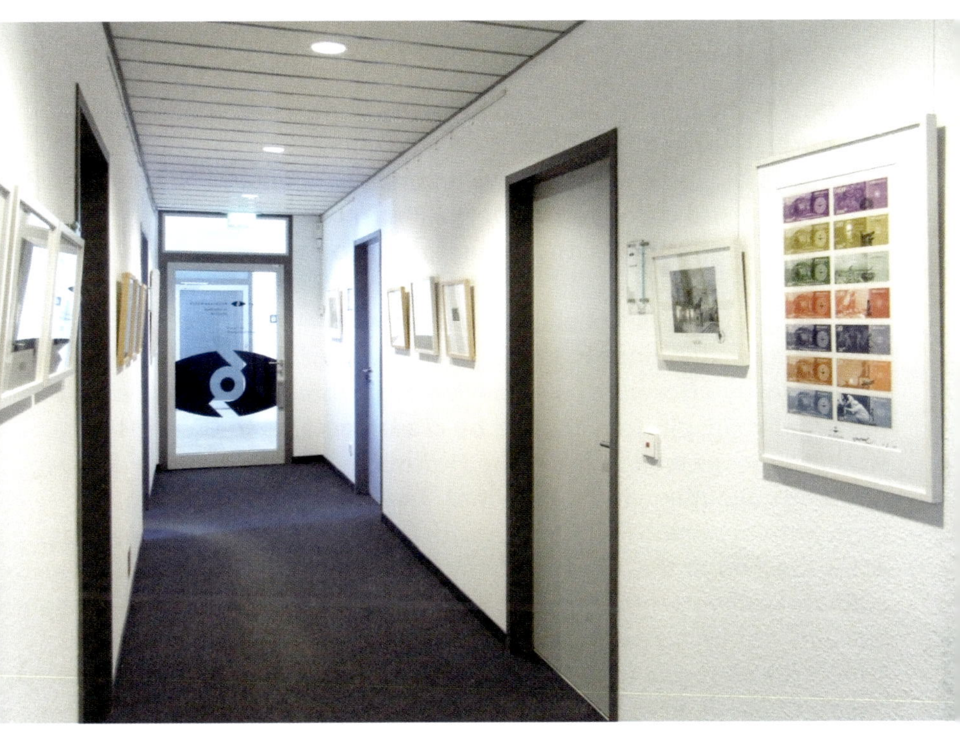

Haupt Rechtsanwälte
Märkisches Ufer 28
D-10179 Berlin
Phone: +49 30 28387521
info@sammlung-haupt.de
sammlung-haupt.de

Opening hours
A guided tour of the collection is possible every first Tuesday of the month at 5 p.m. (approx. 40 minutes). Registration by e-mail or telephone is required.
Sammlung Haupt also houses the meeting room and the corridor of the association of German guarantee banks at Schützenstraße 6a. These can be viewed at 11 a.m. on Saturday of Berlin Gallery Weekend without advance notice or during office hours by calling +49 30 26396540.

Entrance fees
A visit is free of charge.

Arrival by public transportation
The U-Bahn station Märkisches Museum (U2) is only a few minutes away from the office. Leave the underground station in the direction of Märkisches Museum, turn left into Inselstraße, and then right into Märkisches Ufer.

Restaurant tips
There are several simple restaurants in the surrounding streets. Delicious daytime snacks can be found at Käseinsel (kaeseinsel.de, Inselstr. 8a). A side trip to the other side of the Spree is worthwhile, especially when the weather is nice. In approximately fifteen minutes headed east on foot is the hip Holzmarkt. Behind a colorful gate, there is a beer garden, a café, and the trendy Katerschmaus restaurant (katerschmaus.de, holzmarkt.com, Holzmarktstr. 25).

Extra tips
Many Berlin visitors find the East Side Gallery monument 2.5 km away in Berlin-Friedrichshain interesting. The permanent open-air gallery is one of the longest sections of the Berlin Wall still standing and was painted by 118 artists in 1990 (eastsidegallery-berlin.de, Mühlenstr.). If you are in Kreuzberg before visiting the collection, a side trip to the Berlinische Galerie, Landesmuseum für Moderne Kunst, Fotografie und Architektur, is worthwhile (berlinischegalerie.de, Alte Jakobstr. 124–128). Nearby is the spectacular König Galerie (Alexandrinenstr. 118–121) in the former St. Agnes Church.

124 Sammlung Hoffmann

Located in the middle of the Spandauer Vorstadt is likely Berlin's most private collection that is open to the public. Since 1997, it has been possible for art lovers to visit annually changing "installations" in the living and office rooms of the Hoffmanns.

As early as the 1960s, the collector couple Rolf and Erika Hoffmann were interested in contemporary art; they were able to establish lasting relationships at documenta and at museum and art association exhibitions in the Rhineland. Their first purchases were made shortly afterward, as they loved the intellectual challenge and the creative inspiration shaped by close contacts to the art scene. At that time, as well as later, the Hoffmanns tried, with a few exceptions, to collect in a timely manner. They acquired many works from not yet established artists with whom they had personal ties. After the sale of their fashion company van Laack in 1985, the two collectors devoted themselves with even greater dedication to their passion—at first, however, only in private settings and not publically. This changed with the collapse of the GDR, as both had the desire to participate actively in post-reunification cultural changes. In the first years after the fall of the Wall, the Hoffmanns sought to initiate the construction of an art gallery in Dresden designed by Frank Stella. After the project failed, they developed a completely independent concept for today's presentation of the collection, which they were able to implement by discovering and buying the old factory on Sophienstraße. Originally built by H. Mehlich in the last third of the nineteenth century as a residential and commercial complex, sewing machines and later bicycle chains were produced here. In 1995, the Hoffmann family acquired the complex as well as the undeveloped neighboring property on the Gipsstraße side and extensively renovated the entire area. It was extended and redesigned by the architects Becker Gewers Kühn & Kühn into a residential, office, and gallery building. The new throughway between Sophienstraße and Gipsstraße upgraded the entire area, and today it is part of the Hackesche Höfe tourist quarter.

In the entrance area of the collection, visitors encounter sculptures by Richard Serra and Antony Gormley, which, unlike most

Sammlung Hoffmann
Berlin

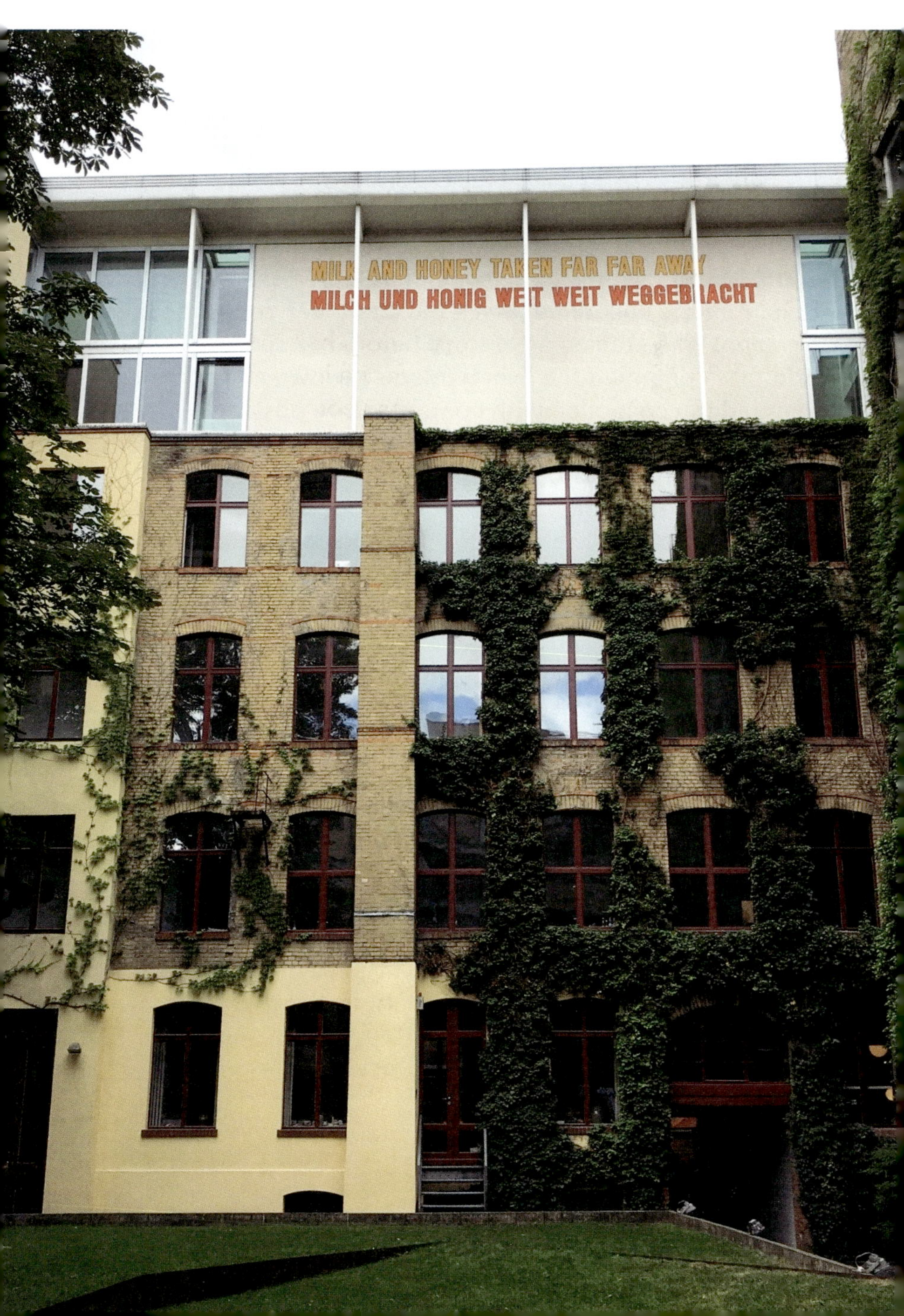

other works, are on permanent view. Visitors are guided through two of the three attic floors in small groups, and selected works of art are explained and discussed. Again and again, glimpses of the charming backyards and the Berlin skyline can be seen. In the private living room, with a little luck, visitors are greeted personally by the lady of the house. The works of art are newly installed annually covering an area of approximately 1,500 m² with differing room layouts. Until 2001, the couple jointly selected the themes and works from the collection. Since the death of her husband, Erika Hoffmann, who studied art history before her success in the fashion world, has continued the joint work on her own and continuously expanded the collection with contemporary positions.

Due to the geographical proximity of their place of residence, Mönchengladbach, to Düsseldorf, the two collectors first intensively studied the works of the ZERO group (Heinz Mack, Otto Piene, and Günther Uecker). Travels to the United States led to the purchase of numerous works by American artists such as Andy Warhol, Jean-Michel Basquiat, Frank Stella, Mike Kelley, Fred Sandback, and Bruce Nauman. With their move to Berlin, the focus was increasingly on Eastern Europe and Asia. The collection includes works by Teresa Murak and photographs by Hiroshi Sugimoto, among others.

In 2018, Erika Hoffmann announced that the Hoffmann Collection had, in fact, found its way to Dresden to complement the holdings there with contemporary works. As part of a generous donation, the Hoffmann family will successively gift approximately 1,200 works of art from 1910 to the present to the Dresden State Art Collections (SKD). For the near future, however, it will still be possible to visit the collection site in Berlin-Mitte, as the transfer to the fifteen Dresden museums is scheduled to last five years.

Sammlung Hoffmann Berlin

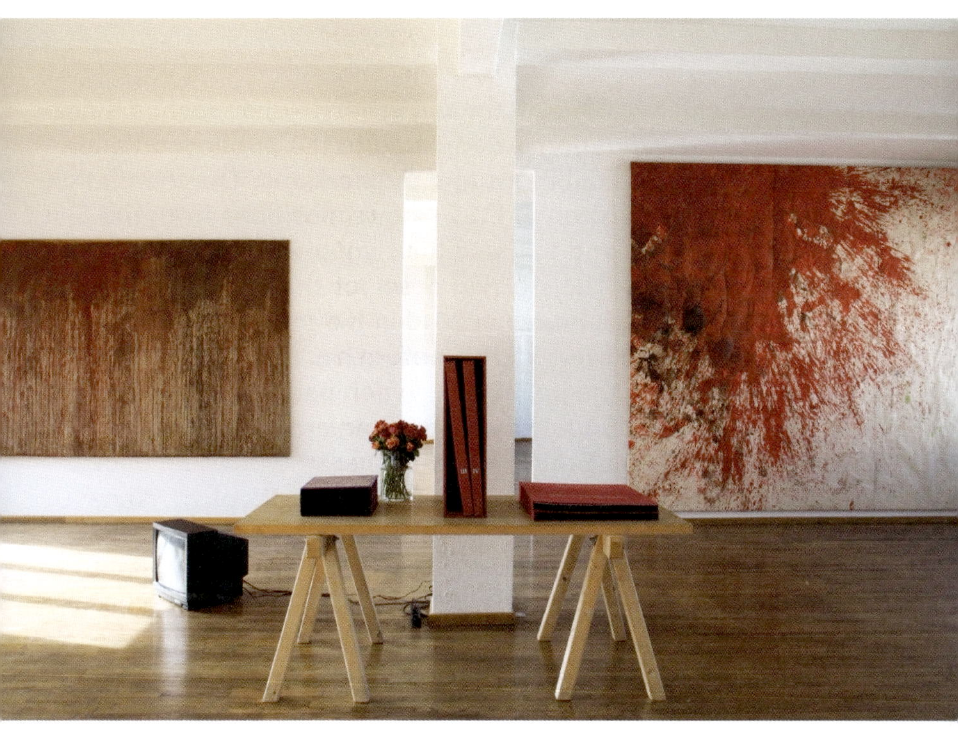

Sammlung Hoffmann
Sophie-Gips-Höfe,
2nd Courtyard, Staircase C
Sophienstr. 21
D-10178 Berlin
Phone: +49 30 28499120
mail@sammlung-hoffmann.de
sammlung-hoffmann.de

Opening hours
Sat 11 a.m.–4 p.m., only after registration (via the website or by telephone) for guided tours in English or German. The collection is closed in August and between Christmas and New Year. The courtyards themselves are open to the public between 9 a.m. and 10 p.m.

Entrance fees
Adults / Children 6 years and older: €10 / €5

Arrival by public transportation
The nearest U-Bahn station is Weinmeisterstraße (U8). Coming from Hauptbahnhof, it is more convenient to take the S-Bahn to Hackescher Markt (S5 direction Strausberg Nord, S75 direction Ostkreuz, S9 direction Flughafen Berlin-Schönefeld).

Restaurant tips
The rustic café bistros Altes Europa (alteseuropa.com; Gipsstr. 11, down-to-earth German cuisine) and Mittendrin (Sophienstr. 19; simple Swabian cuisine and delicious Flammkuchen) are cozy. Much sought after are tables in Barcomi's Deli, where it is possible to find cakes and hearty small bites (barcomis.de; Sophienstr. 21, Sophie Gips Höfe, 2nd Courtyard).

Extra tips
The art quarter of Auguststraße with the me Collectors Room (see p. 130) and the Museum Frieder Burda / Salon Berlin (p. 106) is very close to the Sammlung Hoffmann. The Boros Collection (p. 102), the JULIA STOSCHEK COLLECTION Berlin (p. 140), and the Collection Regard (p. 134) are also close by. Non-residents should take a look at the colorful and lively Hackescher Höfe. The area around Rosenthaler Straße and Münzstraße is also famous for its many small boutiques and designer shops.

128
Kienzle Art Foundation

Through the initiative of collector and gallery owner Jochen Kienzle, the Kienzle Art Foundation is dedicated to the public mediation of art in the form of exhibitions and publications. The foundation aims to examine forgotten or little-known positions from the 1960s to the present and to make their impulses clear for the next generation of artists. The starting point for the foundation's exhibition activities, which began in 2010 in the former gallery rooms of Kienzle, is Jochen Kienzle's art collection. Including the estate of Josef Kramhöller, the collection, which has been continuously expanded since the 1980s, now comprises around 1,000 works of art. Works by Franz Erhard Walther, Jonathan Lasker, Jack Goldstein, David Lamelas, Klaus Merkel, Gary Stephan, Anna Oppermann, Ketty La Rocca, and Emilio Prini are at the heart of the collection, which ranges from Abstract art and Informel to contemporary conceptual tendencies. The committed collector promotes artistic positions that consciously polarize, are of social relevance, and force a change of perspective. He equates the quality of art with its influence on an art-critical discourse and is convinced that art and education are inextricably linked. For this reason, he also sees the mediation of art as an important educational task. Each year, the foundation presents four to five exhibitions in three spacious rooms.

Born into an entrepreneurial family in Freiburg im Breisgau, Jochen Kienzle is the great-grandson of Jakob Kienzle, the founder of Kienzle Uhrenfabriken, one of the world's leading watch manufacturers at the turn of the century. After an apprenticeship as a carpenter, he studied art history and perceptual psychology in Munich. After moving to Berlin, he opened the gallery Kienzle & Gmeiner in Bleibtreustraße together with Anette Gmeiner in 1997. In 2001, Jochen Kienzle took over the sole management of the gallery. In 2009, he founded the Kienzle Art Foundation (a foundation under civil law), of which Kienzle is still a member today.

Kienzle Art Foundation Berlin

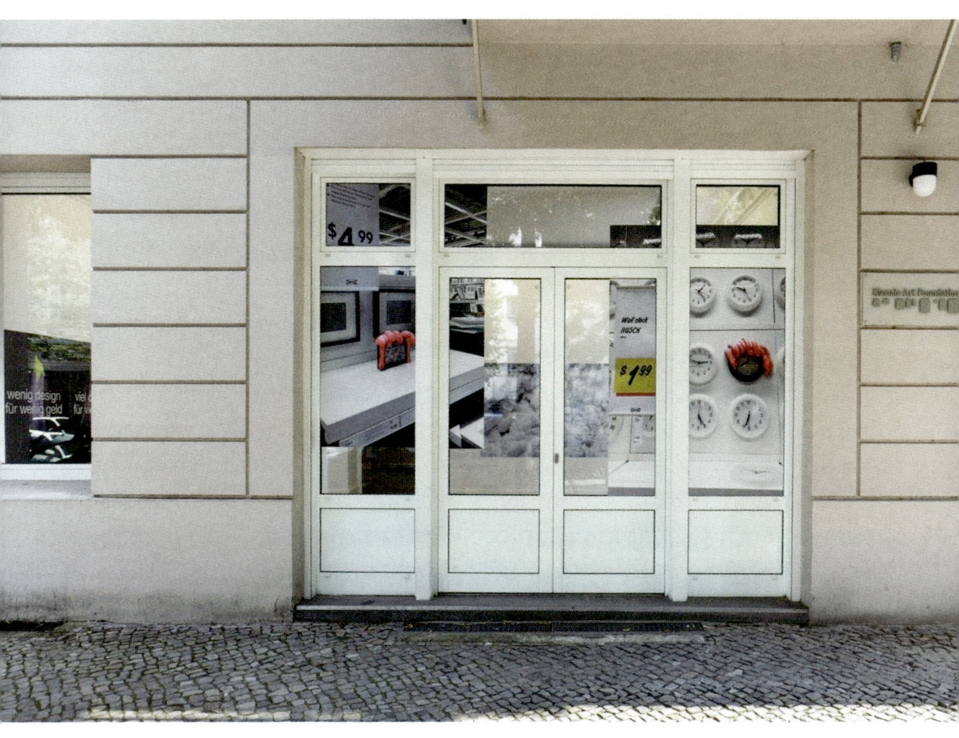

Kienzle Art Foundation
Bleibtreustr. 54
D-10623 Berlin
Phone: +49 30 31507013
office@kienzleartfoundation.de
kienzleartfoundation.de

Opening hours
Thu–Fri 2–7 p.m.,
Sat 11 a.m.–4 p.m. and by appointment
Lectures take place on occasion.

Entrance fees
Free admission

Arrival by public transportation
The Foundation is located near the Savignyplatz S-Bahn station.

Restaurant tips
Anabelas Kitchen serves Mediterranean dishes in a family atmosphere in the evenings (anabelas-kitchen.de; Pestalozzistr. 3; closed Sundays and Mondays). Berlin cuisine is served in the neighborhood tavern Diener Tattersall, which has remained unchanged for decades (diener-berlin.de; Grolmanstr. 47). The traditional Zwiebelfisch bar also has a cult status (zwiebelfisch-berlin.de; Savignyplatz 7–8).

Extra tip
A visit to the Kienzle Art Foundation can easily be combined with visits to the EAM Collection (see p. 112) and Salon Dahlmann (p. 110).

130
me Collectors Room Berlin / Olbricht Foundation

me Collectors Room, the residential and exhibition house built by Thomas Olbricht for his collection, opened its doors in May 2010 and has since enriched the lives of thousands of art lovers in many respects.

The "me" stands for "moving energies" and is intended to point out that this exhibition location is not a museum in the conventional sense, but rather a world of experience open to the public. The desire for adventure, the joy of provocation, and the privilege of being able to assemble completely different things spontaneously becomes visible in this colorful "art laboratory."

The chemist, doctor, medical professor, former chairman of the supervisory board, and heir to the Wella Group was gripped by a passion for collecting as a child. His great uncle, arts patron Karl Ströher, was the driving force behind this impulse.

Beginning with stamps, beer coasters, matchboxes, and toy ambulances, Olbricht has built one of the most extensive private collections in Europe over the last forty years. It includes works from the sixteenth century to the present day, Classical Modernism, as well as Art Nouveau. In addition to such well-known contemporary artists as Elmgreen & Dragset, Maurizio Cattelan, Cindy Sherman, Marlene Dumas, and Andreas Gursky, numerous young positions discovered by Olbricht are also presented. The program of the collection, which oscillates between old and new, is on existential themes such as Eros, death, and transience.

A tour of the exhibition starts on the upper floor in the Wunderkammer Olbricht. It offers insight into the worldview and knowledge of past centuries. The approximately three hundred exhibits include beetle preparations, an amber mirror, a coconut goblet owned by Alexander von Humboldt, and the world's most extensive collection of carved Janus heads. In addition to the restored Green Vault in Dresden, these rooms reflect the concept of the princely

me Collectors Room Berlin / Olbricht Foundation
Berlin

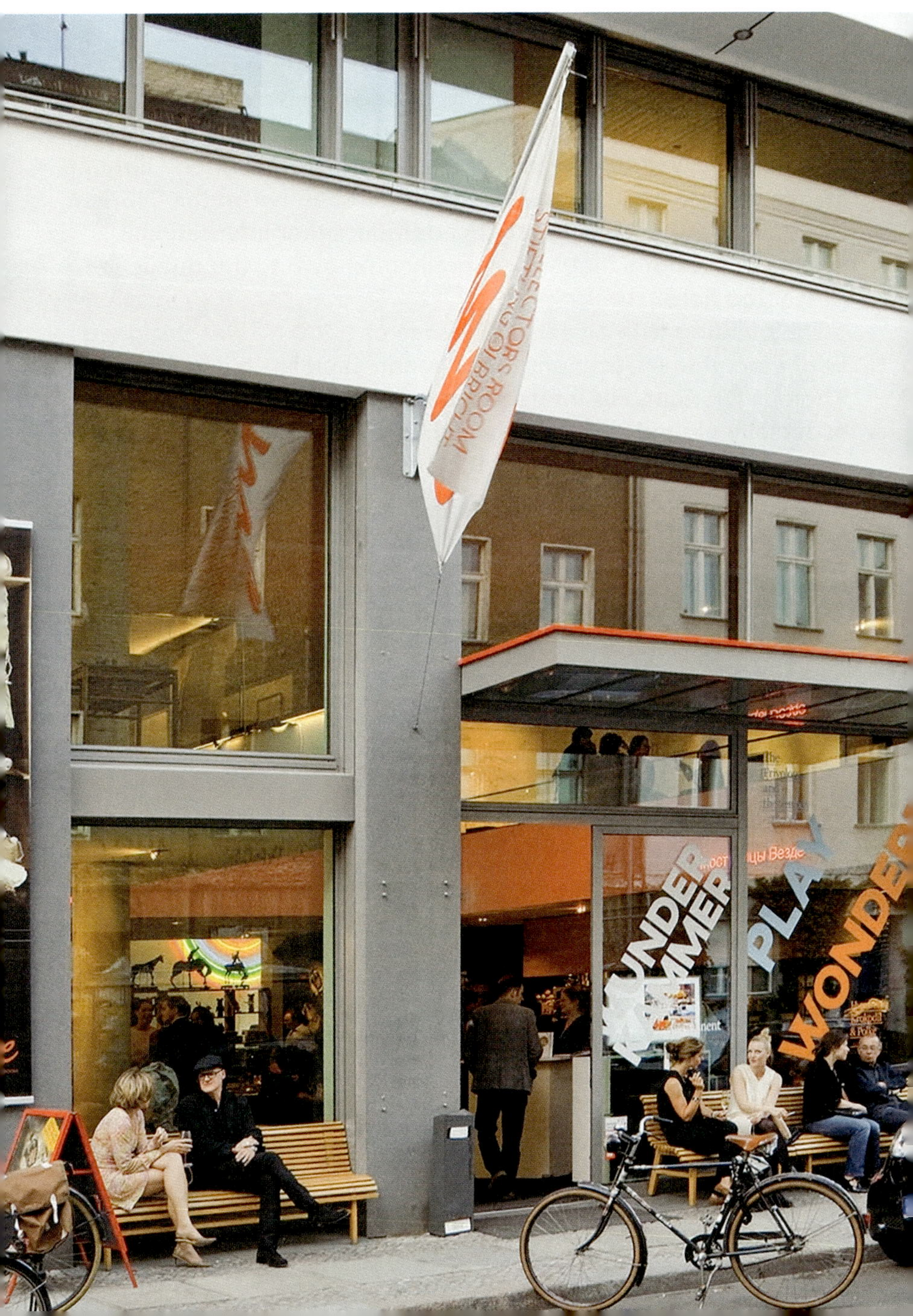

"Wunderkammern" (chambers of wonder), the forerunners of today's museums. The Wunderkammer Olbricht is is a permanent installation whose conception, installation, and supervision are carried out by the Kunstkammer Georg Laue in Munich. Two to three times a year, in the large halls on the ground floor, Olbricht invites various curators to show their perspective on the Olbricht Collection with an exhibition. In addition, other international private collections that are generally unknown to the public are presented here.

The building with an exhibition area of 1,300 m² was designed by Berlin architects Düttmann + Kleymann in close collaboration with Thomas Olbricht. His interest in the Auguststraße location was especially piqued by Klaus Biesenbach, one of the founders of the adjacent KW Institute for Contemporary Art.

me Collectors Room Berlin
Auguststr. 68
D-10117 Berlin
Phone: +49 30 86008510
info@me-berlin.com
me-berlin.com

Opening hours
Wed–Mon noon–6 p.m.
During exhibition changes, the exhibition rooms remain closed for about two weeks.
Every first Saturday of the month at 2 p.m. art:berlin offers public guided tours (€10 including admission). Registration is necessary by calling 030 28096390 or online artberlin-online.de.
Following the guided tours there is a get-together for reflection and discussion in the me Café. There are additional events, guided tours for collectors, and readings (see website).
The me Shop offers catalogs, postcards, and posters about the exhibition, a comprehensive selection of literature on collections and collectors as well as editions and curiosities. In the me Café, daily specials, waffle creations, and vegan snacks are offered.

Entrance fees
Adults / Reduced: €8 / €4
A combination day ticket with the KW Institute for Contemporary Art is also available.

Arrival by public transportation
Starting from Berlin Hauptbahnhof, take bus 142 in the direction of Ostbahnhof to the Tucholskystraße stop. The S3, S7, and S75 trams, as well as the M1 and M6 trams, go to the nearby Oranienburger Straße S-Bahn stop. The underground stations Weinmeisterstraße (U8) and Oranienburger Tor (U6), as well as the S-Bahn station Hackescher Markt (S3, S5, S7, S75), are located near the exhibition building.

Restaurant tips
Approx. 100 m from the collection, Eismanufaktur Berlin will fulfill desires for something sweet (Auguststr. 63). In the Milchhalle (milchhalle-berlin.de; Auguststr. 50) you can relax while enjoying fresh waffles and excellent coffee.

Extra tips
If you would like to briefly immerse yourself in historic Berlin, a visit to Clärchens Ballhaus, a restaurant, beer garden, and ballroom with GDR ambiance, is recommended (ballhaus.de; Auguststr. 24). On the first floor of you can visit a magnificent old Spiegelsaal. On Sunday evenings, regular concerts – mostly classical—take place here for a nominal entrance fee (sonntagskonzerte.de).
Sammlung Hoffmann (see p. 124) and Boros Collection (p. 102), Collection Regard (p. 134), and the Museum Frieder Burda / Salon Berlin (p. 106) are within walking distance.

me Collectors Room Berlin / Olbricht Foundation
Berlin

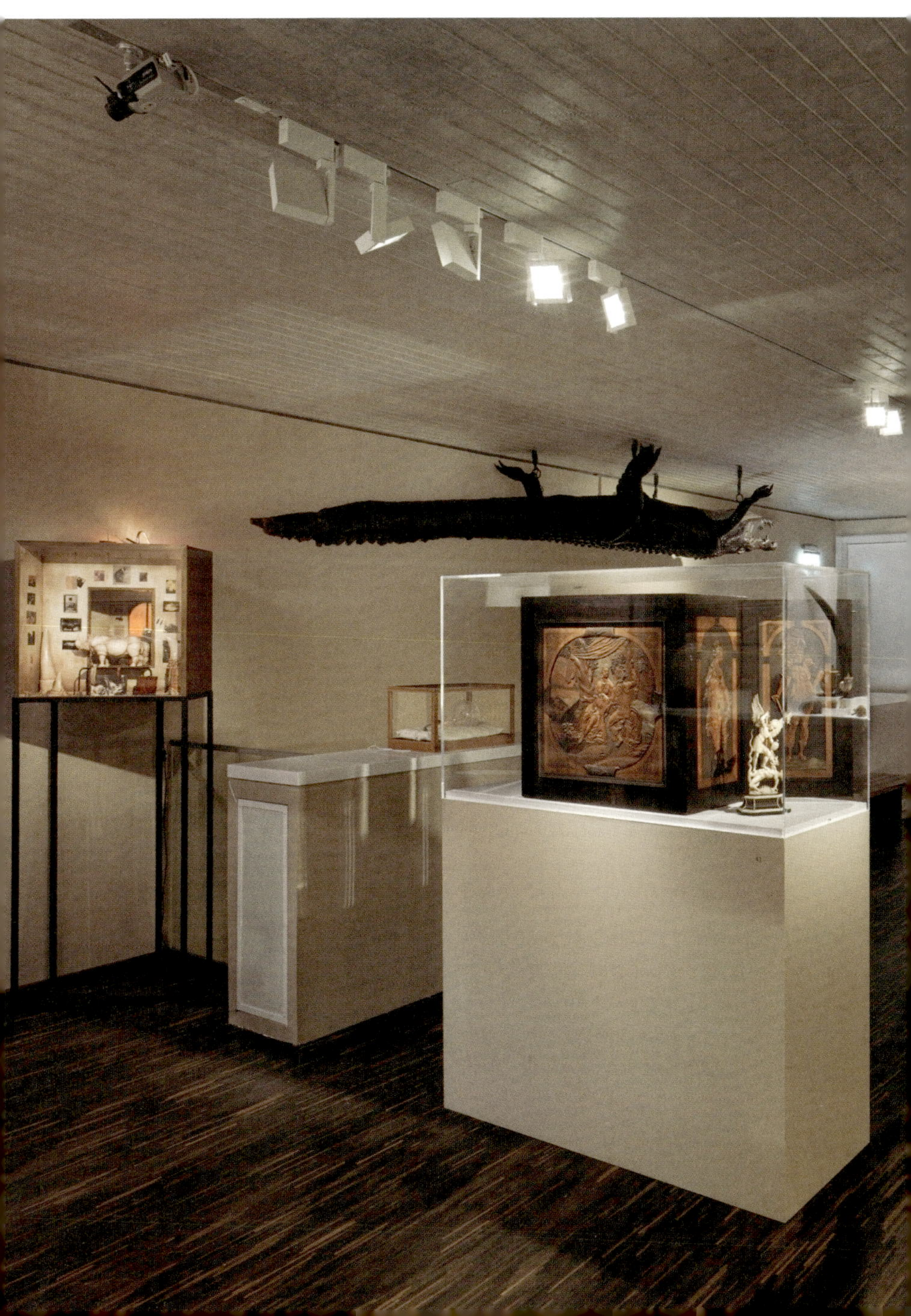

134 Collection Regard

Collection Regard is the photographic collection of Marc Barbey, who has been enthusiastically collecting works from the beginnings of photography to the end of the 1990s since 2005. The focus is on German photography, especially in relation to Berlin. Barbey also follows the subjects of photojournalism and “photographie vernaculaire” with interest. The French term “regard” means “gaze” or “attention,” and the focus is on the selection of artists. The collector’s goal is to show largely unknown photographic works that deserve attention in a curated context. In addition to the extensive archive (approximately 1,200 prints and 17,000 negatives) of Hein Gorny (1904–1967), whose estate it also administers, the Collection Regard comprises several thousand works, including Lotte Jacobi, Siegfried Lauterwasser, Heinrich Riebesehl, Toni Schneiders, Friedrich Seidenstücker, Hans Martin Sewcz, Manfred Paul, Paul Almasy, Bruno Barbey, Dietrich Oltmanns, and Robert Capa. Through targeted cooperation with international institutions, museums, and other collections, his own publications, and the production and sale of exclusive editions, Marc Barbey strives to continuously develop his collection. The Frenchman, who has lived in Berlin since 2003 and previously worked in software distribution, has curated two to three mostly monographic exhibitions annually since 2011 in his former offices. Approximately one-third of the works exhibited come from the collection; the other works are on loan from artists’ or photographers’ archives, most of whom are represented in the collection. In contrast to the classic white cube, the 85 m² collection rooms exude a more homely atmosphere with their classic Danish furniture. Collection Regard, which also sees itself as a “salon” and place for dialogue, thus creates an atmosphere of intimate access to the photographs and offers an opportunity to exchange ideas with the collector and other art and photography enthusiasts.

Collection Regard
Berlin

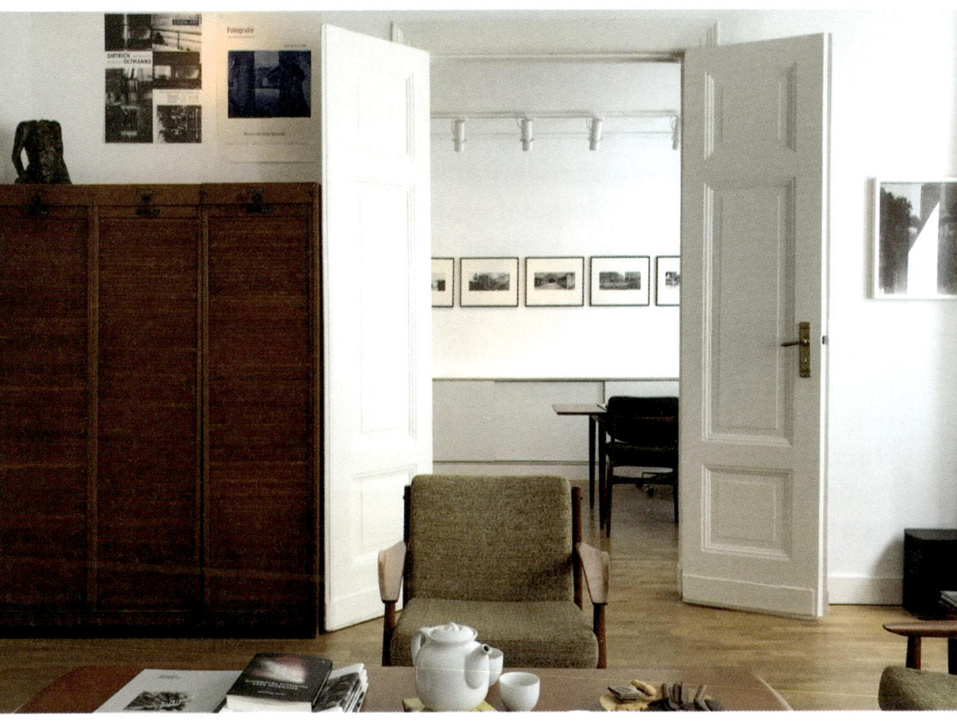

Collection Regard
Steinstr. 12
D-10119 Berlin
Phone: +49 30 84711947
info@collectionregard.com
collectionregard.com

Opening hours
During the exhibitions, the rooms are open every Friday from 2–8 p.m. (except on public holidays) and by appointment. An exciting program of events accompanies the exhibition (artists' talks in the form of "Salons Photographiques" and film screenings, contribution €5 to €7). Details can be found on the website. Marc Barbey regularly leads tours through the exhibitions. Registration is requested.

Entrance fees
Admission is free of charge. The number of visitors is limited to 30 persons at a time.

Arrival by public transportation
The U-Bahn stations Weinmeisterstraße (U8) and Rosa-Luxemburg-Platz (U2) are close to the collection.

Restaurant tips
Numerous cafés, restaurants, and shops are located on Alte Schönhauser Straße around the corner and some side streets. Excellent cheesecake can be enjoyed at the small Five Elephant (fiveelephant.com; Alte Schönhauser Str. 14), tasty Korean cuisine in the simple YamYam (yamyam-berlin.de; Alte Schönhauser Str. 14), authentic Vietnamese dishes in the unusual Qua Phe (Max-Beer-Str. 37). In the evening, the vegan restaurant Kopps is a must for gourmets, who can enjoy innovative vegetable dishes. Also recommended is the extensive weekend brunch buffet (kopps-berlin.de; Linienstr. 94).

Extra tips
You can combine a visit to the Collection Regard with visits to the me Collectors Room Berlin (see p. 130) and the Museum Frieder Burda / Salon Berlin (p. 106). The Alfred Ehrhardt Stiftung is also located in the neighborhood of these collections. In addition to its archival activities, unusual exhibitions and contemporary positions which, following Ehrhardt's work themes, deal with the concept of "nature" and the "constructions of the natural," as well as historical photography and film art by Alfred Ehrhardt, are shown here (alfred-ehrhardt-stiftung.de; Auguststr. 75).

136 Sammlung Scharf-Gerstenberg

Since 2008, the Berlin district of Charlottenburg has been home to the Sammlung Scharf-Gerstenberg in the eastern part of the Stüler building and the adjacent Marstall. Under the title "Surreal Worlds," paintings, sculptures, and works on paper from the holdings of the Foundation of the Dieter Scharf Collection are shown here in memory of Otto Gerstenberg on two floors across an exhibition area of approximately 1,300 m². In 2004, the foundation donated nearly three hundred works of art on permanent loan to the Nationalgalerie of the Staatliche Museen zu Berlin. The latter then commissioned architect Gregor Sunder-Plassmann to convert the eastern Stüler building for the Scharf-Gerstenberg Collection after the Egyptian Museum, which was previously located there, moved to the Museum Island in 2005. The ground floor of the building still contains the columns of the ancient Sahurê Temple and the Kalabsha Gate. German archaeologists saved the Nubian temple of Kalabsha from the Aswan Dam floods in 1963. Eight years later, Germany received the monumental gate from Egypt as a thank you gift. The sandstone blocks from the gate, from circa 20 BC, were found as reused building material in the foundation of the temple. The architectural parts of the Sahurê Temple, built around 2400 BC, were discovered during excavations in Abusir between 1902 and 1908 and installed at their present location in the 1980s.

The Sammlung Scharf-Gerstenberg focuses on Fantastic and Surreal art. The Surrealist movement, founded in Paris in the early 1920s by the French writer, poet, and critic André Breton, sought man's own reality in the unconscious and exploited experiences while intoxicated and while dreaming as a source of artistic inspiration. Almost all followers of Surrealism and their most important predecessors are represented in the collection with selected works. Among the earliest works in the collection are Giovanni Battista Piranesi's depictions of fantastic dungeon architecture and Francisco de Goya's etchings with nightmarish haunted figures. French Symbolism of the late nineteenth century is represented by

Sammlung Scharf-Gerstenberg
Berlin

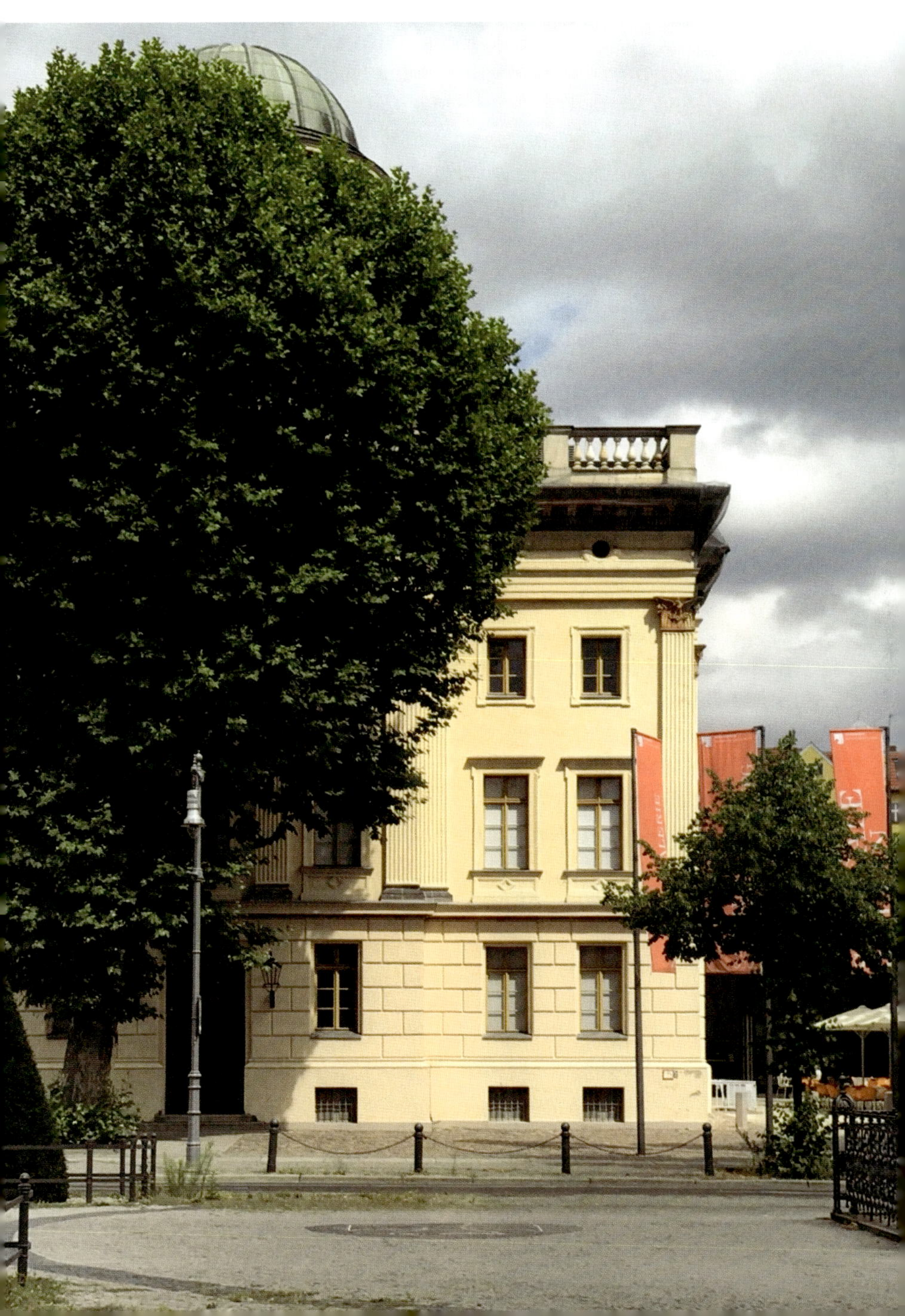

the paintings of Odilon Redon and Gustave Moreau, as well as its German counterpart in the form of Max Klinger's graphic cycles. Surrealists René Magritte, Max Ernst, and Hans Bellmer, as well as Wols and Paul Klee, are represented with larger groups of works. Supplementary special exhibitions are organized annually. The spectrum of the collection is further extended by a film program in the Sahurê Hall, which includes works by Luis Buñuel and Salvador Dalí, as well as contemporary works that reference Surrealism.

The collection has its origins in Otto Gerstenberg's (1848–1935) early enthusiasm for art. Born in South Pomerania, the mathematician and later founder and general director of Victoria Insurance made an impression with his upbeat motto "Go through the world and talk to everyone." In his villa in Berlin-Dahlem, he kept one of the most extensive collections of paintings and prints of his time. The spectrum ranged from his favorite Old Masters to Impressionism. Honoré Daumier's *The Imaginary Illness* (c. 1857) was also part of the collection, as were Edouard Manet's *The Café-Concert* (1878), and Auguste Renoir's *In the Garden* (1885). The collection was either destroyed in the Second World War or taken to Russia as looted art. Today, some of the works in the collection can be found on the upper floor of the Hermitage of St. Petersburg. His passion for collecting was "inherited" by Otto Gerstenberg's grandsons Walter Scharf (1923–1996) and Dieter Scharf (1926–2001). The latter took over the graphic cycles of Giovanni Battista Piranesi, Francisco de Goya, and Max Klinger, among others, which formed the foundation for his collection. From the outset, the collection concentrated on Fantastic and Surreal art and was exhibited in the Neue Nationalgalerie in 2000.

Sammlung Scharf-Gerstenberg Berlin

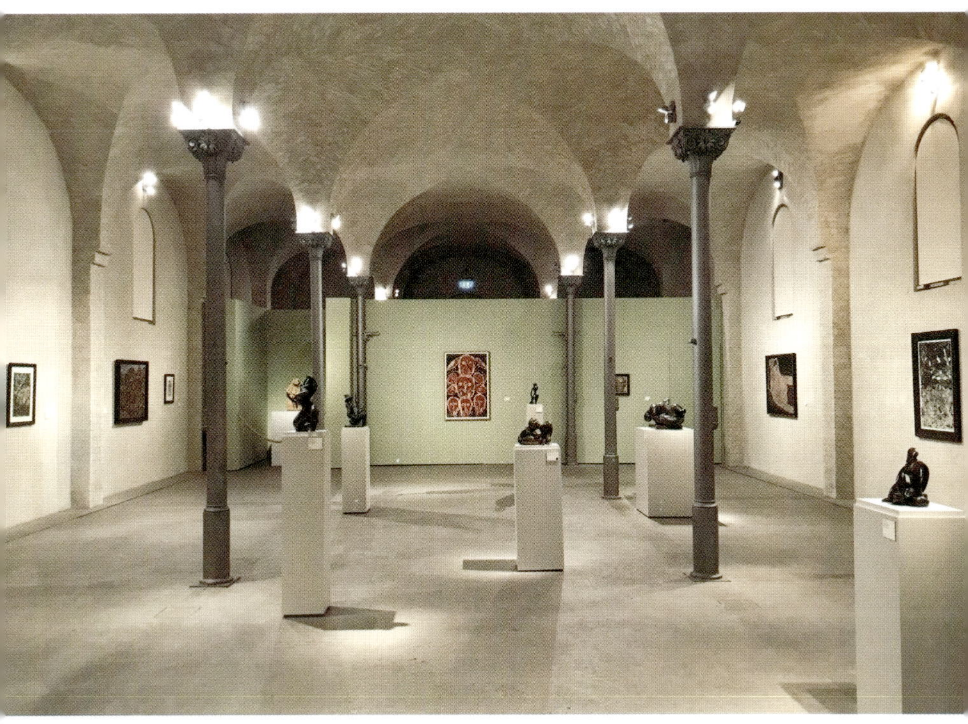

Sammlung Scharf-Gerstenberg
Staatliche Museen zu Berlin
Schloßstr. 70
D-14059 Berlin
Phone: +49 30 266424242
smb.museum/ssg

Opening hours
Tue–Fri 10 a.m.–6 p.m.,
Sat/Sun 11 a.m.–6 p.m.
Public guided tours take place on Saturdays at 3 p.m. (€4 plus admission).
There is a museum shop and a café in the entrance area to the collection.

Entrance fees
Sammlung Scharf-Gerstenberg and Museum Berggruen:
Adults / Reduced / Children and Youths to age 18 as well as Museum Pass Berlin holders:
€10 / €5 / free

Arrival by public transportation
Relatively nearby S-Bahn and U-Bahn stops are Westend (S41, S42, S46), Sophie Charlotte Platz (U2) and Richard Wagner Platz (U7).

Extra tips
Near the Sammlung Scharf-Gerstenberg lies Villa Oppenheim, built in the Neo-Renaissance style and home to the Museum Charlottenburg-Wilmersdorf since 2014. Among other things, the Charlottenburg Art Collection with works by Walter Leistikow, Max Liebermann, and Franz Skarbina and other nineteenth-century artists and the Berlin Secession is presented here (villa-oppenheim-berlin.de; Schloßstr. 55).
In Charlottenburg, art lovers also have a chance to visit the publicly accessible sculpture museum and the workshop gallery of the fourth-generation foundry Noack. Over the past 130 years the foundry has been responsible, for casting sculptures by Ernst Barlach, Henry Moore, and Georg Baselitz among other things. With the addition of the French Bar Brass, in 2018 the Skulpturenforum was enriched to become a place of contemplation. Guided tours through the foundry are possible (skulpturenforum.com; barbrass.de, Am Spreebord 9).
It is also a good idea to visit the Museum Berggruen on the same day, as the admission ticket is valid for both museums (see p. 98). Of course, Charlottenburg Palace with its splendidly furnished rooms, art collections, and gardens also has numerous worthwhile sights; in December, there is a beautiful Christmas market here (spsg.de; Spandauer Damm 10–22).

140
JULIA STOSCHEK COLLECTION Berlin

In addition to the Düsseldorf location (see p. 220), moving image expert Julia Stoschek opened a branch in Berlin-Mitte in 2016. Initially only planned as a pop-up venue, to the delight of all lovers of time-based media art, she has now permanently rented two floors in the building complex of the former Czech cultural center of the former GDR, which was partly used by the Konzulát nightclub after the fall of the Berlin Wall. Berlin architect Johanna Meyer-Grohbrügge transformed the interior of the typical 1969 prefabricated building into an exhibition area of 2,500 m^2. In consultation with the collector, traces of its earlier use were not eradicated, but, if possible, integrated into the presentation concept. Thus, the wood-clad cinema and the former bar were revived. Even the uneasy feeling that many visitors know from traveling to Eastern European countries is still subtly perceptible. Since the opening of her house in Düsseldorf in 2007, Julia Stoschek has made it her task to increase the acceptance of occasionally uncomfortable media art. To make it easier for viewers to access this highly topical art, she and her team put together two to three thematic exhibitions or monographic shows each year for the Berlin branch. Both individual works and groups of works from the Stoschek Collection and supplementary loans or projects created in cooperation with other institutions and artists are shown. This special collection, unique in Europe, comprises 850 works by around 300 artists including Doug Aitken, Ed Atkins, Neïl Beloufa, Hannah Black, Ian Cheng, Melanie Gilligan, Arthur Jafa, Helen Marten, Jon Rafman, Rachel Rose, Frances Stark, Hito Steyerl, Britta Thie, Anicka Yi, Wu Tsang, and Amir Yatziv.

JULIA STOSCHEK COLLECTION Berlin

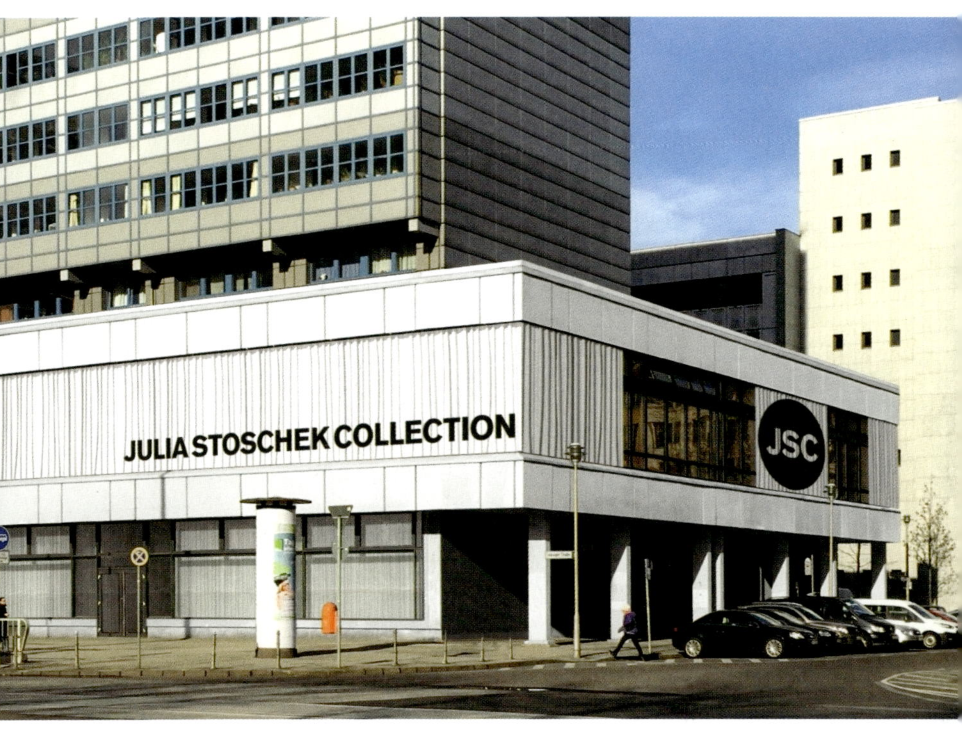

JULIA STOSCHEK COLLECTION Berlin
Leipziger Str. 60
Entrance on Jerusalemer Str.
D-10117 Berlin
Phone: +49 30 921062460
info@jsc.art
jsc.art

Opening hours
Sat/Sun noon–6 p.m. during exhibitions (mostly spring to November/December). Extended opening hours during Gallery Weekend, the Berlin Biennale, and Berlin Art Week.
There are guided tours in German on Sundays and in English on Saturdays at 3 p.m. (€10 including admission). Registration at visit. berlin@jsc.art.

Entrance fees
Adults / Children and teenagers: €5 / free of charge

Arrival by public transportation
The U-Bahn stations Hausvogteiplatz (U2) and Stadtmitte (U2 and U6) are less than 500 m away.

Restaurant tips
In the vicinity of the JSC Berlin, you will find some of the city's long-established culinary institutions. These include the restaurant Lutter & Wegner at Gendarmenmarkt (l-w-berlin.de; Charlottenstr. 56) and the French restaurant Entrecôte (entrecote.de; Schützenstr. 5). You can eat quite well and inexpensively at the modern Thai restaurant Goodtime (goodtime-berlin.de; Hausvogteiplatz 11).

Extra tips
If you plan your visit to JULIA STOSCHEK COLLECTION Berlin early, you can combine it with guided tours of the Feuerle Collection (see p. 114), the Boros Collection (p. 102), or the Hoffmann Collection (p. 124). The historically and architecturally interesting rooms of the Schinkel Pavillon host innovative art exhibitions (schinkelpavillon.de; Oberwallstr. 1). The PalaisPopulaire, which was opened by Deutsche Bank in 2018, features temporary exhibitions from The Deutsche Bank Collection and other major worldwide partner institutions (db-palaispopulaire.de; Unter den Linden 5).

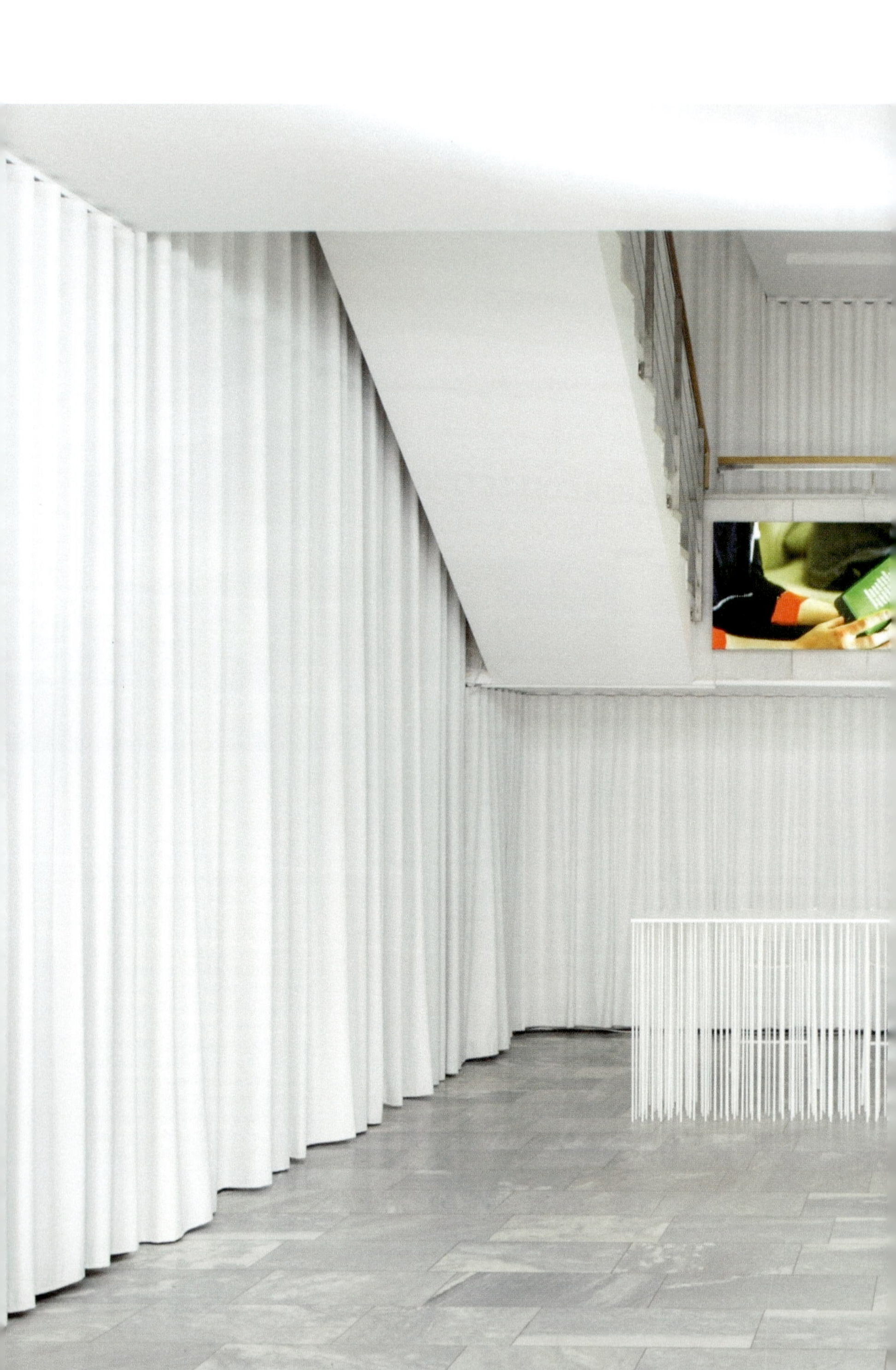

JULIA STOSCHEK COLLECTION
Berlin

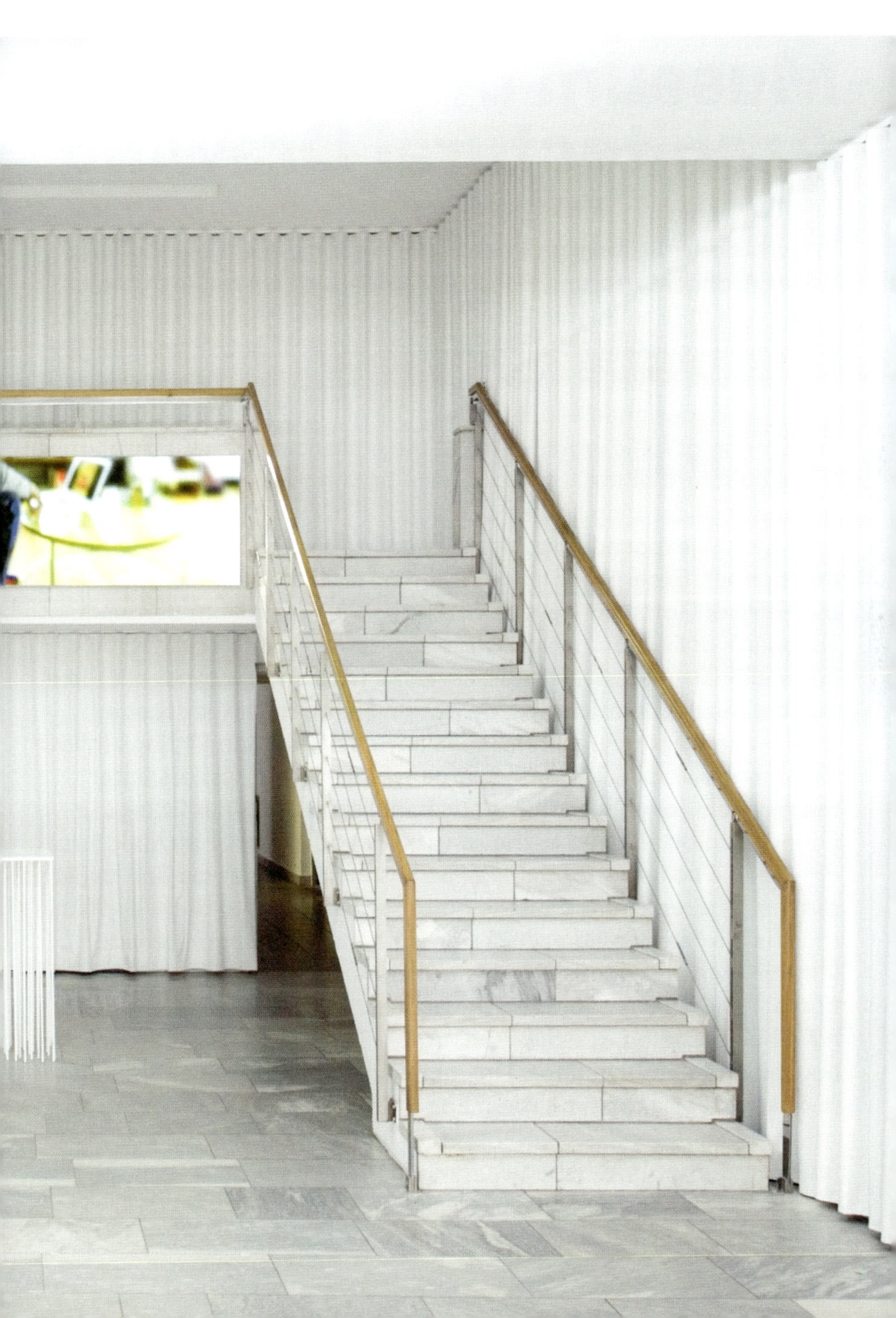

144 Tchoban Foundation – Museum of Architectural Drawing

In the historic brewery grounds of Pfefferberg, near the renowned Aedes Architekturforum, since 2013, friends of art and architecture have been able to admire a building that consistently expresses its mission and content from the outside. Sergei Tchoban and Sergey Kuznetsov of SPEECH, Moscow, and Tchoban Voss Architects, Berlin, have designed a location with ideal conditions for exhibiting and storing graphic works of art at the entrance to the Kunstquartier.

The cubature of the four floors is intended to be reminiscent of a stack of drawing blocks or boxes full of drawings, while the sand-yellow exposed concrete is intended to remind us of parchment paper. Excerpts of three historical architectural drawings by Pietro di Gottardo Gonzaga and Angelo Toselli from Sergei Tchoban's collection, which were transferred to the exposed concrete with structural matrices, served as the basis for the relief-like façade. Inside the museum, the design elements of the façade reappear repeatedly, and the specially designed door fittings follow the same principle. Through a large wooden door, visitors enter the museum foyer, which, with its paneling and walnut fittings, is intended to be attuned to the sensitivity and effect of architectural drawings. The large-format wall panels are hand-carved and depict the motifs already cited on the outer façade. Next to the reception, there is a reference library—a selection from Tchoban's private library—which is accessible to all visitors. On the second and third floors, windowless cabinets with an area of approximately 105 m² have been created as exhibition rooms. The Foundation's archive is housed on the fourth floor. The minimalist glass house on the top floor serves as a meeting room and office.

Born in St. Petersburg and based in Berlin, the Foundation's founder, Sergei Tchoban, developed a passion for architectural drawings in a broader sense, especially those of Old Masters, during his studies at the Russian Academy of the Arts. As a busy

Tchoban Foundation – Museum of Architectural Drawing
Berlin

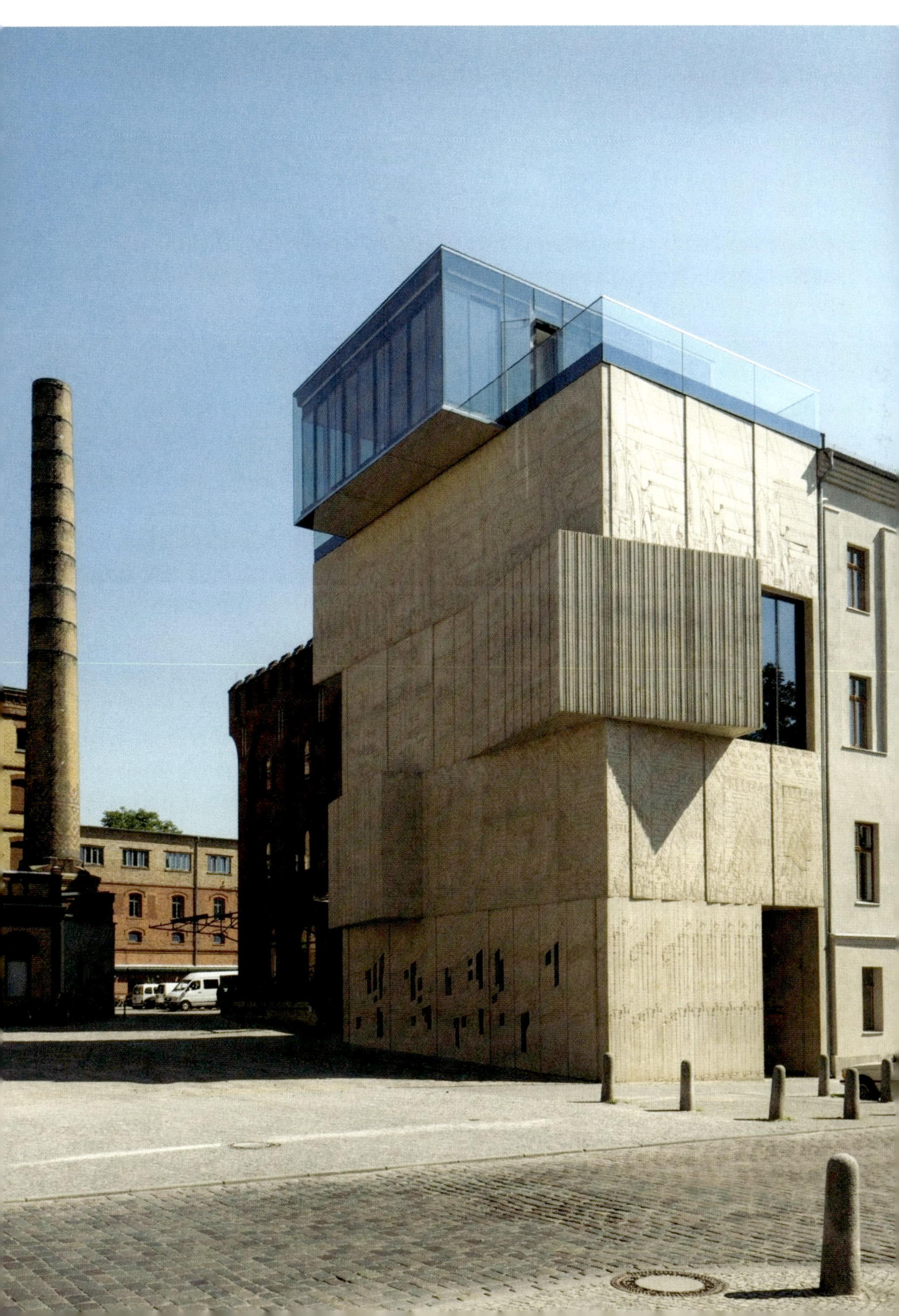

architect in Berlin and also successful in Russia with a Moscow office, he has had exhibitions as an architectural draftsman in numerous countries. The cornerstone for his own collection was laid in 2001 with the acquisition of a drawing by Pietro di Gottardo Gonzaga, an Italian artist from the eighteenth/nineteenth century. It now includes numerous pages from various eras, from Master drawings from the sixteenth century to works by contemporary architects—from Jacques Androuet du Cerceau to Giovanni Battista Piranesi, Hubert Robert, Sir John Soane, Karl Friedrich Schinkel, Frank Lloyd Wright, and Lebbeus Woods. Part of the collection has been incorporated into the Tchoban Foundation, which was founded in 2009. Today, the Foundation's holdings include drawings and visions by internationally leading twentieth and twentieth- and twenty-first-century architects such as Aldo Rossi, Oscar Niemeyer, Gottfried Böhm, Zaha Hadid, Frank Gehry, Daniel Libeskind, Alexander Brodsky, Moon Hoon, and Steven Holl. Of the approximately 2,500 works in the Foundation's collection, about half of the drawings are by Sergei Tchoban himself, some of which are on permanent loan.

The Tchoban Foundation understands its task as creating a relationship between contemporary architectural drawings and the works of great draftsmen and women of the past centuries, while, at the same time, keeping the tradition of hand drawing alive in the computer-influenced present. The Foundation's declared aim is to bring the fantastic and emotionally charged worlds of architectural drawing closer to the general public through exhibitions. To this end, the Foundation presents three exhibitions a year of works from public and private collections in the Museum of Architectural Drawing, which it sponsors, and in return exhibits its treasures in major institutions worldwide. Works from the Foundation's holdings can be viewed as part of a guided tour through the museum archive.

Tchoban Foundation – Museum of Architectural Drawing Berlin

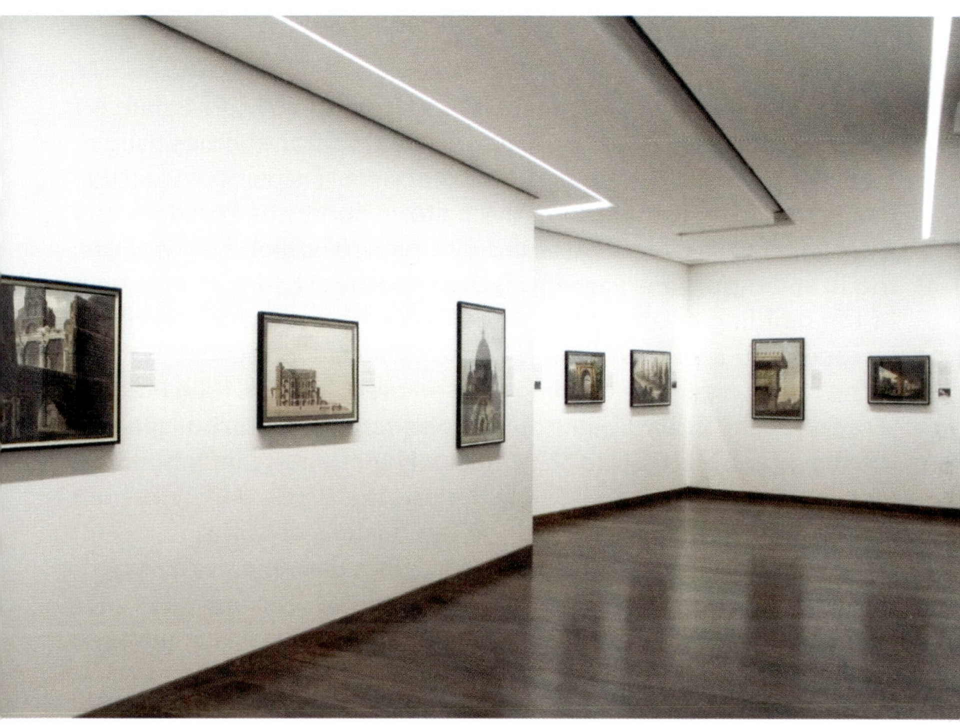

Tchoban Foundation – Museum of Architectural Drawing
Christinenstr. 18a
D-10119 Berlin
Phone: +49 30 43739090
mail@tchoban-foundation.de
tchoban-foundation.de

Opening hours
During exhibitions: Mon–Fri 2–7 p.m., Sat/Sun 1–5 p.m. Guided tours of the museum and the current exhibition are offered for groups of five or more participants (€2 plus admission fee). Individual guided tours with fewer than five participants cost a flat fee of €35. To see the foundation's collection, it is advisable to book a guided tour including a visit to the museum archive (€80, max. five participants). Registration is required for each guided tour (by telephone or at guide@tchoban-foundation.de).

Entrance fees
Adults / Reduced: €5 / €3

Arrival by public transportation
The museum can be reached with the U2 (Senefelderplatz) as well as the M1 and M12 (Zionskirchplatz).

Restaurant tips
Local German cuisine and home-brewed beers are served in the nearby Schankhalle Pfefferberg (schankhalle-pfefferberg.de/braugasthaus; Schönhauser Allee 176; closed Mondays; closed during the day except on weekends). Fans of homemade pasta dishes will get their money's worth at the small Italian Café & Bistrot Gina (Zionskirchstr. 77). The concept store The Store at Soho House Berlin serves unusual vegetarian/vegan snacks during the day (thestores.com/berlin; Torstr. 1).

Extra tips
Numerous exhibitions are presented in the private architecture forum Aedes, which illustrate contemporary architectural and urbanistic visions (aedes-arc.de; Christinenstr. 18–19).
The Sammlung Hoffmann (see p. 124), the Collection Regard (p. 134), the me Collectors Room (p. 130), and the Museum Frieder Burda / Salon Berlin (p. 106) are all within a twenty-minute walk from the Tchoban Foundation.

148
Museum Barberini

With the opening of the Museum Barberini in 2017, Potsdam has attained a top-class art museum. The exhibition themes range from the Old Masters to contemporary art. The reconstructed Palais Barberini is located in the historic center of Potsdam on the Alter Markt. The reconstructed city palace, which now houses the Brandenburg Parliament, is also nearby. The inner courtyard of the building opens to the Alte Fahrt with access to the Havel terraces and a view of the Freundschaftsinsel opposite.

The location and the building have an eventful past. King Frederick II (Frederick the Great) beautified the square, the heart of the residence city, from 1750 to 1777. Italian High Renaissance buildings inspired Frederick II. In 1771/72, he had the Palais Barberini built as a stately townhouse according to the designs of architects Georg Christian Unger and Carl von Gontard. The Baroque palazzo of the same name in Rome served as a model for the palace. In the middle of the nineteenth century, Friedrich Wilhelm IV's royal commission was followed by the addition of two side wings. Even in this epoch, the palace behind the imposing display façade offered not only living space for urban citizens but was also a place of public life and a stage for art and culture. Concerts, lectures, exhibitions, and later, light shows organized by various cultural associations, took place here. The city of Potsdam acquired the Palais in 1912. In 1913, the first municipal facilities such as the registry office, traffic office, and tourist office moved in. During the First World War, the Palais also had a military office and a war welfare office. The municipal public library, a youth hostel, and the registry office remained in the Palais until the time of the Second World War. The building was badly damaged during an air raid in April 1945. The ruins were demolished in 1948. This gave the Alter Markt its socialist function as a place for public announcements and events. Plans for the reconstruction of the center during the GDR proposed a town hall and a theater on the empty property. However, these ideas were not implemented; the Alter Markt served as a public park and parking lot. From 1994 to 2006, the Hans Otto Theater set up an interim venue here. In 2005, the city of Potsdam decided to rebuild the city palace.

Museum Barberini
Potsdam, Brandenburg

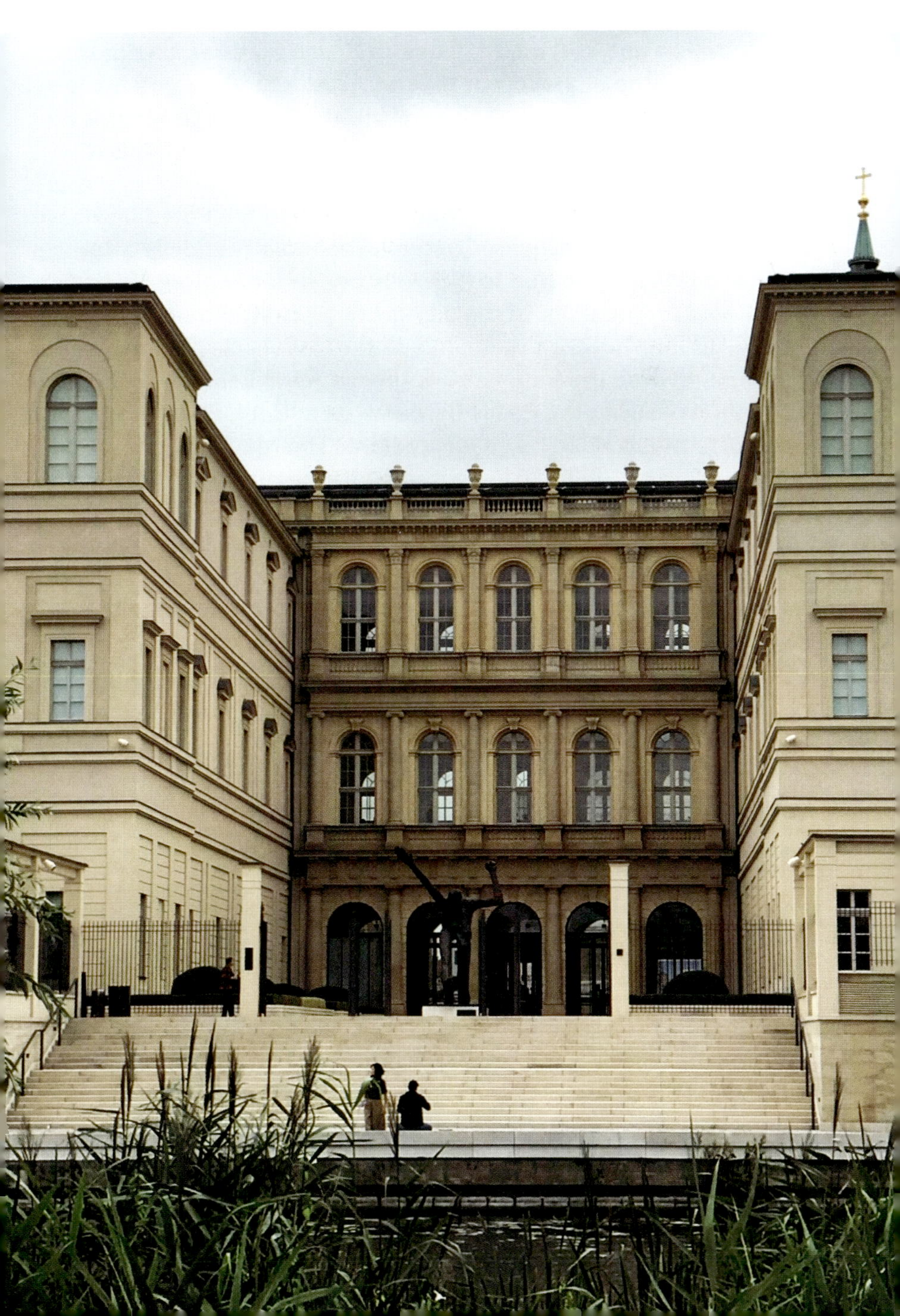

In 2007, patron and software billionaire Hasso Plattner, one of the co-founders of the global corporation SAP, donated twenty million euros for its reconstruction. This gave rise to the plan to restore the entire historic center of Potsdam to its original form, and thus the Palais Barberini was to be reconstructed as faithfully as possible as the "landmark building." Hasso Plattner founded the Potsdam Hasso Plattner Institute for Software Systems Technology shortly after the fall of the Wall, and due to his close ties to the region, his desire to donate an art museum to the city grew. At first, the site of the former GDR Interhotel on the banks of the Havel was planned as the location, but when the Berlin entrepreneur Abris Lelbach renounced his intention of using the Palais Barberini as a hotel, Plattner took the opportunity to build his museum here. The reconstruction was carried out from 2013 to 2016 according to the plans of the Munich/Berlin architects Hilmer & Sattler und Albrecht. Only the façades were reconstructed and the interior was fitted in consideration of modern, purpose-oriented factors. Seventeen exhibition halls (with an area of approximately 2,200 m^2) with the latest technology as well as high ceilings with haunches and oak parquet were created over three floors. As part of the Barberini Digital program, additional

Museum Barberini
Alter Markt, Humboldtstr. 5–6
D-14467 Potsdam
Phone: +49 331 236014499
besucherservice@museum-barberini.com
museum-barberini.com

Opening hours
Wed–Mon 10 a.m.–7 p.m., every first Thursday of the month 10 a.m.–9 p.m. Last admission about one hour before closing time. Special opening hours take place on some public holidays. Except for Tuesdays, the museum offers public guided tours through the current exhibitions daily at 11 a.m., noon and 3 p.m. There is an additional tour every Thursday 5 p.m. (€3 plus admission).
The exhibitions are accompanied by an extensive program of events and education for different age groups with lectures, films, guided tours, and concerts.
The museum is connected to two cafés (to the left of the entrance and adjacent to the bronze sculpture *Jahrhundertschritt* with a beautiful view of the Freundschaftsinsel); a shop is located in the basement.

Entrance fees
Adults / Reduced / Children under 18: €14 / €10 / free of charge
The entrance fee is reduced for the last hour.
Tickets in the online shop and at the museum ticket office have hourly entry times. The number of tickets available for entry times is limited. Waiting times during particularly popular exhibitions can be avoided by purchasing an online ticket in advance.
The audio guide is worthwhile (€2). You can also download the app and use your mobile phone (bring headphones).

Arrival by public transportation
The Museum Barberini is located in the middle of Potsdam, close to the main train station (ten minutes' walk). Therefore, it is best reached by public transport. Leave the main station in a westerly direction either on Friedrich-List-Straße or, if you have passed through the Bahnhofspassage, on Babelsberger Straße, cross the bridge on Friedrich-Ebert-Straße and turn right into Humboldtstraße.

Restaurant tips
The best coffee and sweets are available in the small but hip Buena Vida Coffee Club (buenavidacoffeeclub.de; Am Bassin 7). Cheesecake and hot chocolate are the specialties of the rustic Café Guam (cafe-guam.de; Mittelstr. 38). At Luisenplatz, fans of upscale Asian cuisine will get their money's worth at Chi Keng (chikeng.de; Luisenplatz 3). In the Theaterklause, near Sanssouci Park, food from

information on the works of art and the artists in the main exhibition is provided on the second floor via an audio wall.

The non-profit organization Stadtbild Deutschland, which is committed to the reconstruction of historical buildings, awarded the reconstruction of the Palais Barberini as an art museum "Building of the Year 2016." It was financed by the Hasso Plattner Foundation, which also runs the museum.

Hasso Plattner began to collect art with enthusiasm in the 1970s. The focus is on Impressionism (Auguste Renoir, Claude Monet, and Edvard Munch) as well as on the art of the GDR and German art after 1989 (such as Wolfgang Mattheuer, Werner Tübke, and Bernhard Heisig, as well as Gerhard Richter). Based on the works in the founder's collection, the Museum Barberini presents three main exhibitions per year in cooperation with international museums and private collections. These are each accompanied by one or two smaller exhibitions. Other rooms are usually curated with changing works from the Museum Barberini's collection. In the inner courtyard of the U-shaped building, Wolfgang Mattheuer was given a historical monument with the installation *Jahrhundertschritt* (1984), a five-meter sculpture.

regional and seasonal products with organic quality can be found (theaterklause-potsdam.de; Zimmerstr. 10–11).

Extra tips
When the weather is good, it is worth taking a stroll along the newly formed banks of the Havel (accessible via the southeastern exit of the museum) and visiting Freundschaftsinsel. As part of the former BUGA grounds, the latter invites you to linger in its gardens, including the herb garden, and spend time among the various sculptures. The small Brandenburgische Kunstverein Potsdam e. V. is also located here (bkv-potsdam.de).
In the Villa Schöningen, changing art exhibitions are shown in historical rooms parallel to the permanent exhibition on the history of the house and the Glienicke Bridge (villa-schoeningen.de).
On the way from or to Berlin, a detour to the Liebermann Villa at Wannsee, where small exhibitions are presented, is worthwhile. The gardens and terrace offer a wonderful refuge on sunny days (liebermann-villa.de; Colomierstr. 3, 14109 Berlin).

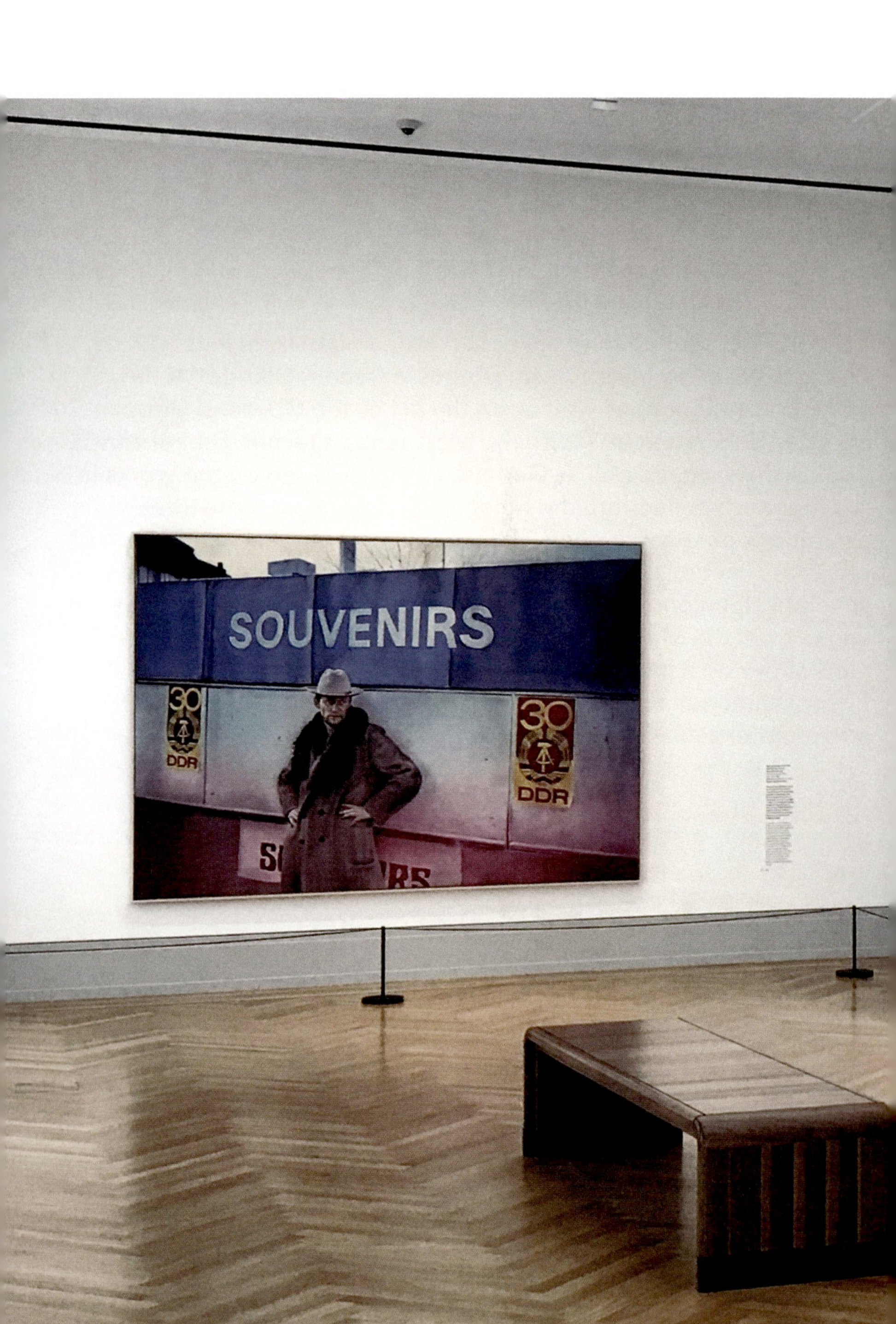
SOUVENIRS
30
DDR
30
DDR

Museum Barberini
Potsdam, Brandenburg

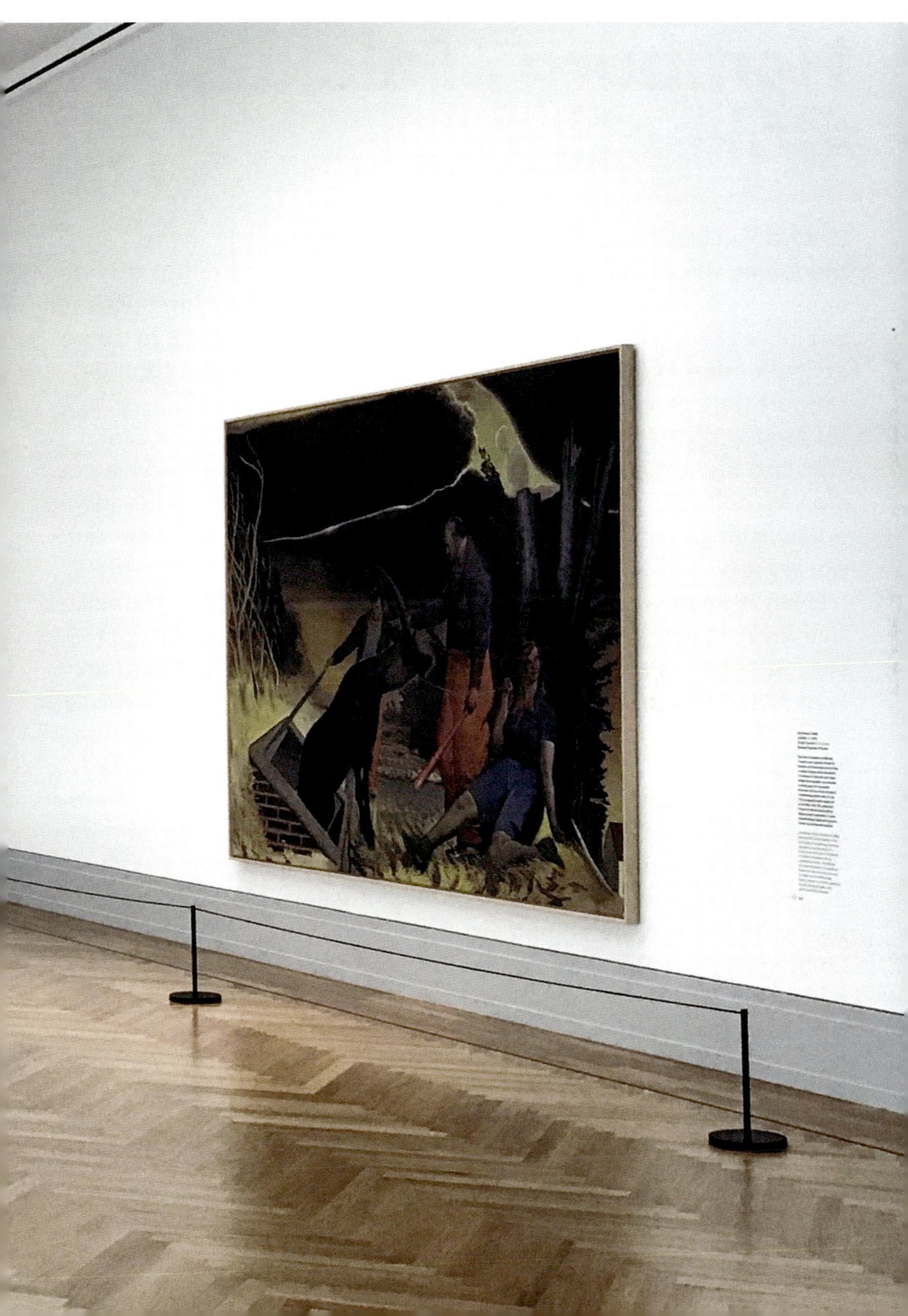

154 Deichtorhallen Hamburg / Falckenberg Collection

Harald Falckenberg, lawyer, author, professor of art theory, and managing director of a family business specializing in gas station accessories, collected works by the Hamburg artist Horst Janssen while he was still a student. However, the decision to build up an art collection and to become personally involved in contemporary art only came about in 1994. After initially acquiring works by renowned artists such as Robert Rauschenberg, Frank Stella, Gerhard Richter, and Sigmar Polke, he radically reoriented his passion for collecting in 1996—particularly as a result of his friendship and exchange with Werner Büttner—and purchased more contemporary art.

From 1996 onwards, the first collection room, the Pump Haus, built in 1767 and located on the periphery of Hamburg Airport, served simultaneously as a veritable experimental stage and art warehouse. After the house was demolished, a new location was found south of the Elbe. Since 2001, the Falckenberg Collection has been housed in a hundred-year-old former Phoenix-Werke factory building in Hamburg-Harburg. In 2007, Harald Falckenberg acquired one of the buildings and commissioned Berlin architect Roger Bundschuh to completely redesign the complex. The result differs significantly from conventional museum architecture. The play with the ever-changing visual axes is a perceptual challenge. On five levels, which are accessed by a bright central staircase, the collection, temporary exhibition, and depot are organically placed next to each other, without a stringent sequence, across an area of 6,500 m^2. The new premises enabled Harald Falckenberg to present larger installations and multimedia projects in areas designed specifically for this purpose.

The Falckenberg Collection comprises over 2,000 works by international avant-garde artists, including groups of works by Martin Kippenberger, Werner Büttner, and Albert Oehlen, as well as large

Deichtorhallen Hamburg / Falckenberg Collection
Hamburg

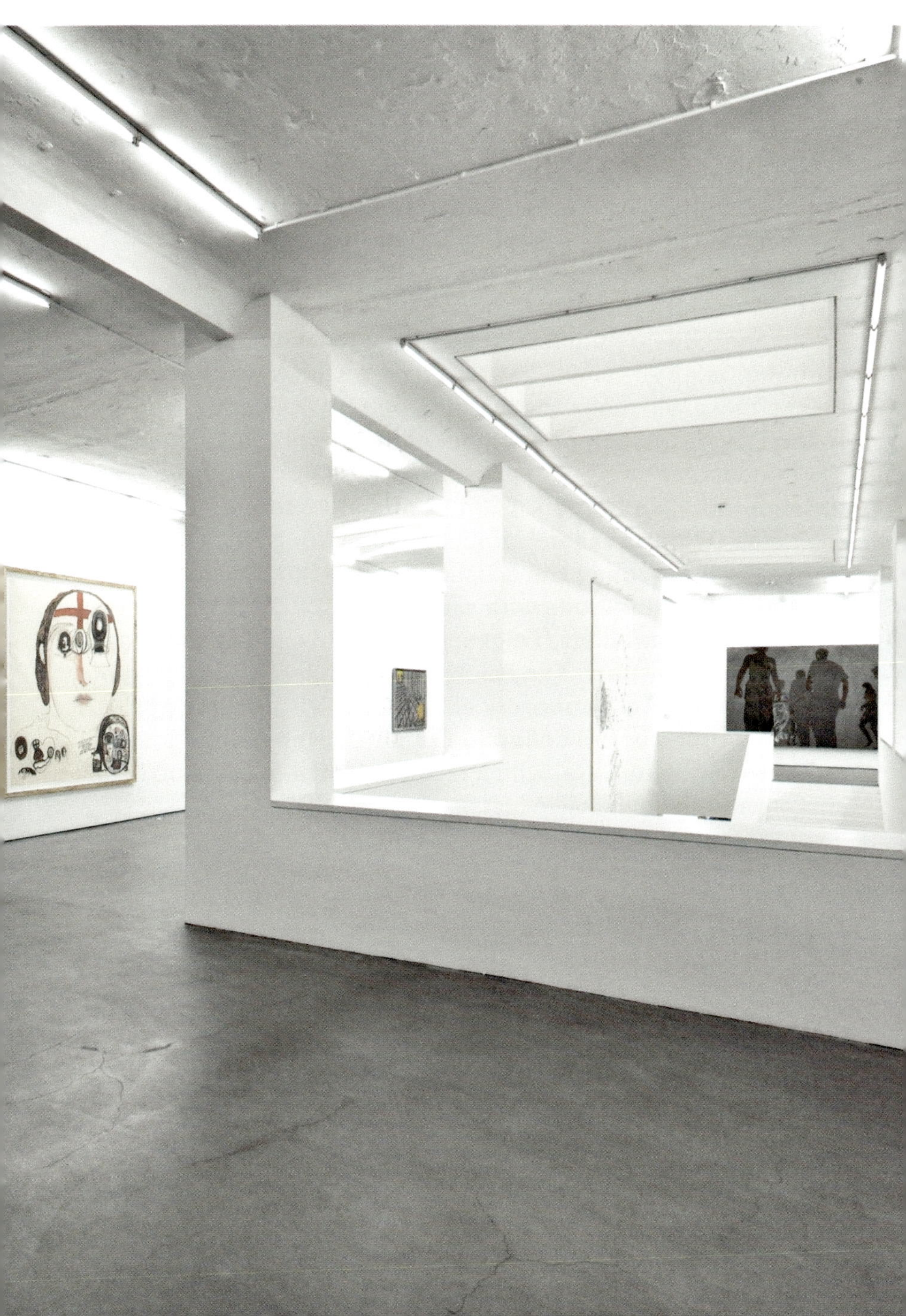

installations by Jonathan Meese, Thomas Hirschhorn, John Bock, Jon Kessler, Mike Kelley, and Gregor Schneider. Other works, including pieces by John Baldessari, Dieter Roth, Robert Longo, Franz West, Daniel Richter, Paul McCarthy, and Richard Prince, hang in the comprehensible display and storage rooms of the basement. Personally interested in history and social developments, Falckenberg attaches great importance to art that also reflects these themes.

At the end of 2010, the Hamburg Bürgerschaft (Hamburg's Parliament) decided in favor of a long-awaited cooperation with the Deichtorhallen. The agreement stipulates that Harald Falckenberg will make the building and his collection available to the Deichtorhallen on permanent loan until 2023. Since 2011, the Phoenix factory buildings in Hamburg-Harburg have belonged to Deichtorhallen Hamburg GmbH and are operated by it under the name Deichtorhallen Hamburg / Sammlung Falckenberg. Under the direction of the artistic director Dirk Luckow, two to three special exhibitions with artists who are often not represented in the Sammlung Falckenberg or only with a few works take place every year. The Falckenberg Collection is occasionally presented anew in temporary exhibitions. Visitors can get an overview of the entire collection as part of the guided tour of the collection on Saturdays, which includes a visit to the mobile storage shelves and the expansive installations.

Deichtorhallen Hamburg / Falckenberg Collection
Hamburg

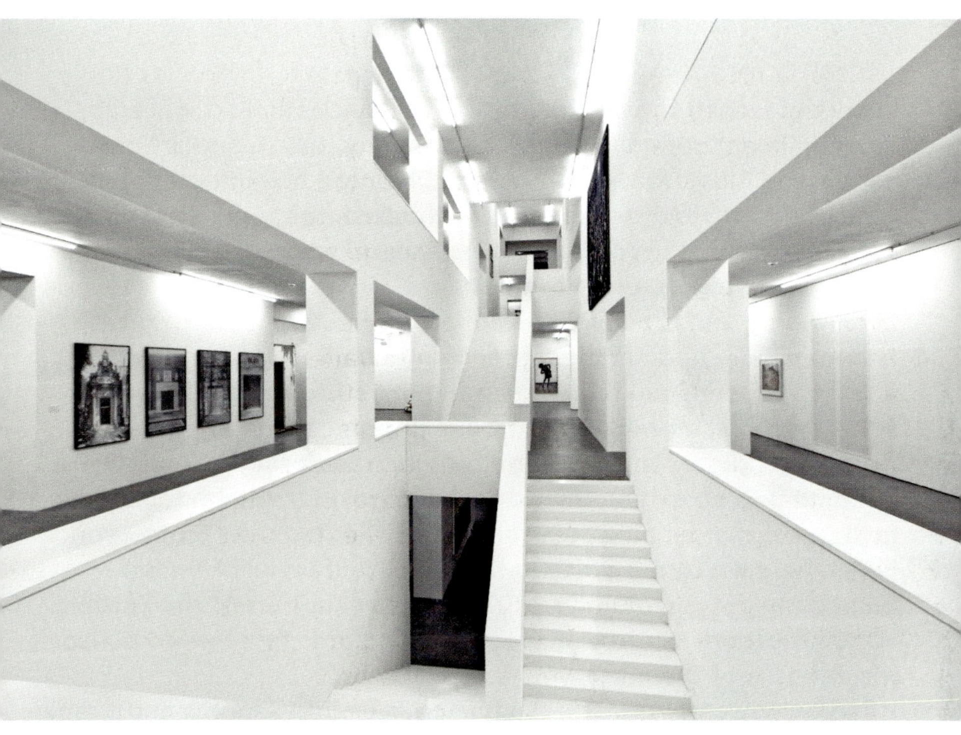

Deichtorhallen Hamburg / Falckenberg Collection
Wilstorfer Str. 71, Tor 2
D-21073 Hamburg-Harburg
Phone: +49 40 32506762
sammlungfalckenberg@deichtorhallen.de
sammlung-falckenberg.de
deichtorhallen.de/sammlung-falckenberg

Opening hours
Thu–Sun as part of public guided tours, which require booking an online ticket. Guided collection tours take place on Saturdays at noon (early registration is advisable). The respective exhibition can also be visited every first Sunday of the month from noon–5 p.m. (without registering).

Entrance fees
Adults / Reduced / Children under age 18: €15 / €12 / free (public guided tours)
Adults / Reduced / Children under age 18: €10 / €6 / free (first Sunday of the month)

Arrival by public transportation
The collection can be reached easily by S-Bahn from Hamburg. You can take the S3 towards Neugraben as well as the S31 towards Harburg Rathaus. Harburg is also reachable by various regional and long-distance Deutsche Bahn trains. At the S-Bahn station, follow the signs to Moorstraße/City. Behind the exit, keep left, and a small ramp leads you to Moorstraße. Cross the ramp and follow the street along the shopping center to the next intersection. Turn left into Wilstorfer Straße. After about 200 m you will see the black gated entrance and on the right, a black door leading to the collection.

Parking
Except on Sundays, parking is possible during the day in the Phoenix-Center car park (entrance Wilstorfer Str. 69) next to the factory building.

Restaurant tip
Silo16, a stylish restaurant with a bar and lounge, offers Italian cuisine and good wines served directly on the waterfront in a former granary (silo16.com; Schellerdamm 16).

Extra tip
The Kunstverein Harburger Bahnhof is located directly above tracks 3 and 4 in the Harburg long-distance train station. In the formerly magnificent and first class waiting room, exhibitions of contemporary art are regularly shown (kvhbf.de; Hannoversche Str. 85).

158
Museum Modern Art

Lovers of Constructive, Concrete, and Conceptual art will enjoy the significant commitment of the collector, artist, and art professor Jürgen Blum (1931–2015). Although only a few internationally renowned artists are presented in Hünfeld (for example Ludwig Wilding, Matthias Will, Karl-Heinz Adler, Rupprecht Geiger, and Eugen Gomringer), there is plenty of room for possible discoveries in charming and creatively designed surroundings.

Jürgen Blum opened the museum in 1990 in the historic Gaswerk, a listed Art Nouveau building dating to 1907. On his initiative, several artists, as well as numerous citizens of Hünfeld, made financial and personal contributions to transform the unused building into an exhibition space and expand it with extensions. In about three decades, Jürgen Blum collected over 3,000 works, which he gave to the Stiftung Museum Modern Art Hünfeld – Sammlung Jürgen Blum in 2007. With the support of the Förderverein Museum Modern Art Hünfeld e. V., this foundation is also the sponsor of the museum.

Today, you can view works of art in over thirty rooms and even in two former gas boilers on an area of approximately 1,000 m^2 and take a walk in the adjacent sculpture garden. Since its reopening in 2014, the Museum has been showing an extensive selection of works from the museum founder's collection as a permanent exhibition in rotation. At the same time, changing special exhibitions of contemporary art in various styles are presented, some of which are on loan and directed by the invited artists. Visitors thus have an opportunity to rediscover the liveliness and diversity of the art shown here time after time. Concrete art thematizes seeing, training our perception and gaze. In memory of Jürgen Blum, visitors and artists will continue to be invited to take an active part in this experiment, which Blum would probably have called "conscious living."

Museum Modern Art
Hünfeld, Hesse

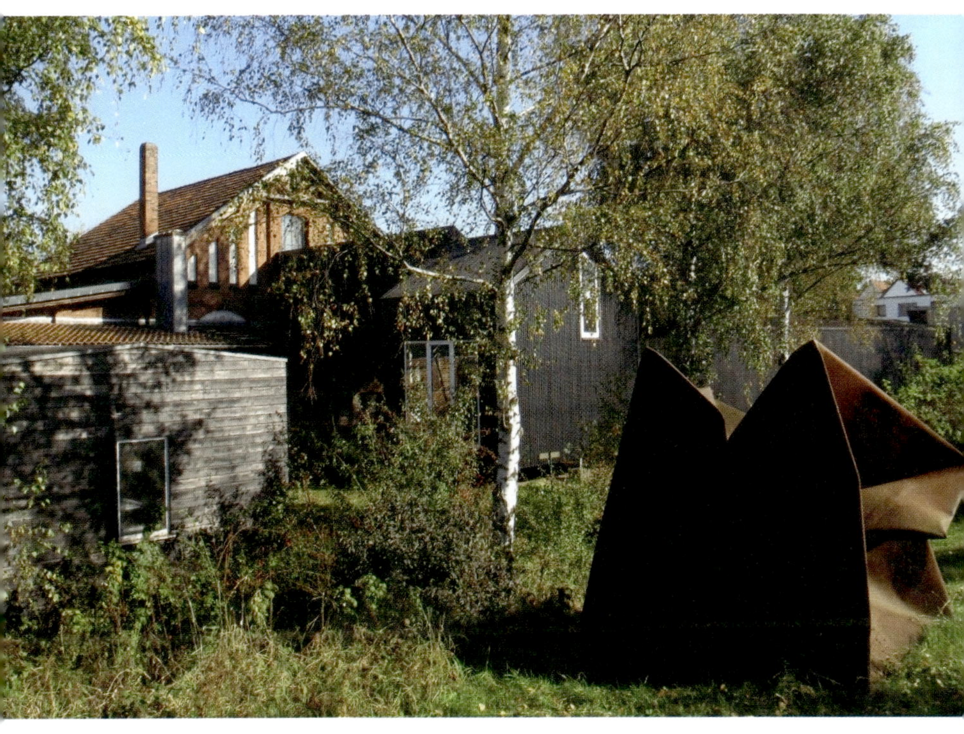

Museum Modern Art
Altes Gaswerk in Hünfeld
Hersfelder Str. 25
D-36088 Hünfeld
Phone: +49 151 40470183
peter.liebau@museum-modern-art.de
museum-modern-art.de

Opening hours
Thu–Sun 3–6 p.m. and by appointment

Entrance fees
Adults / Reduced / Family ticket: €3 / €1 / €6
Guided tours are possible by appointment by telephone (€25 plus admission).

Arrival by public transportation
Hünfeld can be easily reached by a local train from Fulda. You can reach the museum on foot in about ten minutes from the train station, but you can also take the bus lines 70 and 71 to the bus stop Hünfeld Nordend.

Parking
Parking is available in the courtyard.

Restaurant tips
Gasthof Schützenhof serves classic German dishes in a rural ambiance (schuetzenhof-huenfeld.de; Fuldaer Berg 3). Ristorante Pizzeria La Bella Vita offers good pizzas and other Italian specialties (ristorante-labellavita.de; Konrad-Adenauer-Platz 2). In the city café Hünefeld-Spanish Röhn, there are delicious cocktails and tapas as well as coffee from their own roasting (rhoentapas.de; Hauptstr. 15; Tue–Sat from 5 p.m.). Distinctive wines can be enjoyed in the attractive Via Regia wine cellar (vinothek-viaregia.de; Brunnenstr. 9; Fri/Sat from 5 p.m.).

Extra tips
Jürgen Blum founded the Open Book project in Hünfeld in 1996. Over 145 building façades permanently display works of concrete poetry, a literary-artistic movement initiated by Eugen Gomringer. The words here are no longer just carriers of meaning, but are used as visual and phonetic design elements. The homeowners were able to choose “their texts” from various suggestions, which were then artistically applied by Blum himself. If traveling in the area by bicycle, it is worth exploring the Kegelspielradweg. Here Jürgen Blum’s idea of having plaques with inscriptions in Rhöner Platt attached along the route to recall the local dialect, which is increasingly being forgotten, was implemented.

160 KUNSTHAUS TAUNUSSTEIN / Sammlung Haas van Gemmern

The collector couple Dr. Irene Haas and Ulrich van Gemmern have created an oasis of encounters with art in Niederlibbach, one of ten districts of Taunusstein, a town of 500 people. Their shared passion for collecting began in 1996, with the purchase of a work by Rolf Behm and, to date, the couple has acquired over 200 works. The collection focuses on paintings and sculptures created after the Neue Wilde. Over the last two decades, the collectors have remained true to their personal tastes: intense colors, decisive brushstrokes, abstract-expressive forms, and figurative pictorial content. Among the favorite artists of Haas and van Gemmern are Jean Y. Klein, Reinhard Stangl, Katrin Kampmann, Hans-Hendrik Grimmling, Bernd Kirschner, and Walter Stöhrer. The collection also includes works by SEO, Helge Leiberg, Helmut Middendorf, Edgar Diehl, Evelyn Hellenschmidt, Hans Scheib, Elvira Bach, and Felix Droese. After the sale of their marketing and PR firm in 2011 and the resulting loss of walls for the large-format works, a new location was sought for the Sammlung Haas van Gemmern. On a plot of land in the village where the couple has been living since 2004, a minimalist cube was created as an exhibition building. The commission to civil engineer Andreas Mayer and architect Siglinde Bothe was clearly defined: Nothing was to distract from the art, and no curves were to be used. Inside the building, which opened in 2016, there are four levels on three floors, two of which are 600 m^2 each and are used for exhibitions. A calm language of color and form reigns with reduced use of materials, whereby the strongly colored works in the collection are particularly accentuated.

KUNSTHAUS TAUNUSSTEIN / Sammlung Haas van Gemmern
Taunusstein, Hesse

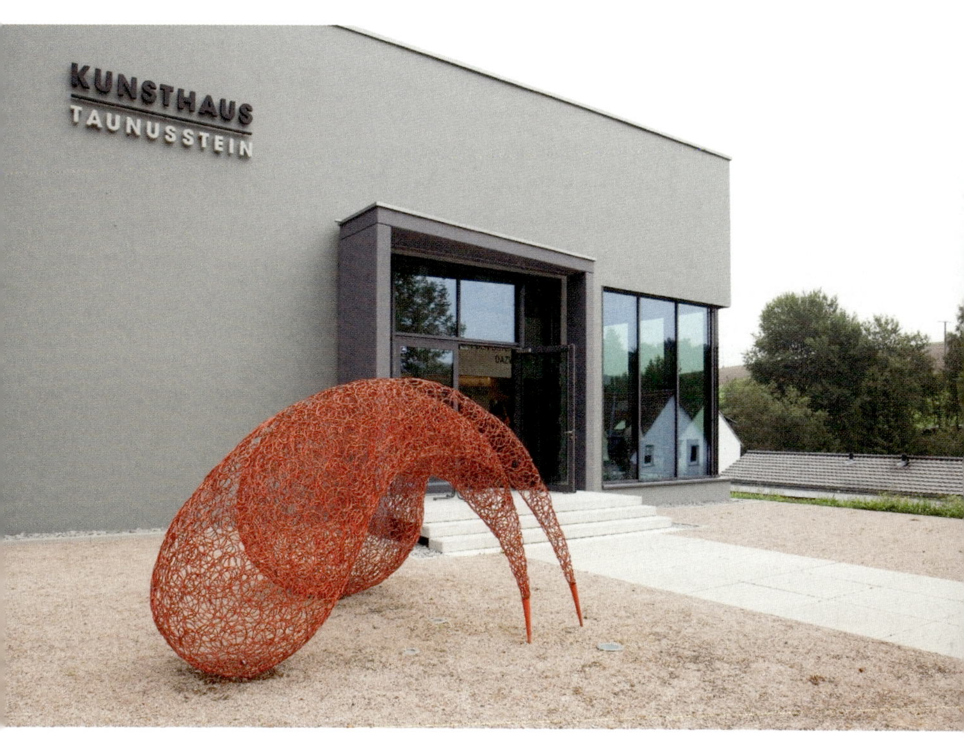

KUNSTHAUS TAUNUSSTEIN / Sammlung Haas van Gemmern
Hauptstr. 1A
D-65232
Taunusstein-Niederlibbach
Phone: +49 151 21749270
info@kunsthaus-taunusstein.de
kunsthaus-taunusstein.de

Opening hours
Sat/Sun 4–6 p.m. during exhibitions
The indicated opening hours may vary in exceptional cases. Visitors are advised to check these on the website, Facebook, or by telephone before a visit.
The Kunsthaus is closed during the summer months.
Group visits can also be arranged outside regular opening hours.
The collectors offer public guided tours during the exhibition on the first Sundays of the month at 4 p.m. (€7 plus admission). Additional cultural events are communicated on the website.

Entrance fees
Adults / Reduced / Children up to age 12: €7 / €5 / free

Arrival by public transportation
Unfortunately, arrival by public transportation is quite complicated. There is a connection at irregular intervals with the call bus 270 from the Idstein station or from the Hahn bus station (phone: 06124 7265913, register at least ninety minutes before departure).

Restaurant tips
In summer, a magnificent view can be enjoyed over Wiesbaden from the terrace of Gollner's auf der Burg Sonnenberg, where Austrian cuisine is served (gollners.de; Am Schlossberg 20, 65191 Wiesbaden). French cuisine is served at Les Deux Dienstbach, run by two sisters (les-deux-dienstbach.de; Untere Albrechtstr. 16, 65185 Wiesbaden; open only on weekday evenings). Café Maldaner, the first Viennese coffeehouse to be opened outside Vienna, is a Wiesbaden institution (maldaner1859.de; Marktstr. 34, 65183 Wiesbaden).

Extra tips
Museum Wiesbaden is known for its art (especially for the paintings of Alexej von Jawlensky and Abstract Expressionism) and natural history collection (with butterflies from Maria Sibylla Merian) (museum-wiesbaden.de; Friedrich-Ebert-Allee 2, 65185 Wiesbaden). The Nassauische Kunstverein Wiesbaden is located close by in an old villa (kunstverein-wiesbaden.de; Wilhelmstr. 15, 65185 Wiesbaden).

162 Schloss Kummerow

Schloss Kummerow was completed in 1730 by the von Maltzahn family in the late Baroque style and expanded one hundred years later by a landscape park designed by Peter Joseph Lenné. The estate was orphaned time and again due to the fate of its owners. After the First World War, the house was extensively renovated and experienced a new heyday in the Weimar Republic and during National Socialism. After 1945, the castle was occupied by the Soviets and converted into a quarantine camp for refugees and former forced laborers. In the ensuing forty years, until 1993, the community used the castle. A Konsum grocery store with a restaurant, the mayor's office, a primary school, a kindergarten, and a secondary school have all been located here. In 1985, it became the property of the Deutsche Post (postal and telecommunications monopoly of the GDR). In 1993, the castle was sold as private property and was to be converted into a hotel. In 2011, the castle became the property of Torsten Kunert at an auction. During a renovation that lasted several years, the building sins that had taken place over decades were removed. About one-third of the renovation costs were financed by subsidies from the EU and other public institutions. Today, a limited nonprofit company is the leaseholder and operator of the unusual exhibition site.

Since the opening of the Schloss Kummerow photographic collection in 2016, a visit to "Mecklenburg Switzerland" has been well worth the trip for art lovers. The permanent exhibition from the over 2,000 photographs of Torsten Kunert's private collection fits perfectly into the renovation concept of the manor house and enters into a dialogue with the preserved traces of the house's eventful history. Bizarre patterns and peeling paint, demolition scars, and Jungpionier (Young Pioneers) slogans from the times when the expropriated aristocratic castle was a polytechnic secondary school are included in the presentation. Wall writings such as "Thinking is the first civic duty" by Walter Ulbricht or "Thälmann Pioneers honor their blue scarf" are still clearly visible. For the real estate entrepreneur and collector Kunert, both the collection and the house have autobiographical references. Having grown up in the GDR, he wore these scarves himself as a teenager.

Schloss Kummerow
Kummerow, Mecklenburg-Vorpommern

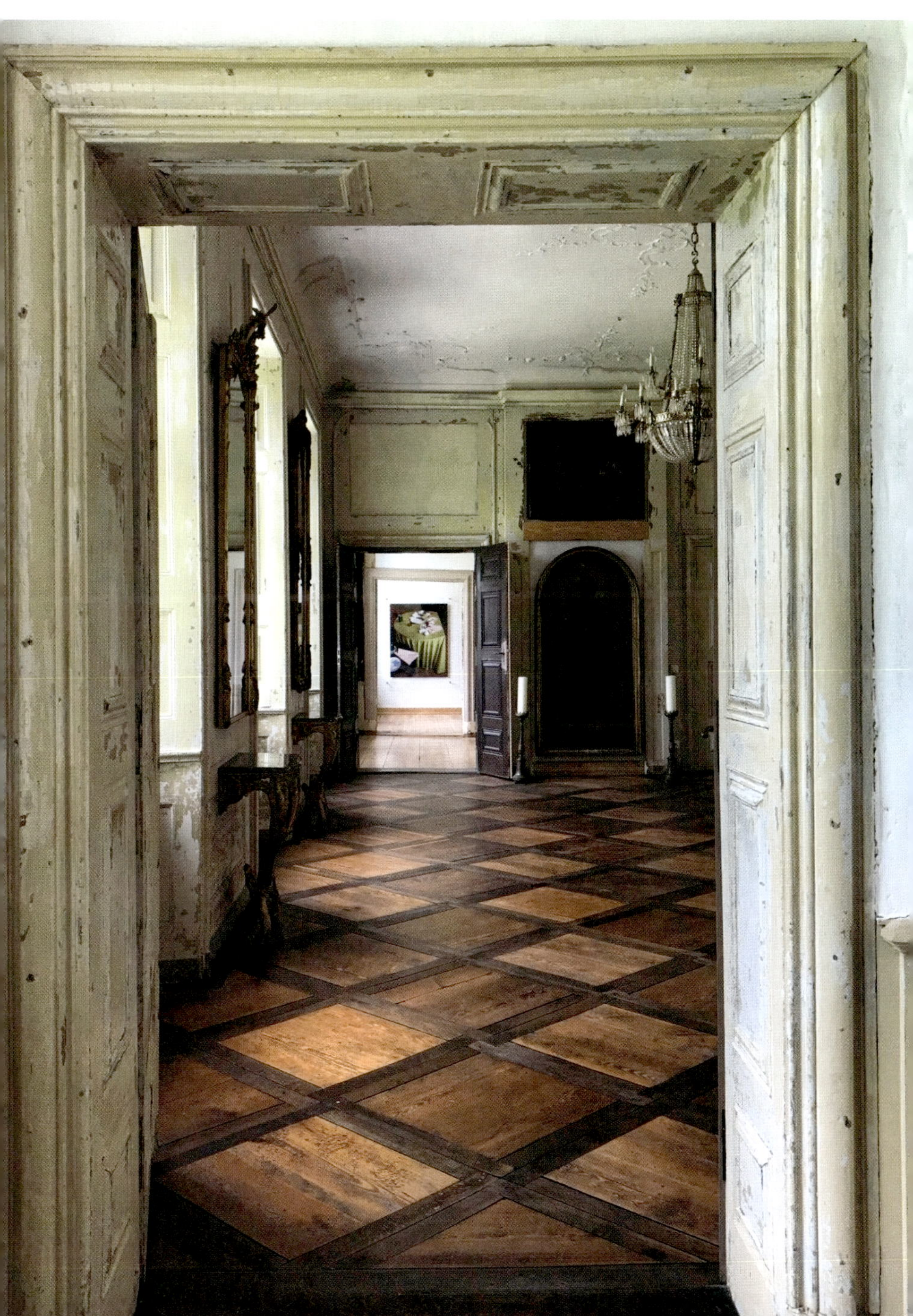

The Torsten Kunert Collection is one of the leading private photographic collections in Germany. The focus is on the period from the Second World War to the present day, and it is continuously expanded by new positions. Within this orientation, photographs taken during the time of the GDR by today's renowned representatives of East German photography form the heart of the collection. They document the past and lingering lives of people in the former GDR region. In recent years, an essential addition to the collection has been the purchase of comprehensive collections of anonymous photography on the history of documentary and product photography.

The first presentation of the collection with many large-format works was so successful that at present only a few are exchanged from time to time. The five-meter *Because the Night* (2012) by Richard Mosse, Michael Wesely's six-meter exposure with water lilies from 2014/15, the chronology of a high school class since 1977 by Werner Mahler, and the almost five-meter museum image *16.777.216 Farben* (16,777,216 Colors, 2010) by Adrian Sauer are the attractions of the exhibition spread over three floors. But *Afghan Girl* (1984) by Steve McCurry and numerous documentary photographs of performances by Marina Abramović are also on display, along with photographic works by Hiroshi Sugimoto, Wolfgang Tillmans, Bernd and Hilla Becher, Thorsten Brinkmann, Thomas Ruff, and Candida Höfer. Some video works are permanently shown in four smaller rooms. Part of the total area of over 3,500 m^2 is also a small room in which three special exhibitions per season are shown.

An extension planned for 2020/21 in the abandoned former stable will allow a more comprehensive presentation of time-based works curated by Torsten Kunert's daughter Aileen. Other outbuildings will also house a community office, a café, a museum shop, holiday apartments, and a kindergarten.

Schloss Kummerow
Kummerow, Mecklenburg-Vorpommern

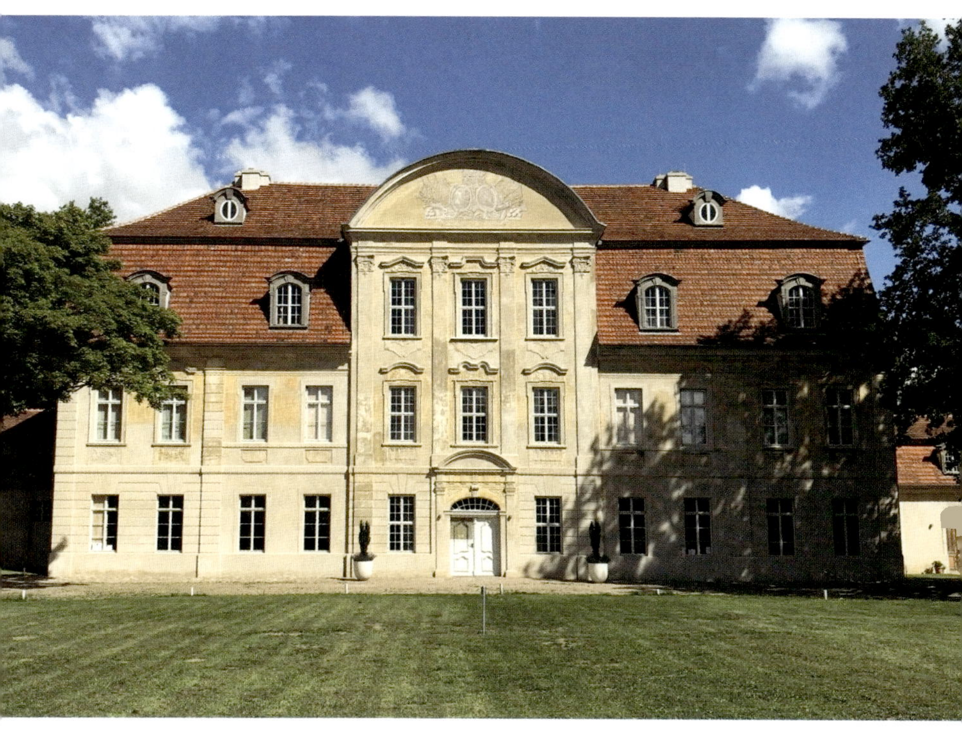

Schloss Kummerow
Dorfstr. 114
D-17139 Kummerow
Phone: +49 399 52235180
post@schloss-kummerow.de
schloss-kummerow.de

Opening hours
Mid-April to end May Fri–Sun 11 a.m.–5 p.m., June to end September Wed–Sun 11 a.m.–5 p.m., October Fri–Sun 11 a.m.–5 p.m. and public holidays
Guided tours (also in English) and a visit to the castle outside regular opening hours are possible by arrangement. Historical tours are offered on Saturdays at 2 p.m. (€5 plus admission).
During the summer months, concerts and readings occasionally take place.

Entrance fees
Adults / Special exhibition only / Adolescents (ages 14–18) / Children: €7,50 / €2,50 / €1 / free

Arrival by public transportation
From the Malchin train station, take bus 407 in the direction of Grammentin Dorf to Kummerow after prior reservation. With the launch of the blue-and-white fleet from Malchin, in summer a trip to the castle is possible during a lake cruise on Wednesdays and Fridays (1000seen.de/kummerowersee).

Parking
Sufficient parking spaces are available to the left of the castle.

Restaurant tips
During the summer months, cakes and other snacks are offered in the afternoon at the Gutscafé Pohnstorf (gutshaus-pohnstorf.de/cafe.html; Alt Sührkow). The Romantik Hotel Gutshof Ludorf serves Mecklenburg and Pomeranian dishes (gutshaus-ludorf.de; Rondell 7, Ludorf/Müritz). Gourmets will appreciate Restaurant Moshack in the Teterow railway station (restaurant-moshack-teterow.de). Also in Teterow, fantastic cuisine is offered at the Gasthaus Stadtmühle, a former water mill (stadtmuehle-teterow.de; Mühlenstr. 1, 17166 Teterow).

Extra tips
In Basedow, a visit of the unusual castle and the church is worthwhile. A visit to the castle can be combined with an excursion to the Till Richter Museum (see p. 166), the Wesenberg Sculpture Park & Künstler Bei Wu (p. 168).

166
Till Richter Museum – Schloss Buggenhagen

Since 2013, contemporary art has been on display in Schloss Buggenhagen on a protrusion of land at Peenestrom in the nature park on the island of Usedom in Vorpommern. Once the ancestral seat of the Buggenhagen family, the castle was built around 1840 as a classicist manor house in the style of the buildings on Pariser Platz in Berlin. From 1260 to 1945, the Buggenhagen family, one of the oldest noble families in Pommern, continuously owned the manor. From 1995 to 2002, it was used as a hotel. After the hotel stood empty for several years due to bankruptcy, Dr. Till F. A. Richter bought and renovated the property for his museum project. As founder and director of the museum, the Bremen-born fashion designer and scientist has turned his passion into a vocation.

The collection of the Till Richter Museum comprises several hundred works of all media by over one hundred artists from Europe, America, and Asia. The focus is on young artists who have extraordinary potential. But also more established artists such as Lev Khesin, Miguel Aragon, Gerhard Mantz, Gregorio Iglesias Mayo, and Said Baalbaki are represented in the collection. Selected works from the collection can be seen permanently in the approximately 50 m² Cabinet on the upper floor. The group exhibition there changes every October. Otherwise, the mostly monographic presentations are equipped with loans from artists, galleries, and other collectors. Each year, Till Richter organizes more than ten exhibitions on an exhibition area of approximately 1,000 m². Videos are shown in a small cinema. Richter's impressive first purchase, a wooden sculpture by Gerhard Mantz acquired at the age of seventeen in 1990, has a place of honor in the office. With his museum, Till Richter would like to offer young artists a springboard for their careers. With the Rising Stars Residency scholarship holder, every year, an artist is invited to live and work in the castle and to present an exhibition in the circa 400 m² main area of the ground floor from August until the winter break.

Till Richter Museum – Schloss Buggenhagen
Buggenhagen, Mecklenburg-Vorpommern

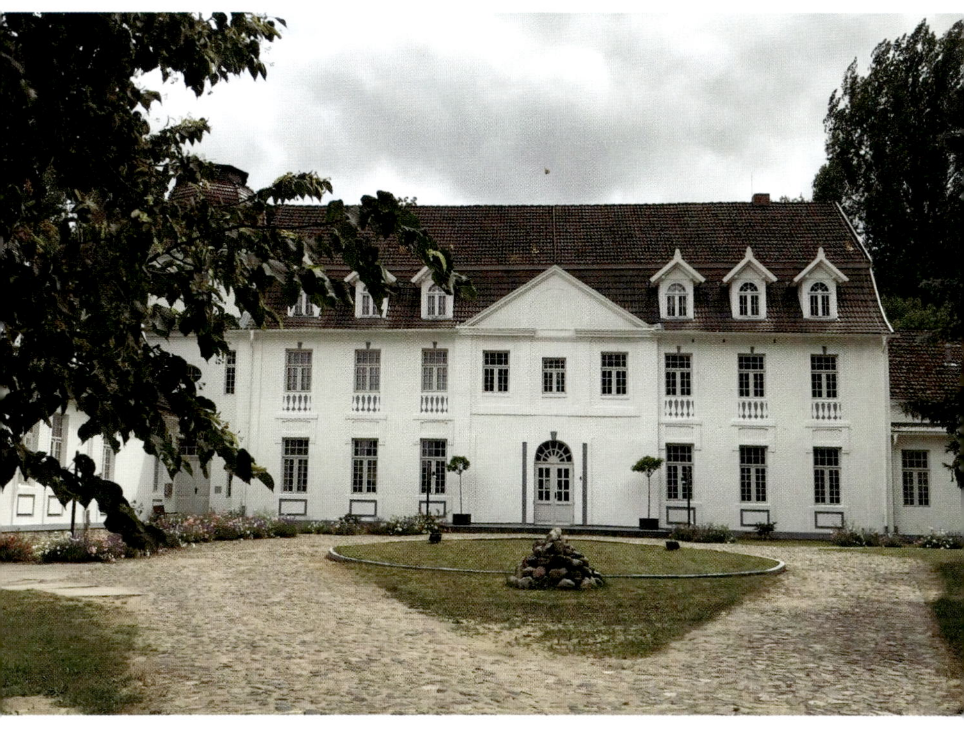

Till Richter Museum – Schloss Buggenhagen
Straße des Friedens 6
D-17440 Buggenhagen
Phone: +49 38374 551919
till.richter@tillrichtermuseum.org
tillrichtermuseum.org

Opening hours
Mid-April to the end of December Thu–Sun 11 a.m.–6 p.m., on public holidays noon–6 p.m. and by appointment during the winter break.
During the exhibition, Dr. Till Richter personally guides the visitors through the house daily at 3 p.m. (€15 including admission, duration circa two hours).
Lectures, concerts, and readings are held as well as museum educational cooperation projects for school classes.

Entrance fees
Adults / Reduced: €10 / €5

Arrival
A visit is only possible by car.

Restaurant tips
In Greifswald, delicious meals can be enjoyed at Büttner's Restaurant (buettners-restaurant.de; Am Hafen 1a, 17493 Greifswald-Wieck; a reservation is recommended).
In the eco-shop Lassaneria, there are nut cakes and vegan dishes on Fridays starting at 6 p.m. (Markt 11, 17440 Lassan). Homemade cakes are served at the Peenestrom Café (Wendenstr. 19, 17440 Lassen).

Extra tips
Seminars and concerts are held in the Klanghaus am See from the European Academy of Healing Arts (eaha.org; Am See 1, 17440 Klein Jasedow).
The Caspar David Friedrich Centre is an exhibition venue for contemporary artists and a documentation site on the life and work of Caspar David Friedrich (caspar-david-friedrich-gesellschaft.de; Lange Str. 57, 17489 Greifswald).
One hundred sculptures can be seen in the Skulpturenpark Katzow e. V., initiated by the sculptor Thomas Radeloff (skulpturenpark.wixsite.com/skulpturenparkkatzow; Dorfstr. 45, 17509 Katzow).
The Historisch-Technische Museum Peenemünd, deals with the history of the Peenemünde Army Research Center and the rockets built there between 1936 and 1945, such as the V2 rocket developed by Wernher von Braun (museum-peenemuende.de; Im Kraftwerk, 17449 Peenemünde).
A visit to the Till Richter Museum can be combined with an excursion to Schloss Kummerow (see p. 162) and the Sculpture Park Wesenberg & Künstler Bei Wu (see p. 168).

168
Sculpture Park Wesenberg & Künstler Bei Wu

The Sculpture Park Wesenberg and the estate Künstler Bei Wu are located directly at the idyllic Weißen See in the Mecklenburg Lake District at the southern entrance of the Müritz National Park. Since 2016, it has been possible to explore outdoor sculptures and visit numerous exhibition rooms, including the artist's studio, during the summer months. The idea of founding an artists' colony between the cities of Neustrelitz, Mirow, and Wesenburg came to David Ng, an architect born in Hong Kong and trained in Great Britain, after he bought the property in 2007. Together with the city, local offices, and the district, he implemented his plan for an exhibition site and sculpture park, and in 2015 acquired 20,000 m^2 of the adjoining forest from the community in addition to the 60,000 m^2 property. This area is now the sculpture park. In the same year, the estate was transferred to the Peter Wilmot Thompson Stiftung, which promotes exchanges between Australian and German artists, runs the Australian Indigenous Art Center Bei Wu (White Sea in Chinese), and collects contemporary sculptures. The history of the estate is as exciting as that of its two founders, David Ng and Peter Thompson: Discovered and built by a Hamburg piano builder at the beginning of the twentieth century, it only later became a place of amusement for Ufa cinema stars and, in GDR times, a children's home. Today, more than twenty large sculptures by Michael Kutschbach, Johann Carrera, Benjamin Storch, Laurence Edwards, Fré Ilgen, Takayuki Daikoku, and Alan Chan can be found in the wooded area crossed with paths. The foundation owns some of the sculptures, others are on loan and can be purchased. The exhibition building has a presentation area of over 1,000 m^2. Half of this space is used for permanent exhibitions, and the Inge King Memorial Galerie pays tribute to the outstanding work of the Berlin-born Australian sculptor. Photographs of her works of art and some original works in six rooms illustrate

Sculpture Park Wesenberg & Künstler Bei Wu
Wesenberg, Mecklenburg-Vorpommern

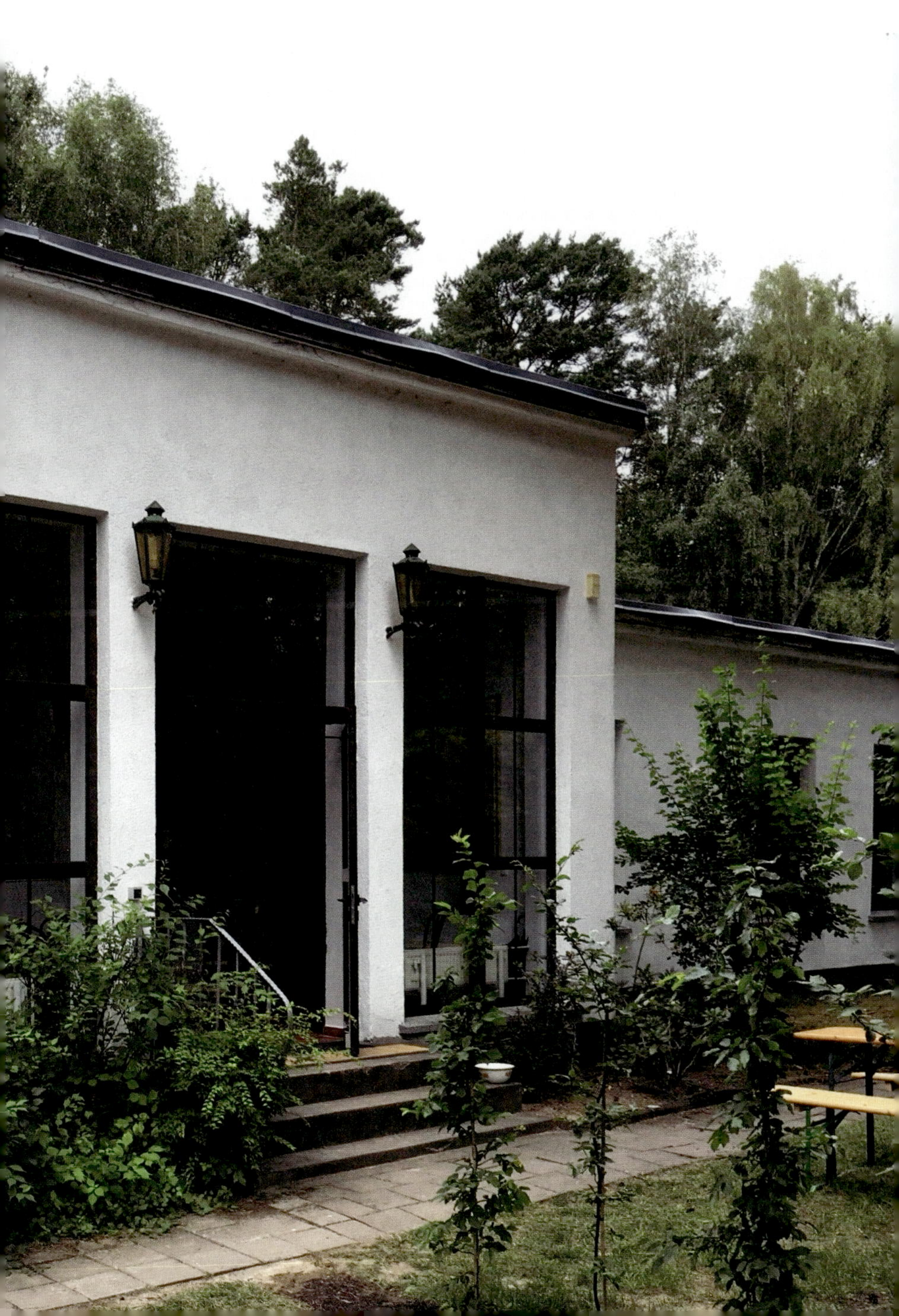

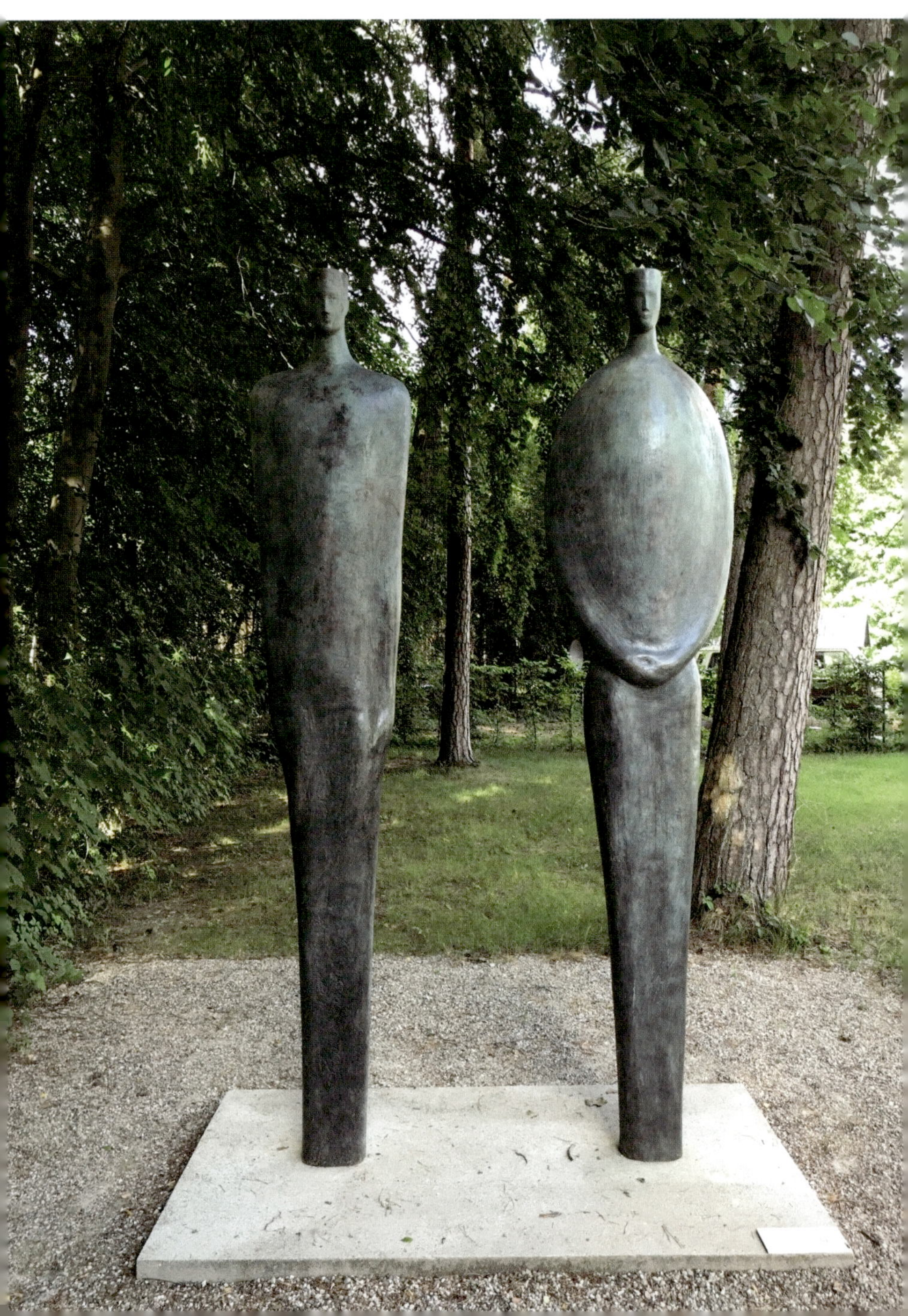

her contribution to the development of sculpture in Australia from 1951 until her death in 2016. In addition, some works by Australian artist Erwin Fabian, born in Berlin in 1915, are on display. The other rooms are used as artists' studios and for temporary exhibitions of German and international artists. A particular focus is on contemporary Australian Indigenous art, which is a particular preference of Australian collector Peter Thompson, who lives predominantly in Hong Kong.

Sculpture Park Wesenberg & Künstler Bei Wu
Am Weißen See 3
D-17255 Wesenberg
Phone: +49 39832 262466
info@park-residenz-bei-wu.de
kuenstlerbeiwu.com

Opening hours
Tue–Sun 10 a.m.–4 p.m., beginning of May to end of October
Guided tours and programs with artists are offered every month. The sculpture park and the artists-in-residence take part in the Mecklenburg cultural programs Kunst:Offen during Whitsun and Kulturherbst in September. At the end of June, there is an annual music festival with the in-residence orchestra and composers. Café Bei Wu, furnished in Viennese style, offers coffee and cake during the opening hours of the sculpture park.

Entrance fees
Free admission to the exhibitions
The cost of the programs varies.

Arrival by public transportation
The journey by public transport is only possible every two hours with the HANSeatic Railway from Neustrelitz. From the Weißer See stop, it is a fifteen-minute walk along the lake to the sculpture park.

Arrival by car
Some navigation systems guide visitors to a cul-de-sac at the beach restaurant. It is therefore advisable to enter "Wesenberg 17255" and follow the signs once there. Parking spaces are available on the property and in the public parking lot by the lake.

Restaurant tips
The Alte Kachelofenfabrik serves innovative dishes (basiskulturfabrik.de; Sandberg 3a, 17235 Neustrelitz). Regional kitchen is offered at Fürstenhof (ideenreich-graphicmanufaktur.de; Markt 3, Neustrelitz). The QuerBeet restaurant offers tasty organic meals (querbeet-restaurant.de; Useriner Str. 9, Neustrelitz).

Extra tips
A detour to the sculpture Schlosskirche Neustrelitz and the adjacent castle garden is worthwhile (bildhauermuseen.de/ausstellungen/plastikgalerie_schlosskirche.html; Hertelstr. 2, Neustrelitz). The Schloss Mirow museum is located directly on the lake (mv-schloesser.de/location/schloss-mirow; Schlossinsel 1, Mirow).

172
Hall Art Foundation / Schloss Derneburg Museum

In the summer of 2017, after almost ten years of reconstruction, Schloss Derneburg opened a top-class private collection to the public. Northern Germany's largest private museum looks back on a varied history. The former Derneburg manor house was donated to the Hildesheim church in 1143. Seventy years later, Augustinian women from Holle founded a monastery here, which was dissolved at the beginning of the fourteenth century and given over to the Cistercian Reform Order in 1441. During the Reformation, the estate was a Lutheran abbey for young women before being returned to the Cistercians in 1651. At the beginning of the nineteenth century, the monastery was dissolved, and in 1814, the English and Hanoverian king, King George III, gave it to Count Ernst of Münster in recognition of his merits as a result of the annexation of the principality of Hildesheim to the new kingdom of Hanover. The Count commissioned the architect Georg Ludwig Friedrich Laves to rebuild and create an English landscape garden before his son Georg Herbert Count of Münster converted the monastery building into a palace between 1846 and 1848. During the Second World War, it was used as a military hospital and, until 1952, it was a retirement home for displaced persons. When the Count of Münster reclaimed his castle rooms, the state of Lower Saxony acquired the castle's land in 1955. However, the castle itself remained in possession of the Münster family, who sold it to the painter and sculptor Georg Baselitz in 1975. Baselitz lived and worked here until 2006. The US-based couple Christine and Andrew Hall and their foundation bought the castle from Baselitz and, in 2008, the adjacent unused farm buildings from the state of Lower Saxony and had the entire complex extensively rebuilt and renovated by the Berlin- and Munich-based architect Tammo Prinz.

The Schloss Derneburg Museum is one of four exhibition venues worldwide with which the Hall Art Foundation, founded in 2007,

Hall Art Foundation / Schloss Derneburg Museum
Derneburg, Lower Saxony

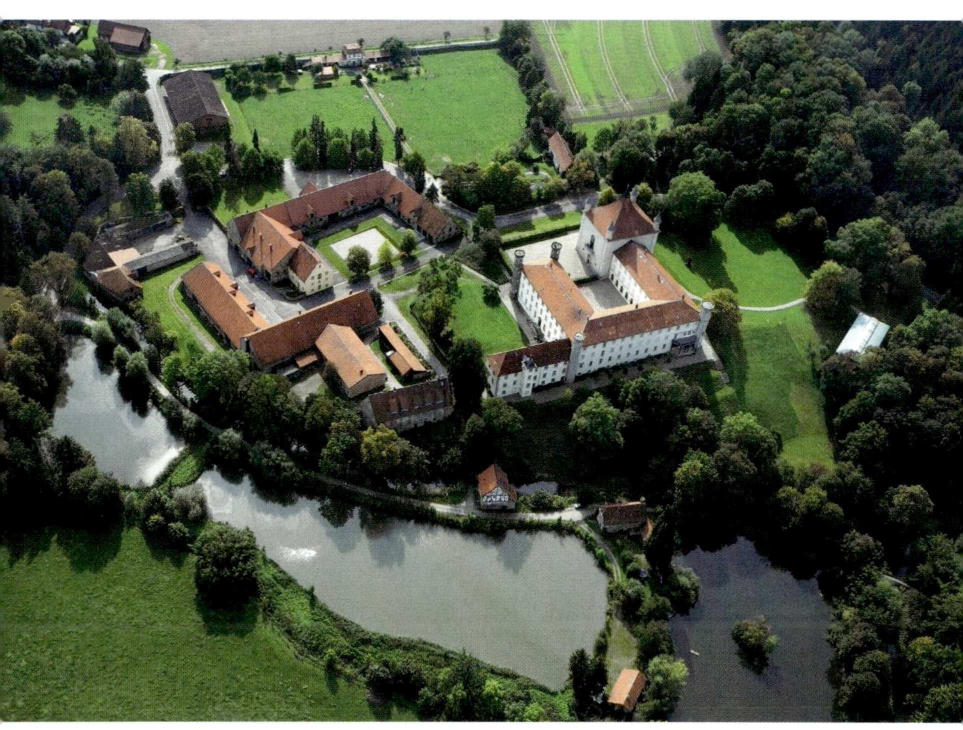

Hall Art Foundation / Schloss Derneburg Museum
Schlossstr. 1
D-31188 Derneburg
Phone: +49 5062 9640294
derneburg@hallartfoundation.org
hallartfoundation.org/location/schloss-derneburg
hallartfoundation.org

Note
The meeting point for the viewing tour is not in the castle itself, but in the visitor center 1.5 km away (Astenbeck 42, 31188 Holle).

Opening hours
The castle can only be visited as part of a group tour booked online in advance. It is possible to take part in short tours (two hours) on Wednesdays, Saturdays, and Sundays for €30 at 3 p.m. For visitors with great stamina, however, the five-hour tour at 11 a.m. on Saturdays is recommended. For €75, it also includes lunch in the former studio of Georg Baselitz (which was originally a kitchen for the monks) amidst his wall pencil sketches. During all of the tours, visitors can expect to be on their feet and climb numerous stairs. In the winter months, there are no guided tours.
At the beginning of every tour, one is welcomed with coffee and biscuits in the visitor center. There is a small exhibition on the upper floor.

Arrival by public transportation
The regional train Erixx (in the DB network) usually stops hourly in Derneburg. If you do not want to walk almost 2 km on Bahnhofstraße in a westward direction to the visitor center, you should get off in Hildesheim and take a taxi. For the way back, you can order a taxi from the museum guide or walk 1.2 km from the castle back to the Derneburg station. Transportation from the visitor center to the castle is easily arranged on site.

Parking
Parking is available in front of the visitor center and on Schlossstraße (the parking lot is about 100 m behind the entrance to the castle on the left-hand side).

provides visitors with access to postwar works and contemporary art. The Hall Art Foundation and Hall Art Collection comprise around 5,500 works by several hundred artists, including Joseph Beuys, Georg Baselitz, Eric Fischl, A.R. Penck, Franz West, Richard Artschwager, Malcolm Morley, Ed Ruscha, and Andy Warhol. The Halls have been intensely interested in the works of German postwar artists for many years, and in 2004 they acquired 120 masterpieces by artists, most of whom were friends with Baselitz, such as Markus Lüpertz, Anselm Kiefer, and Jörg Immendorff, as well as numerous Renaissance prints and African sculptures through the purchase of the Baselitz collection.

During the year of its opening, seven exhibitions were on view in the castle itself and in the surrounding buildings on a total of 10,000 m^2. Andrew Hall, who emigrated from England to the United States thirty years ago and earns his living as a commodities and Wall Street trader, is a skilled and experimental "co-curator" of the unusual hangings and temporary exhibitions. The large-format works by Julian Schabel, one of the favored artists, as well as the window installation by the American Spencer Finch in the entrance hall of the castle are on permanent display. The rooms of Austrian action artist Hermann Nitsch and some of the sculptures of the British artist Antony Gormley have found their home in the castle as well.

It is crucial to the Halls to collect in depth, which is why they possess extensive groups of works by artists who inspire them and constantly keep them busy.

Hall Art Foundation / Schloss Derneburg Museum
Derneburg, Lower Saxony

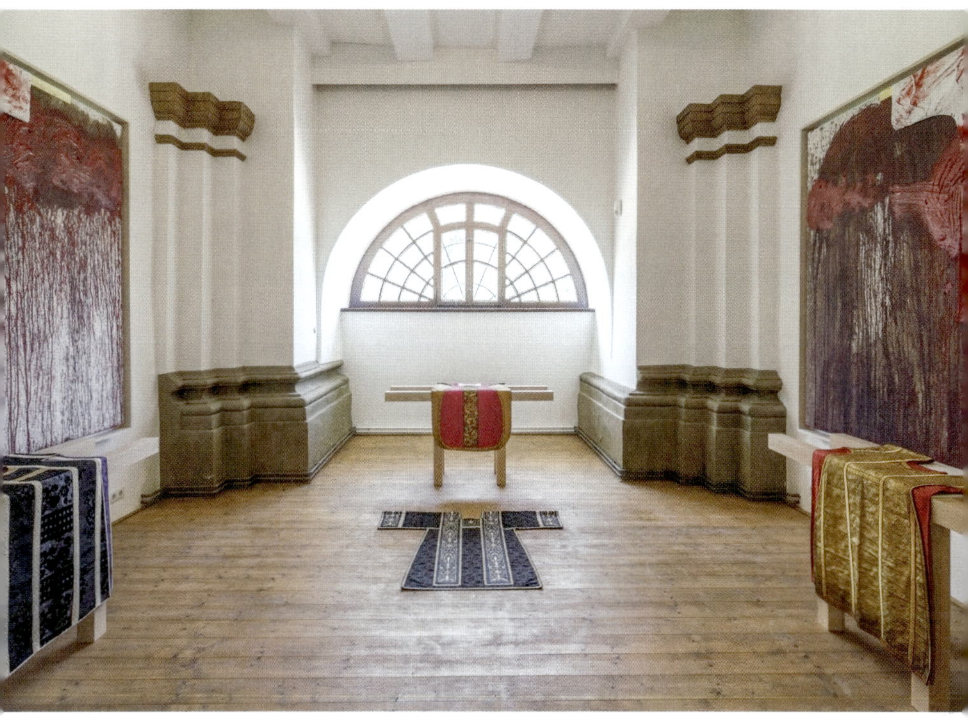

Restaurant tips
Cakes and snacks are offered in the Glashaus, the former greenhouse of the castle nursery directly opposite the entrance to the castle. Opening hours vary (derneburg.de/cafe-im-glashaus).

Extra tips
If you have enough energy for a short walk in the woods after visiting the castle, you should definitely walk a few of the 100 m on the Laves-Kulturpfand. After having crossed the meadow behind the small red house opposite the entrance to the castle, one discovers a small path at the edge of the forest on the right between two bigger fir trees. Following this path, keep left at the next fork, you reach the top of the hill and stand in front of a small Doric temple built in 1827 by Georg Ludwig Friedrich Laves on behalf of Count Ernst of Münster. The building called the "tea temple" served the count as a vantage point. Inside, there was a room with a fireplace in which Münster celebrated the English custom of drinking tea. Continuing on, through the fence it is possible to see the count's pyramid-shaped mausoleum, which he commissioned from Laves in 1893, the year of his death. He opted for a tomb in the geometric-symmetrical formal language of Egyptian architecture, which today seems strange and mystical in this environment, but was frequently used in classicism. Those who have traveled far should spend the night in Goslar or Hildesheim. In Goslar, the imperial palace with the Henry Moore sculpture, as well as the Möncheahaus Museum (moenchehaus.de, Mönchestr. 3) are recommended sites to visit. In Hildesheim, a trip to the reconstructed old town with the Mariendom (Domhof 17), which reopened in 2014 is worthwhile. The bronze doors date back to 1015. A visit to the UNESCO protected St. Michaeliskirche (Michaelisplatz 2) is also recommended.

176 Kunstmuseum Celle mit Sammlung Robert Simon

Visitors to the "first twenty-four-hour art museum in the world" can experience two different museums in Celle at the same location. During the day, large-format paintings, objects, and light art are shown on three floors of approximately 1,000 m^2 of exhibition space. As dusk falls, international light art takes over behind and on the façade and, using 1,272 light emitting diodes, makes the building shine in dazzling colors.

The collector and gallery owner Robert Simon is the creative director, museum founder, donor, and honorary director of the museum. Growing up in Kassel, Simon came into contact with art at an early age through documenta artists who lived in his uncle's hotel. As a child, he was already collecting works by Joseph Beuys. And so it came as no great surprise that in 1981, while studying business administration, he and his wife founded the gallery Kö 24 in Hanover specifically to promote young artists, alongside his work in the management of an insurance group. Since 1985, he has passionately dedicated himself exclusively to art.

The collection of around 1,000 works of art that Robert Simon has successively contributed to the Robert Simon Kunststiftung since it was founded in 2000 reflects his personal preferences and professional connections. Part of the collection is based on donations from artists who were convinced by Simon's exhibition and collection concept. The works in the collection range from the early twentieth century to the present, and the focus is on the 1960s. In addition to a collection of multiples by Joseph Beuys, works by Ralph Fleck, Dieter Krieg, Molitor & Kuzmin, Regine Schumann, Timm Ulrichs, and Ben Willikens are represented. There is also painting from Lower Saxony with works by professors and graduates of the Braunschweig Art Academy. The collection also includes drawings from the 1920s by representatives of New Objectivity. Showcases by Peter Basseler permanently fill a room

Kunstmuseum Celle mit Sammlung Robert Simon
Celle, Lower Saxony

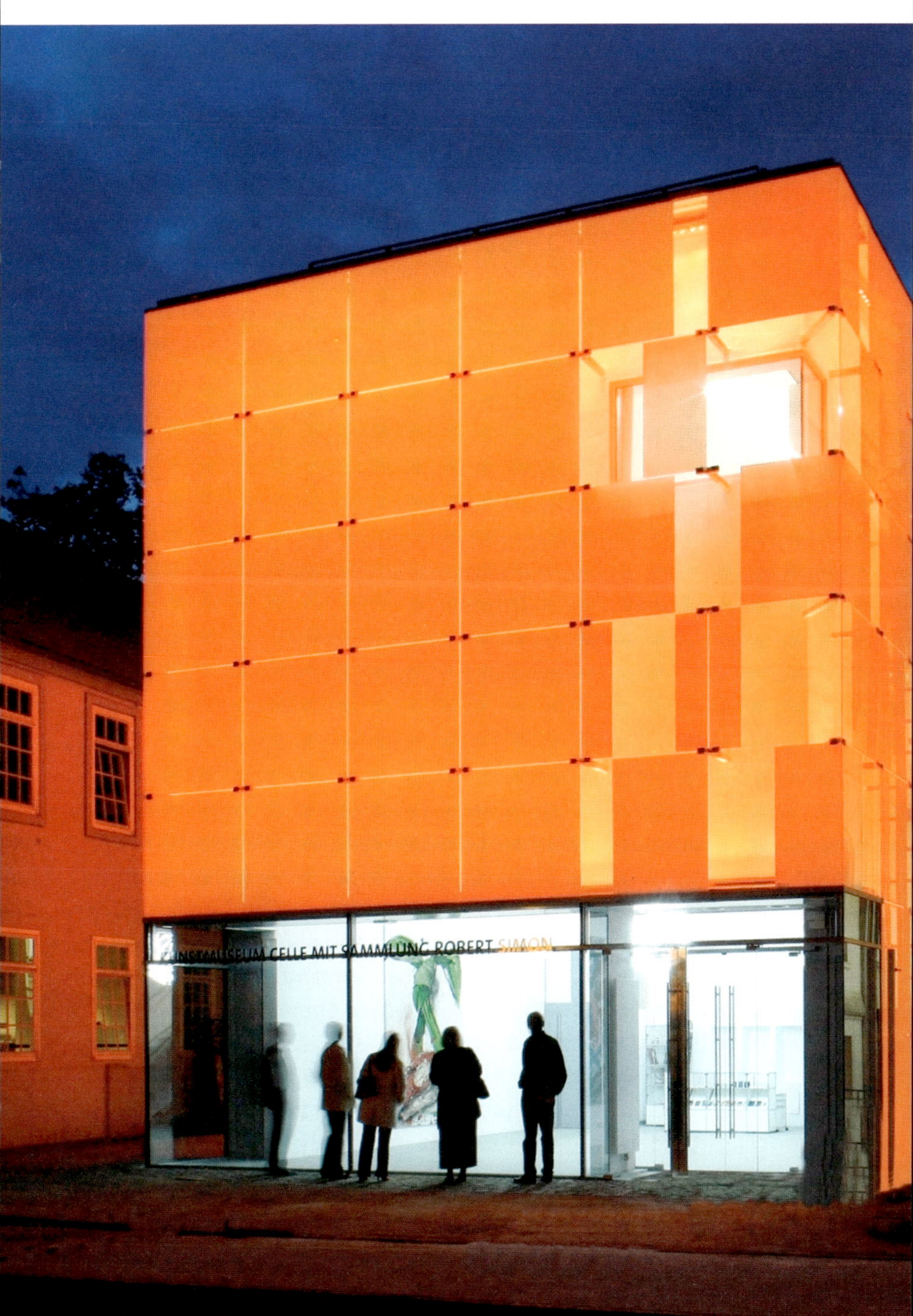

with absurd scenes. Simon and his curator plan three exhibitions from the collection and three special exhibitions a year. The latter is curated partly with works from the collection, but often with loans. Numerous works of site-specific art are created for the exhibitions. In the inner courtyard next to the Celle Market stands the pair of *Feuerwerk für Celle* (Fireworks for Celle, 2006) sculptures by Otto Piene. The famous ZERO artist also created the light room, which was specially designed for the museum in 2001. The museum's "nocturnal side" includes works by Vollrad Kutscher, Francesco Mariotti, Otto Piene, Klaus Geldmacher, and Brigitte Kowanz.

The museum is spatially affiliated to the Bomann Museum, supported by the Kunst-Stiftung Celle and the Simon Kunststiftung. The land and buildings belong to the city of Celle, which cooperates closely with the two foundations and has granted the right of use to the foundation. Robert Simon had the concept of the twenty-four-hour art museum patented in 1998, and its present form was created after extension and conversion work by the architects Ahrens and Grabenhorst in 2005/06.

His desire to bring art and light art in particular closer to the general public is illustrated not only by the founding of the museum but also by his initiation of the Mile of Sculptures in Hanover and the Lichtkunstbahnhofs (Light Art Train Station) in Celle. In public space, too, he invites rail passengers to engage with art. As soon as they get off the train in Celle, they are greeted by bright benches, walls, and illuminated works of art by Francesco Mariotti, Albert Hien, and Timm Ulrichs. Hans Kotter's *Triple Tube* (2012) even fills its own room in the station building. In the installation *Lichtspieltheater* (2012) by Vollrad Kutscher, passersby trigger colorful LED lighting with motion detectors as they walk through the station underpass. Robert Simon has succeeded in financing the costs for the art, with which the simple station complex was upgraded during an extensive renovation, through sponsored money. Simon is also the founder of the 10,000 euro German Light Art Award, which was given to light artist Brigitte Kowanz in 2018.

Kunstmuseum Celle mit Sammlung Robert Simon
Celle, Lower Saxony

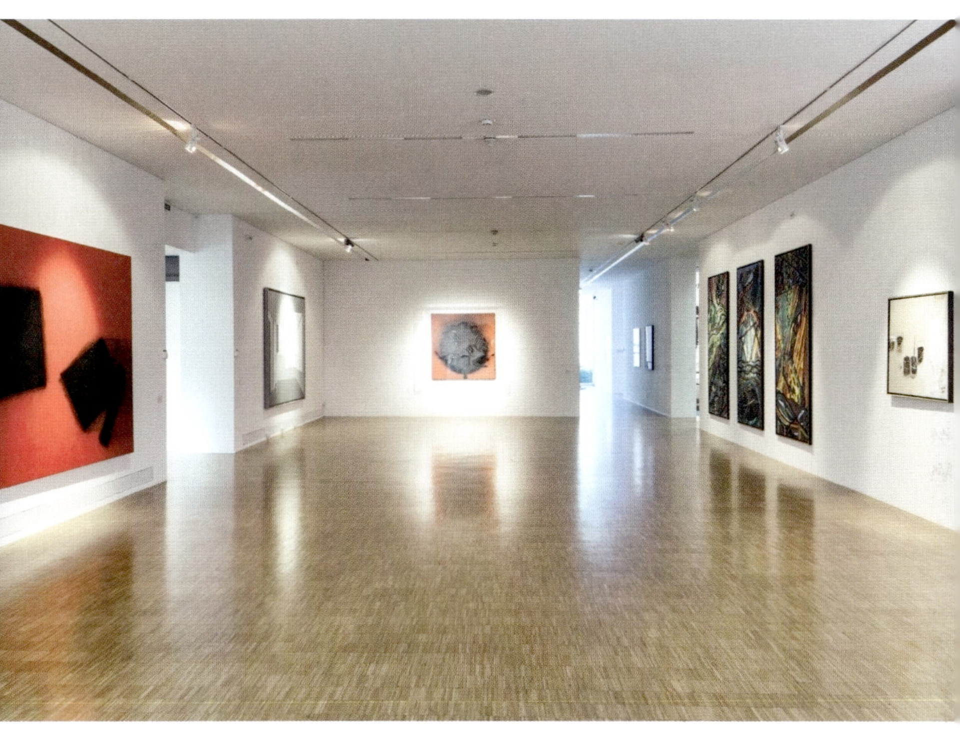

Kunstmuseum Celle
mit Sammlung Robert Simon
Schlossplatz 7
D-29221 Celle
Phone: +49 5141 124521
kunstmuseum@celle.de
kunst.celle.de

Opening hours
Tue–Sun 11 a.m.–5 p.m.
International light art can be discovered daily outside at dusk. There are guided tours and evening tours of the collection, exhibitions, and light art as well as workshops for children and adults. The exhibitions are accompanied by lectures, concerts, and special events.

Entrance fees
Adults / Reduced / Children and students €8 / €5 / free
Combined ticket (Bomann-, Kunst- und Residenzmuseum; valid for two days): €12 / €8

Arrival by public transportation
From the Celle station it is less than ten minutes to Schlossplatz with bus 9, 12, 13, 300, or 800.

Restaurant tips
In the Kanzlei Café, enjoy a pause among numerous works of art (Kanzleistr. 6). Likely the best bread in Germany and sweets can be found at the Rönitz bakery (roenitz-brot.de; Großer Plan 5). Gourmet cuisine is served in the Restaurant Palio in the Althoff Hotel Fürstenhof (fuerstenhof-celle.com; Hannoversche Str. 55/56).

180 Museum DKM

Founded in 1999 by Dirk Krämer and Klaus Maas, the Foundation DKM maintained the Gallery DKM in Duisburg's inner harbor until 2011 and the Museum DKM since 2009. It promotes the realization of new works of art, has the works of art from the Collection DKM on display in the museum, and comprises four sub-foundations: the Ernst Herrmann Archiv Foundation, the Foundation Ulrich Rückriem – Five Rooms, the Ulrich Rückriem Museum Foundation, and the Ulrich Rückriem Sinsteden Foundation.

The Museum DKM, which opened in Duisburg's city center in January 2009, was designed by Swiss architect Hans Rohr on an industrial site of the 1960s and consists of three buildings extending over five levels. For this purpose, an original residential and commercial property with a front building and courtyard wing was completely redesigned and extended with a new building. In more than fifty individual rooms and several sculpture courtyards, several hundred works and artifacts from the DKM Collection from different times, as well as cultural and geographical contexts, are presented over 2,700 m^2 of exhibition space. On display are works of modern art since the 1960s (for example by Blinky Palermo, Erich Reusch, Ulrich Erben, and Richard Long), photographs, contemporary and ancient artifacts from Asia (Pakistan, China, India, Iran, Japan, Cambodia, and Thailand), as well as objects from Egyptian antiquity and vessels that trace up to 5,000 years of cultural history.

The staged thematic ensembles and the arrangement of the rooms enable exciting dialogues between art and architecture. The meditative views of Far Eastern-styled courtyards underscore the desire of the donors to let the collection have a silent effect. On the ground floor of the old building, temporary exhibitions take place several times a year. The remaining areas were designed for the permanent exhibition.

Museum DKM
Duisburg, North Rhine-Westphalia

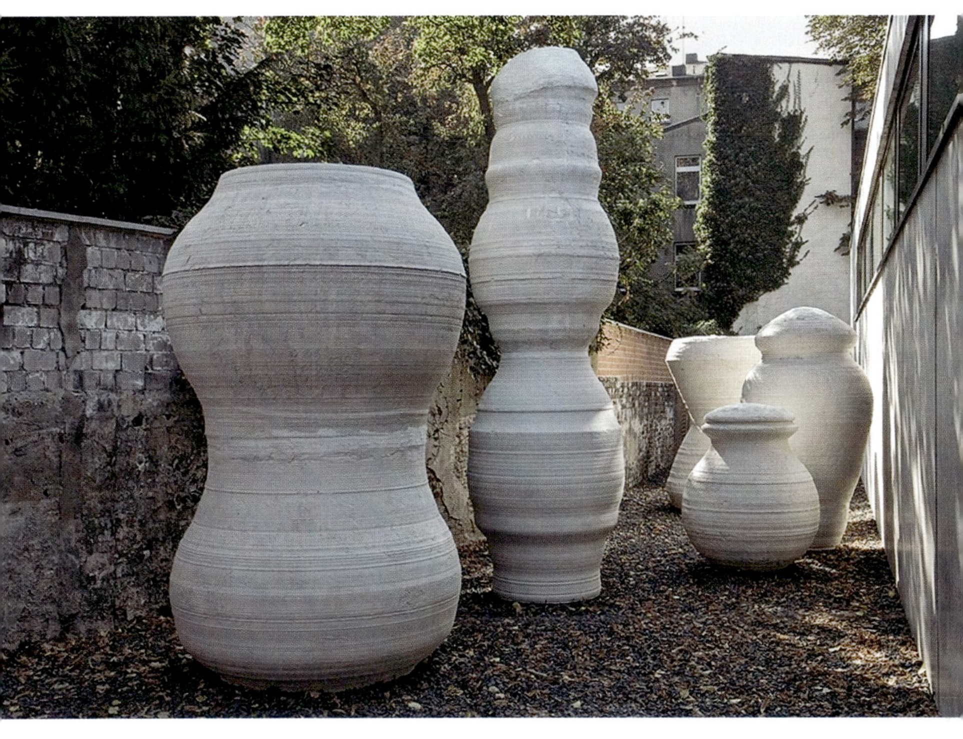

Museum DKM
Güntherstr. 13–15
D-47051 Duisburg
Phone: +49 203 93555470
mail@museum-dkm.de
museum-dkm.de

Opening hours
Sat/Sun and public holidays noon–6 p.m., every first Friday of the month noon–6 p.m., Mon–Fri by appointment only
Public tours take place by appointment on the first Friday of the month at 4 p.m. (€6 plus admission). Additional tour dates are listed on the website. In the foyer of the museum, there is a small modern café with a reading corner.

Entrance fees
Adults / Reduced: €12 / €6

Arrival by public transportation
The Museum DKM is located in the center of the city of Duisburg between Kant Park with the Lehmbruck Museum and the main train station.

Extra tips
A visit to the Museum DKM should be combined with one to the Lehmbruck Museum, which has an excellent collection of international modernist sculptures, and the Kant Park with over forty large sculptures on display (lehmbruckmuseum.de; Friedrich-Wilhelm-Straße 40). A visit to the MKM Museum Küppersmühle of Modern Art is also recommended (see p. 208).

182 Draiflessen Collection

In the middle of a quiet residential area in the small Westphalian town of Mettingen, visitors have been coming across an elegant event and museum complex designed for the Draiflessen Collection by Essen-based Nattler Architekten for several years now. After its private foundation in 2009 by the Brenninkmeijer family, the Draiflessen Collection became a nonprofit public art museum with regular exhibitions and art education in 2017. Every year, two major exhibitions on various themes are shown across an area of almost 900 m^2. The epoch-spanning exhibitions are partly equipped with works from the collection and partly with loans from other institutions and artists. Some of the guiding principles of the Draiflessen Collection are the conceptual considerations that works should always be oriented towards people, address socially relevant themes, and pose questions with a research-based artistic perspective. There are also some contemporary works of art in the Draiflessen Collection, including a major work by Julian Rosefeldt. The expansion of this area through further purchases from the respective temporary exhibitions is planned.

Since September 2012, the Draiflessen Collection has included the Liberna Collection compiled by Bernard Brenninkmeijer (1893–1976)—Liberna is a combination of *Liber* (book) and Bernard—an extensive collection of valuable manuscripts, miniatures, books, prints, and drawings from the fifteenth to seventeenth centuries on permanent loan. The collection consists of around 4,000 objects, including famous incunabula—such as Sebastian Brant's *Narrenschiff* (1494), the *Nuremberg Chronicle* (1493), the *Koberger Bible* (1483), and Albrecht Dürer's *Apocalypse* (1498)—as well as highlights of the printing art of later years such as the *Elzevier Bible* or a complete *Blaeu Atlas,* both from the seventeenth century. A Luther Bible bound in the same century and now open to the public in the study room presents itself in an unusual garment, namely in shark leather dyed in black. The collection of prints and drawings includes numerous German and Dutch masters; the main focus, however, is on Albrecht Dürer and Rembrandt van Rijn. Together with the Liberna Collection, the book and graphic collection is one of the

Draiflessen Collection
Mettingen, North Rhine-Westphalia

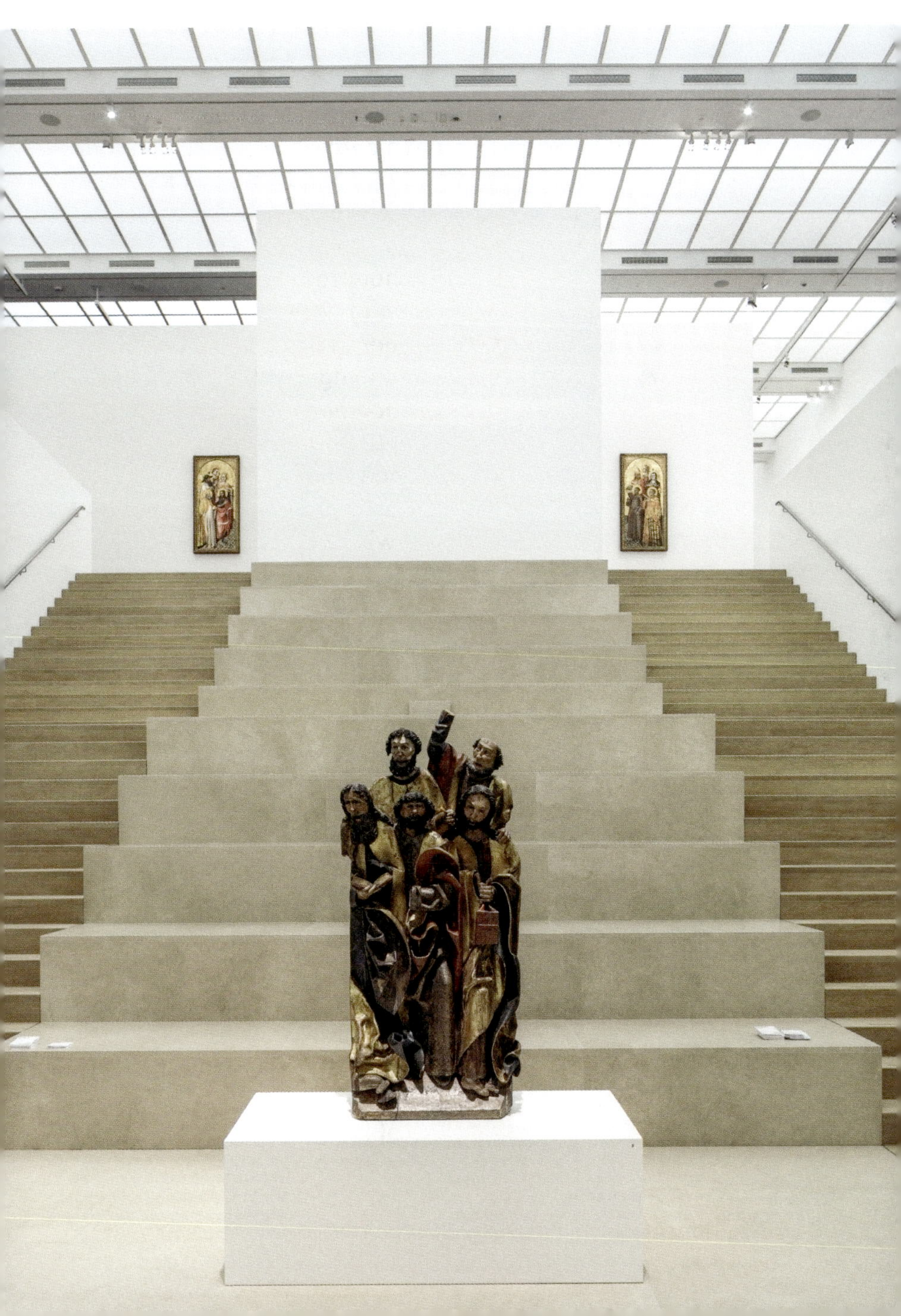

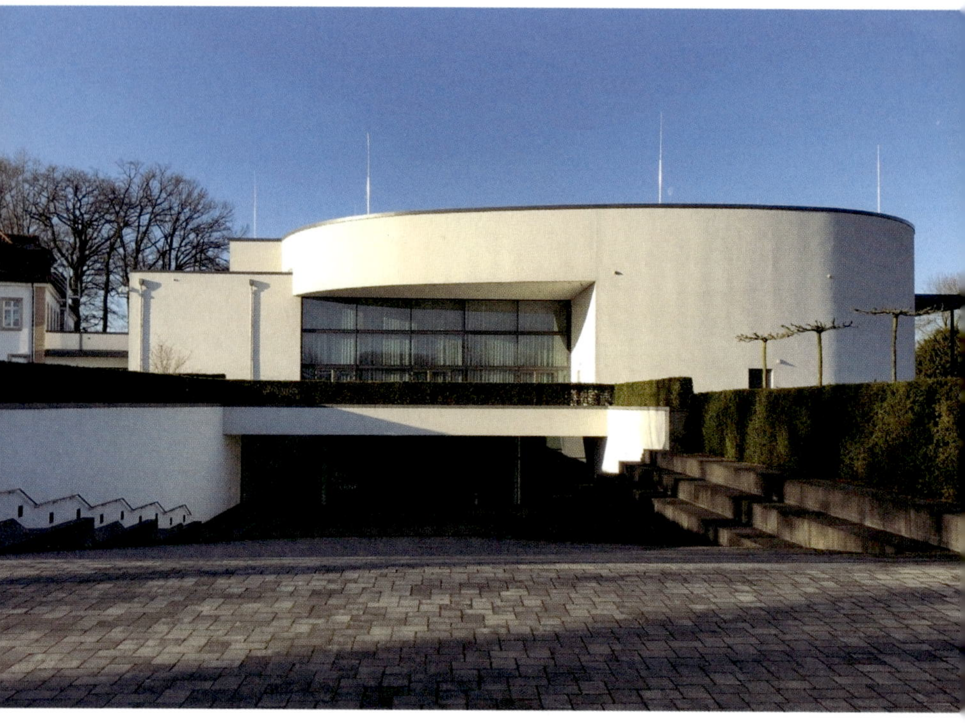

Draiflessen Collection
Georgstr. 18
D-49497 Mettingen
Phone: +49 5452 91680
info@draiflessen.com
draiflessen.com

Opening hours
Wed–Sun 11 a.m.–5 p.m., Saturdays as well as every first Thursday of the month 11 a.m.–9 p.m. On Sundays (3–4 p.m.) and every first Thursday of the month (7–7:45 p.m.), there are free public guided tours. Individual guided tours can be booked starting with three participants (€12 incl. admission). Guided tours for children, adolescents, and school groups are also available.
The highly recommended visit to the cabinet exhibitions in the Liberna study hall is only possible with a guided tour and after registration up to three days before the desired date (tel: +49 5452 9168 3500 or info@draiflessen.com).
Numerous workshops for children, as well as irregular concerts and other events, take place.
The museum also has a small shop and a coffee bar.

Entrance fees
Adults / Reduced / Teenagers under 18: €12 / €6 / free
Combined tickets for the exhibition without a guided tour and cabinet exhibition with a guided tour (only after registration): €15/ €12 as well as exhibition with a guided tour and cabinet exhibition with a guided tour (only after registration): €16 / €13.

Arrival by public transportation
A visit is possible by bus S10 from the Osnabrück main station. From the bus stop Schultenhof, Mettingen, you can reach the museum in about ten minutes.

Restaurant tips
The tastefully decorated WOHN BAR serves delicious cake and good coffee (wohn-bar.eu; Burgstr. 11; open every afternoon).
At Foto Heyday Café, there are homemade cakes and spelt crêpes (Markt 16, Wed–Sun open afternoons, also Saturday mornings).

Extra tips
Mettingen is home to a range of remarkable half-timbered and sandstone buildings. The numerous Tüötten villas are a unique local feature.
Since 1962, the Tüöttenmuseum has been housed in the inner courtyard of the former Hotel Telsemeyer and today's town hall, which is run by the Heimatverein (mettingen-tourismus.de; Sunderstr. 2). The small but worth-seeing Otto Modersohn Museum Tecklenburg is dedicated to the work of Otto Modersohn (ommt.de; Markt 9, D-49545 Tecklenburg; limited opening hours in the winter months).

most important libraries for the seventeenth and eighteenth centuries worldwide. Fortunately, access to some collection highlights is possible during registered guided tours in the specially equipped Liberna study hall. In the future, three small cabinet exhibitions will take place annually in the fully air-conditioned study hall, which can only be entered with shoe covers. This working, storage, and cabinet exhibition room, designed in muted tones by the exhibition and interior designer Astrid Michaelis, are a delight for art and architecture fans alike and should be visited.

The ancestors of the founding family Brenninkmeijer belonged to the so-called Tüötten, Westphalian wanderers who traveled through Germany and Northern Europe especially in the seventeenth and eighteenth centuries to trade linen. With the decision to build Draiflessen on the site of a former production plant, the entrepreneurial family deliberately referred back to their Westphalian roots and their hometown of Mettingen. An ancient farmhouse in the small town between Münster and Osnabrück is the original home of the Dutch Catholic family Brenninkmeijer, whose forefathers Clemens and August Brenninkmeijer founded the internationally renowned textile company C&A in Sneek, the Netherlands, six generations ago in 1841. The choice of location was made in response to the desire to expand the region's cultural offerings with an art museum away from urban areas. The name "Draiflessen" is a word construction derived from the old secret language of the Tüötten. Its two word stems "drai" (meaning three, trinity, turning, trading) and "flessen" (meaning flax, linen, home), express important themes to the founding family: their close connection with Westphalian origins, their Christian faith, and their entrepreneurship, which began in the textile trade at that time. The varied history of the company is documented in changing exhibitions in the same complex. The DAS Forum—DAS stands for Draiflessen, Archiv (archive), and Sammlung (collection)—, which opened in November 2018, was conceived within the Draiflessen Collection as a new place for study, research, and dialogue on a wide variety of issues relating to family businesses.

186
Langen Foundation

Since 2004, art and architecture fans have been able to visit the Langen Foundation's exhibition house on the site of the Rocket Station Island Hombroich. Behind a bright, slightly curved concrete wall hides an architectural jewel designed by Tadao Ando that thrills minimalism fans at any time of day or year.

The Rocket Station Island Hombroich is part of the visionary plan of Karl-Heinrich Müller, founder of the nearby Museum Insel Hombroich, to transform the NATO anti-aircraft base, which was shut down in 1993, into a place where art and nature come into synthesis. Tadao Ando, who first visited the Rocket Station in 1994, had already worked on a concept by Karl-Heinrich Müller, Erwin Heerich, Oliver Kruse, and Katsuhito Nishikawa, which was presented at the Architecture Biennale in Venice in 1996. The plan, which was largely implemented by 2001, provided for the removal of the purely military elements, the redesign of the existing buildings, and the construction of new buildings by Heerich and Nishikawa. The history of the place was consciously preserved and transferred into a cultural use. The arch, through which today a path lined with cherry trees leads to the entrance of the Langen Foundation, was realized in 1998/99 as one of the first buildings. When Tadao Ando's plans were first presented to the founder Marianne Langen in 2001, the enthusiasm of the Japan enthusiast was so great that the commission to revise the original design quickly followed. The laying of the foundation stone for this last and largest work of art in her collection took place in 2002.

Surrounded by earthen walls planted with grass, the complex of light gray, layered concrete, glass and steel girders consists mainly of two architecturally different, interconnected building complexes that masterfully blend into the flat landscape: the above-ground, elongated concrete structure surrounded by a glass jacket, and two concrete beams connected at a forty-five-degree angle, which sunk deep into the ground. As initially planned, the seemingly sacred exhibition space inside the concrete core is mostly reserved for temporary exhibitions from the Langen Foundation's Japan collection. In the exhibition areas Modern I and Modern II,

Langen Foundation
Neuss, North Rhine-Westphalia

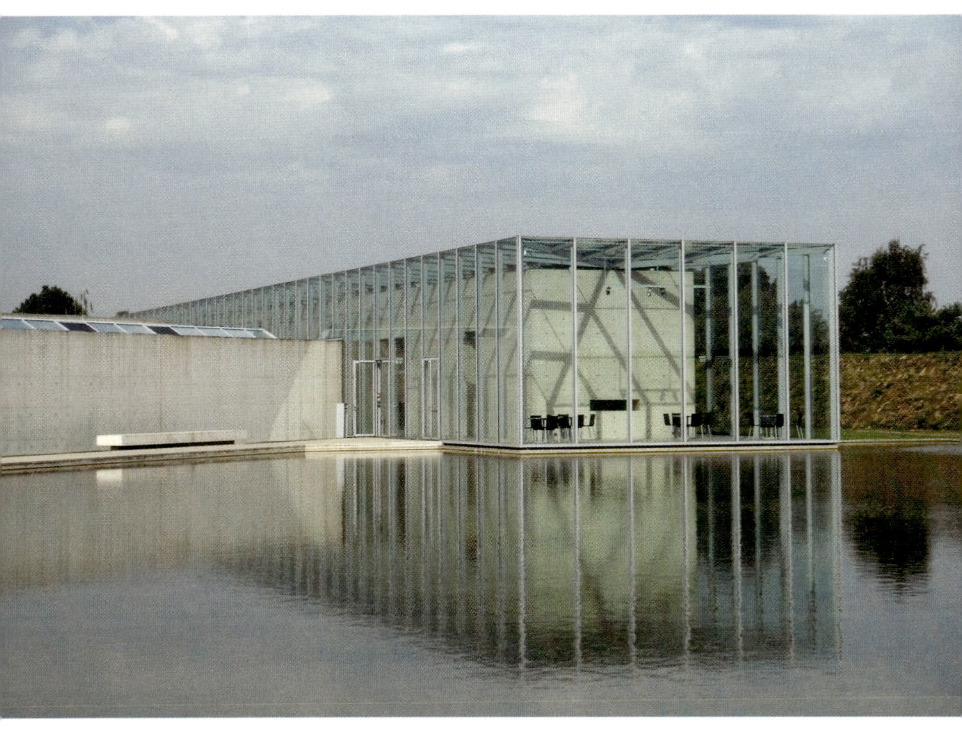

Langen Foundation
Raketenstation Hombroich 1
D-41472 Neuss
Phone: +49 2182 570115
info@langenfoundation.de
langenfoundation.de

Opening hours
Daily 10 a.m.–6 p.m., closed during periods of exhibition installation. From April to November, public guided tours take place every first Sunday of the month at 3 p.m. (€6 plus admission).

Entrance fees
Adults / Reduced / Family ticket: €8 / €5 / €19
Combined ticket with the Insel Hombroich and the Skulpturenhalle (sculpture hall):
Adults / Reduced: Mon–Fri €20; Sat/Sun €25 / Mon–Fri €12,50; Sat/Sun €15

Arrival by car
Coming from Düsseldorf, drive in the direction of Neuss and follow the A57 to the Neuss-West junction, where you turn onto the A46 in the direction of Heinsberg / Aachen / Neuss-Holzheim / Neuss-West. At the fork after 100 m, stay left and take the A46 towards Aachen. Attention: Google Maps and also some navigation systems lead drivers the wrong way: take the exit 14 / Grevenbroich-Kapellen or Kapellen and follow the brown signs to the Rocket Station Island Hombroich. The parking lot is behind the Langen Foundation.

Arrival by public transportation
From the S-Bahn station Neuss-Süd, take bus 869 in the direction of Grevenbroich Bahnhof or from the stop Neuss Landestheater, take bus 870 in the direction of Jüchen Schulzentrum to the stop Neuss Bergerhof. You can also take the regional train to Kapellen Wevelinghoven station and from there, take bus 869 in the direction of Neuss Stadthalle/Museum to the Neuss Bergerhof stop. Then follow the Bergerweg, which turns off the main road, in a northwesterly direction. Cross Lindenweg and you will see the Ando building on your left. For timetables or directions, enter "Langen Foundation" as the destination in the search field at vrr.de.

which are up to eight meters high, curated special exhibitions with loans from other private collections of modern or contemporary art or artists are shown in individual or group exhibitions. A total area of 1,300 m^2 is available for the two temporary exhibitions each year. Supported by deliberate daylight control, a fascinating interplay between inside and outside, light and shadow, art and nature, as well as massiveness and lightness can be experienced in the building.

The Viktor and Marianne Langen Collection has its origins in the 1950s and today consists of around 350 works of Japanese art from the twelfth to twentieth centuries and about one hundred objects from other non-European cultures. Until a few years ago, another focus of the collection was the art of the twentieth century with a focus on classical modern art. The entrepreneur and engineer Viktor Langen (1909–1990) had a keen instinct for the exceptional. As a collector couple, Marianne and Viktor Langen had a simple strategy: they collected “the present,” as Viktor Langen put it, and bought works that spontaneously impressed them. They did not seek art expertise, did not ask about the importance of the artists, but relied on their own judgment. “Art is not a luxury, but a need” was the credo. The collector couple’s enthusiasm for Japan was aroused in the early 1960s during numerous business trips. Over the decades, a Japan collection was created that is unique in Europe, including scroll paintings, folding screens, and sculptures.

The construction costs were financed without external funds by Marianne Langen, who died shortly before the opening of the house. Her heirs have assumed the task of preserving the foundation in the spirit of the legacy of Viktor and Marianne Langen. Although the Langen Foundation is part of the Hombroich cultural area as an art foundation, it operates independently in terms of organization and program.

Langen Foundation
Neuss, North Rhine-Westphalia

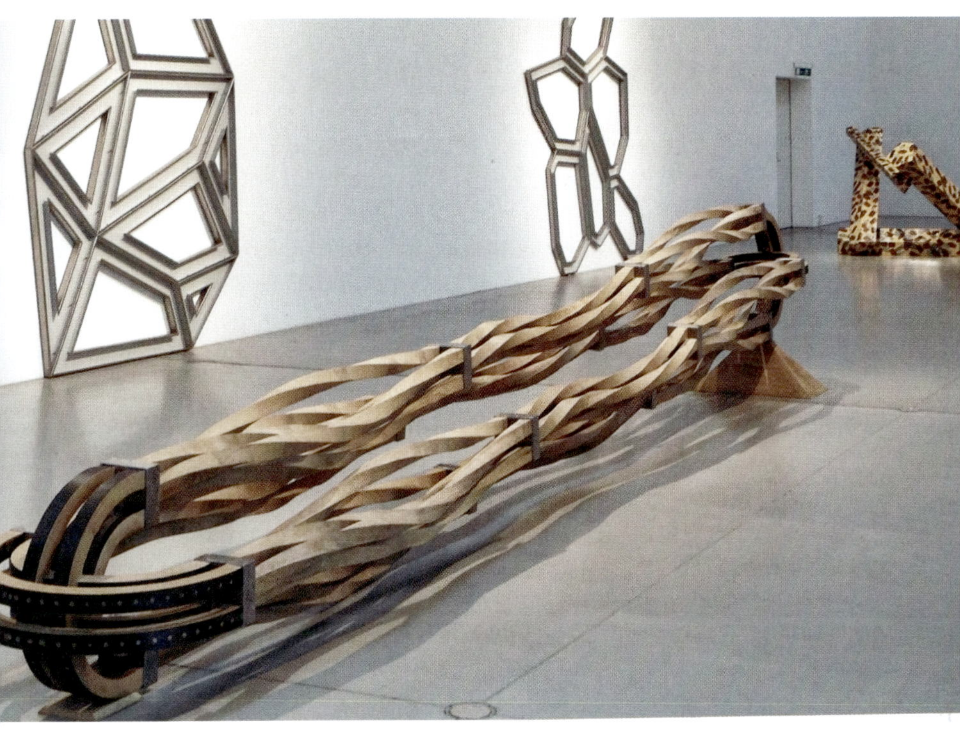

Extra tips
It is a good idea to visit the Langen Foundation in the morning and then Insel Hombroich, where you can enjoy a hearty local buffet for lunch. From the Langen Foundation, it takes about twenty minutes to walk to the Museum Insel Hombroich (see p. 190). Numerous additional events take place within the program of the Insel Hombroich Foundation at the Rocket Station Island Hombroich. Public guided tours of the Rocket Station Island Hombroich are offered every first Sunday of the month from February to November at 1 p.m. (€7.50 plus admission). The meeting point is the guardhouse at the entrance of the Rocket Station Island Hombroich. A visit to the Thomas Schütte Foundation's Skulpturenhalle (sculpture hall), completed in 2016, is also recommended. In the architecturally unusual exhibition room, changing sculpture exhibitions are presented (thomas-schuette-stiftung.de; Lindenweg, corner Berger Weg). On the way from the Langen Foundation via the Skulpturenhalle to Insel Hombroich, one crosses the Kirkeby-Feld. The "field," named after Per Kirkeby, consists of five buildings by the Danish artist. Exhibitions and art installations are regularly shown in the ensemble Drei Kapellen and the Feld-Haus – Museum für Populäre Druckgrafik, which is run by the Clemens Sels Museum in Neuss (inselhombroich.de/en/visit/general; clemens-sels-museum-neuss.de; Berger Weg 5). As part of the Lower Rhine Music Festival, classical concerts usually take place in September at the Langen Foundation (see niederrhein-musikfestival.de).

Restaurant tips
Sophisticated German and Asian cuisine is prepared at the long-established, family-run restaurant Drei Könige. A highlight is the monthly changing Amuse Bouche menu, which is offered on Thursday evenings. In Tanja's Bistro, small snacks are served (drei-koenige.net; Neusser Str. 49, 41516 Grevenbroich; closed Mondays).

190 Museum Insel Hombroich

Düsseldorf real estate agent Karl-Heinrich Müller (1936–2007) developed the concept of Museum Insel Hombroich based on Paul Cézanne's leitmotif, "Art parallel to nature," which corresponded to his desire for a presentation of his collection in decentralized exhibition pavilions within green surroundings. In 1982, he discovered the wild park landscape in the Erft floodplains between Neuss and Grevenbroich, a perfect location for the realization of his vision. The geometric gardens were laid out in 1820 when the de Weerth family of industrialists from Wuppertal moved into the Rosa Haus, a country estate located here.

The collector found support for his plans in the Düsseldorf Art Academy from three artists who were closely associated with the project for the long term: Gotthard Graubner (1930–2013), who stayed partly on the foundation's premises until his death and curated the permanent presentation of the collection; Anatol Herzfeld (1931–2019) had his studio here; and Erwin Heerich (1922–2004) designed eleven pavilions distributed throughout the grounds as walk-in sculptures.

During the first construction phase, the Orangerie, the Graubner Pavillon, and the Hohe Galerie were built. In 1984, the collector succeeded in acquiring the much larger adjacent property and had it carefully recultivated from an agricultural landscape into a lush park and floodplain by landscape architect Bernhard Korte. For the new terrain, Karl-Heinrich Müller had further sculptures designed by Erwin Heerich, which, as in previous years, were converted by the Düsseldorf architect Hermann H. Müller into buildings made of brick typical of the region.

In this second construction phase, the labyrinth, the cafeteria, the tower, the Tadeusz Pavilion, the Snail, the Twelve Room House, and the cashier's office were built. In 1987, the twenty-five-hectare area was opened to the public. In 1994, Karl-Heinrich Müller also acquired the Rocket Station Island Hombroich, a former NATO air defense base with facilities for launching medium-range missiles,

Museum Insel Hombroich
Neuss, North Rhine-Westphalia

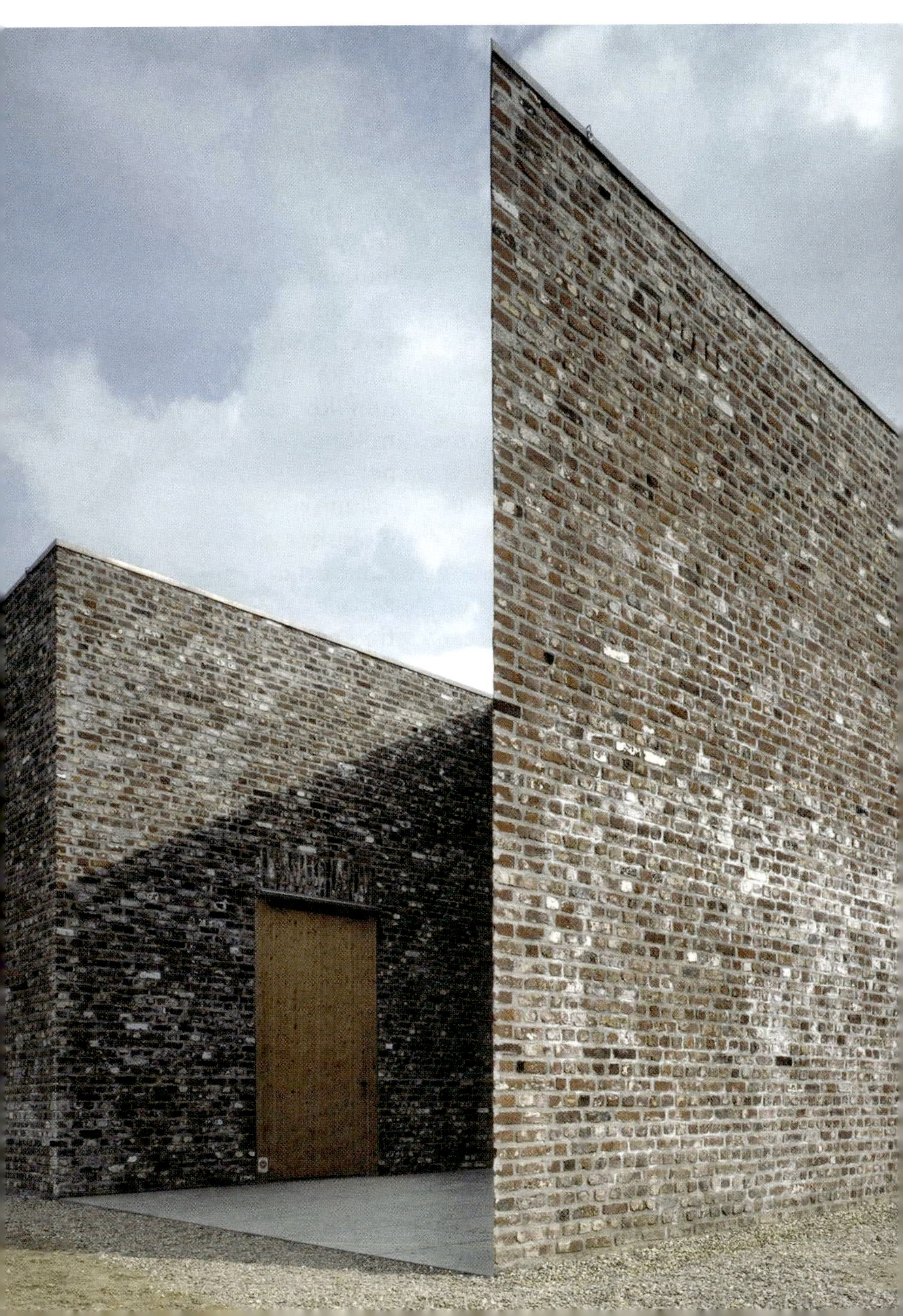

which had been shut down since the disarmament negotiations in 1989 and is located near Museum Insel Hombroich. In the newly founded Rocket Station Island Hombroich and the later extended Kirkeby-Feld, Müller created a kind of interdisciplinary laboratory for the synthesis of natural sciences, spirituality, philosophy, art, music, and literature. In addition to Erwin Heerich, artists and architects such as Katsuhito Nishikawa, Oliver Kruse, Dietmar Hofmann, Tadao Ando, Álvaro Siza, Raimund Abraham, and Per Kirkeby were commissioned to plan the archives, residential and exhibition buildings, studios, seminar rooms, and overnight accommodations. In 2018, the futuristic Haus für Musiker (house for musicians), developed directly for the Rocket Station site, was completed. The design was by the Austrian-American architect Raimund Abraham (1933–2010) from the mid-1990s.

In the early years, Karl-Heinrich Müller initially acquired works by Joseph Beuys, Ulrich Rückriem, Jean Dubuffet, and Antoni Tàpies for his collection, but subsequently resold some of them. Later works by Hans Arp, Jean Fautrier, Yves Klein, Alexander Calder, Lovis Corinth, and Kurt Schwitters were added. He also supported his friends Erwin Heerich, Gotthard Graubner, and Norbert Tadeusz with purchases of their works. Antiquity treasures from China, Persia, Africa, and Oceania can also be found in the collection.

Gotthard Graubner presents the approximately eight hundred exhibits in the Museum Insel Hombroich according to a unique exhibition concept that eschews a chronological and style-based order. Rather, exciting interactions between the works of old cultures and modern European art are staged. There are no signposts on the site, the pavilions are not numbered, the works of art are not inscribed. Visitors to the pavilions should take their time and interact with the works of art in a candid and unobserved manner.

In 1996, Karl-Heinrich Müller brought the Rocket Station Island Hombroich, the so-called Kirkeby-Feld, and the Museum Insel Hombroich together with the art collection to the Stiftung Insel Hombroich, which today looks after the over sixty-hectare cultural area Hombroich. The nonprofit Stiftung Insel Hombroich was founded by the merger of Karl-Heinrich Müller, the Rhein-Kreis Neuss, and the city of Neuss, and to a lesser extent with financial support from the state of North Rhine-Westphalia. This alliance creates the basis for the dynamic ensemble to continue to develop in the future in the spirit of its founder.

Museum Insel Hombroich
Minkel 2
D-41472 Neuss-Holzheim
Phone: +49 2182 2094
stiftung@inselhombroich.de
inselhombroich.de

Opening hours
April to September, daily 10 a.m.–7 p.m., October to March, daily 1 a.m.–7 p.m.
Last admission of the day and the café closing take place one hour before the museum closes. During storm warnings by the German Weather Service, the museum closes partially or entirely for safety reasons.
Every first Sunday of the month from February to November, public guided tours of the Museum Insel Hombroich take place at 11 a.m. (€7.50 plus admission). The meeting point is the museum's ticket office. The art educators are all artists themselves and, depending on their background, bring individual focal points to the tours. On the same days, at 1 p.m., public guided tours of the Rocket Station Island Hombroich are offered (€7.50 plus admission). The meeting point is the guardhouse at the entrance of the Rocket Station Island Hombroich. The cafeteria offers a free buffet with simple regional food.

Entrance fees
Adults / Reduced / Family ticket / Children under age 6 and Art:card holders: Mon–Fri €1; Sat/Sun and on public holidays €20 / Mon–Fri €7,50; Sat/Sun and on public holidays €10 / Mon–Fri €35; Sat/Sun and on public holidays €45 / free
Combined ticket with the Langen Foundation and the Skulpturenhalle (sculpture hall): Adults: Mon–Fri €20; Sat/Sun €25 / Reduced: Mon–Fri €12,50; Sat/Sun €15

Arrival by public transportation
From the S-Bahn station Neuss-Süd take bus 869 in the direction of Kapellen Wevelinghoven Bf / Grevenbroich Bahnhof or from the stop Neuss Landestheater take bus 870 in the direction of Jüchen Schulzentrum to the Neuss Insel Hombroich stop. It is also possible to take the regional train to the Kapellen Wevelinghoven station and from there take bus 869 in the direction of Neuss Stadthalle / Museum to the stop Neuss Insel Hombroich. For timetables, enter "Insel Hombroich" as your destination in the search query on vrr.de.

Extra tips
You should combine your visit to the Museum Insel Hombroich with a detour to the Langen Foundation (see p. 186), the Kirkeby-Feld, the Skulpturenhalle, and a tour of the Rocket Station Island Hombroich. The latter offers a fascinating mixture of crude legacies from the military era with experimental, artistic field experiments and fascinating architecture. It is a good idea to check the Calendar section of the Insel Hombroich website when planning your visit. The venues and opening hours of the Hombroich cultural area change frequently.
On the website of the Rhein-Kreis Neuss, you will find information about Kultohr, a service that offers maps and short, concise information about the most important cultural features of the region via mobile phone (rhein-kreis-neuss.de).

194 Kunsträume from the Michael Horbach Foundation

Since 2011, the Michael Horbach Foundation has been showing exhibitions of contemporary photography and painting in the former gallery and studio complex of Monika Sprüth and Rosemarie Trockel in a backyard in Cologne's Südstadt district. The initiator of Kunsträume Michael Horbach pursues cultural and social concerns with his exhibition and collecting activities. The collector, patron, photographer, former gallery owner, and successful entrepreneur sees the location as a meeting place. Michael Horbach founded the foundation in 2000 after he sold his company, HORBACH Wirtschaftsberatung (business consultancy). "A just world is possible" is the guiding principle under which all charitable projects sponsored by the Michael Horbach Foundation can be summarized. It is particularly committed to cultural projects. In addition to organizing exhibitions, the foundation also awards a photography prize worth 10,000 euros every two years, which is preferably given to socially committed artists. In addition, three-month scholarships are awarded to young foreign photographers. The artists have a studio at their disposal to live and work in.

Michael Horbach has been collecting photography for almost two decades. His passion is focused on positions that could be assigned to—in the broadest sense—a modern, contemporary "Humanist Photography." He evaluates the mostly black-and-white photographs against the utopia of a better world and whether the photographers have successfully implemented this claim in their images. Contemporary photography from South America and Cuba is primarily represented, with photographers such as Juan Carlos Alom, Pep Bonet, Raúl Cañibano Ercilla, Arien Chang Castán, Thomas Dorn, Miquel Frontera, Cristina García Rodero, Flor Garduño, Frank Gaudlitz, Jan Grarup, Alberto Diaz Guttierrez (Korda), Lucana (Ana Lucia Perez Tobón), Beat Presser, Sebastião Salgado, Alfredo Sarabia, and Marcos Zimmermann. Nude photography

Kunsträume from the Michael Horbach Foundation
Cologne, North Rhine-Westphalia

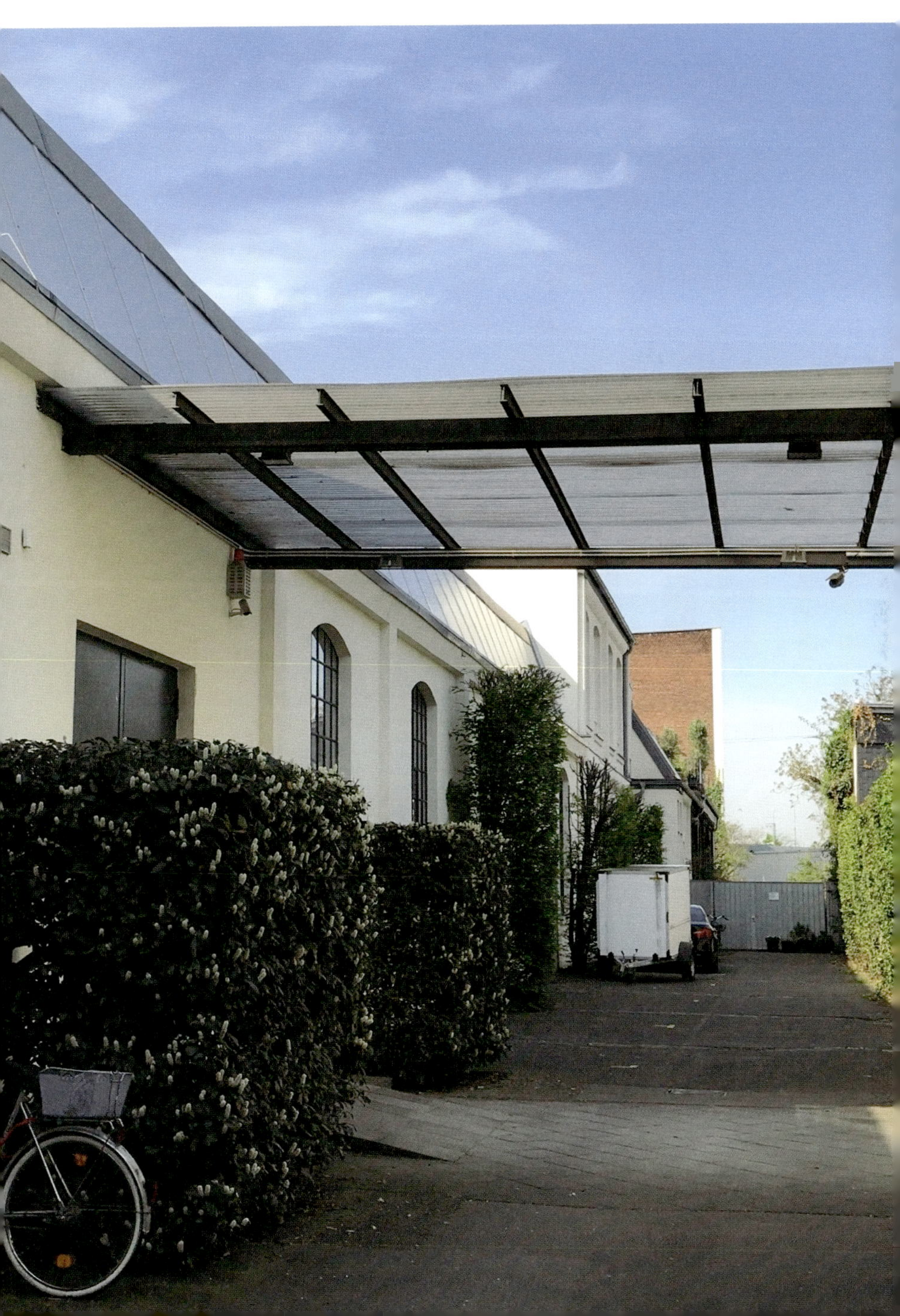

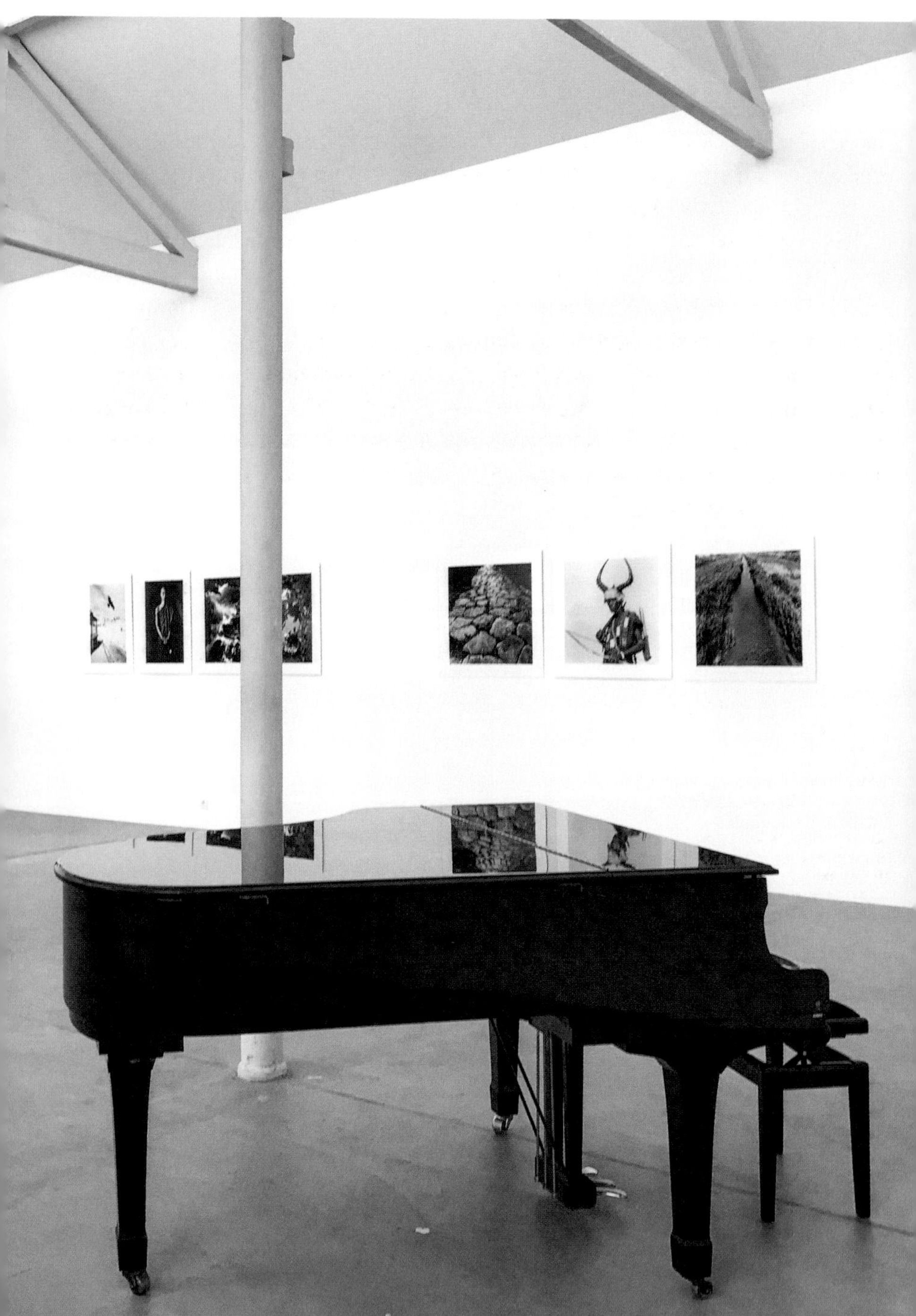

from artists Helmut Newton, Jock Sturges, Olaf Martens, Herlinde Koelbl, Lee Friedländer, and Thomas Karsten is another focal point of the collection. In painting, Michael Horbach represented Heinz Zolper, Blalla W. Hallmann, Thomas Huber, Werner Wefers, Dieter Teusch, Edgar Tezak, Karl Heidelbach, and Peter Angermann in his Horbach Gallery from 1986 to 1991.

The restored brick building, which Horbach acquired in 2010, used to be the headquarters of the Cologne police equestrian squadron, followed by a laundry before it was converted into a gallery and studio building. In the future, Michael Horbach will permanently display works from his collection in at least one of the foundation's rooms. At irregular intervals, the entire exhibition space will be filled with pieces from the collection. On average, eight exhibitions are organized each year in the approximately 750 m^2 foundation rooms.

Kunsträume from the Michael Horbach Foundation
Wormser Str. 23 (rear courtyard)
D-50677 Cologne, Germany
Phone: +49 221 29993378
info@michael-horbach-stiftung.de
michael-horbach-stiftung.de/kunstraeume

Opening hours
Wed and Fri 3:30–6:30 p.m., Sun 11 a.m.–2 p.m. as well as by appointment
Guided tours, events, and concerts are held at irregular intervals in the exhibition rooms.

Entrance fees
Free admission

Arrival by public transportation
From Cologne's main station you can reach Chlodwigplatz in fifteen minutes with tram 16 (direction Bonn/Bad Godesberg). From there, it is a ten-minute walk to the foundation.

Restaurant tips
Casa di Biase in Cologne's Südstadt offers Italian cuisine (casadibiase.de; Eifelplatz 4; closed Sundays). Those seeking a typical Kölsch pub should visit the Gasthaus zur Eule (gasthaus-zur-eule.de; Alteburger Str. 299; closed Tuesdays). The Persian restaurant Oxin is on the same street (Alteburger Str. 35; noon only by request, closed Mondays). Near Chlodwigplatz, the coffee bar of the nonprofit organization Kunsthaus KAT18 offers vegetarian lunch dishes as well as coffee and cake from Tuesday to Saturday (kunsthauskat18.de; Kartäuserwall 18).

Extra tip
Very close to the foundation, Berlin artist Katharina Grosse sprayed the Chlodwigplatz U-Bahn station with a colorful wall painting. The Museum Ludwig is internationally known for its top-class collection and outstanding temporary exhibitions (museum-ludwig.de; Heinrich-Böll-Platz). The Kolumba—the art museum of the Archdiocese of Cologne—, designed by Peter Zumthor, is particularly exciting for architecture fans (kolumba.de; Kolumbastr. 4).

198
KAT_A

Initiated by art collector Andra Lauffs-Wegner, KAT_A, an abbreviation for Kunst am Turm_Andra, is a forum for contemporary international art. Since the end of 2014, installations, sculptures, video works, paintings, and photographs have been presented in the interior and exterior spaces of the spacious grounds around the historic tower in the Bad Honnef district of Rhöndorf. Now a partner in the Rabenhorst ("Rotbäckchen") company, Andra Lauffs-Wegner accompanied her father as a child on museum and gallery visits and grew up amid her parents' collection with essential works by European artists from the 1960s and 1970s, Pop Art, Arte Povera, Conceptual Art, and Minimalism. As a student, she bought her first sculpture, *Sleeping Woman* (1970) by George Segal, which is still her favorite work. Today, the business economist and art historian, who wrote her diploma thesis at the end of the 1970s on "Modern Art as Capital Investment," is primarily concerned with photographic and object art as well as conceptual works. She collects both established and young artists, with whom she creates personal relationships as much as possible. Her collection of over 400 works also includes artists from the post-digital generation such as Simon Denny, Yngve Holen, and Anne Imhof, who won the Golden Lion for the German Pavilion at the 2017 Venice Biennale. Michael Sailstorfer, Anna K. E., Katharina Grosse, Isa Genzken, and Yves Klein are also represented in the collection. Among the photographers are Thomas Ruff, Stan Douglas, Candida Höfer, Thomas Struth, Annette Kelm, Wolfgang Tillmans, and Katharina Sieverding.

Andra Lauffs-Wegner had been involved in committees of various art institutions for some time, when, as she was walking her dog, she noticed renovation work in the historic Hedwig House, which had been unused for years. She rented the building and put her plans for a private exhibition space into concrete terms. The heart of the 400 m^2 exhibition space is the former dining room on the ground floor of the building, which was used as a military hospital during the Second World War and later as a Müttergenesungswerk (a facility of the German Maternal Convalescence

KAT_A
Bad Honnef, North Rhine-Westphalia

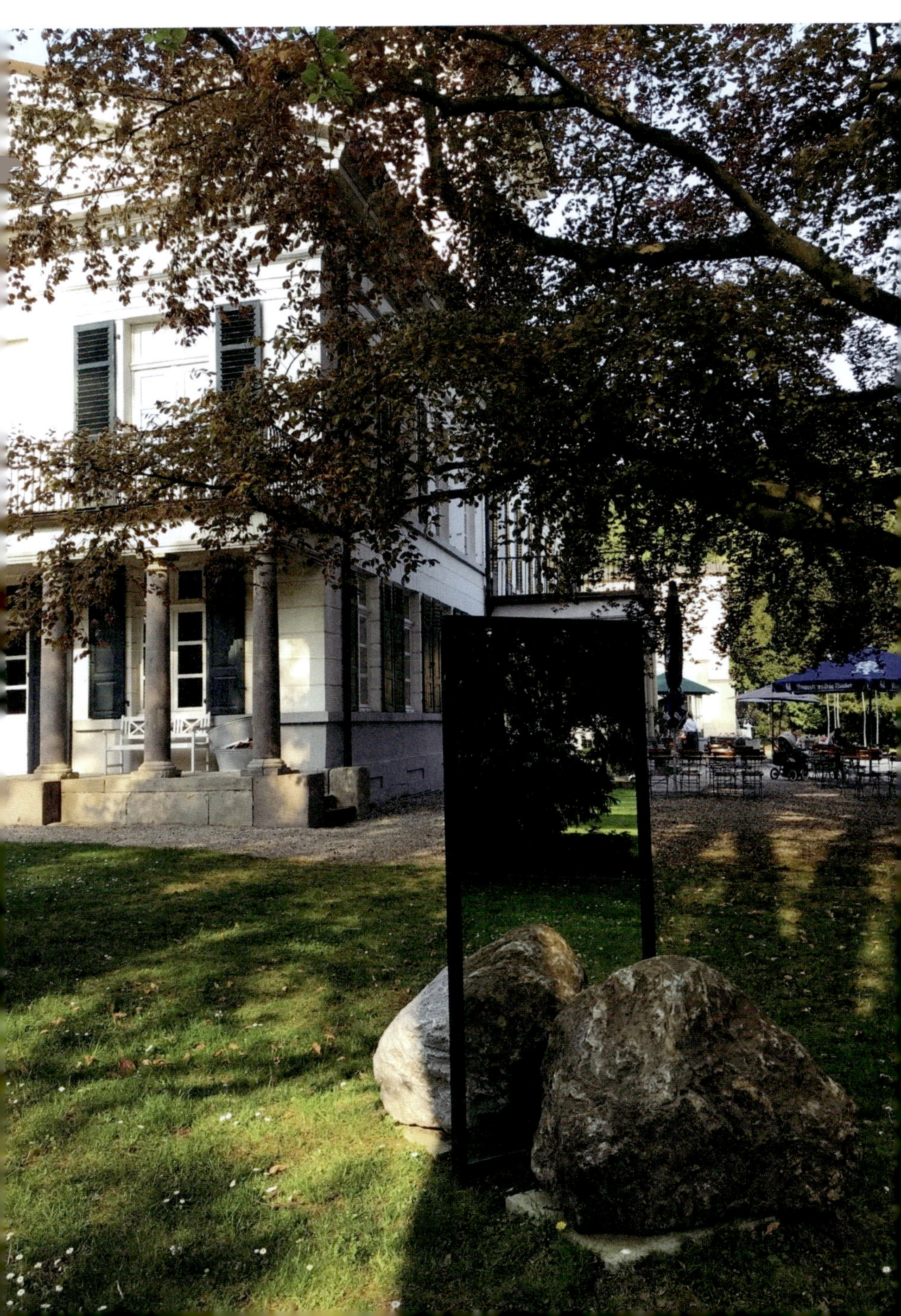

Movement). With its raw, unpainted walls, a spacious room structured by two columns and a partial wall offers a grandiose stage for the annually changing, mostly thematic exhibitions. The former chapel of the Müttergenesungswerk, only a few steps away, also belongs to the KAT_A exhibition space. Here, the 1.7-ton installation *Untitled* (2014) by Tatiana Trouvé is located next to a light object by Ólafur Elíasson. Upon entering the chapel, one notices that Andra Lauffs-Wegner particularly appreciates the play with artistic interventions that put familiar perceptions to the test. The temporary exhibitions curated by her, in which positions of internationally established and young artists from the collection are placed in new contexts, also often raise current art-historical questions.

In addition to the exhibition rooms of KAT_A, there is a publicly accessible park from the former Villa Merkens, which, with its rare, old trees, provides an attractive setting for more than ten objects and sculptures from the collection. Immediately visible is the palm installation *Neusilber* (New Silver, 2015) by David Zink Yi, made of aluminum and stainless steel and positioned in front of the terrace of the restaurant of the classicist villa Haus im Turm. There are also two sculptures by Alicja Kwade, the sculptures *HB-DAA* (2007) by Michael Sailstorfer, several interactive garden benches by Jeppe Hein, and the round bench *Chelsea Kramer* (2013) by Michaela Meise.

KAT_A
Bad Honnef, North Rhine-Westphalia

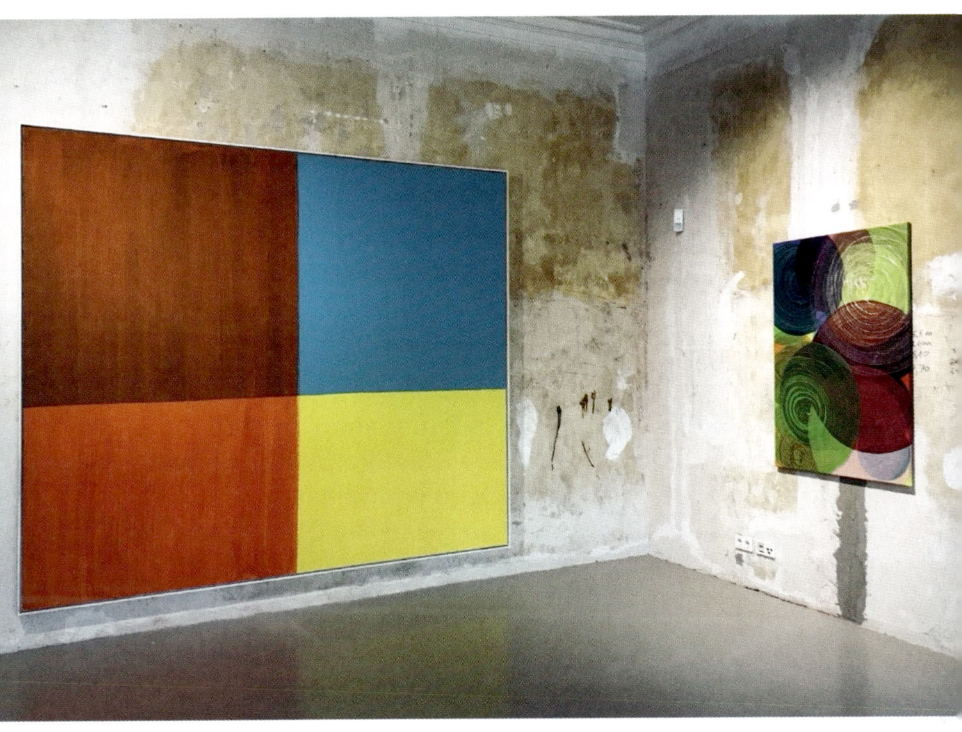

KAT_A
Drachenfelsstr. 4–7
53604 Bad Honnef-Rhöndorf
Fax: +49 2224 10606
info@kat-a.de
kat-a.de

Opening hours
Visitors to the exhibition must register at least one day in advance on the ticketing page of the website (kat-a.de/tickets). Visitors are usually guided through the exhibition by art collector Andra Lauffs-Wegner. At CAFÉ KAT_A, visitors can enjoy coffee and use the small library by appointment.

Entrance fees
Adults / Groups of five or more / Students: €10 / €7 / free of charge
The entire proceeds from ticket sales are doubled by KAT_A and donated to an art institution.

Arrival by public transportation
The station Bad Honnef-Rhöndorf can be reached either by tram line 66 or by regional train. From there it is only a few minutes' walk to KAT_A. From Drachenfelsstraße, cross the courtyard between the wine shop and the Haus im Turm restaurant.

Parking
Parking is available in the area.

Restaurant tips
The Haus im Turm restaurant serves German and Mediterranean cuisine with a view of the sculpture park (hausimturm.de; Drachenfelsstr. 4–7; Wed–Sun evenings and for lunch on weekends). The Café Profittlich is famous for its legendary Herrentorte, and a corn-flour bread created by Federal Chancellor Adenauer (cafe-profittlich.de; Drachenfelsstr. 21; closed Mondays). Vier Jahreszeiten Biomarkt & Bistro offers wholefood cuisine and cakes (naturkost-vierjahreszeiten.de; Rhöndorfer Str. 40). Fish lovers will be thrilled by the French restaurant Chamai (restaurant-chamai.de; Löwenburgstr. 35, closed Tuesdays). The best ice cream in the region can be found in the Eis-Atelier (eis-atelier.com; Rheinpromenade 6).

Extra tips
On the other side of the Rhine is the architecturally interesting Arp Museum Bahnhof Rolandseck. The bar area in the museum bistro designed by Anton Henning is definitely worth checking out (arpmuseum.org; Hans-Arp-Allee 1, 53424 Remagen). A journey into German history can be made in the Adenauerhaus (adenauerhaus.de; Konrad-Adenauer-Str. 8c).

202
Skulpturenpark Köln

Not far from the Zoobrücke, there is an artistic open-air treasure on the banks of the Rhine. Thanks to the unparalleled commitment of Michael and Eleonore Stoffel, a sculpture park was established here in 1997 as a meeting place for people, art, and nature. The City of Cologne provided the site, and everything else was the responsibility of the Gesellschaft der Freunde des Skulpturenparks Köln (Society of Friends of the Cologne Sculpture Park) initiated by Michael Stoffel. After the death of Eleonore Stoffel, who, until 2007, dedicatedly cared for the legacy of her husband, who died in 2005, the Skulpturenpark Köln Foundation, founded in 2008, now continues the tradition of the KölnSkulptur exhibition series in the spirit of its patrons. This is done with the help of the Michael und Eleonore Stoffel Förderstiftung and the City of Cologne, which supports the sculpture park as a cultural institution with annual financial compensation in the form of an operating grant.

The Skulpturenpark Köln changes continuously and is reopened every two years in a redesigned form under the care of independent curators. The contemporary sculptures artfully integrated into the 35,000 m^2 park are either permanent loans from the Sammlung Stoffel or temporary loans from various art institutions and artists. Some of the works are new productions and were made by the artists especially for the area. More than forty-five selected sculptures by established and young artists enter into a dialogue with each other in this natural environment. Works by internationally renowned artists such as Anish Kapoor, James Lee Byars, Dan Graham, Jenny Holzer, Rosemarie Trockel, Bernar Venet, Per Kirkeby, and Thomas Schütte can be found, as well as numerous more recent positions such as sculptures by Andrea Büttner and Claudia Comte. The KölnSkulptur exhibitions are intended not only to present the modern manifestations of the medium of outdoor sculpture but also to reflect sociopolitical themes.

Skulpturenpark Köln
Cologne, North Rhine-Westphalia

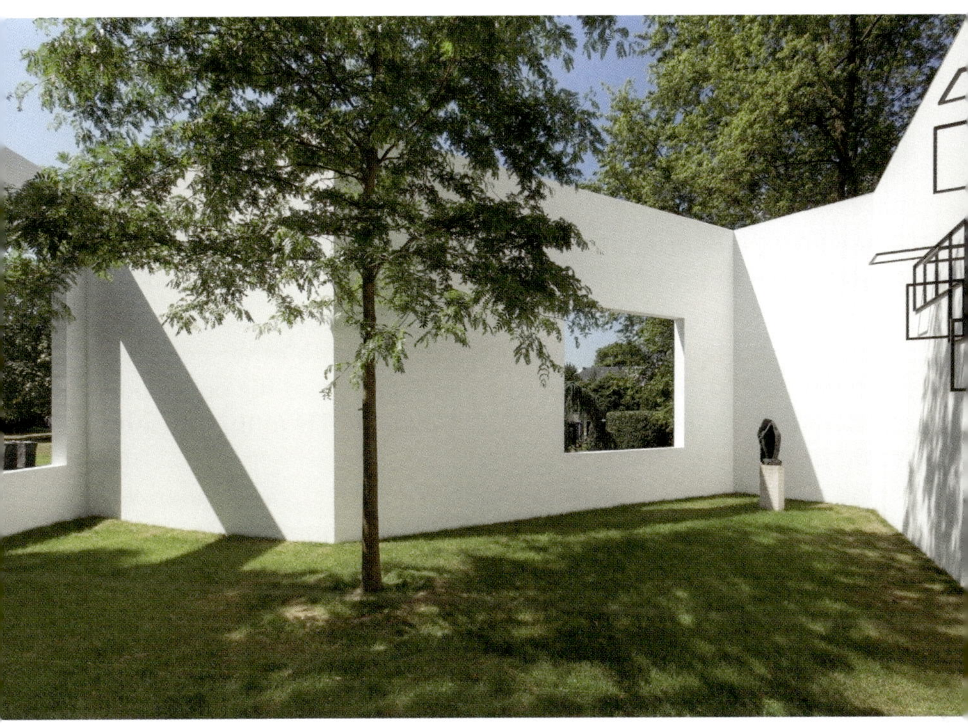

Skulpturenpark Köln
Riehler Str. (main entrance)
D-50668 Cologne
Phone: +49 221 33668860
info@skulpturenparkkoeln.de
skulpturenparkkoeln.de

Opening hours

April to September daily 10:30 a.m.–7 p.m., October to March daily 10:30 a.m.–5 p.m.
Public tours take place every first Sunday of the month at 3 p.m.; €8 / reduced €2. Meeting point: park entrance on Riehler Straße. QR codes at the respective exhibits accompany the visit to the exhibition with text and, in part, audio contributions.

Entrance fees

Free admission

Parking

Skulpturenpark Köln is located north of the main railway station on the left bank of the Rhine at the corner of Konrad-Adenauer-Ufer/Zoobrücke. Parking is available under the Zoobrücke and in the Zoo multistory car park.

Arrival by public transportation

From Dom/Hauptbahnhof, take tram 16 to Reichenspergerplatz or tram 18 to Riehl Zoo/Flora. From the station, it is a half-hour stroll along the Rhine to the sculpture park.

Restaurant tips

In the eastern corner of the sculpture park, it is possible to enjoy fine regional and international cuisine as well as excellent wines with a beautiful view at Richters Restaurant am Rhein (richters-koeln.de; Konrad-Adenauer-Ufer 115). Exceptional Italian cuisine is offered in the Zippiri Gourmetwerkstatt (zippiri.de; Riehler Str. 73; closed Tuesdays). Creative, down-to-earth gourmet dishes are served in the evening in the stylish NADA restaurant (nadakoeln.de; Clever Str. 32; closed Sundays and public holidays). In the cool LADEN EIN, an inexpensive stationary pop-up restaurant, guests are served and surprised with new concepts by different chefs every two weeks (laden-ein.com; Blumenthalstr. 66; closed Sundays).

Extra tip

A visit to the sculpture park can be combined with a visit to the art spaces of the Michael Horbach Foundation (see p. 194).

204 Foundation Conceptual Art with SCHROTH COLLECTION

Since 2007, industrial engineer, inventor, and entrepreneur Carl-Jürgen Schroth opened his home, and his living room, in the former Marienschule in Soest several times a year. There he presented his latest purchases in dialogue with other collection items. Since 2016, he has been showing parts of his collection in his own exhibition room, the ROOM SCHROTH in the Museum Wilhelm Morgner.

The city fathers of the medieval city of Soest were faced with the urgent task of renovating the aging Morgnerhaus multipurpose building. Looking for a permanent home for his steadily growing collection, Carl-Jürgen Schroth took the opportunity for a successful public-private partnership and supported the city financially with the renovation. Together, they tackled the task of developing the house into a full-fledged museum and a place for culture and education. The federal government and the state of North Rhine-Westphalia also supported the concept. Since the reopening of the house as Museum Wilhelm Morgner, up to four temporary exhibitions have been organized annually by the Foundation Conceptual Art in the 280 m^2 ROOM SCHROTH, in addition to special exhibitions and the permanent presentation of the eponym's work. Every two years, the foundation uses the entire house for a few summer months. During the exhibitions, the holdings of the SCHROTH COLLECTION are often supplemented by loans.

Carl-Jürgen Schroth was interested in art as a student and later trained his eye by visiting museums and exhibitions. He began to acquire his first works of art in the 1970s. While, in the beginning, it was mostly smaller works that thematized geometric analyses of nature, by the end of the 1980s his interest shifted to works that referred to the ideas of Concrete, Constructive, (Post)Minimalist, and Conceptual art and, because of their dimensions and materials, went beyond the private sphere. What has remained is the desire to

Foundation Conceptual Art with SCHROTH COLLECTION
Soest, North Rhine-Westphalia

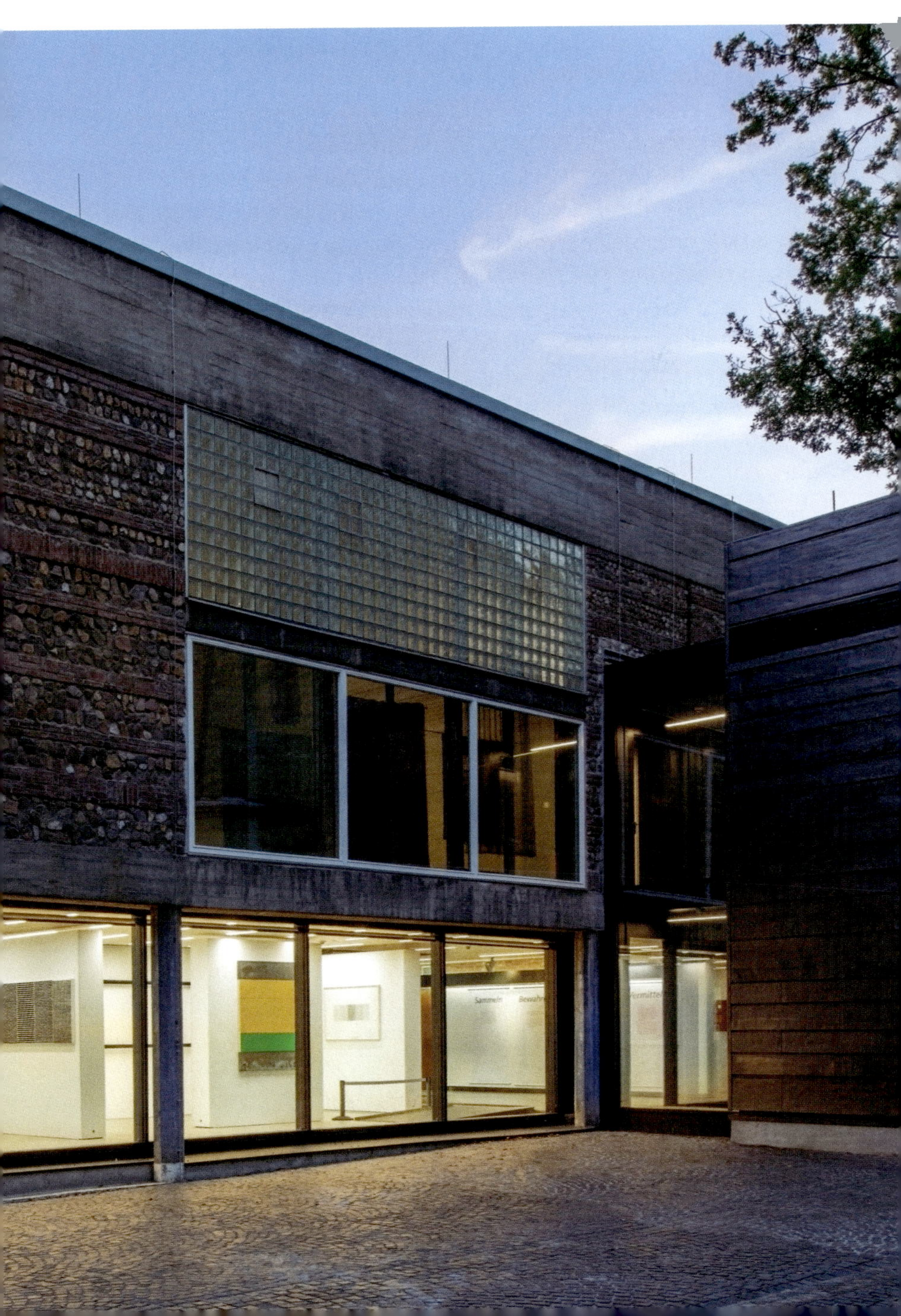

establish a personal relationship with each individual work and to cultivate a friendly relationship with the artists.

Today, the collection comprises over 430 works by around ninety artists, including Frank Gerritz, Winston Roeth, Ulrich Rückriem, Beat Zoderer, Heiner Thiels, Stefana McClure, Jill Baroff, Victor Vasarely, Günter Umberg, Günther Uecker, Hartmut Böhm, Daniel Buren, and François Morellet. These include light installations based on mathematical rules or measured data, works dealing with the theme of space, and conceptual works dealing with literature and printing in a reduced form.

To preserve the collection for the long term, Carl-Jürgen Schroth established the Foundation Conceptual Art in 2014, which serves as an independent, legal, and nonprofit foundation for the preservation, administration, and presentation of art from the SCHROTH COLLECTION.

Foundation Conceptual Art with SCHROTH COLLECTION
ROOM SCHROTH im Museum Wilhelm Morgner
Thomästr. 1
D-59494 Soest
Phone: +49 2921 1031131 (Museum)
museen@soest.de /
museum-wilhelm-morgner.de
info@skk-soest.de /
skk-soest.de

Opening hours
Tue–Fri 2–5 p.m., Sat/Sun 11 a.m.–5 p.m.

Entrance fees
Adults / Reduced: €2 / €1
There are irregular public guided tours through the ROOM SCHROTH exhibitions.

Parking
Parking is difficult in the medieval alleys. You should follow the parking guidance system from Soest. The nearest parking garage is Isenacker / P3. On Thomästraße, there are also some parking spaces.

Arrival by public transportation
The Soest railway station is 1 km away from the museum.

Restaurant tips
The Pilgrimhaus hotel and restaurant, the oldest inn in Westphalia, serves hearty, regionally influenced dishes (pilgrimhaus.de; Jakobistr. 75). Rustic cuisine and home-brewed beer can be found at Brauhaus Zwiebel (brauhaus-zwiebel.de; Ulricherstr. 24). In the small restaurant FachWerk, delicious meals delight diners (fachwerk-soest.de; Am Seel 5). Homemade ice cream is available near the railway station at the Soest ice cream factory (eismanufaktur-soest.de; Brüdertor 4; closed in winter). The café and restaurant Paradies in the Stadtpark offers spelt cake and other organic farming delicacies (paradies-soest.de; Stadtpark 1).

Extra tips
A side trip to the Wiesenkirche, which is one of the most beautiful late Gothic hall churches in Germany and houses a famous window with the scene of the Westphalian Last Supper, as well as to the Dombauhütte with its attached green sandstone museum is always worthwhile. Soest residents are also proud of their almost completely preserved city wall. Even today, you can walk around the city on the wall and take a look at the green gardens of the old town (see soest.de). Anyone arriving in the city from Soest railway station will experience the spiritual charisma of the light art object *Ein Pilgerstab für Soest* (A Pilgrim's Staff for Soest, 2016) created by the Cologne artist duo Ursula Molitor and Vladimir Kuzmin.

Foundation Conceptual Art with SCHROTH COLLECTION
Soest, North Rhine-Westphalia

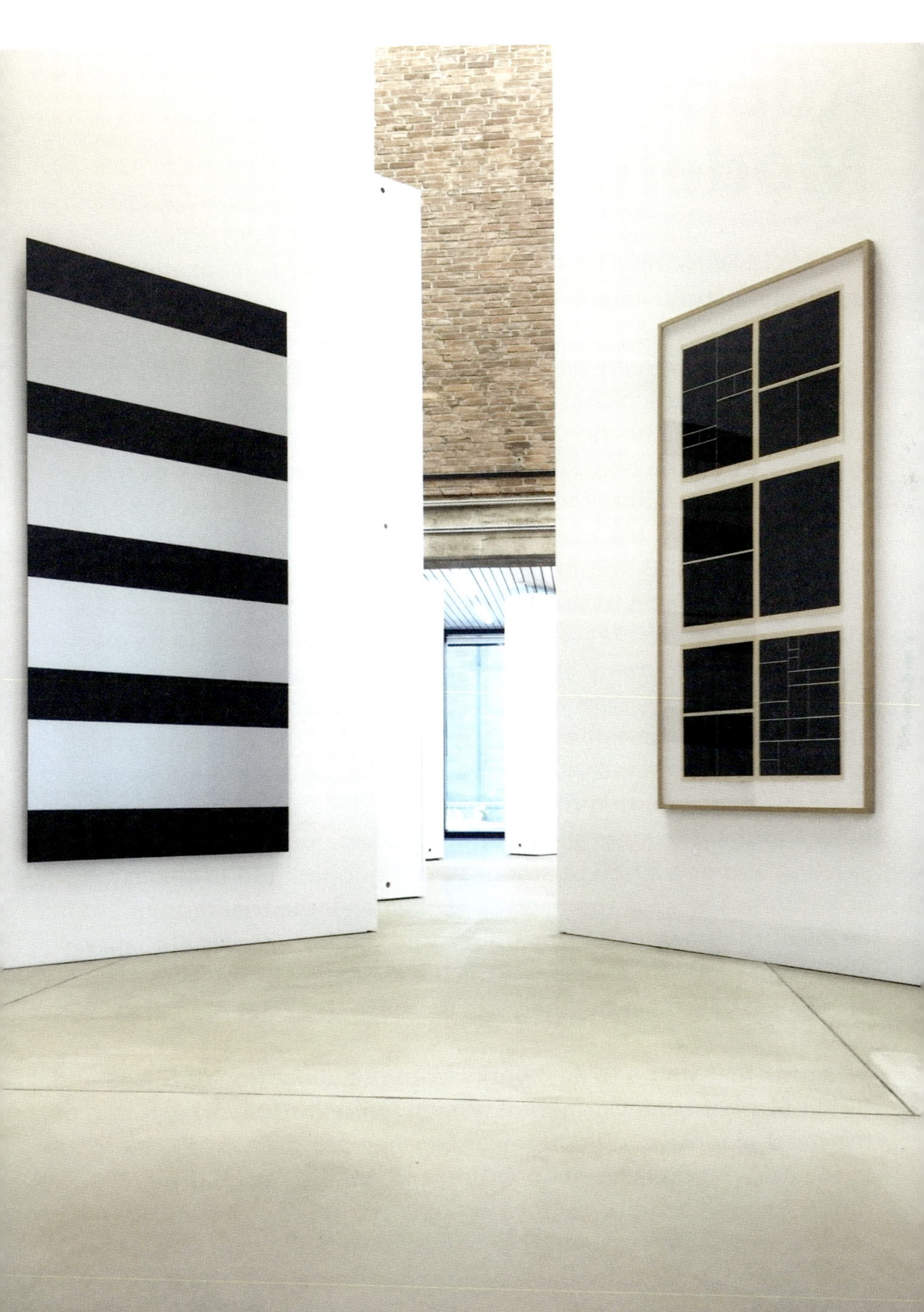

208
MKM Museum Küppersmühle of Modern Art

The MKM Museum Küppersmühle of Modern Art is located on the lively cultural mile in Duisburg's inner harbor. According to a master plan developed by the British architect Sir Norman Foster, the abandoned industrial harbor was transformed into a multifunctional service park as part of the International Building Exhibition Emscher Park (1989–1999). Swiss architects Herzog & de Meuron were awarded the contract for the elaborate conversion of the former Küppersmühle mill and storage building. Between 1997 and 1999, they gutted the rooms and created a three-story building with around 3,600 m^2 of exhibition space within the historic brick façade. An addition to the building in the form of a staircase made of terracotta concrete, which represents a work of art in its own right, has thrilled many visitors. The architecture of the entire building captivates with its clarity and reduction to the essentials and will also be continued in the extension of the museum, which is to be completed in 2020. As before, Herzog & de Meuron's design is based on that of the MKM and the architecture of the inner harbor. The steel silos from the 1930s, located between the existing and new brick buildings, will be connected to the exhibition floors. The silos themselves remain an industrial monument in terms of their external appearance and their original materiality. A viewing platform is planned for the roof zone of the silos. The new four-story main building will increase the exhibition area by a further 2,500 m^2.

The MKM is home to key works from the collection of Sylvia and Ulrich Ströher from Darmstadt, which, with 2,000 works, is one of the most extensive collections of German art after 1945. The focus at the MKM is on Informel painting and painting from the 1970s to the 1990s, but sculpture, drawing, and photography are also presented. Almost everything that has written German art history is represented, especially the "founder generation" of the Informel.

MKM Museum Küppersmühle of Modern Art
Duisburg, North Rhine-Westphalia

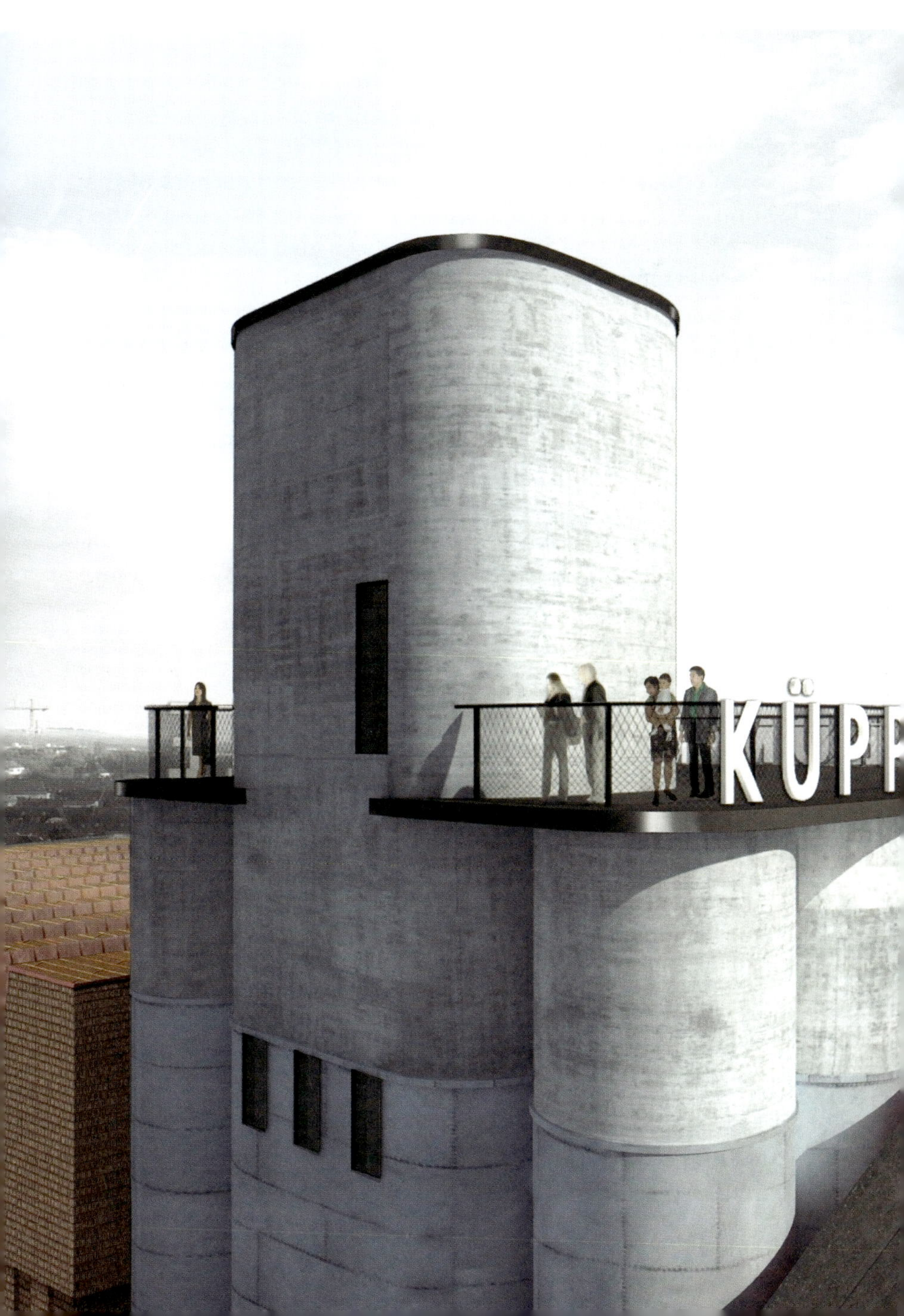

The collection contains numerous works from various creative phases by internationally renowned artists such as Georg Baselitz, Anselm Kiefer, Markus Lüpertz, Gerhard Richter, K. O. Götz, Imi Knoebel, Markus Lüpertz, and Candida Höfer. The extension will make it possible to present the oeuvres and careers of the collection's artists within a broader context. In the future, the presentation of the permanent collection will also be supplemented by up to four temporary exhibitions each year: retrospectives of renowned artists, thematic group exhibitions, presentations of current developments of individual artists, or the art scene of a country.

Since the museum was founded in 1986, the Stiftung für Kunst und Kultur e. V., located in Bonn Bad Godesberg, has been responsible for the overall organization and conception of the MKM (stiftungkunst.de). It is financed almost exclusively by sponsors from the business world and by donations. The extension is funded by the private MKM Foundation founded by Sylvia and Ulrich Ströher.

MKM Museum Küppersmühle of Modern Art Duisburg, North Rhine-Westphalia

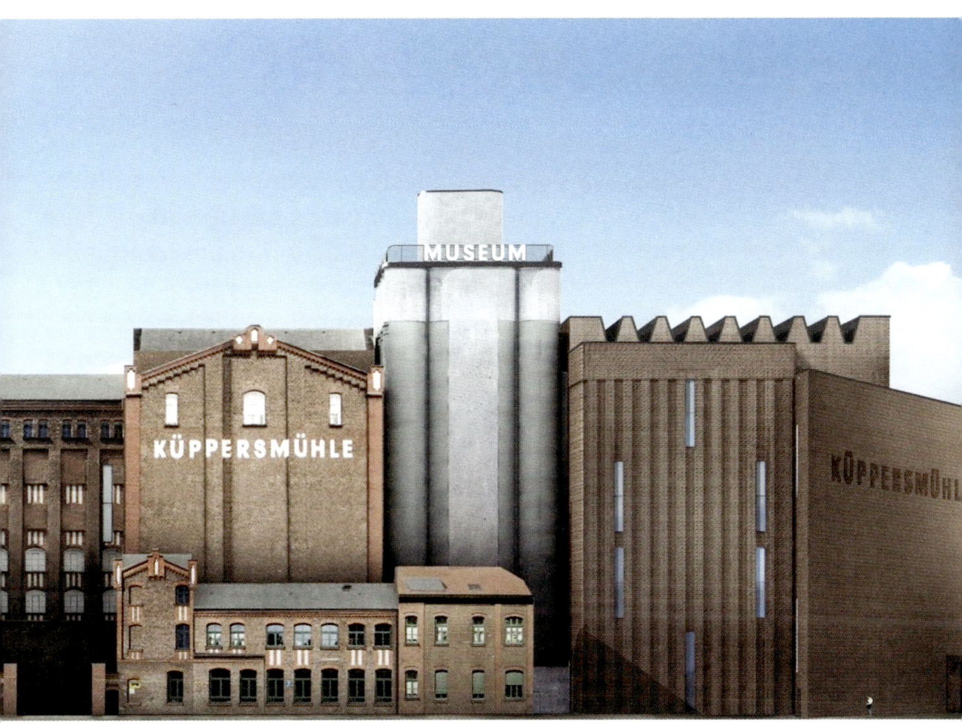

MKM Museum Küppersmühle of Modern Art
Duisburg Inner Harbor
Philosophenweg 55
D-47051 Duisburg
Phone: +49 203 30194811
office@museumkueppersmuehle.de
museum-kueppersmuehle.de

Opening hours
Wed 2–6 p.m., Thu–Sun 11 a.m.–6 p.m., holidays 11 a.m.–6 p.m. Public guided tours of the current exhibition and the collection, which are included in the admission fee, take place every Sunday at 3 p.m.

Entrance fees
Adults / Reduced / Children and students ages 6 and over / Special exhibition only:
€9 / €4.50 / €2 / €6

Parking
Visitors can park free of charge for three hours in the parking lot opposite the MKM, if they have their ticket validated in the MKM.

Arrival by public transportation
From the Duisburg main station, for example, take bus line 934 in the direction of Duisburg Betr. Am Unkelstein to the Hansegracht stop.

Restaurant tips
The inner harbor area in Duisburg is an excellent example of a successful structural change in the Ruhr area. There are numerous restaurants near the museum. The museum complex is home to the upscale Küppersmühle Restaurant. Here, innovative regional dishes can be enjoyed with a wonderful view of the inner harbor (kueppersmuehle-restaurant.de; Philosophenweg 49–51). Delicious Thai cuisine is served in the small Amazing Thai Restaurant (amazingthai.restaurant; Stresemannstr. 2).

Extra tips
For drivers, a trip to the impressive industrial monument in the Duisburg-Nord Landscape Park is worthwhile, particularly as part of an informative guided tour. In the evening, an impressive light installation bathes the blast furnace in spectacular light (landschaftspark.de; Emscherstr. 71). A visit to the MKM can be easily combined with a visit to the DKM Museum in the city center (see p. 180).

212 Museum Schloss Moyland

The Museum Schloss Moyland successfully combines art, culture, and nature. In addition to the historical moated castle and gardens, the heart of the museum, which is embedded in the Lower Rhine landscape, is a collection of modern and contemporary art—the world's largest collection of works by Joseph Beuys is housed here—as well as special international exhibitions. The existence of the multifaceted collection is based on the commitment and former private collection of the brothers Hans (1929–2002) and Franz Joseph (born 1933) van der Grinten. The brothers began to enthusiastically collect art as early as 1950. Coming from an agricultural family, they studied art history and organized numerous "stable exhibitions" in empty parts of the buildings on their parents' farm in Kranenburg. Here they also organized the first solo exhibition of their friend Joseph Beuys. Over the ensuing decades, they became the biggest collectors of his work. Early on, Beuys advised them to collect photographs, English etchings, and Art Nouveau, as well as contemporary Lower Rhine artists. With sure instinct and great passion, a collection of drawings, paintings, sculptural objects, and prints from the nineteenth century to the modern era was created. Eagerly searching for a suitable home for their huge collection, Johannes Rau, the then Prime Minister of North Rhine-Westphalia, fulfilled their lifelong dream of having their own museum. Perhaps this support can even be seen as a late redemption; after all, it was Rau who as NRW's Minister of Science in 1972 expelled Professor Beuys from the Düsseldorf Art Academy. In 1990, with great political support, the van der Grinten brothers—as donors of the art collection, the Joseph Beuys Archive, and the museum library together with the federal state of North Rhine-Westphalia and the Steengracht family—founded the "Stiftung Museum Schloss Moyland, Sammlung van der Grinten, Joseph Beuys Archiv des Landes Nordrhein-Westfalen." The state provided the financial foundation for the reconstruction of the palace and is still responsible for most of the operating costs. The couple Baron and Baroness von

Museum Schloss Moyland
Bedburg-Hau, North Rhine-Westphalia

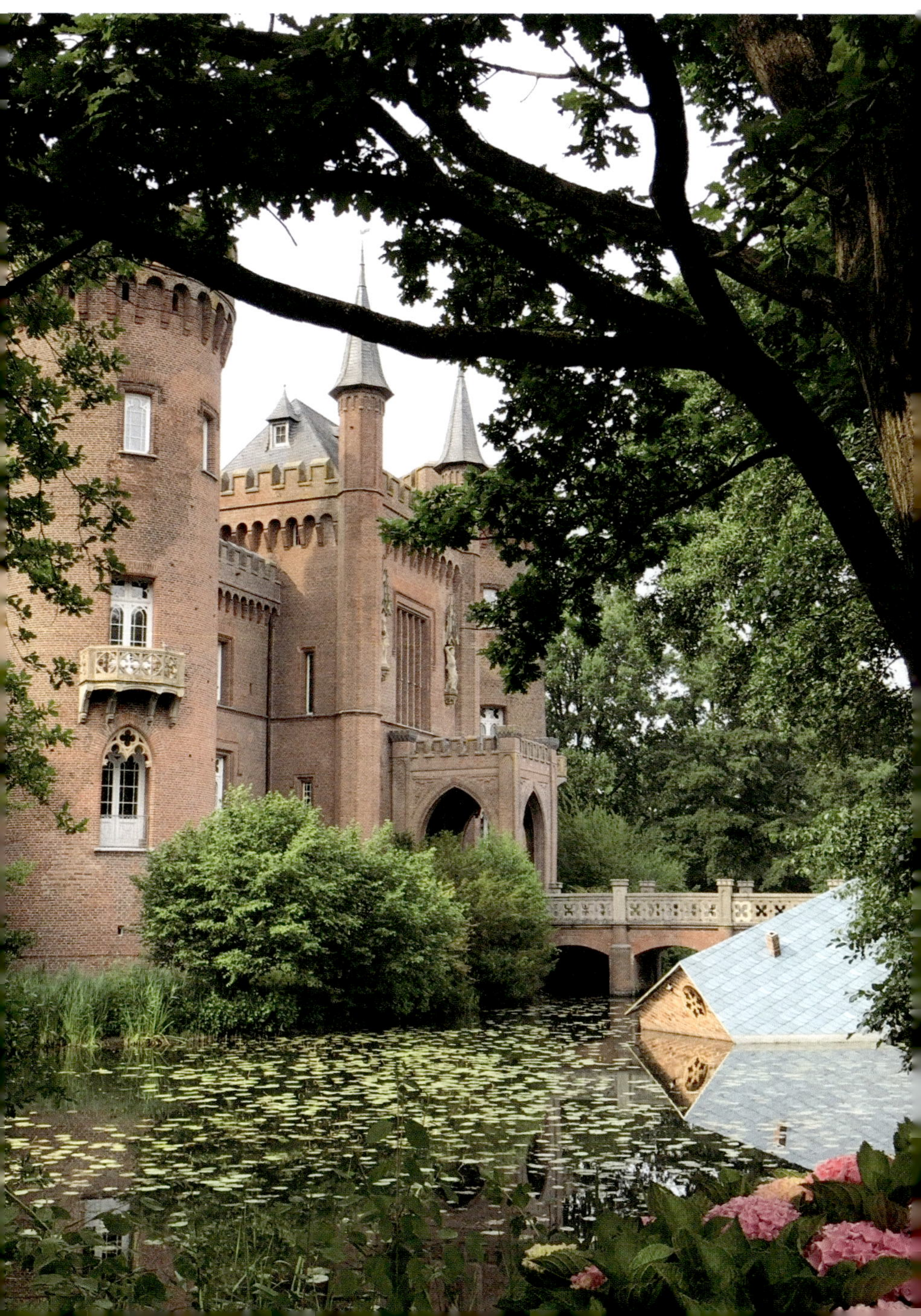

Steengracht donated the castle and the park. In the nineteenth century, Cologne Cathedral architect Ernst Friedrich Zwirner redesigned Moyland Castle in neo-Gothic style. Until 1945, it was the residence of the von Steengracht family, who had acquired the complex in 1766. After the castle was bombed and destroyed in the Second World War, it stood empty and fell into ruin. Until the end of the 1980s, no donors could be found for its restoration. And so, the establishment of the foundation and the associated cooperation of three different interest groups was not an undisputed or problem-free idea, but a great win for all lovers of art. The museum was opened in 1997 after reconstruction under the direction of architect Karl Ebbers. Previously, the garden had been laid out according to historical traditions. Presently, it combines a landscape garden with a sculpture park in which over sixty works by James Lee Byars, Erwin Heerich, Eduardo Chillida, and other sculptors can be found. The Förderverein Museum Schloss Moyland e. V., founded in 1987, still accompanies and supports the work of the museum; the district of Kleve and the community of Bedburg-Hau are also involved in museum operations. The two collectors as artistic directors essentially shaped the Museum Schloss Moyland in the development and early phase. They now had an opportunity to place the collection with works from the eighteenth century in a spiritual relationship with the works of Joseph Beuys and to add further exhibits. In 2010, a new concept for presentation of the collection's contents was executed, as well as a redesigned palace interior by architectural office Hilmer & Sattler und Albrecht. The quite dense Moyländer Hängung by the van der Grinten brothers has been abandoned. With its reopening in 2011, the museum was transformed from a collector's museum into a museum with an art collection and exhibition program. Nevertheless, the works from Joseph Beuys acquired by the brothers are still a major focus of the 115,000 works today. In addition to individual works of modern art, there are entire complexes of works by other artists such as André Thomkins, Rudolf Schoofs, Erwin Heerich, and James Lee Byars.

Since 2011, thematic and monographic exhibitions, as well as changing presentations of the art collection, have been the main components of the museum program. Before entering the castle, it is possible to first visit the former stables on the right, where special exhibitions are shown twice a year in the modern exhibition hall. The castle itself can be visited on three levels: in the basement, sculptures from the eighteenth century to the present day are permanently on display. The history of the castle is presented in another room. On the ground floor, there are temporary exhibitions related to the collection. The second floor is exclusively devoted to works by Joseph Beuys with thematic exhibitions that change twice a year. On the third floor, next to the art workshop, is the ascent to the North Tower. A view of the surrounding area can be enjoyed after ascending 194 steep stairs leading to a viewing platform.

Museum Schloss Moyland
Am Schloss 4
D-47551 Bedburg-Hau
Phone: +49 2824 9510-60
info@moyland.de
moyland.de

Opening hours
April–September Tue–Fri 11 a.m.–6 p.m., Sat/Sun 10 a.m.–6 p.m., October–March Tue–Sun 11 a.m.–5 p.m.
The North Rhine-Westphalia Joseph Beuys Archive can be visited by appointment.
On Sundays and public holidays, various public guided tours take place in the afternoon (€3 plus admission).
There are also special and family tours, workshops for children and adults, as well as readings and concerts. The annual Herb Garden Festival and the Arts and Crafts Christmas Market and other special day events are very popular.
There is a café and a shop in front of the castle.

Entrance fees
Adults / Reduced / Family ticket (including sculpture park and gardens): €7 / €3 / €15

Arrival by public transportation
From the train stations Kleve or Xanten, take bus 44 in the direction of Moyland to the castle. The entrance is behind the large car park on the left.

Parking
There is a large car park in front of the castle. The entrance and the castle itself can be reached in a few minutes.

Restaurant tips
Regional dishes are served in the modern Landgasthof Westrich (landgasthof-westrich.de: Bienenstr. 26). Traditional dishes are offered at the Ratskeller Kalkar at the Marktplatz (ratskeller-kalkar.com; Markt 20, 47546 Kalkar). Authentic Japanese cuisine can be tasted at Fujiyama (fujiyama-kleve.de; Hoffmannallee 1, 47533 Kleve).

Extra tips
A visit to the restored Museum Kurhaus Kleve is particularly recommended. From 1957 to 1964, Joseph Beuys' studio was located in the then empty Kurhaus. The museum is also home to the estate of the Rhineland sculptor Ewald Mataré, Beuys's teacher (museum-kurhaus.de; Tiergartenstr. 41, 47533 Kleve).

216 Philara Collection

With the rooms of the Philara Collection, opened in the summer of 2016, art collector and real estate agent Gil Bronner has created a special place for lovers of contemporary art in the Düsseldorf district of Flingern. Gil Bronner inherited his ability to deal with sophisticated art. His parents, Dan and Cary, were art enthusiasts and began collecting early on, primarily works of classical modern art. Cary Bronner comes from Israel, Dan from the Czech Republic. Both initially lived in Israel and came via detours to Düsseldorf, where Gil was born in 1962. The fact that Gil Bronner thinks long-term and will pass on his enthusiasm for art to his descendants is guaranteed, as the name of his collection already consists of the first names of his children Philip and Lara.

He began building up his collection in the mid-1990s. Although his initial interest was in the Leipzig School artists, more than twenty years ago he set himself the task of promoting local, up-and-coming artists because of his strong ties to the Düsseldorf Art Academy. In 2006, Bronner acquired the former Leitz building in Düsseldorf-Reisholz and converted it into a studio house, which was used by Düsseldorf Art Academy artists and classes. There he organized temporary exhibitions in one room with works by his favorites, which he also regularly purchased. Since 2008, three, and later five, temporary exhibitions per year have been organized, each with a presentation from the collection. In 2014, Bronner had the opportunity to acquire a 6,000 m² site in Düsseldorf-Flingern, including the accompanying industrial halls near the galleries he frequently visited. Initially planned for a different use, it was not long before Gil Bronner decided to create a permanent home for his collection here. After the complex reconstruction of the former glass factory in a backyard, hidden and cleverly integrated into the urban structure, the collection rooms with an exhibition area of approximately 1,700 m² were created with flexible usage. Commissioned with the task, Düsseldorf planning office Sieber Architekten has succeeded in paying tribute to the character of the industrial halls. In addition to the crane runway, part of the railway tracks which used to supply the Glaswerkstatt

Philara Collection
Düsseldorf, North Rhine-Westphalia

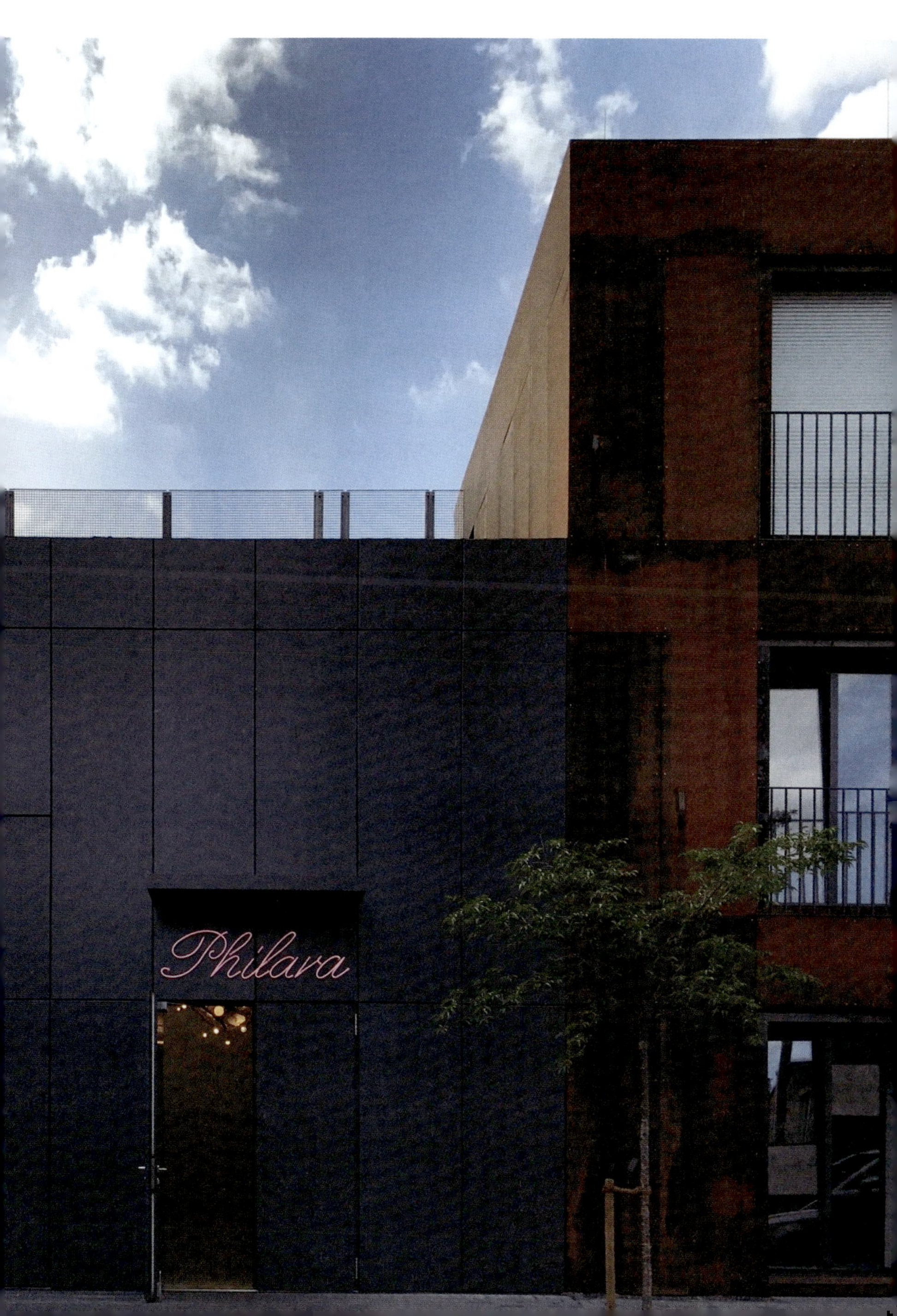

Lennartz are preserved. The floor plan of the exhibition area seems sacral, and the rooms are deliberately designed in a labyrinth-like manner. In addition to the large exhibition hall, the ground floor houses twelve cabinets for paper works (Bronner's particular preference) and for new media, and three rooms for temporary exhibitions. On the upper floor, there are four smaller cabinet rooms and a 550m^2 sculpture garden on the roof of the hall. Three guest studios and a kitchen with private rooms can be reached via a separate entrance.

Every year, up to four temporary exhibitions are curated in the approximately 200 m^2 rooms with loans or works from the collection. The exhibition hall and the cabinets are dedicated to the irregularly rotating presentation of the collection's holdings. Rooms and installations specially constructed for the site by individual artists are also shown here. Particularly exciting is the permanent walk-in installation *Artichoke Underground* by the Americans Jonah Freeman and Justin Lowe, which was exhibited in the Unlimited Section of Art Basel in 2014. Old architectural elements such as a staircase and a column are cleverly embedded in the installation. The salt room in the basement, which is part of the work in which visually attractive salt crystals are "grown," is built into the existing track section.

Today, the constantly growing art collection comprises over 1,400 works of various genres such as painting, sculpture, installation, photography, and drawing. The decisive feature of the collection's presentation is the juxtaposition of local newcomers with established artists such as Thomas Ruff, Andreas Gursky, Hans-Peter Feldmann, and internationally active artists such as Alicja Kwade, Gregor Hildebrandt, Tomás Saraceno, Kris Martin, Pae White, Rashid Johnson, and Monika Sosnowska. The lack of labels is intentional; instead, visitors receive an overview plan.

Both the building and the collection belong to Gill Bronner himself. The reconstruction of the area and the maintenance of the collection were or are being financed by the Cary and Dan-Georg Bronner Foundation, which is headed by Gill Bronner.

Philara Collection
Düsseldorf, North Rhine-Westphalia

Philara Collection

Birkenstr. 47
D-40233 Düsseldorf
Phone: +49 211 24862721
info@philara.de
philara.de

Opening hours

The Philara Collection is only accessible from Friday to Sunday with guided tours. A tour lasts about 75 minutes and is included in the price. To register, you will be asked to purchase an online ticket. However, last-minute visitors are usually able to arrange a booking on site. On Thursdays, the collection can be visited without a guided tour and without registration. Individual guided tours can also be booked in other languages.
Thu 4–8 p.m., without a guided tour
Fri tours start at 2 p.m. and 4 p.m. (at 4 p.m. in English if required)
Sat tours start at 2 p.m. and 4 p.m.
Sun tours start at noon and 3 p.m.
The collection is closed on Christmas holidays, New Year's Eve, New Year's Day, and Rose Monday. In August, the collection is closed for summer break.
Book presentations, performances, concerts, and other events are held regularly (see philara.de/en/program).
The café and restaurant Glas Lennarz is located in the collection rooms and is permanently equipped with works of art by Tobias Rehberger and Nevin Aladağ (open Thursdays to Sundays).

Entrance fees

Adults / Reduced (incl. Art Card Düsseldorf / Düsseldorf Card)
€10 / €5

Arrival by public transportation

The collection can be reached on foot in about fifteen minutes from the Düsseldorf main station by leaving the station to the right on Worringer Straße and then turning right into Ackerstraße and right again into Birkenstraße. Alternatively, take the tram 708 (direction Heinrichstr.) or 709 (direction Gerresheim) to the Birkenstraße stop (the stop is on Ackerstr). Then turn right into Birkenstraße. The collection can be reached on foot via the S-Bahn stop Wehrhahn with regional long-distance trains.

Parking

The collection has only limited parking space in the courtyard for visitors with reduced mobility. Since parking in the area is complicated, public transport is recommended.

Restaurant tips

The nearby Café Hüftgold offers homemade cakes and snacks all day long (cafehueftgold.de; Ackerstr. 113). The familiar living room of Italian Cucina Vitale impresses with its simple but tasty cuisine (vitaleonline.de, Ackerstr. 168b).

Extra tips

In the surrounding streets, there are numerous young galleries and several off-rooms as well as the spaces of designers and film companies.

220 JULIA STOSCHEK COLLECTION

In a listed factory building, since 2007, Düsseldorf-Oberkassel has been home to Germany's largest collection of time-based media art. Julia Stoschek impressively presents annually changing exhibitions from her collection of videos, photographs, and installations on two floors across a total area of 2,500 m^2.

Julia Stoschek discovered the reinforced concrete building at the end of 2004 during a walk down Schanzenstraße. The industrial building was constructed in 1907 for Die Bühne GmbH and initially used for the production of theater equipment, later by a bed and mattress factory, and after the Second World War until 2002 by the frame and slat manufacturer F. G. Conzen. It was only waiting to be awakened from its slumber. Julia Stoschek had Kuehn Malvezzi, an architectural firm in Berlin, convert the building into a unique art repository and exhibition venue with unpretentious simplicity.

To meet the requirements of both monument protection and light-sensitive media art, a kind of new building was created within the existing building. The exhibition floors are redesigned for the temporary exhibitions and optimally adapted to the various works of art. In the successful concept of room sequences, the sounds of the works are isolated from each other with the help of glass walls so that the video art does not have to be presented in individual cells—as is usually the case.

Germany's youngest major collector was born in 1975 and initially studied business administration. As the great-granddaughter of company founder Max Brose, together with her father and siblings, she is a Brose Fahrzeugteile GmbH & Co. KG shareholder.

Julia Stoschek is now considered so competent in the field of video and performance art that she has been a member of the board of trustees of KW Institute for Contemporary Art in Berlin since 2004 (deputy chairwoman since 2017), of the acquisition commission of the Kunstsammlung Nordrhein-Westfalen since 2011, and on the board of trustees at the MOCA Museum of Contemporary Art in Los Angeles since the end of 2018. Julia Stoschek was

JULIA STOSCHEK COLLECTION
Düsseldorf, North Rhine-Westphalia

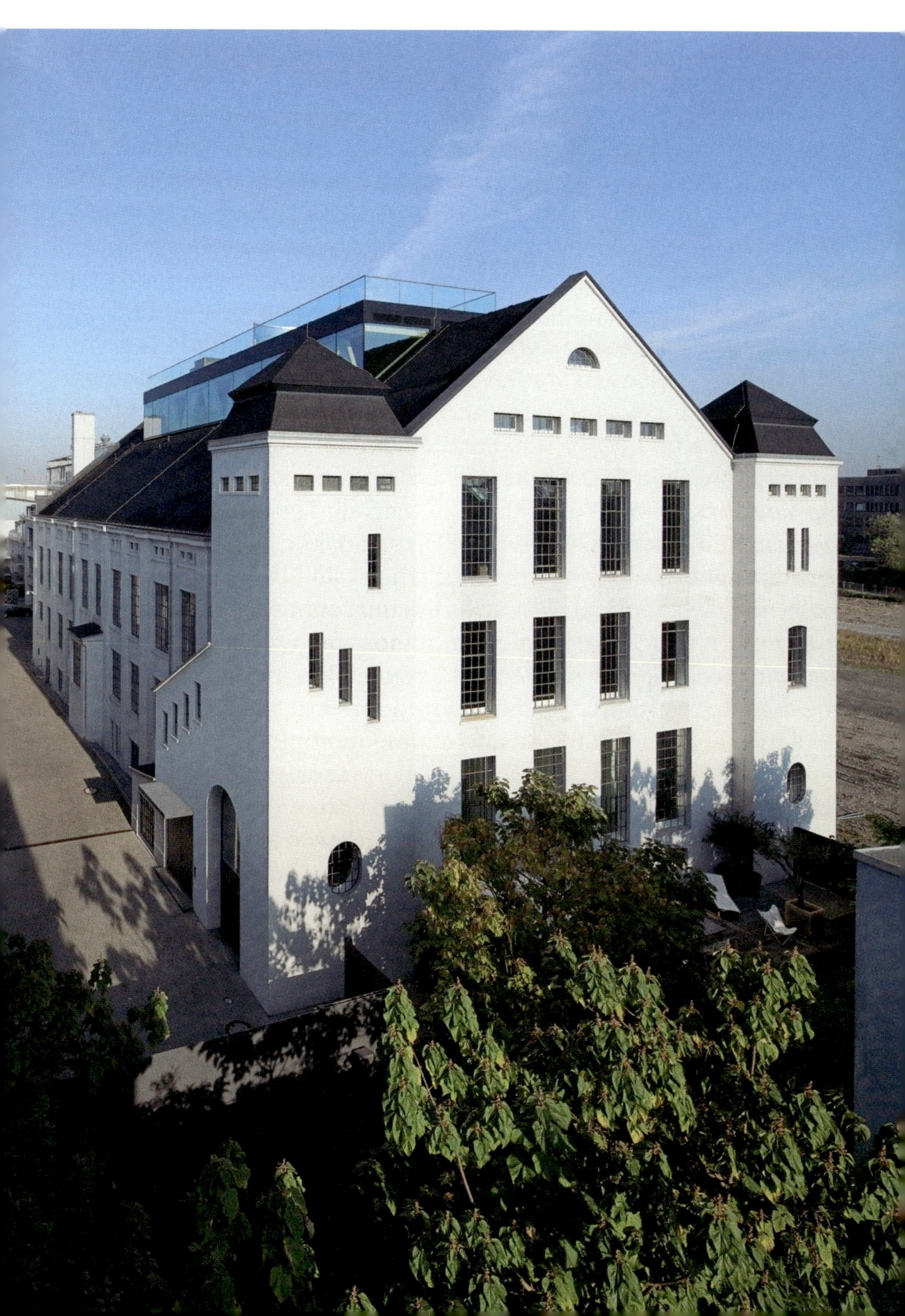

awarded the ART COLOGNE Prize 2018 for her mediation work in the field of time-based media art.

Her first video work, Aaron Young's *High Performance* (2000), was purchased in 2004. Stoschek's purchases initially focused not only on contemporary works but also on the classics of the media art genre, especially from the 1960s and 1970s, such as Marina Abramović or Gordon Matta-Clark. Today, she is particularly enthusiastic about promising talents from the younger generation, such as Ian Cheng and Britta Thie. She seeks out new additions to the collection primarily during her travels to the United States as well as during visits to studios and galleries. It is important to her to include real key works or entire groups of works in the collection. In just a few years, she has succeeded in compiling a collection of more than 850 works—including pieces by Tony Oursler, Pipilotti Rist, Franz West, Anthony McCall, Thomas Ruff, Thomas Demand, Ed Atkins, Cyprien Gaillard, and Hito Steyerl—which surprises with its quality and creative presentation even those who were initially skeptical. The scientific elaboration of the contents, the identification of art-historical references within the collection, and the disclosure of references between the individual works are the main focal points. Further central aspects of the collection's activities are the expansion and supplementation of the collection's holdings, restoration, and conservation support, as well as art education. In the early years, only works from the collection were presented in Düsseldorf; today, Julia Stoschek enters into numerous exciting collaborations with international museums and other art institutions. In addition to its Düsseldorf location, the JULIA STOSCHEK COLLECTION opened a branch in Berlin-Mitte in June 2016 (see p. 140), making it Germany's first private collection with two publicly accessible exhibition venues.

JULIA STOSCHEK COLLECTION
Düsseldorf, North Rhine-Westphalia

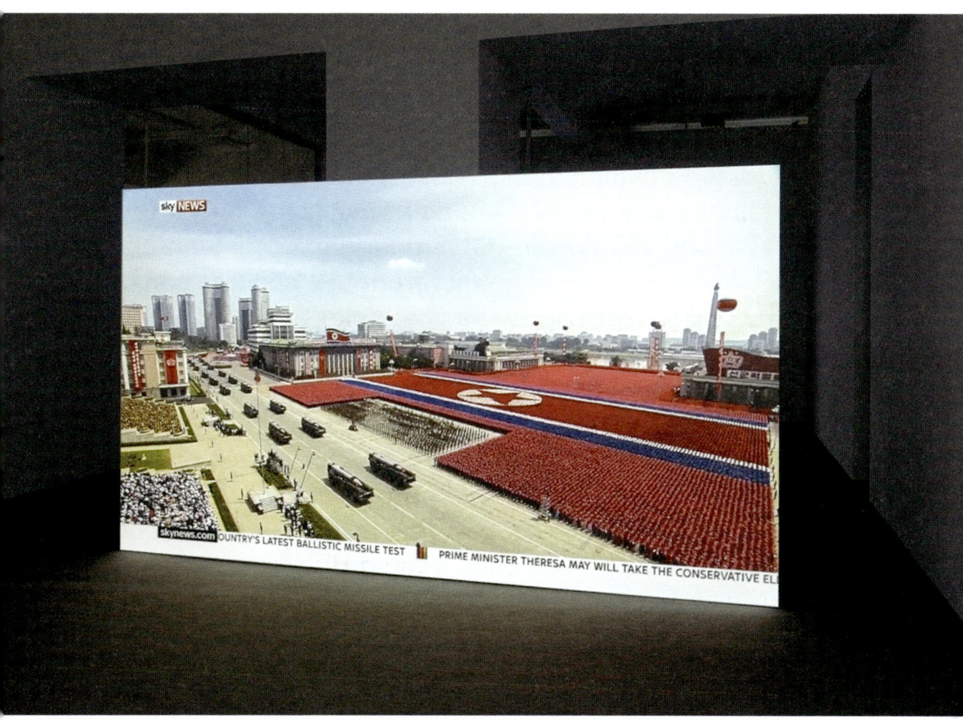

JULIA STOSCHEK COLLECTION
Schanzenstr. 54
D-40549 Düsseldorf
Phone: +49 211 5858840
info@jsc.art
jsc.art

Opening hours
Sun 11 a.m.–6 p.m.
During the installation periods, the rooms remain closed for several months. Guided tours with a maximum of 25 persons are offered. They take place every fourteen days on Sundays at 11 a.m. and 1 p.m. (€10). Registration is necessary and can be done on the website. Coveted, versatile evening events are regularly offered. In addition to the exhibitions, STUDIO 54 presents a film program on selected works from the collection.

Entrance fees
Free admission

Arrival by public transportation
The nearest U-Bahn station is Belsenplatz (U70, U74, U75, U76, U77).

Restaurant tips
The lively Brasserie Hülsmann (brasserie-huelsmann.de; Belsenplatz 1; unfortunately closed Sundays and Mondays) offers tasty and rather hearty French cuisine. The old-established Muggel is a successful mixture of street café, restaurant, and pub. The basement houses the last "classic" art house cinema of its kind in Düsseldorf (cafe-muggel.de; Dominikanerstr. 4). Super delicious Italian ice cream is available in the modern and tastefully furnished Gelateria La Romana (gelateriaromana.com/de/49-eisdielen-dusseldorf.php; Barmer Str. 35).

Extra tips
In order to not miss the exciting presentations and events in the field of media art, subscribing to the collection's newsletter under the heading "Visitor Information / Newsletter" on the website is recommended. It is also worth visiting the KAI 10 / ARTHENA FOUNDATION, a private funding institution that organizes three to four exhibitions a year (kaistrasse10.de; Kaistr. 10). An art trip to Düsseldorf can easily be combined with a stay at the Langen Foundation (see p. 186) and the Museum Insel Hombroich (p. 190) near Düsseldorf-Neuss.

224 Sculpture Park Waldfrieden

In 2008, with the opening of the sculpture park, a dream came true for world-famous and award-winning British artist Tony Cragg, who lives and works in Wuppertal. Situated in a fourteen-hectare forest, the park surrounds Villa Waldfrieden, a building constructed from 1947 to 1950 according to the guidelines of anthroposophical architecture. Kurt Herberts, lacquer manufacturer and art collector, commissioned architect Franz Krause to design an organic building, and so the outer form of the villa was designed in reference to the random outlines of an inkblot on a sheet of paper. In preceding years, the landlord had succeeded in protecting Willi Baumeister and Oskar Schlemmer from persecution by the National Socialists by hiring the artists, who had been defamed as “degenerate,” in his factory between 1937 and 1944. Villa Waldfrieden, which housed a large art collection during Kurt Herberts’s lifetime, was not used for some time after his death in 1989. Since 2006, it has belonged to the Cragg Foundation, which lovingly restored the impressive villa. For the opening of the park, Tony Cragg, in collaboration with Wuppertal architect Rudolf Hoppe, designed a new, approximately 240 m^2 separate glass building with a small terrace that serves as a modern exhibition center for outdoor and indoor sculptures. In 2013, the interior space for temporary exhibitions was enlarged with the opening of the 170 m^2 second exhibition hall below the entrance area. The three closed, seven-meter walls now also allow the hanging of works of art. In 2017, Tony Cragg and Rudolf Hoppe created an impressive third exhibition hall for the upper area, where a magnificent view over an “infinity lawn” opens up to the Wupper Valley. The glass walls of the third hall enclose an oval base. In the three pavilions, a total of five alternating, high-caliber monographic exhibitions of internationally renowned sculptors and other artists take place each year. Since the opening, works by Mario Merz, Eduardo Chillida, Jean Dubuffet, Richard Long, John Chamberlain, Jean Tinguely, Henry Moore, Imi Knoebel, and Norbert Kricke, among others, have been presented on loan.

Sculpture Park Waldfrieden
Wuppertal, North Rhine-Westphalia

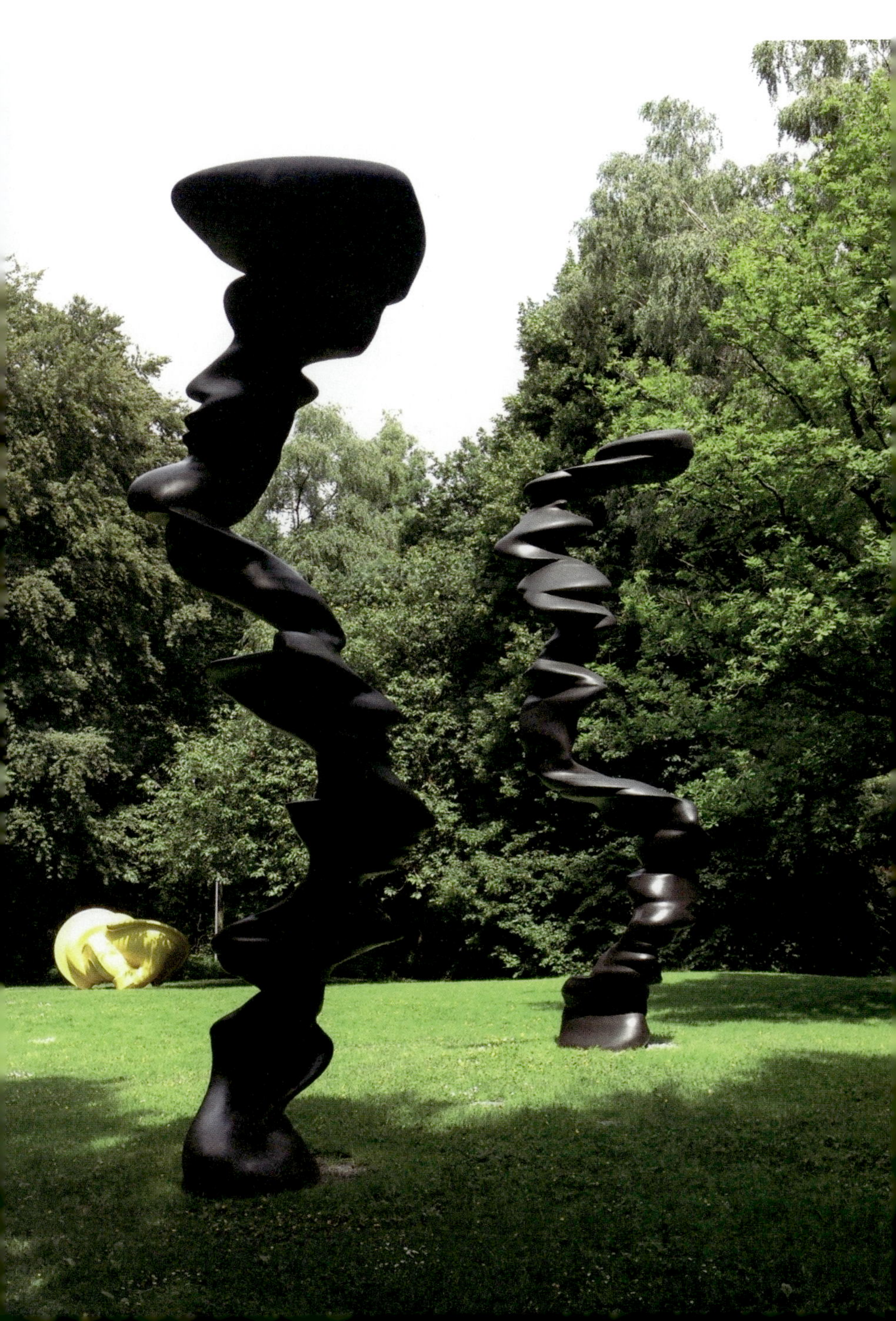

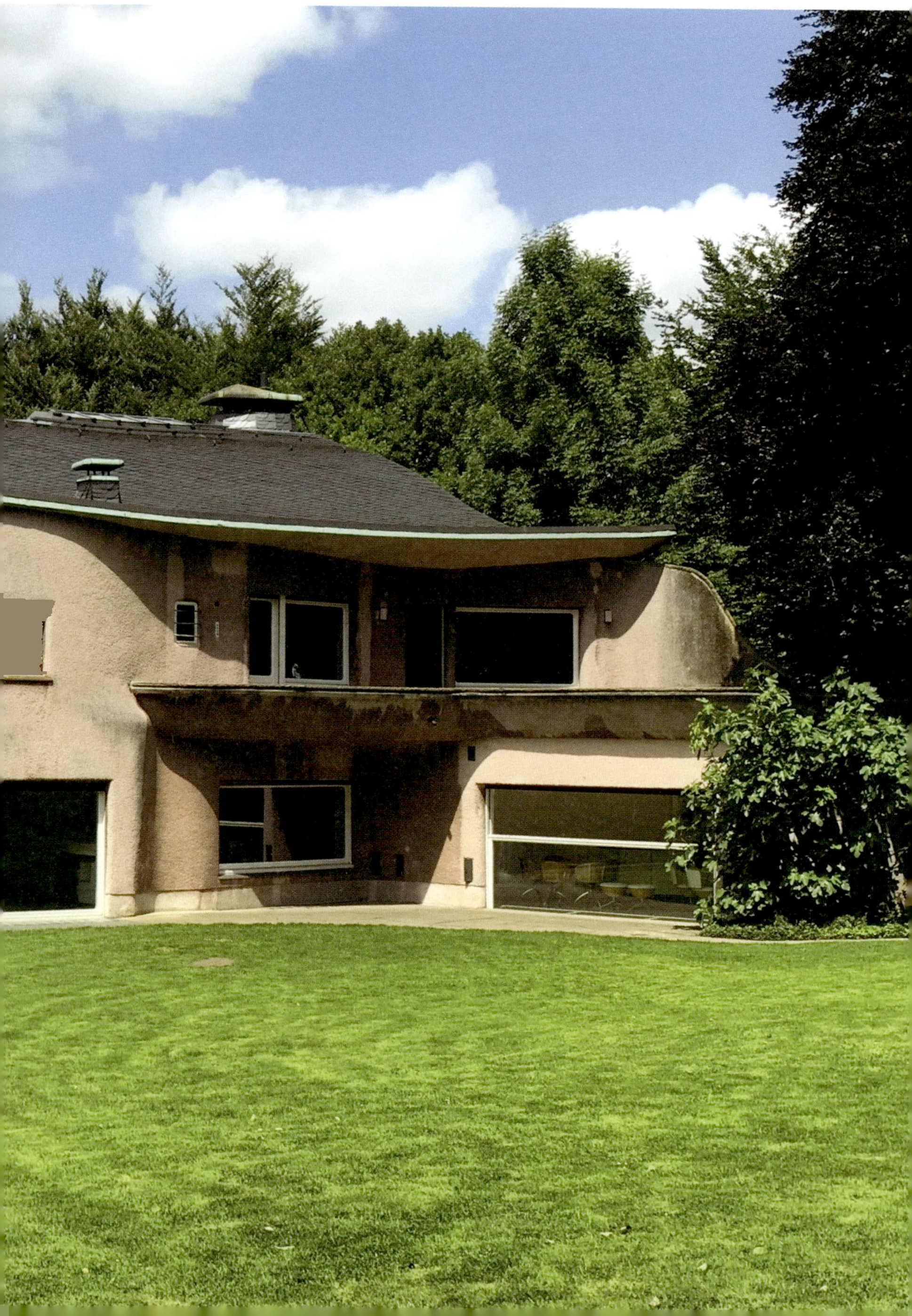

Sculpture Park Waldfrieden
Wuppertal, North Rhine-Westphalia

The Cragg Foundation is continuously expanding its collection of important sculptures. The focus is on modern and contemporary art. On a tour through the ever-changing park, situated on a slope, one encounters about forty sculptures. The mostly permanently installed works by Tony Cragg and several other artists such as Wilhelm Mundt, Jaume Plensa, Hede Bühl, Hubert Kiecol, Richard Deacon, Jonathan Monk, Per Kirkeby, Eva Hild, and Markus Lüpertz blend harmoniously into their natural surroundings.

Sculpture Park Waldfrieden
Hirschstr. 12
D-42285 Wuppertal
Phone: +49 202 47898120
mail@skulpturenpark-waldfrieden.de
skulpturenpark-waldfrieden.de

Opening hours
March to October: Tue–Sun 10 a.m.–7 p.m.; November to February: Fri–Sun 10 a.m.–5 p.m.
In the former gardener's cottage, which is located at the entrance to the sculpture park, visitors are spoiled with delicious cakes at Café Podest during the park's opening hours.

Entrance fees
Adults / Reduced / Children and students: €12 / €9 / free of charge
Public guided tours are available on Saturdays at 3 p.m. and Sundays at 11 a.m. (€4 plus entrance fee).
There are numerous events and programs for children and youth groups.

Arrival by public transportation
From the main station, take bus 628 direction Sedanberg to Bendahler Straße/Hesselnberg, walk right through Gemsenweg and turn right into Hirschstraße (see wsw-online.de for timetable information).

Extra tips
As part of the Klangart series, there is music playing regularly in the park during the changing seasons from spring to late summer. The top-class concerts take place either outdoors or in the new exhibition pavilion (skulpturenpark-waldfrieden.de/klangart and galeriepalette.de).
An opportunity to visit the inside of the beautiful Villa Waldfrieden unfortunately only exists with a little luck on the Tag der Architektur (Architecture Day, in June) and on the Tag des öffentlichen Denkmals (Day of Public Monuments, in September); registration takes place directly at the sculpture park.
A visit to the Von der Heydt Museum is also worthwhile. The focus of the collection is sixteenth- and seventeenth-century Dutch painting and nineteenth- and twentieth-century painting (vdh.netgate1.net; Turmhof 8).

228 Kunstraum am Limes / Zeitgenössische Kunst

In the late 1990s, a visit to Galerie Erhard Klein in Bad Münstereifel, which ended with the purchase of a painting by Sigmar Polke, sparked a new passion in Dr. Axel Ciesielski. From that point on, he spent his free time almost exclusively at art fairs, galleries, and museums and began to train his eye. In addition to numerous works by Sigmar Polke (around two hundred prints and multiples with one copy each of the artist's editions), large formats by K. O. Götz, Blinky Palermo, Erwin Wortelkamp, and Katharina Sieverding, a collection of works by Imi Knoebel and, more recently, politically motivated works by Felix Droese have also found their way into the collection. Little by little, younger contemporaries have also joined the collection: Gereon Krebber, Jorinde Voigt, Frank Gerritz, and Alicja Kwade. Inspired by the idea that his growing collection should be available both to his employees at WEPA Apothekenbedarf GmbH & Co KG and to the broader public, in 2009 Ciesielski had two former beverage halls near his company converted into the Kunstraum am Limes in the middle of the industrial district of Hillscheid. Rather inconspicuous from the outside, the rooms are bright and spacious inside. Particularly impressive is the vast gable room with works from various phases by Imi Knoebel, including the only model of the legendary Room 19 and the eight-part work *Schwules Bild* (Gay Picture, 1976). Despite the extensive exhibition area of approximately 1,200 m², after only a few years the two halls were too small and a modern portal extension was commissioned. The cube-like new building of concrete and glass, inaugurated in 2017, houses the entrance hall as well as two differently cut rooms for temporary exhibitions. A staircase leads from the foyer to a gallery, from which one has a beautiful view of the Westerwald landscape. A glass sculpture with elaborate mirroring effects by Gereon Krebber is permanently installed here.

Kunstraum am Limes / Zeitgenössische Kunst
Hillscheid, Rhineland-Palatinate

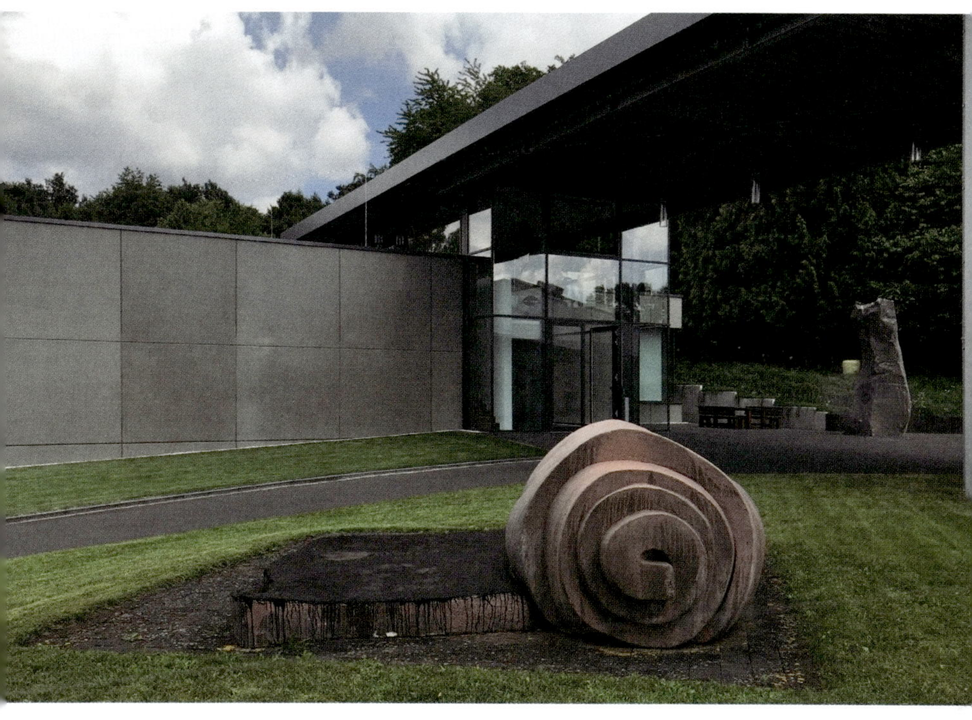

Kunstraum am Limes / Zeitgenössische Kunst
Am Limes 2
D-56204 Hillscheid
Phone: +49 2624 9432169
info@kunstraum-am-limes.de
kunstraum-am-limes.de

Opening hours
Visits by appointment

Entrance fees
€5 incl. a guided tour

Arrival by public transportation
It is difficult to get to the Kunstraum with public transportation.

Restaurant tips
In the restaurant Die Traube, sophisticated cuisine is served in a historic half-timbered house (dietraube-vallendar.de, Rathausplatz 12, 56179 Vallendar; closed Sundays and Mondays). The restaurant Zur Burg Grenzau offers German home cooking (Burgstr. 13, 56203 Höhr-Grenzhausen; +49 2624 950175).

Extra tips
In Koblenz, a visit the Ludwig Museum in the Deutschherrenhaus is worthwhile (ludwigmuseum.org; Danziger Freiheit 1, 56068 Koblenz). The Keramikmuseum Westerwald provides an overview of the history of ceramics (keramikmuseum.de; Lindenstr. 13, 56203 Höhr-Grenzhausen). Between April and October, art exhibitions are organized in the former NATO ammunition depot b-05 in Montabaur (kunst-kultur-natur-forum.de; Im Stadtwald, 56410 Montabaur). If the weather is fine, it would be worthwhile for car drivers to visit the „im Tal" park, which is accessible at any time. Initiated by the sculptor Erwin Wortelkamp, around forty artists have redesigned the landscape, which is characterized by a stream, pastures and wooded areas, and integrated their site-specific art works (im-tal.de; Schulstr. 18, 57635 Hasselbach). The Marienstatt Cistercian Abbey, considered Germany's first Gothic church on the right bank of the Rhine, is a beautiful place of silence (abtei-marienstatt.de; 57629 Marienstatt).

230
G2 Kunsthalle / Hildebrand Collection

Opposite Thomaskirche, on the fourth floor of a bunker-like building at the corner of Dittrichring and Gottschedstraße, is the G2 Kunsthalle, which in recent years has established itself as a permanent fixture in Leipzig's cultural life. The private collection of real estate entrepreneur Steffen Hildebrand focuses on twenty-first-century contemporary painting, expanded to include sculpture, drawings, prints, and other media. The collection activities focus on young art from Leipzig. Important positions from the so-called New Leipzig School are represented, including paintings by Neo Rauch, David Schnell, Matthias Weischer, Christoph Ruckhäberle, Rosa Loy, Jochen Plogsties, and Tilo Baumgärtel, which are essential components of the collection. Works by national and international artists such as Stephan Balkenhol, Daniel Richter, Gregor Hildebrandt, Alicja Kwade, Tomás Saraceno, Raymond Pettibon, Judith Bernstein, and Rebecca Horn form a second core of the continually growing collection.

Steffen Hildebrand's interest in Leipzig art dates back to 1988 when the then twenty year old had his parents give him a painting by Jost Giese. However, the fact that this was a GDR artist was unknown to the Frankfurt native at the time. Hildebrand first got to know Leipzig in 1990, when he came to the city to install a computer system. He fell in love with the metropolis and moved here a few years later. At the end of the 1990s, Hildebrand began to collect more actively, because in Leipzig he came across a young art scene around the teachers and graduates of the Academy of Visual Arts Leipzig. Thus, he came into direct contact with artists and bought their works at a time when they were still affordable. When, in 2013, he came across the prefabricated building erected between 1986 and 1989, which was initially to be used as a VEB data processing center during the final phase of the redevelopment of the Kolonnadenviertel neighborhood, Hildebrand saw great potential in it as a private exhibition hall, despite its unattractive appearance. With the purchase, he took over the existing rental contracts, had

G2 Kunsthalle / Hildebrand Collection
Leipzig, Saxony

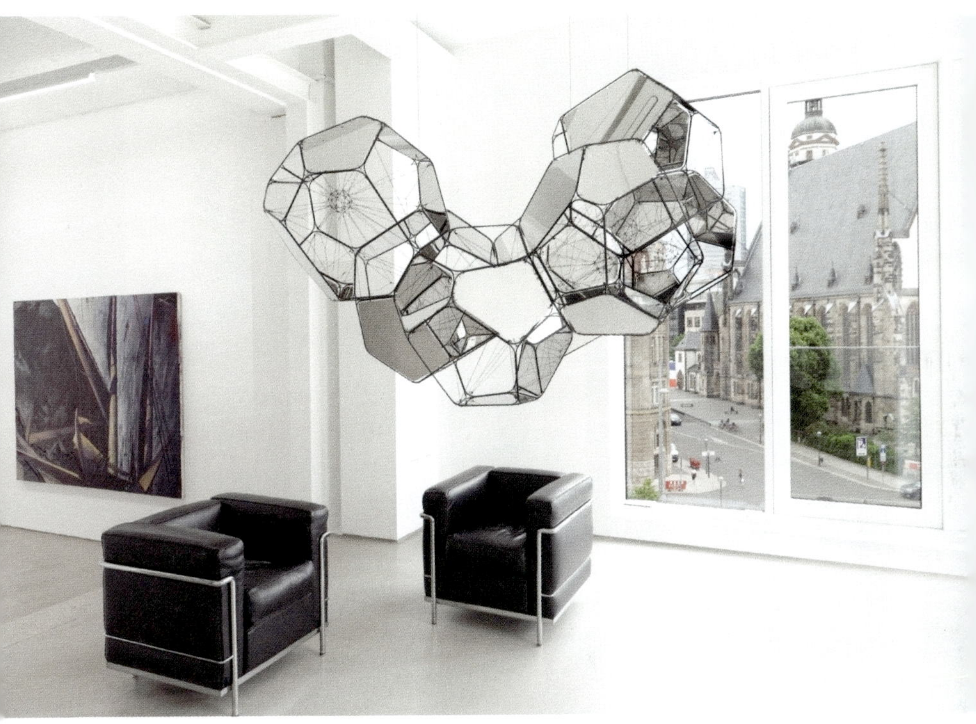

G2 Kunsthalle / Hildebrand Collection

Visitor entrance:
Dittrichring 13
D-04109 Leipzig
Phone: +49 341 35573793
info@g2-leipzig.de
g2-leipzig.de

Opening hours

A visit is possible with a guided tour or Wednesdays without a guided tour. The guided tours in German and English take place from Thursday to Monday (approx. 45 minutes, registration required, max. fifteen participants). Registration for the guided tours is via the online visitor portal (g2-leipzig.de/en/buchungsportal).
Wed 3–8 p.m. (visit without a guided tour, no advance reservation required) In summer, visitors can visit the exhibition in the project room on the third floor after the guided tour of the collection. Artist's talks, book presentations, and other events take place regularly.

Entrance fees

Adults / Reduced / Children under 14 and art students: €5 / €3 / free of charge (cash only, incl. a guided tour, except for special tours)

Arrival by public transportation

From the Thomaskirche stop (tram 9, bus 89), it is only a few meters to the G2 Kunsthalle. From the S-Bahn Markt stop (S1, S2, S3, S4, S5), it is a five-minute walk to the collection.

Parking

The Marktgalerie parking garage (Thomaskirchhof) is only 200 m away from the G2 Kunsthalle.

Restaurant tips

The Max Enk restaurant, located in the historic dining hall of the Städtisches Kaufhaus, is a delight for gourmets and art lovers alike (max-enk.de; Neumarkt 9–19). The same company also owns Pilot restaurant, which is part of the Leipzig Schauspielhaus. Surprising innovative dishes are served in a relaxed atmosphere (enk-leipzig.de/index.php/gastronomie; Bosestr. 1). Diagonally opposite, sushi variations and other Japanese cuisine are served in the Sakura Kaiten Sushi Bar (sakura-leipzig.de; Bosestr. 4). On the top floor of The Westin Hotel, overlooking the city center, gourmets are pampered with the cuisine passion légère© from patron Peter Maria Schnurr (westin-leipzig.de/restaurant-falco; Gerberstr. 15). The Galerie für Zeitgenössische Kunst café is redesigned every three years by artists (gfzk.de/orte/cafe; Karl-Tauchnitz-Str. 9–11).

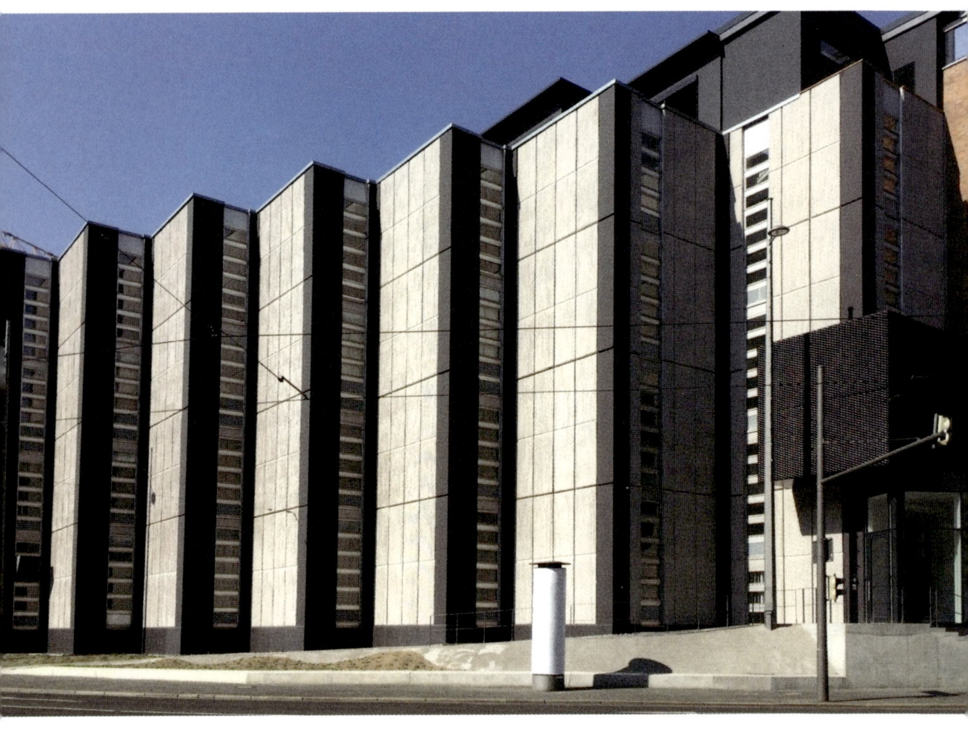

Extra tips

The Museum der bildenden Künste Leipzig (MdbK), built according to the plans of architects Hufnagel / Pütz / Rafaelian, exhibits works of art from the late Middle Ages to the present day (mdkb.de; Katharinenstr. 10). The Grassi Museum für Angewandte Kunst presents changing exhibitions on arts, handicrafts, and design, as well as photography and architecture of international standing (grassimuseum.de; Johannisplatz 5–11). In the Galerie für Zeitgenössische Kunst (GfZK), postwar art is shown in the form of collection presentations and temporary exhibitions (gfzk.de; Karl-Tauchnitz-Str. 9–11). Exhibitions take place irregularly at the art spaces Werkschauhalle and Spinnerei archiv massiv in the world-famous Leipziger Baumwollspinnerei. A visit to the complex is particularly worthwhile during the spring and autumn gallery tours, as many of the artists also open their studios (spinnerei.de; Spinnereistr. 7). Tech-savvy visitors should consider a detour to the Kunstkraftwerk Leipzig, which has been developed into the European hotspot for digital art since 2016. The focus is on immersive art projects that combine various art forms and technologies (kunstkraftwerk-leipzig.com; Saalfelder Str. 8b). The Thomaskirche, located diagonally opposite the G2 Kunsthalle, is particularly famous for the tomb of Johann Sebastian Bach and his monument in front of the church as well as the performances of the Thomanerchor, and for its beautiful stained glass windows, designed by David Schnell a. o., whose paintings are also represented by the Hildebrandt Collection (thomaskirche.org; Thomaskirchhof).

the previously bright-pink-and-red concrete shell painted in a more discreet gray and white, and transformed the entire fourth floor into a spacious, minimalist exhibition area of approximately 1,100 m^2 with four rooms. Hildebrand had a small glass bastion built into the façade opposite St. Thomas's Church, much to the delight of the original architect, who had planned exactly such a connection to the city, but had not received approval in GDR times.

Since the opening of the G2 Kunsthalle (G2 is the abbreviation for the official address, Gottschedstr. 2) in 2015, selected works from the Hildebrand Collection have been presented in a permanent exhibition on approximately two-thirds of the total area. In addition to the work of Tomás Saraceno, works by Neo Rauch, Matthias Weischer, and Paule Hammer are also shown. As a non-profit limited company, the G2 Kunsthalle has also set itself the statutory goal of promoting young up-and-coming artists. Thus, the G2 Kunsthalle realizes at least two special exhibition projects a year, primarily curated with artist loans or with loans from other collections and institutions, in cooperation with artists. These exhibitions are monographic or show two mostly new positions. In the past, Katrin Heichel, Sebastian Burger, Stefan Guggisberg, Stefan Behlau, Dennis Loesch, and Oskar Rink have been on view. A third annual special exhibition will feature works from the collection. Since 2017, exhibition projects by master students or classes of the Academy of Visual Arts Leipzig have also taken place on the third floor of the G2 Project Room for a few weeks each year. The difference between the rooms on the two floors could not be greater, which makes a visit to both floors particularly exciting and worthwhile. Since 2017, the G2 Kunsthalle, in cooperation with the Academy of Visual Arts Leipzig, has also awarded the G2 Kunsthalle's Meisterschülerpreis every year. This prize, endowed with 10,000 euros and one year of studio use in the Kunsthalle building, proves a commitment to support artists directly.

234 Museum Gunzenhauser

In 2003, renowned Munich gallery owner and collector Dr. Alfred Gunzenhauser transferred a large part of his private collection to a Chemnitz-based foundation. Previously, the then General Director of the Chemnitz Art Collections, Ingrid Mössinger, had proposed a separate building in the city as the future permanent venue for the presentation of Dr. Alfred Gunzenhauser's collection. The former headquarters of the Chemnitzer Sparkasse was chosen as the exhibition venue. From 1928 to 1930, the bank building was one of the first skyscrapers in Chemnitz to be designed in the New Objectivity style by Martin Helmert and built by Fred Otto, head of the municipal planning and building control office at the time. To add an avant-garde structure to the Chemnitz building landscape, everything decorative was deliberately omitted and light travertine was used for the façades. The land and the building were transferred to the Gunzenhauser Foundation by the Chemnitz Sparkasse. The generous support provided by the Ostdeutsche Sparkassenstiftung in the Free State of Saxony and the Sparkasse organization was for the necessary restoration of the listed buildings. With the help of other sponsors, the former Sparkasse building was transformed into the Gunzenhauser Museum from 2005 to 2007 by the Berlin architect Volker Staab. Opened at the end of 2007, it was the first collection museum in the new German states. The Chemnitz Art Collections run the administration.

The top-class collection comprises almost 2,500 works by important artists of the twentieth century. The decision of Alfred Gunzenhauser, who died in 2015, in favor of Chemnitz was a stroke of luck for the city—after all, the art collections lost almost 1,000 works of classical modern art during the National Socialist era. Since Gunzenhauser was particularly interested in Expressionism and bought the first works by Otto Dix as early as 1964, represented him, and collected his entire oeuvre throughout his life, the museum's reputation is based on two extensive groups of works in addition to other Expressionist paintings: with 380 works

Museum Gunzenhauser
Chemnitz, Saxony

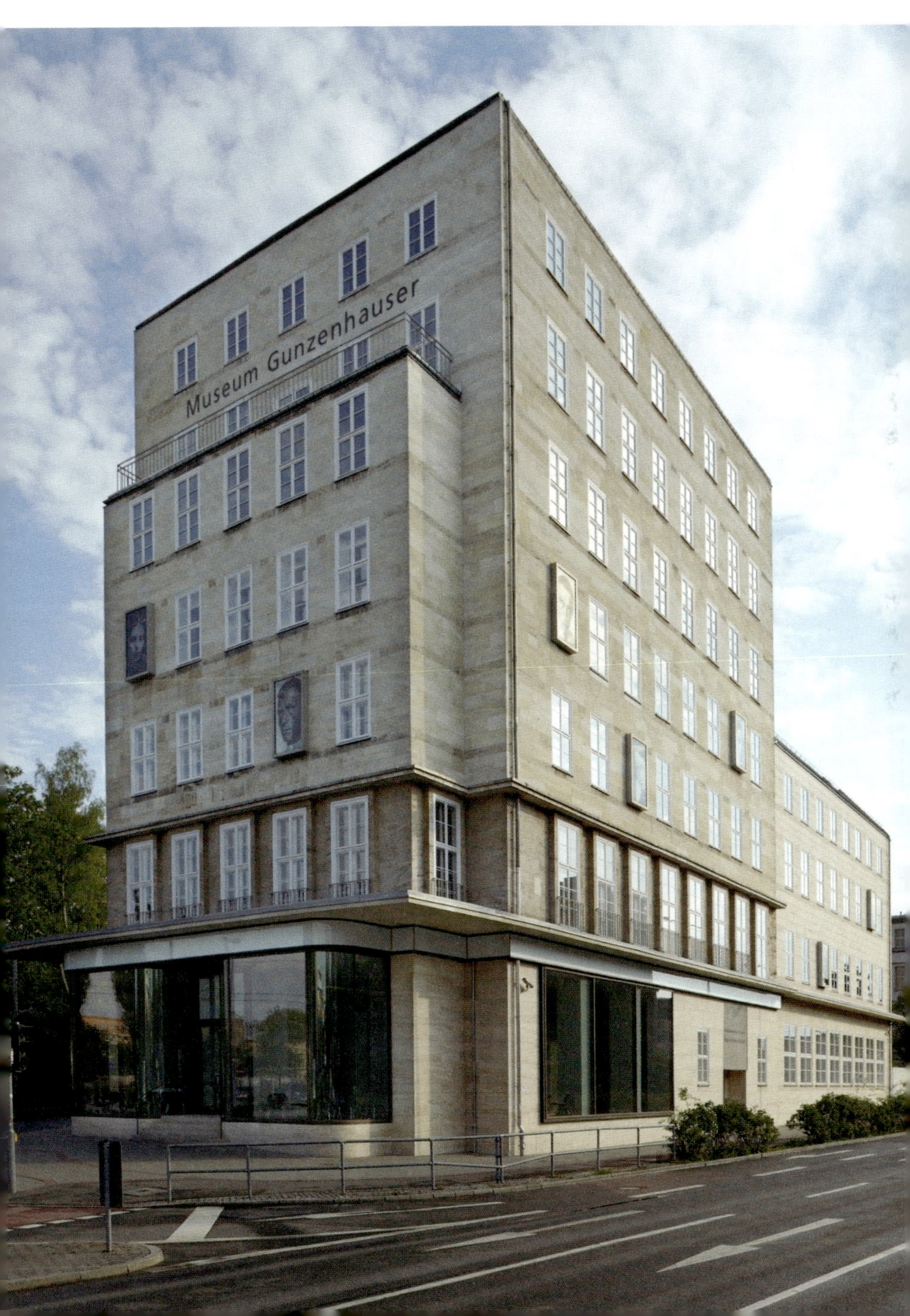

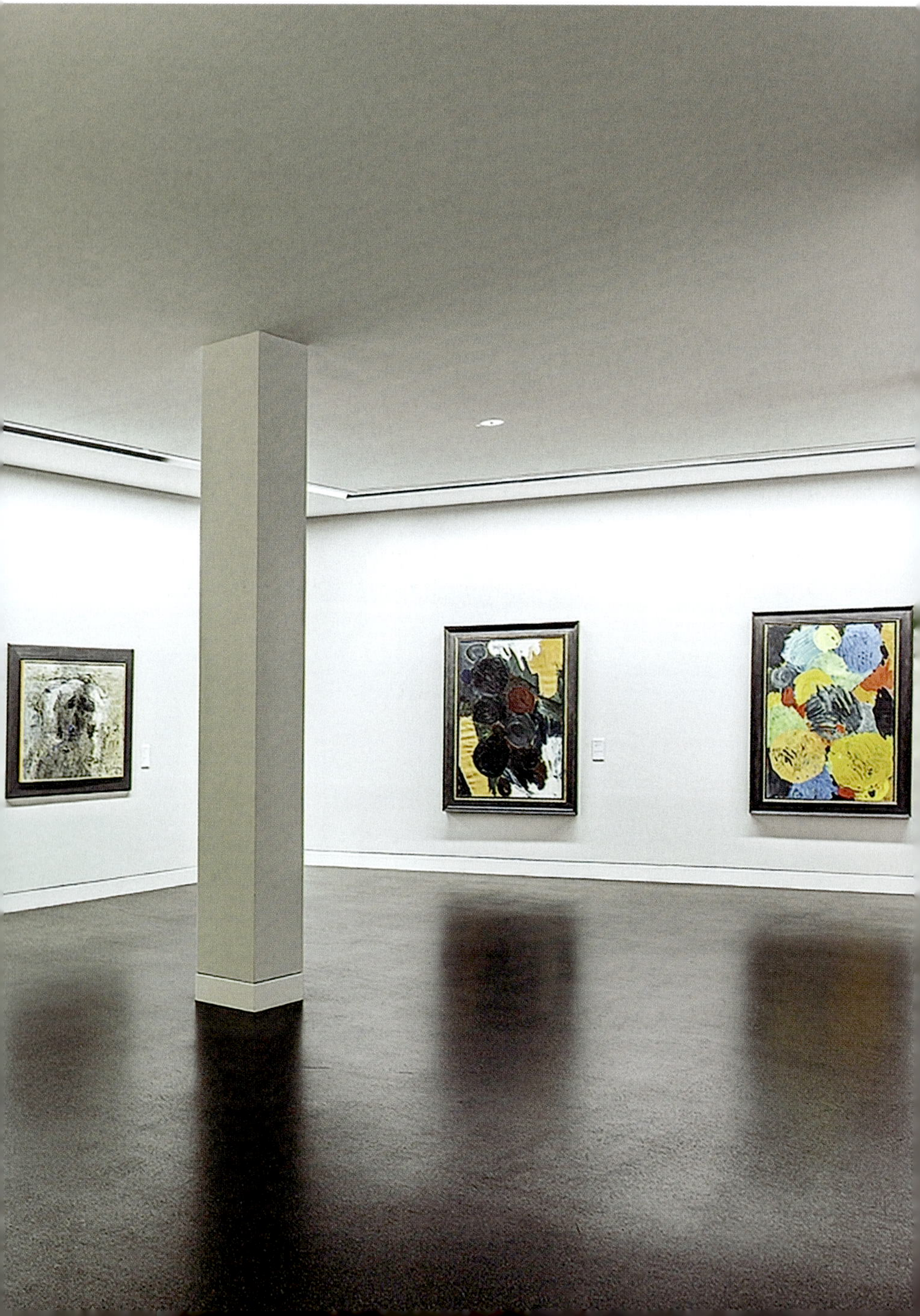

by Otto Dix, it has one of the world's largest collections of the painter's works, as well as a large number of works by Alexej von Jawlensky. The collection of around 270 artists is rounded off by numerous positions in Abstract and Figurative art created before and after the Second World War. These include works by artists such as Willi Baumeister, Fritz Winter, Ernst Wilhelm Nay, Bernhard Schultze, and Emil Schumacher as well as Karl Hofer, Johannes Grützke, Horst Antes, Klaus Fußmann, Karl Horst Hödicke, and Rainer Fetting. Alfred Gunzenhauser's open-mindedness was also directed at artists who created their works in the GDR, such as Gerhard Altenbourg, Strawalde, Max Uhlig, and Albert Ebert. A spectacular red staircase connects the four exhibition floors, which offer a total area of approximately 2,300 m². The works of Dix and Jawlensky form the core of the permanent exhibition, which is usually presented on the two upper floors of the museum and in which changes are also made. In addition, two large and four smaller special exhibitions are shown annually on the two lower floors as part of the Young Contemporary Art from Saxony series.

Museum Gunzenhauser
Chemnitz Art Collections
Falkeplatz
(corner between Stollberger and Zwickauer Str.)
D-9112 Chemnitz
Phone: +49 371 4887024
gunzenhauser@stadt-chemnitz.de
kunstsammlungen-chemnitz.de

Opening hours
Tue, Thu–Sun and public holidays except December 24 and 31
11 a.m.–6 p.m., Wed 2 p.m.–9 p.m.
Public guided tours, special tours, and other events are offered.

Entrance fees
Adults / Reduced / Children under 18: €7 / €4,50 / free
There are different, interesting combination tickets for several museums in the Chemnitz Art Collections (incl. Henry van de Velde Museum).

Arrival by public transportation
From the station, you can reach Falkeplatz with tram 1 (direction Schönau) and tram 4 (direction Hutholz).

Parking
Inexpensive parking can be found at Am Wallgraben.

Restaurant tips
Right next to the Chemnitz Art Collections at Theaterplatz, innovative cooking can be found at the Heck-Art restaurant. There, guests dine surrounded by works from Chemnitz artists (restaurant-heck-art.de; Mühlenstr. 2; closed Sun/Mon). Creative dishes are served near the Schlossberg Museum at the max louis restaurant, which is housed in a former spinning mill (max-louis.de; Schönherrstr. 8).

Extra tips
It is worth visiting the Henry van de Velde Museum at the same time—it is very interesting even if it is sparsely furnished. The villa (1902/03), designed by the Belgian artist Henry van de Velde for entrepreneur Herbert Eugen Esche, is rightly classified by architecture lovers as a monument of European rank (Parkstr. 58; Wed and Fri–Sun 10 a.m.–6 p.m.). The main building of the Chemnitz Art Collections on Theaterplatz is home to an excellent collection of Expressionist work (Theaterplatz 1). Friends of medieval and religious art will find what they are looking for in the restored rooms of the Schlossbergmuseum (Museum für Stadtgeschichte) and the nearby Schlosskirche (Schlossberg 12). Local contemporary art is shown in the Neue Sächsische Galerie (neue-saechsische-galerie.de; Moritzstr. 20).

238
Gerisch Sculpture Park

In 2007, with commitment and open-mindedness, Herbert and Brigitte Gerisch created the sculpture park in Neumünster as a new place for art in the heart of Schleswig-Holstein. The former CEO of the BIG BAU Group, who died in 2016, had a vision of transforming the former textile and leather center of the northern-most federal state into a "city of modern sculpture." Founded in 2001, the Gerisch Foundation aimed to create an internationally oriented sculpture park. Relationships to the natural environment as well as the vulnerability of the individual are fundamental themes in the collection. The examination of images which display a longing for nature and the concept of the Arcadian at the beginning of the twenty-first century is fascinating. The ancient art myth Arcadia represents the epitome of idyllic existence and thus a counter-world to the constraints of society and culture. Visitors can ponder the question of how art processes images of nature today during a walk along the little Schwale river, which leads past the exhibits and the reform garden laid out in 1925 by landscape architect Harry Maasz.

In May 2002, the first sculpture was unveiled by the Gerischs, then still in the private garden of their villa: *Kissing Birds* (1999/2000) by Tel Aviv-born artist Menashe Kadishman. It formed the starting point of the collection, which currently comprises over thirty objects. Some sculptures were carefully integrated into the garden after their creation (including works by Pit Kroke, Horst Antes, Markus Lüpertz, Magdalena Abakanowicz, Bogomir Ecker, Brigitte Kowanz, and Carsten Höller), others are site-specific works created in relation to the spatial environment. This was the case, for example, with the work *Annie* (2007) by Olaf Nicolai. With this installation, which consists of screen prints behind glass and gives the fence the appearance of a living-room curtain, the street front is separated from the three-hectare park.

The continually growing collection of modern and contemporary outdoor art is supplemented by three temporary exhibitions a year. In an exhibition area of approximately 700 m², divided between the artfully renovated Villa Wachholz, which was built by

Gerisch Sculpture Park
Neumünster, Schleswig-Holstein

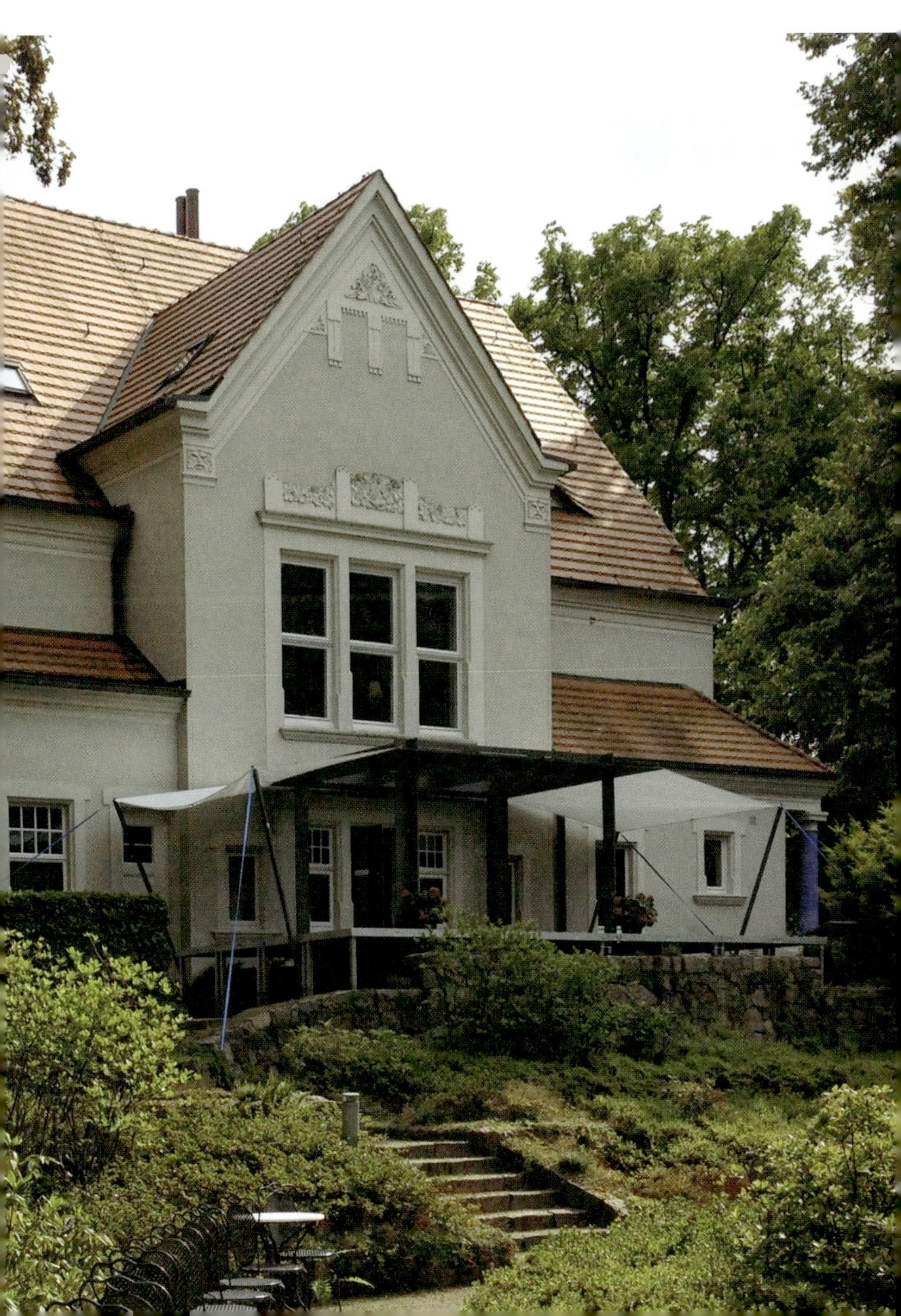

Hans Schnittger in 1903, the Gerisch Gallery and the art pavilion Remise, historical overviews and coordinated positions in the form of sculptures, paintings, graphics, and video art are shown. These exhibitions are often created in cooperation with other international art institutions.

Herbert Gerisch Foundation
Brachenfelder Str. 69
D-24536 Neumünster
Phone: +49 4321 555120
kontakt@gerisch-stiftung.de
herbert-gerisch-stiftung.de

Opening hours
Wed–Sun 11 a.m.–6 p.m.; April–September, additionally Sat/Sun 11 a.m.–7 p.m. and by appointment. Winter break from Christmas to mid-March.
Guided tours are offered every Sunday (€9 / €5 incl. admission). Interesting lectures, discussions, readings, guided tours, and concerts are announced on the website. During museum opening hours, Café Harry Maasz on the ground floor of the villa offers homemade cakes and snacks in a cozy, private atmosphere.

Entrance fees
Adults / Reduced / Family ticket / Children to age 15: €8 / €5 / €10 / free (cash only)

Parking
The nearest parking can be found in the City Parkhaus (Brachenfelder Str. 20) or the car park at the AOK (Rudolf-Weißmann-Str. 13).

Arrival by public transportation
About a twenty-minute walk from the train station to the sculpture park.

Restaurant tips
In the Blechnapf restaurant, located in an old factory building, tasty Mediterranean and Holstein dishes are served (restaurant-blechnapf.de; Gartenstr. 10). It is possible to enjoy a wonderful Sunday brunch with a reservation in the restaurant L.O.K.S, located somewhat outside the city. In the evening, international and regional meals are offered here (loks-restaurant.de; Einfelder Schanze 3).

Extra tip
Little known outside Schleswig-Holstein, but worth seeing for art lovers is the NordArt, which takes place every year from June to September/October. Since 1999, the 22,000 m² hanger of the Büdelsdorfer Carlshütte foundry, founded in 1827 and shut down in 1997, offers an extraordinary venue for art with an 80,000 m² sculpture park (nordart.de; Vorwerksallee 3, 24782 Büdelsdorf near Rendsburg).

Gerisch Sculpture Park
Neumünster, Schleswig-Holstein

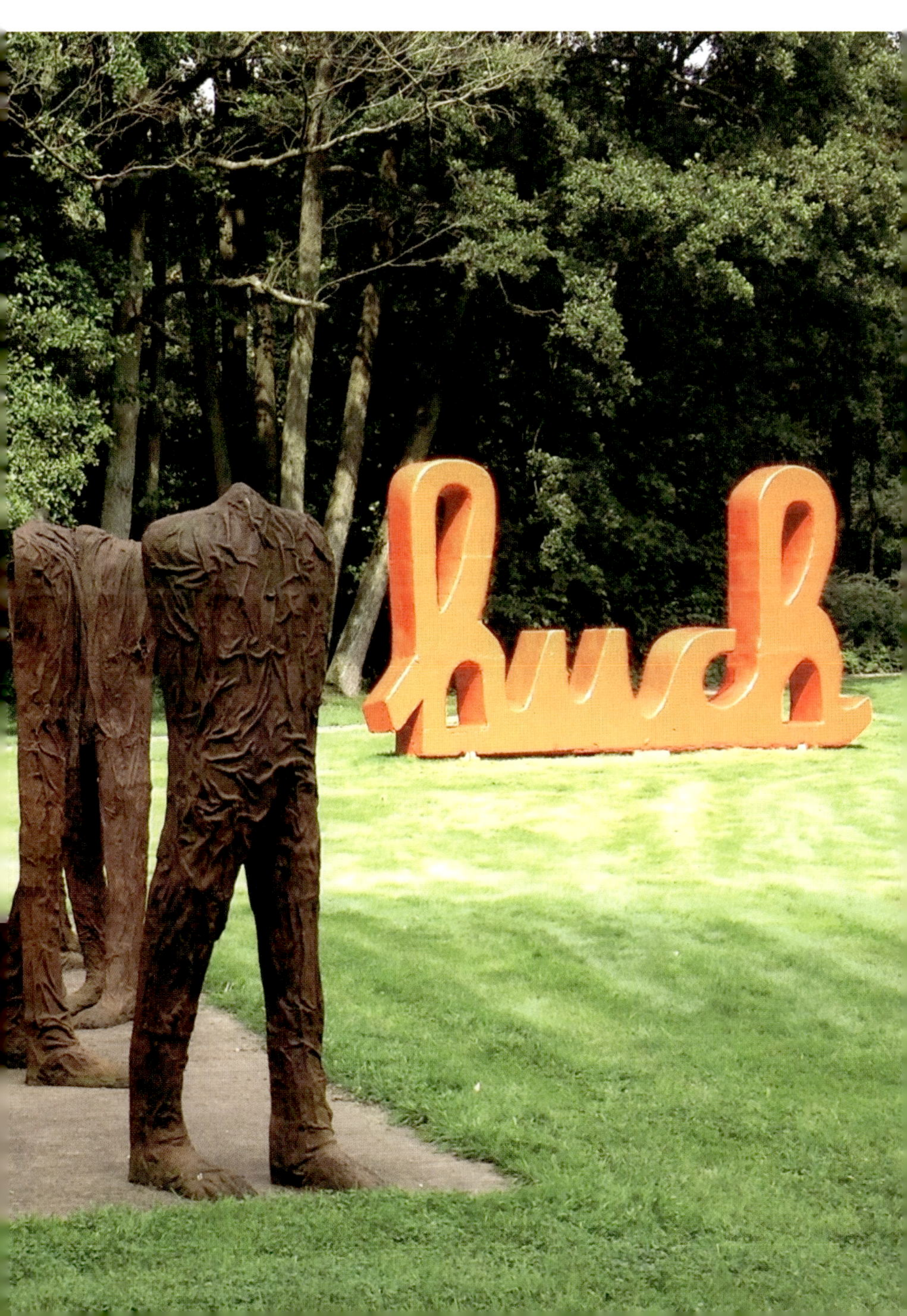

242 Museum Kunst der Westküste

The North Frisian island of Föhr has a cultural “lighthouse” with international appeal in the form of the nonprofit foundation museum in Alkersum. Based on the historical collection of paintings by museum founder Prof. Dr. mult. h. c. Frederik Paulsen, it collects researches, and mediates art that deals with the theme “sea and coast.” The collection is dedicated to art created between 1830 and 1930 in the four countries bordering the North Sea: Norway, Denmark, Germany, and the Netherlands. Norwegian landscape painting is represented by works by Johan Christian Dahl and Edvard Munch, but also by paintings by German artists who have discovered the “wild nature” of the high north country since the 1820s.

There is also a focus on the famous painters from the Skagen artist colony, including Anna and Michael Ancher, Peder Severin Krøyer, Viggo Johansen, and Christian Krohg. North German painting is represented in the collection with large groups of works by Hans Peter Feddersen and Otto H. Engel. Expressionist artists such as Erich Heckel, Emil Nolde, and Max Beckmann were enthusiastic about the German North Sea coast, as was German Impressionist Max Liebermann, who spent every summer in the Netherlands from the 1870s until the First World War. In addition, Dutch colleagues such as Henrik Willem Mesdag and Jozef Israëls, but also Piet Mondrian and Jan Toorop, are presented. Since the opening of the museum, the original collection of 480 works has grown to over 720. In recent years, German and international contemporary art in a wide variety of media, especially photography by Thomas Wrede, Jochen Hein, Nan Hoover, Joakim Eskildsen, Anja Jensen, Martin Parr, Gerhard Richter, Trine Søndergaard, Mila Teshaieva, Fiona Tan, Yinka Shonibare, and Volker Tiemann, has also found its way into the collection.

The choice of the unusual location and the theme of the museum’s collection can be inferred from the founder’s family history. Born in Sweden in 1950, chemist and business economist Frederik Paulsen now resides in Switzerland. The headquarters of the

Museum Kunst der Westküste
Föhr, Schleswig-Holstein

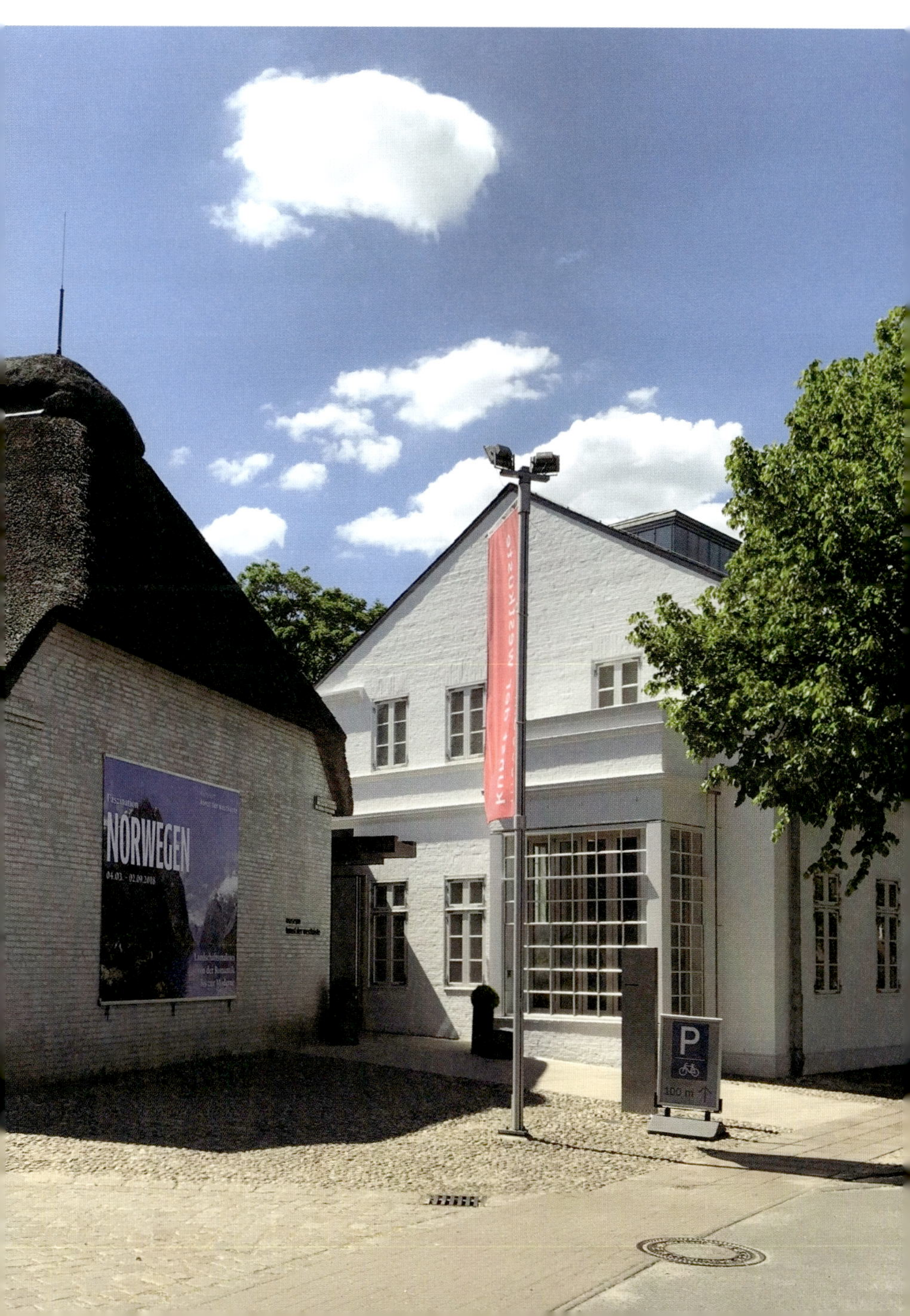

pharmaceutical company Ferring, originally founded by his father, Dr. med. Frederik Paulsen Senior, in the 1950s in Malmö, is located in Copenhagen. Today, Frederik Paulsen junior is chairman of the board of directors of Ferring. Paulsen senior's parents are from Föhr. The close connection to the island is evident: the company name Ferring is derived from the name of the island, because the inhabitants of Föhr are called Feringen in the Frisian language, i.e., "Föhrer." In 1961, Paulsen Senior bought his mother's parental home in Alkersum on Föhr, near which the museum is located. In 1988, he founded the Ferring Stiftung, which promotes the Frisian language, culture, and region. Frederik Paulsen Junior is also very active in various cultural and scientific institutions.

The "daylight" museum, designed by architect Gregor Sunder-Plassmann from Kappeln/Schlei as a multiunit building ensemble, opened in 2009—just in time for Frederik Paulsen Senior's hundredth birthday. The award-winning museum complex, run by Det Paulsen Legaat gGmbH, harmoniously combines tradition and modernity. Avant-garde, white-plastered hall cubes alternate with a newly erected, large thatched exhibition hall as well as converted historic Frisian houses and a glass corridor with presentation booths. The six hall buildings comprise an exhibition area of 900 m^2. The entire complex also includes a museum garden and the Grethjens Gasthof, rebuilt in the style of a Scandinavian mansion around 1900. The name goes back to Margaretha Dorothea Hansen, known as Grethjen, who ran an inn here, which was the residence and meeting place for various artists from Germany and Denmark. One of them, Otto H. Engel, was the co-founder of the Berlin Secession. He stayed in the inn every summer between 1901 and 1907, and his paintings of Föhrer women in traditional costumes and historic Frisian houses earned him a reputation as "the painter of Föhr."

Museum Kunst der Westküste
Föhr, Schleswig-Holstein

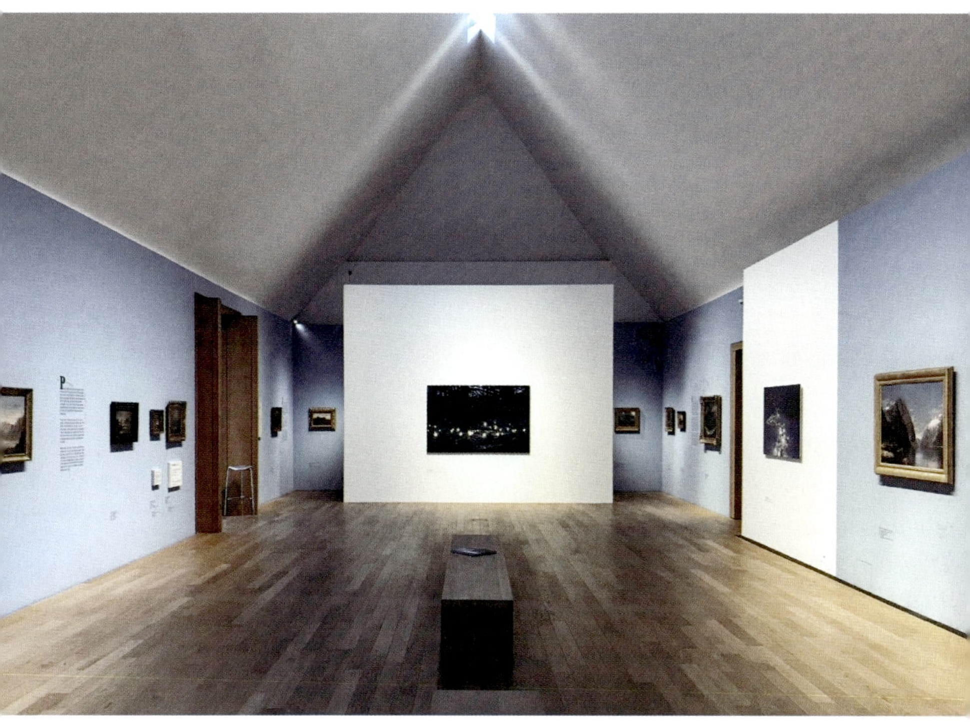

Museum Kunst der Westküste
Hauptstr. 1
D-25938 Alkersum
Phone: +49 4681 747400
info@mkdw.de
mkdw.de

Opening hours
March to October Tue–Sun 10 a.m.–5 p.m., November to early January Tue–Sun noon–5 p.m., closed from the second week of January to end of February
Public guided tours take place on Sundays and Tuesdays at 1:30 p.m. (registration for the tour: +49 4681 747400 or info@mkdw.de; €4 plus admission).
There are numerous workshops for children, teenagers, and adults as well as other events.
The museum has a shop and the café-restaurant Grethjens Gasthof. The restaurant also offers favorite dishes by artists who are represented in the exhibitions.

Entrance fees
Adults / Reduced / Children up to age 18: €8 / €4 / free. Combined tickets with the Friesenmuseum are also available.

Arrival by public transportation
The museum can be reached by bus lines 1 and 2 from the harbor or Wyk. From the bus stop at the harbor in front of the W.D.R. building, there is an art shuttle bus to the museum at 1 p.m. on some weekdays between April and September. The return trip is at 3:30 p.m. (€4 round trip).

Parking
The museum has two parking areas. These are not directly next to the building, but on the same side of the road about 100 and 150 m further in the direction of Utersum.

Restaurant tips
The NAMINE WITT Genusshandwerk Föhr is an innovative mixture of restaurant, café, wine bar, and delicatessen (namine-witt.de/bistro; Alkersumer Stieg 4, 25938 Nieblum). Fish and lamb dishes are served at Alten Landhaus (landhaus-nieblum.de; Bi de Süd 22; 25938 Nieblum). The stattBar serves not only coffee and cake but also works of art in correspondence with exhibitions at the Museum Kunst der Westküste (Westerstr. 1, 25938 Wyk auf Föhr).

Extra tip
In the lovingly designed Friesen-Museum: Dr.-Carl-Häberlin, visitors can learn something about the history of Föhr (friesen-museum.de; Rebbelstieg 34, 25938 Wyk auf Föhr).

Austria

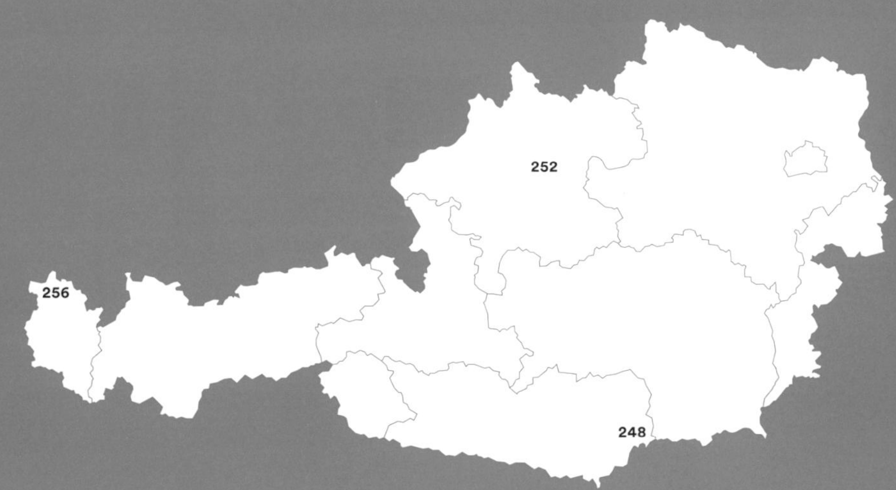

248
Museum Liaunig

In the seclusion of South Carinthia, one finds the Museum Liaunig embedded in the landscape. The existence of this unusual exhibition site is due to entrepreneur Herbert W. Liaunig, who built up an impressive collection of contemporary art over the last five decades. He was inspired by school friends interested in art and later acquaintances with artists, which had a lasting influence on his nuanced understanding of art.

From the beginning, Liaunig's collection concentrated on Austrian contemporary art after 1945. Additionally, earlier works by painters and illustrators such as Herbert Boeckl, Werner Berg, Gerhart Frankl, Oskar Kokoschka, Anton Kolig, Wilhelm Thöny, Anton Mahringer, and Alfred Wickenburg, among others, were purchased. From 1985, sculpture also emerged as a favorite collection theme. Thus, in addition to sculptures by Austrian artists, there are works by international stars such as Tony Cragg, Anthony Caro, and Matt Mullican. New works on paper and paintings have been added in recent years, so that the collection now ranges from Josef Albers, Antonio Calderara, and Joan Miró to Robert Motherwell and Georges Mathieu.

At the end of August 2008, Herbert W. Liaunig fulfilled a long-standing wish by opening a museum in his hometown of Neuhaus. In the center of a high plateau, the museum lies like a sculpture in the mountainous, lush, green landscape. Seen from the neighboring hill, the minimal building, designed by Viennese architectural firm querkraft, calls to mind a half-buried UFO. This unique complex was awarded the Austrian Museum Prize in 2011 and listed as a historic monument in 2012. Due to the collection, which has grown to 3,500 works, the museum was expanded by around 2,500 m^2 to a total of 7,500 m^2 (usable area) in 2014 according to plans by the same architectural office. Reopened in 2015, the museum now boasts a large exhibition hall, a graphics room, a display repository in the entrance area, a multifunctional special exhibition room, a sculpture repository, three underground showrooms, and a sculpture garden. In the daylight-flooded "minimalist museum tube," annually changing exhibitions from the collection are shown. In the

Museum Liaunig
Neuhaus, Carinthia

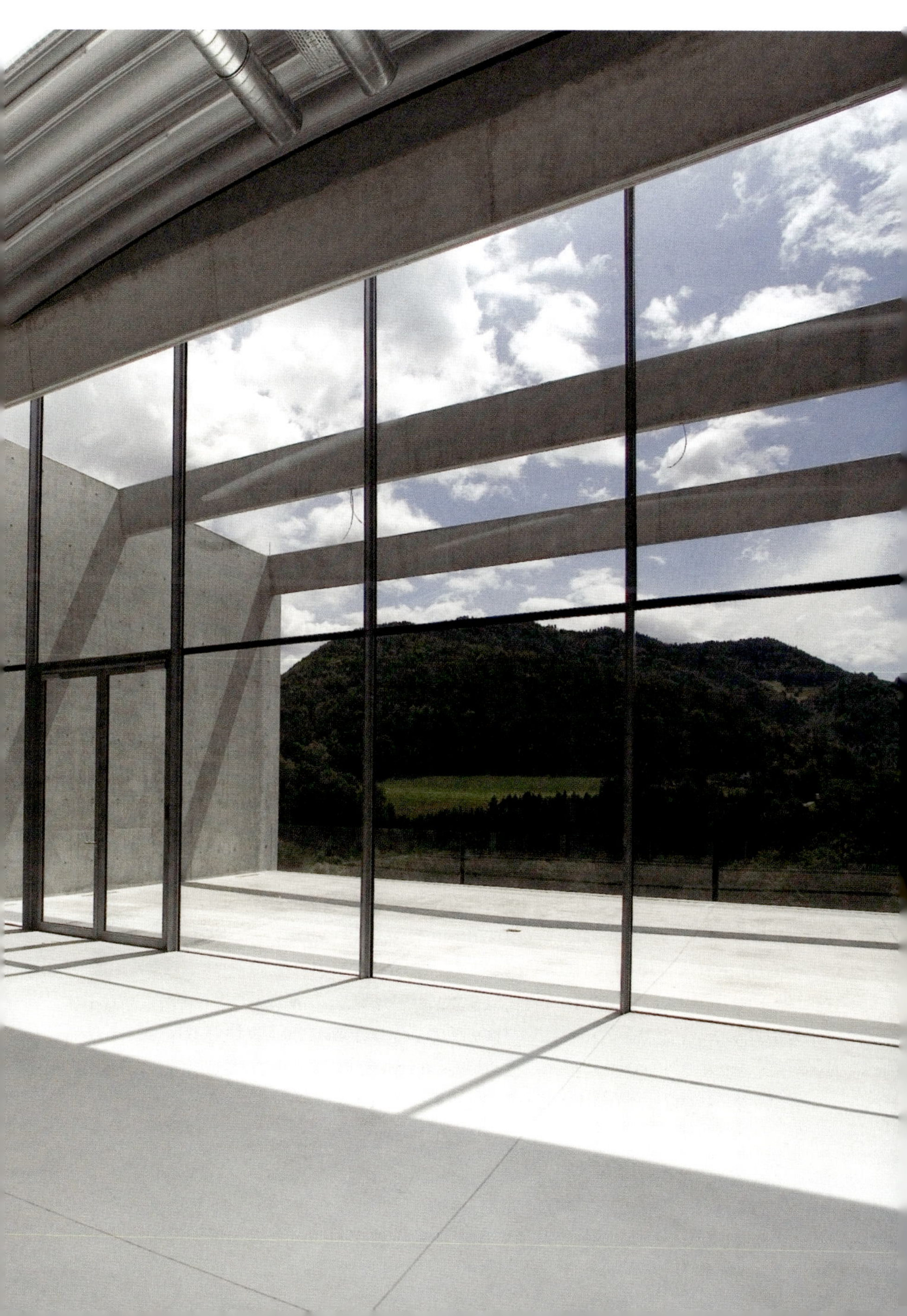

triangular special exhibition space, which also forms the framework for the chamber music series sonusiade, the exhibition series *Alte Freunde* (Old Friends), partly showing works on loan, will be continued, in which two to three exhibitions per season present artists who have been friends with Herbert Liaunig since the beginnings of his collection activities. As a contrast to modernism, visitors can expect several surprises in the underground rooms. Herbert Liaunig collects not only art but also rare historical and important ethnological objects.

A narrow entrance with a light installation by Brigitte Kowanz leads to a dark blue annex in which the quite impressive exhibition *Gold der Akan* (Gold of the Akan) is generally presented. The gold objects, which are satisfying in their formal richness and the expressiveness of their style, are historically and artistically significant testimonies of various tribes of the Akan ethnic group who live in West Africa in areas of the southern half of Ghana as well as in the southeast of the Ivory Coast. With around six hundred objects, the collection is one of the largest of its kind in the world. In the two new underground showrooms, historical collections from the Liaunig family are alternatingly shown. For example, in 2018, Herbert Liaunig's stamp collection (rare Austrian and Lombardo Venetian postage and newspaper stamps from 1850–1867) as well as parts of the Liaunig silver collection, with over eighty selected sacral and profane pieces of silver (from 1490–1830), were exhibited here.

If the visitors yearn for fresh air and a view of nature after diving into the rooms embedded in the hills, a visit to the sculpture park is a good idea when the weather is fine. The park, opened in 2016, together with the round sculpture depot, which is not dissimilar to the Pantheon, invites visitors to view Austrian and international sculptors and object artists from modern times to the present day.

Museum Liaunig
Neuhaus, Carinthia

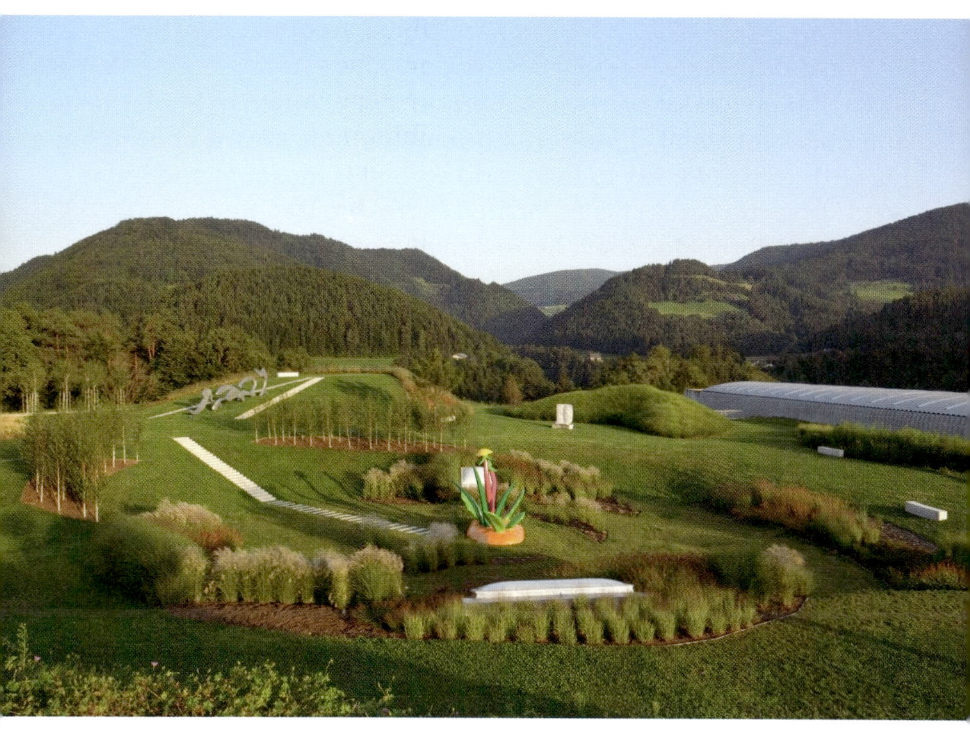

Museum Liaunig
A-9155 Neuhaus
Phone: +43 4356 21115
office@museumliaunig.at
museumliaunig.at

Opening hours
The museum is open from the beginning of May until the end of October, Wed–Sun, 10 a.m.–6 p.m.
Only for children ages 12 and over.
The sculpture park is only open during good weather. Highly recommended public guided tours take place Wed–Sun at 11 a.m. and 2 p.m. (included in the entrance fee).
Individual guided tours can be booked.
As part of the chamber music series sonusiade, classical concerts take place four times during the season.
There is also a café and shop in the museum.

Entrance fees
€15 for all exhibitions incl. sculpture park / €6 for temporary exhibitions / €11 for school children in class groups

Arrival by public transportation
Take the regional express from the Klagenfurt railway station to Bleiburg. From the Bleiburg railway station, you can reach the museum by Go-Mobil (gomobil-kaernten.at; registration at +43 664 6036039150; starting from Lavamünd registration at +43 664 6036039473).

Restaurant tips
The culinary offerings in the region are very limited. Near the museum, typical Carinthian cuisine is served in the Gasthof Hartl (hartl-wirt.at; Neuhaus 3). At the Landgasthof Hafner, regional specialties are also served (hadnwirt.info, Oberdorf 14). In Bleiburg, the Brauhaus Breznik is worth recommending for dinner (breznik.9150.at, 10. Oktoberplatz 9, 9150 Bleiburg).

Extra tips
Not far from the museum you can visit the St. Paul Benedictine monastery, famous for its Romanesque basilica (stift-stpaul.at; Hauptstr. 1, 9470 St. Paul). The Werner Berg Museum in Bleiburg, established after the artist's death in 1981, is also worth a visit. It shows annually changing exhibitions (wernerberg.museum; 10. Oktoberplatz 4, 9150 Bleiburg).

252 Museum Angerlehner

In Thalheim, an unassuming suburb of Wels, Austrian industrialist and collector Heinz J. Angerlehner fulfilled his dream of bringing his enthusiasm for art to the world when his museum opened in 2013. After directing his company, Ferro-Montagetechnik (FMT), for almost three decades, he resigned from operative business activities in 2007, acquired the company property including office and hall complex in 2009, and founded Angerlehner Museums GmbH in the same year. The design for the conversion of the former factory and assembly hall came from the Upper Austrian offices of Wolf Architektur, which won an international competition. The result, which was ingeniously devised together with the collector, is captivating with its clarity and generosity. From the outside, the building presents itself with a black, iridescent metal façade; from the inside, visitors can expect airy exhibition rooms with deliberately set perspectives and views. The former function of the building is referenced by components such as a huge overhead crane weighing ten tons. A distinctive feature of the architectural concept is the 50 m long show depot with 161 extendable registers suspended on both sides and a hanging area of around 6,000 m^2. A glass wall provides art lovers with insights into the collection in addition to the respective exhibitions. More than thirty-five years of passion for contemporary art form the basis of the Angerlehner Collection. The focus of the private collection, which comprises around 3,000 works, is on Austrian painting from 1945 onwards, which are supplemented by drawings, photographs, and sculptures. In a conscious commitment to his own region, Heinz J. Angerlehner pays special attention to works by Upper Austrian artists. There is an additional interplay created by national and international art positions. There is no stringent collection concept; the works in the collection were all selected based on personal enthusiasm. Great names of Austrian contemporaries such as Arnulf Rainer, Xenia Hausner, and Hermann Nitsch are represented, as are young up-and-coming artists. Heinz J. Angerlehner has repeatedly participated in the performances of Irene Andessner; they can now be discovered in photographs in

Museum Angerlehner
Thalheim bei Wels, Upper Austria

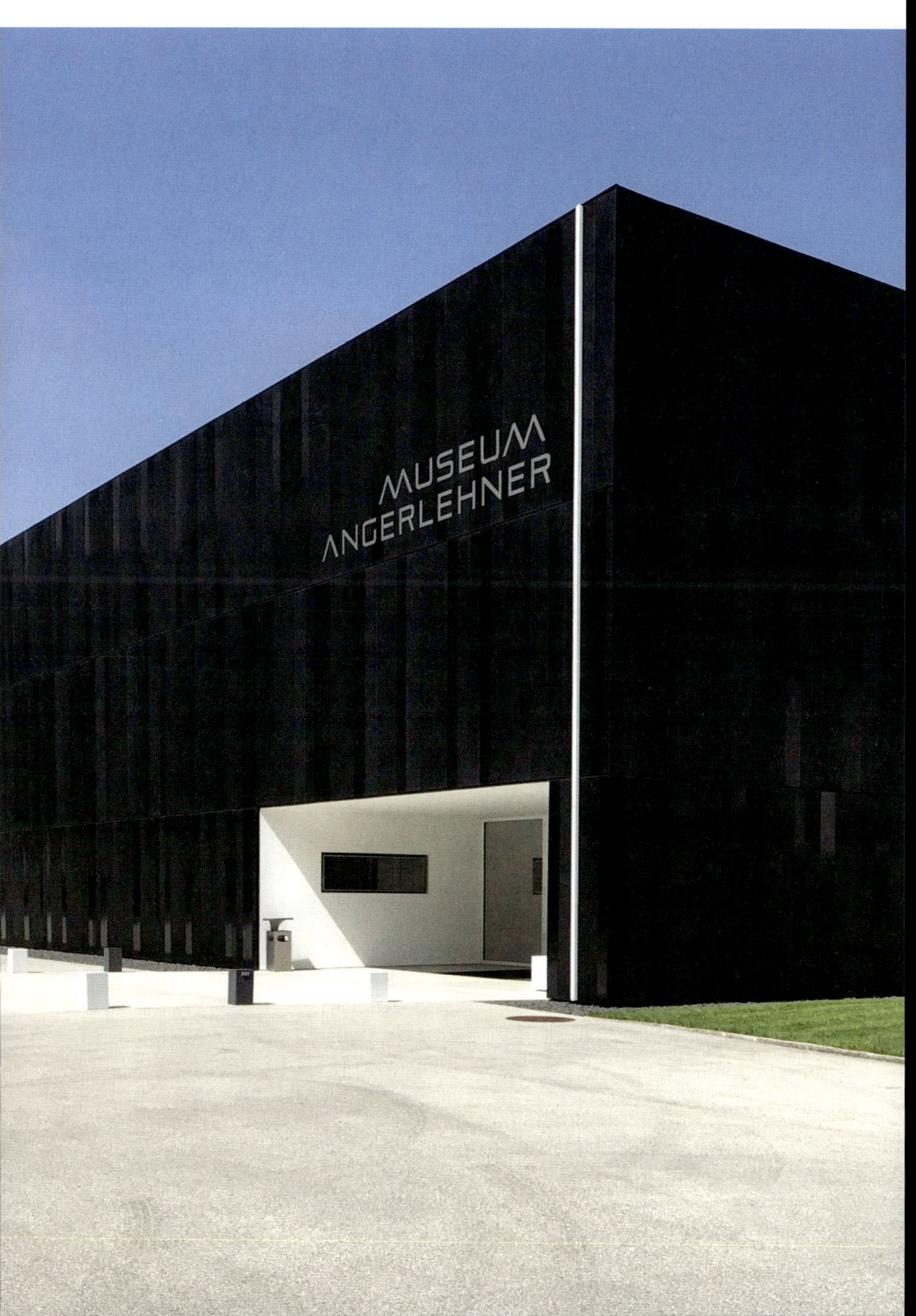

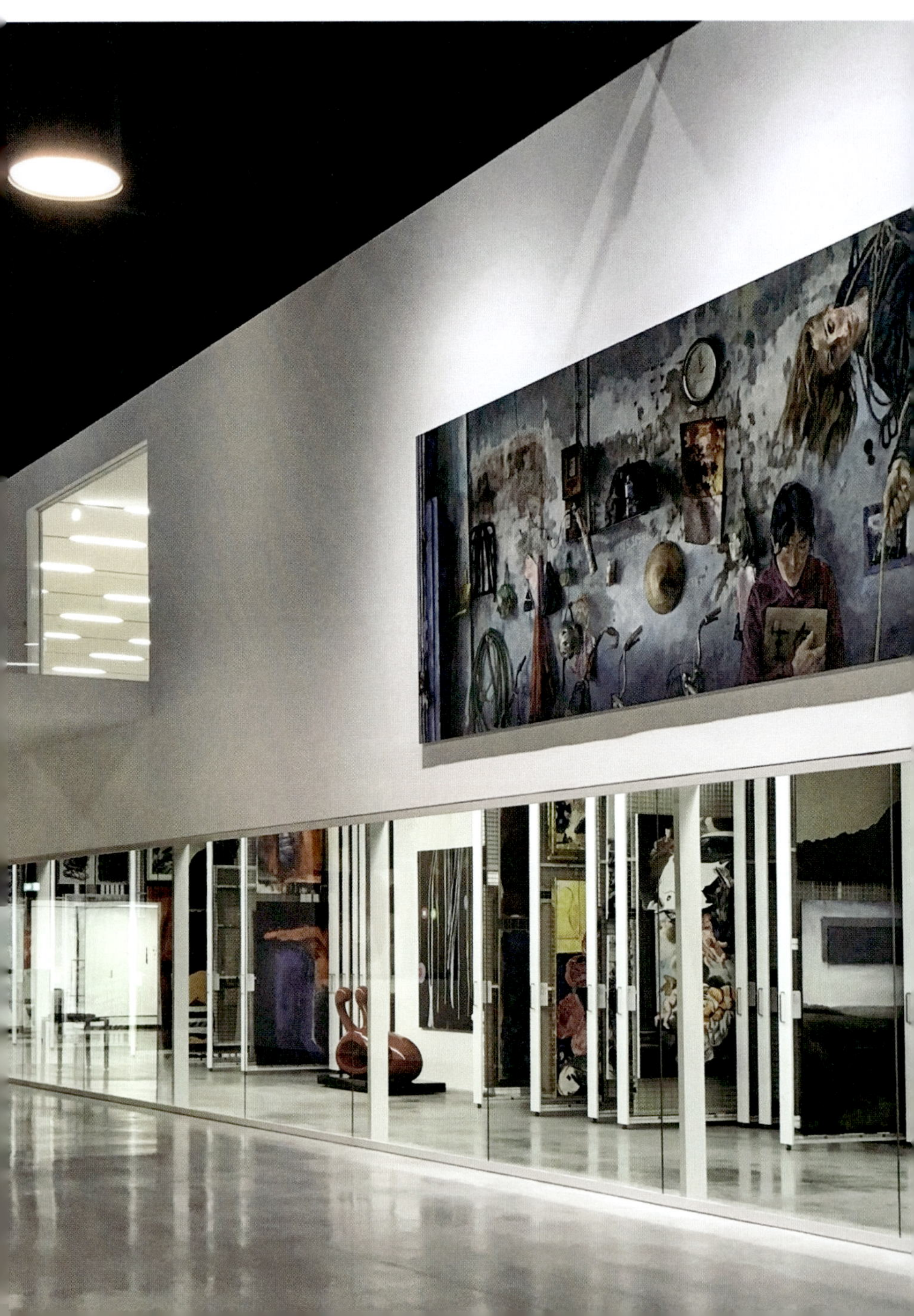

the collection. International stars such as Tom Wesselmann, Andy Warhol, and Roy Lichtenstein are also represented among the five hundred artists.

The 2,500 m² exhibition space is quite actively used. Two temporary exhibitions per year are presented in the 1,200 m² main room, four in the upper four rooms, and as many as five in the small salon. Most of the exhibits come from the collection, which is effectively supplemented by loans.

Museum Angerlehner
Asheter Str. 54
A-4600 Thalheim near Wels
Phone: +43 7242 2244220
office@museum-angerlehner.at
museum-angerlehner.at

Opening hours
March–September: Sat / Sun 10 a.m.–6 p.m., in August it is only possible to visit by appointment.
October–February: Sat / Sun 10 a.m.–5 p.m.
On some Sundays, public guided tours are offered (€5 plus admission; see website for dates; only if a minimum number of participants take part). Registration is necessary at least two days in advance (kunstvermittlung@museum-angerlehner.at or by telephone). Individual art tours can also be booked outside opening hours. Occasionally, concerts or other events take place. There is a comprehensive educational program for school classes.

Entrance fees
Adults / Reduced / Children up to 12 years: €10 / €8 / €5

Arrival by public transportation
Take the regional train from Wels central station to Grünau im Almtal and get off at Wels Messe. It is important to press the "stop request" button! Cross the railway bridge and turn left to the museum. Or take bus 16 to Welldorado and walk over the Angerlehner Steg bridge to the museum.

Extra tips
If you are traveling by car, the Kremsmünster Abbey is definitely worth a visit (preferably as part of a guided tour). Additionally, the church, library, observatory, imperial hall, and the fishponds are also worth seeing. The Stiftsschank serves home-style cuisine (www.stiftsschank.at; Stift 1, 4550 Kremsmünster).
Nicely presented and especially exciting for children are the Evolutionsmuseum Schmiding (evolutionsmuseum.at; access via Zoo Schmiding, Schmidinger Str. 5, 4631 Krenglbach) and the Welios Science Center (welios.at; Weliosplatz 1, 4600 Wels).

256
Kunst im Rohnerhaus

In 1996, entrepreneur Alwin Rohner and his family founded the Rohner Privatstiftung as a private institution for cultural impulses. The sociopolitical goal of the foundation and the personal concern of Alwin Rohner to make the public aware of the down-to-earth achievements and standing of Vorarlberg artists over time, to promote the shaping of opinions, social criticism, and tolerance in today's world. On this occasion, the private Rohnerhaus in Lauterach was opened to the public in 2000. It was built under the perspective of "living and working under one roof." In addition to the four exhibition floors with an exhibition area of approximately 500 m^2, the home of the founders also houses two apartments for family members. The foundation runs the museum, is the tenant of the exhibition rooms, and owns part of the collection of around 1,000 works. It contains works by Vorarlberg artists from the seventeenth century to the present day such as Oswald Baer, Albert Bechtold, Hubert Berchtold, Stefanie Hollenstein, Edmund Kalb, Angelika Kauffmann, Herbert von Reyl-Hanisch, and Rudolf Wacker. The collection, which has been assembled over forty years, focuses on the important artistic movements of Vorarlberg in the last century. It is important for the collector to show that from the very beginning, female artists from Vorarlberg were involved in the emergence of Expressionism, New Objectivity, Geometric Abstraction, and Realism parallel to the international developments in the visual arts. The second and third floors are entirely occupied by the collection, with the exhibition at the top being replaced only every five years and the one on the second floor every two years. On the ground floor and the basement, annually changing special, mostly themed, exhibitions are presented, which are supplemented by individual loans. It is important to the collector that at all exhibitions the works of art relate to each other over time. The restrained architecture is also intended to contribute to this concept.

Kunst im Rohnerhaus
Lauterach bei Bregenz, Vorarlberg

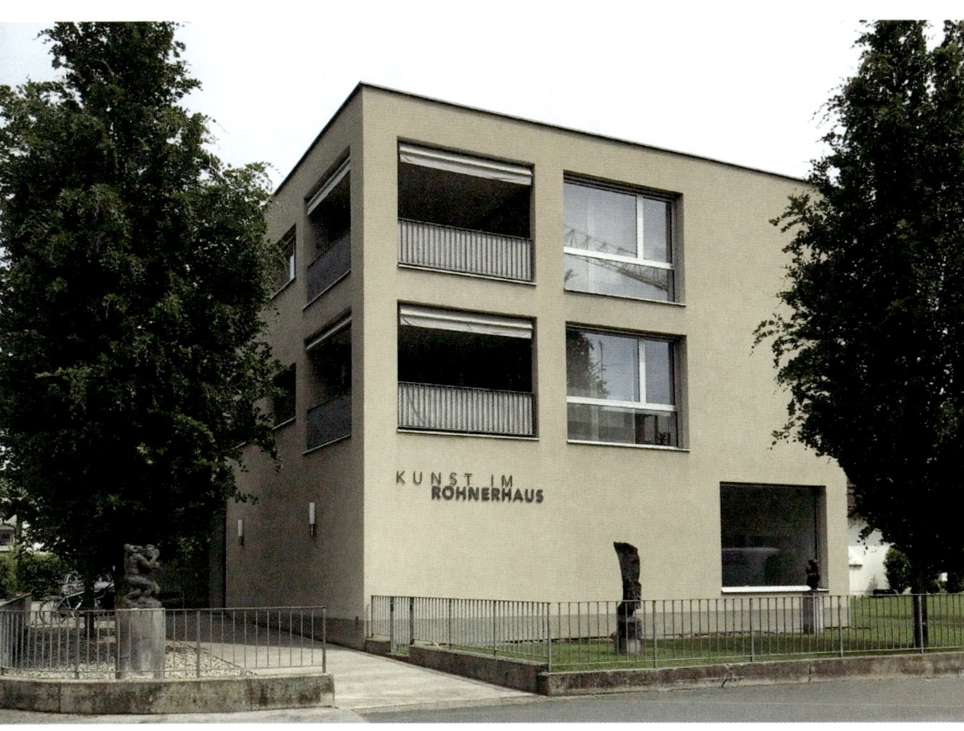

Kunst im Rohnerhaus
Kirchstr. 14
A-6923 Lauterach
Phone: +43 676 7032873
info@rohnerhaus.at
rohnerhaus.at

Opening hours
Open every first Sunday of the month with free admission from 10:30 a.m.–5 p.m. On all other days, visits and, if desired, guided tours by a family member are possible by appointment.

Entrance fees
Visit incl. guided tour €6

Arrival by public transportation
From Bregenz, you can take the S1 to Lauterach. From the station, follow Bahnhofstraße south and then turn left into Kirchstraße.

Parking
There is a parking lot on Kirchstraße, approx. 50 m after the museum.

Restaurant tip
On weekdays, gourmets can pamper themselves in the immediate vicinity at the Gault Millau toque-awarded Restaurant Guth (restaurantguth.at; Wälderstr. 10).

Extra tips
The Kunsthaus Bregenz, designed by Peter Zumthor, is a must-see for its architecture alone (kunsthaus-bregenz.at; Karl-Tizian-Platz, A-6900 Bregenz). The nonprofit Kunstraum Dornbirn, housed in a historical assembly hall, shows exhibitions of contemporary art (kunstraum-dornbirn.at; Jahngasse 9, 6850 Dornbirn). Dornbirn is also home to the FLATZ Museum, which shows works by the Austrian performance artist Wolfgang Flatz (flatzmuseum.at; Marktstr. 33, 6850 Dornbirn; open only Friday afternoons and Saturdays). The same building houses the exhibition room of vai (Vorarlberger Architektur Institut). The Swiss side of the region also attracts visitors with its unusual exhibition venues. In the Forum Würth Rorschach, changing art exhibitions (initiated by the Würth Collection) and a sculpture garden can be visited free of charge (wuerth-haus-rorschach.ch; Churerstr. 10, CH-9400 Rorschach; see also p. 62).
With its extraordinary underground exhibition rooms, the art space THE VIEW offers very extraordinary encounters with contemporary art (the-view-ch.com; Fruthwilerstr. 14; CH-8268 Salenstein; booking a guided tour is absolutely required).

Switzerland

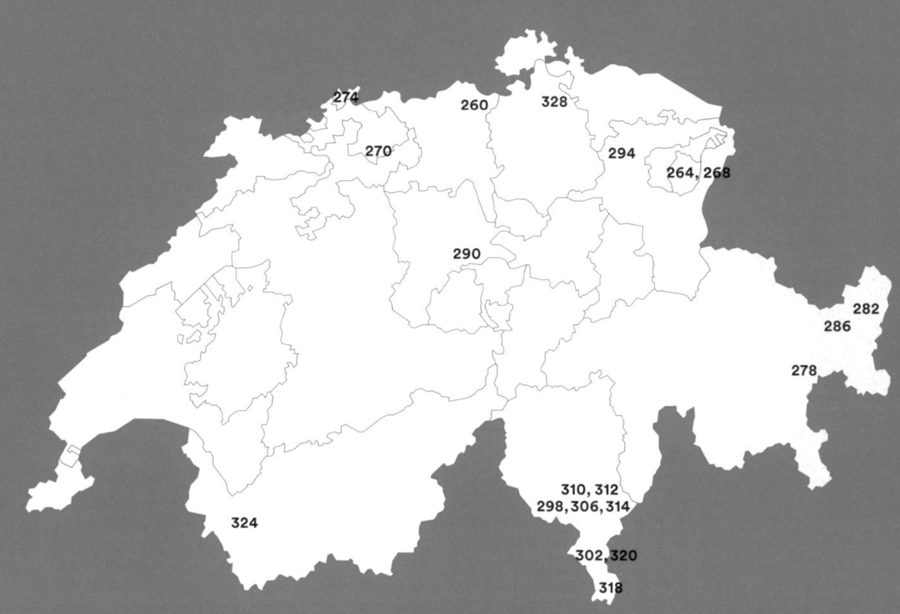

260 Museum Langmatt

Since 1990, the small Museum Langmatt has been in the thermal bathing town of Baden in Canton Aargau. The will of John Alfred Brown, the last descendant of Sidney and Jenny Brown, left the Villa Langmatt, the park-like property, and the valuable collection of his parents to the city. Baden architect Karl Moser, who worked with his partner Robert Curjel in Karlsruhe from 1888 to 1915, built the residential house, which was later extended, and the park in 1900/01. As was customary in the Art Nouveau era, the architect, who wanted to create a Gesamtkunstwerk, also influenced the interior.

To understand the origins of the museum, a short excursion into its history is worthwhile: Sidney Brown's father, Charles, was appointed as an engineer and moved from England to Winterthur in 1851. Thanks to his inventions, his employer, Gebrüder Sulzer, became one of the most important machine manufacturers in Switzerland. Sidney Brown, who was trained as an engineer at the Technikum Winterthur, married Jenny Sulzer, a member of the company's founding family in 1896. An interest in art and other cultural endeavors was awakened early on in both. The resourceful engineer and the industrialist's daughter, who had studied painting, were ideal complements to each other in the construction of the collection and the design of the villa and garden. Even today, particularly attentive visitors can discover traces of their various talents throughout the rooms. On the upper floor, one can marvel at a bathroom that was ultramodern for its time and a unique central vacuum cleaner device, while at the same time enjoying the home furnishings, wall design, and picture hanging, which were obviously executed with great attention to detail.

The foundation stone for the couple's art collection was laid as early as 1896 on their honeymoon: In Paris, they acquired works by Eugène Boudin and Paul Désiré Trouillebert. After that, in keeping with the prevailing taste in German-speaking Switzerland at the time, attention was initially focused on artists of the Munich Secession. Supported by the young Winterthur painter Carl Montag, who lived in Paris, their interest shifted back to French art and culture in 1904. The Museum Langmatt still houses the first Swiss private collection of paintings of French Impressionism and its predecessors. Starting with Camille Corot and Eugène Boudin, the collection ranges from Edgar Degas, Claude Monet, Pierre Auguste Renoir, Camille Pissarro, and Alfred Sisley to Paul Cézanne and Paul Gauguin. Additionally, there are individual works by Gustave Courbet, Odilon Redon, Pierre Bonnard, and the American Mary Cassatt, who lived in France. To keep the house alive, four to five varied special exhibitions are organized each year. In addition to the collection exhibitions, the focus is on shows of contemporary figurative painting.

To support the Sidney and Jenny Brown Foundation, which is responsible for maintaining the museum, the Freunde Museum Langmatt association was founded before the museum opened. The federal government, the canton, the city, and several companies took part in the necessary construction measures. Today, the city and canton still bear part of the operating costs.

Museum Langmatt
Stiftung Langmatt
Sidney and Jenny Brown
Römerstr. 30
CH-5401 Baden
Phone: +41 56 2008670
info@langmatt.ch
langmatt.ch

Opening hours
March to November Tue–Fri 2–5 p.m.; Sat/Sun 11 a.m.–5 p.m. Public holidays have individual opening hours. Guided tours, workshops for school classes, academic lectures, discussions with artists, readings, concerts, and other cultural events are organized regularly. The diverse program can be found on the website. Like the park, the museum café with a terrace is open from Tuesday to Friday at noon and on weekends from 10 a.m.

Entrance fees
Adults / Reduced / Adolescents under 18 and Museum-Musées holders: CHF 12 / CHF 10 / free

Parking
Parking is available on the street or, for a fee from 1 p.m. onwards on the ABB-Gelände Verenaäcker opposite.

Arrival by public transportation
Bus 9 in the direction of Roggebode/Kraftwerk runs from the upper bus stop at the railway station directly to the Museum Langmatt. You can also reach the museum by foot in about ten minutes. Coming from the railway tracks, keep left at the SBB counters and walk past the Post auto station along Bahnhofstrasse. This extends into Parkstrasse. Following the signs, turn left into Römerstrasse. The museum is on the right side.

Restaurant tips
It is possible to dine quite well at the upscale restaurant Grand Casino, not far from the museum. The weekly lunch offer is especially recommended (restaurant.grandcasinobaden.ch; Haselstr. 2). In the south of the city center, the Restaurant Roter Turm serves excellent innovative regional dishes. This unique location enables the successful integration of people with disabilities (restaurant-roterturm.ch; Rathausgasse 5; closed Sundays).

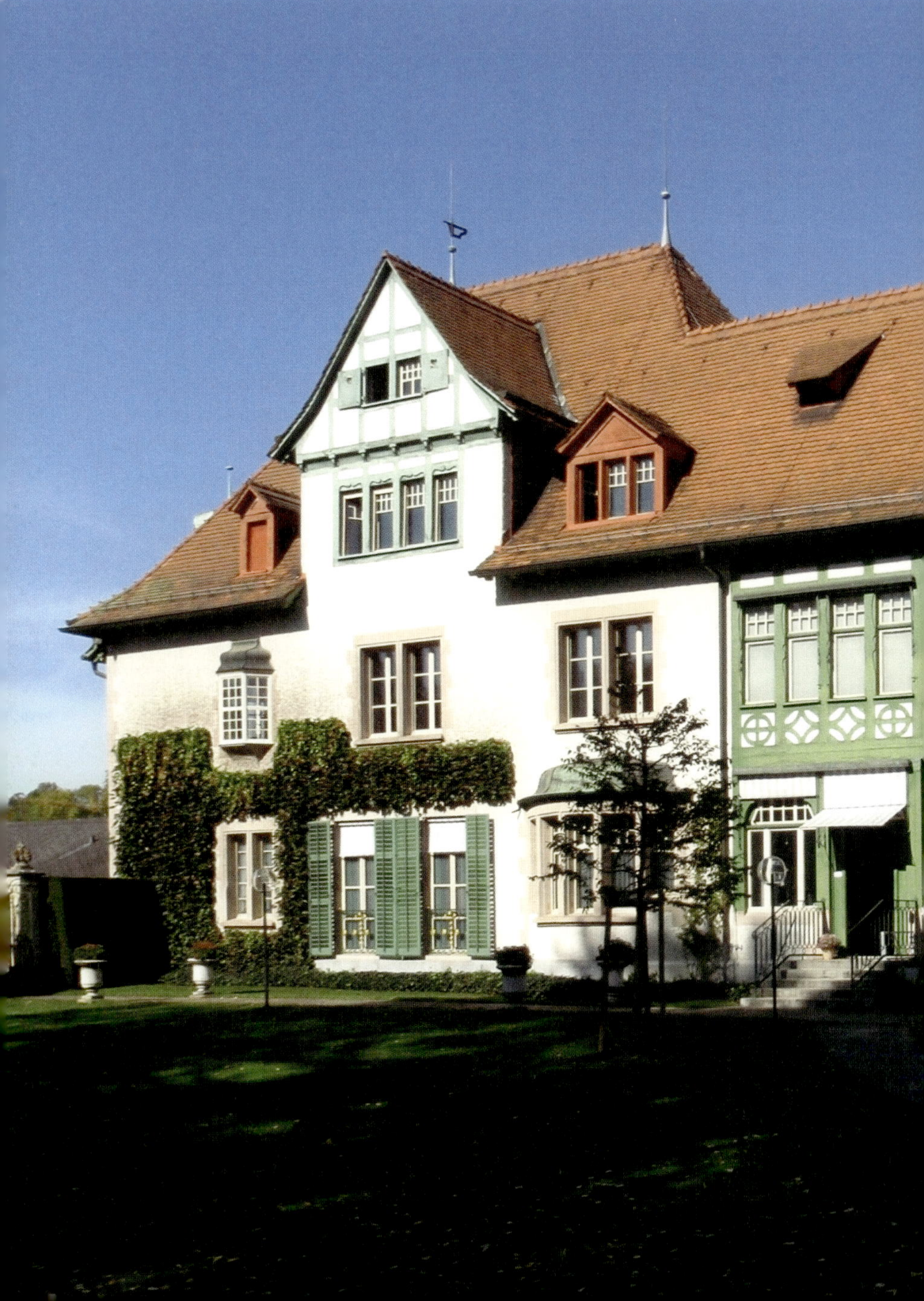

Museum Langmatt
Baden, Aargau

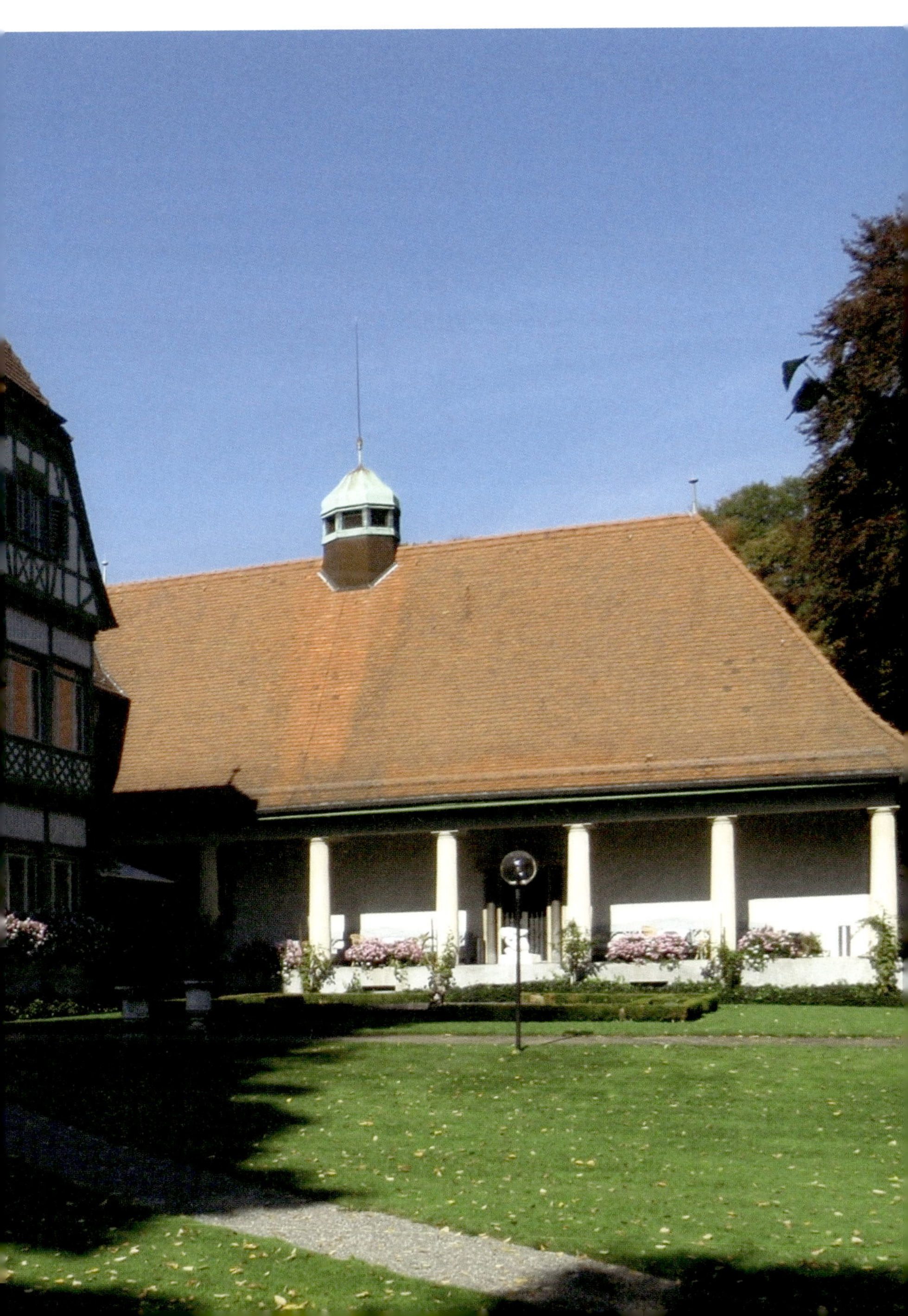

264 Kunstmuseum Appenzell

Appenzell is not only known for its cheese, houses painted with cows, and traditional costume figures, but also for its art and culture. The village owes this to industrialist and visionary Heinrich Gebert (1917–2007). Together with his brother Klaus, he took over his parents' tinsmith shop at a young age and developed it into the famous sanitary company Geberit. In the 1950s, his personal friendship with Appenzell painter Carl Walter Liner led to a commitment to modern art, which began with the establishment of a collection of his and Carl August Liner's works. Carl Walter Liner (1914–1997) was one of the most important Swiss representatives of the colorist tradition. He developed a unique language of color in his expressive landscape and figure paintings and his lyrical, gestural, and geometric abstractions. His father, Carl August Liner (1871–1946), began painting rural landscapes and portraits of the Appenzell citizens in 1906. He is one of the most important Swiss representatives of late Impressionism. In the early 1970s, Heinrich Gebert combined modern art and modern production facilities for the first time in Switzerland in the groundbreaking project "Art in the Factory." After retiring from active business life, he supported numerous projects with the foundations he established and wanted to initiate both a traditional and modern understanding of culture in the canton of Appenzell Innerrhoden. With the donation of more than 1,000 paintings, drawings, watercolors, and gouaches by Carl August and Carl Walter Liner by Heinrich Gebert, Katharina Liner-Rüf, and others in 1997, around 200 works of classical Modern and contemporary art from Heinrich Gebert's personal collection were donated to the precursor of the today's Heinrich Gebert Kulturstiftung Appenzell in 1998. Since 1996, Heinrich Gebert and his board of trustees had been searching for land and planning an adequate building for the foundation's collection.

The Appenzell convent Sta. Maria der Engel provided the foundation with a plot of land close to the railway station. Gebert invited the Zurich architects Annette Gigon und Mike Guyer to design the Museum Liner Appenzell (today Kunstmuseum Appenzell).

Kunstmuseum Appenzell
Appenzell, Appenzell Innerrhoden

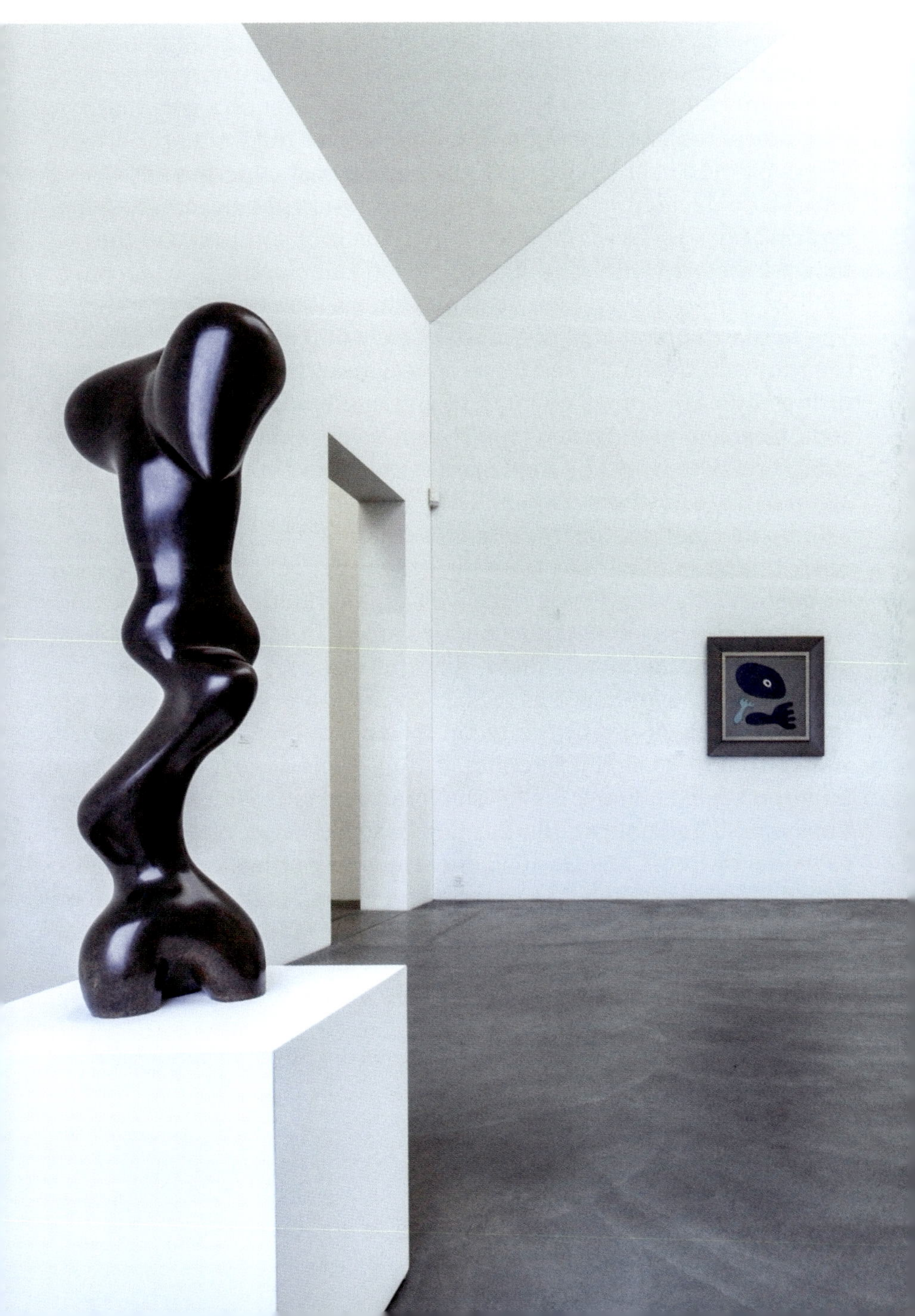

The museum, opened in 1998, was primarily dedicated to the work of father and son Liner, as well as twentieth-century and contemporary art. All the rooms have been designed in such a way that they are suitable for changing exhibitions from different art periods. The exhibition halls have bright walls and a cast concrete floor, into which daylight falls through high and wide gables, creating the typical "zigzag shape" of the building. The roof surfaces and the façades are clad with sandblasted chrome steel sheets, which have not lost their radiant power even after more than twenty years. The total exhibition area of approximately 650 m^2 is divided into ten rooms between 30 and 50 m^2. Every year, three monographic or thematic exhibitions on modern and contemporary painting, sculpture, and photography are shown. Every second year, a special exhibition with works by the Liners is presented in the Kunstmuseum or the Kunsthalle Ziegelhütte.

Since its creation, the foundation's collection has grown continuously thanks to donations from the private art collection of Heinrich Gebert and his wife, Myriam, as well as other donations and acquisitions. Today, the collection contains around 1,400 works by the Liners and approximately three hundred works by the Swiss and international avant-garde as well as contemporary art. In addition to the two Liners, also represented in the collection are Piet Mondrian, Hans Arp, Ernst Ludwig Kirchner, Antoni Tàpies, Ernst Wilhelm Nay, Eduardo Chillida, Frank Stella, Sam Francis, Pierre Alechinsky, Sean Scully, Willi Baumeister, Markus Lüpertz, and Hugo Weber, as well as works by Swiss and German contemporary artists such as Kerim Seiler, Dominik Stauch, Margret Eicher, Frank Badur, Stefan Steiner, Gottfried Honegger, Stefan Inauen, Robert B. Käppeli, and Beat Zoderer, among others. On the south side of the museum, there is a sculpture by George Rickey and in the entrance foyer a mobile by Alexander Calder.

Kunstmuseum Appenzell
Appenzell, Appenzell Innerrhoden

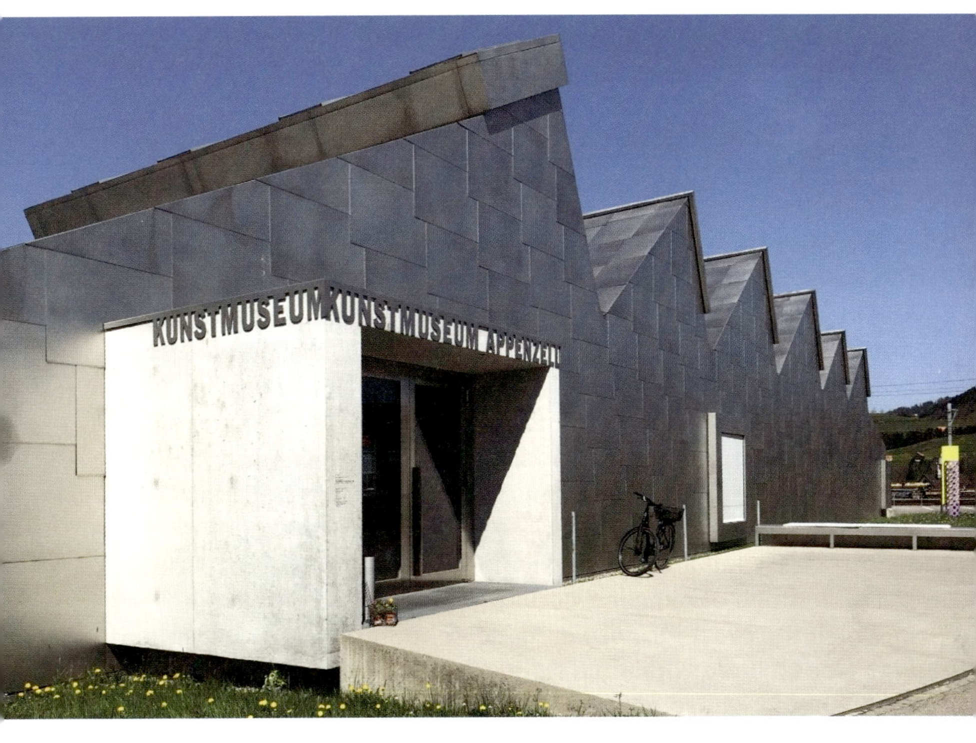

Kunstmuseum Appenzell
Unterrainstr. 5
CH-9050 Appenzell
Phone: +41 71 7881800
info@kunstmuseumappenzell.ch
h-gebertka.ch

Opening hours
April to October Tue–Fri 10 a.m.–noon and 2–5 p.m., Sat/Sun 11 a.m.–5 p.m.
November to March Tue–Sat 2–5 p.m., Sun 11 a.m.–5 p.m.
For adults, public guided tours take place on the first Sunday of the month at 2 p.m. (regular admission prices apply). Additional guided tours and workshops are offered for children.

Entrance fees
Kunstmuseum Appenzell: Adults / Reduced / Family ticket / Children (under age 10): CHF 9 / CHF 6 / CHF 19 / free
Both museums: Adults / Reduced / Family ticket / Children (under age 10): CHF 15 / CHF 10 / CHF 32 / free

Arrival by public transportation
Kunstmuseum Appenzell is located near the Appenzell railway station.

Parking
Please use the public parking spaces in the village, for example, next to the Gringel schoolhouse, 100 m south of the Kunstmuseum.

Restaurant tips
In the northern city center, the Drei Könige restaurant offers Appenzell specialties under a 500-year-old wooden ceiling. It is also worth descending to the restored cellar, which has been restored in a minimalistic style (drei-koenig.ch; Hauptgasse 26). Creative cuisine is served in the Marktplatz restaurant (marktplatz-appenzell.ch; Kronengarten 2; closed Sun–Tue).

Extra tips
If you stay three nights or longer in the same accommodation in Appenzell, you will automatically benefit from the Appenzell Holiday Card. In addition to free admission to the museums, it also offers numerous other advantages. The Flauderei is the experience shop of Goba AG, one of the smallest mineral water producers in Switzerland. The shop, which is completely redesigned four times a year, offers drinks and hand-picked souvenirs (flauderei.ch; Hauptgasse 21). The sculptures *Table* (2008) and *Rotating Plate* (2005) by Appenzell-born artist Roman Signer can be seen on Adlerplatz.

268
Kunsthalle Ziegelhütte

Appenzell owes another cultural highlight to Heinrich Gebert's generosity; the Kunsthalle Ziegelhütte, opened in 2003, is an exhibition house, concert hall, social meeting place, and industrial monument at the same time. In 1500, the first lime kiln was put into operation in the Appenzell brickworks; in 1566, six years after the great fire in Appenzell, the brickworks was rebuilt with the kiln still in use today. From 1958 onwards, no bricks were produced, but bricks were still sold until 1981. After that, the building stood empty and was to be demolished. To preserve the historic building, Appenzell's oldest industrial monument, in 1999 the heirs sold the brickworks to the Carl Liner Vater und Sohn Foundation (now Heinrich Gebert Kulturstiftung Appenzell). From 2001 to 2003, the brickworks was transformed into a multifunctional cultural center by the St. Gallen architectural office of Robert Bamert. A new building made of exposed concrete as a "house within a house," in which the most modern climatic conditions were guaranteed, was placed under the main ridge of the brick building. This exhibition wing, in whose conception Zurich office Tilla Theus was also involved, forms a bridge over the preserved brick kiln from 1566. In this way, the contrast between the wood smelting works and the concrete art cube can be spatially experienced. The circular kiln, which is entered on the ground floor and has a new iron platform, is the central object in the hall-like interior and venue for various events. The lighting control was an elementary part of the conversion concept, in which the natural light falls through a roof skylight along the exhibition walls through two floors into the hall on the ground floor. The three exhibition floors of the fair-faced concrete building, which are approximately 430 m^2 in size, are used for the art exhibitions. These change three times a year, and circa sixty works by Carl Walter Liner from the collection of the foundation are permanently presented in the event section of the Ziegelhütte.

Kunsthalle Ziegelhütte
Appenzell, Appenzell Innerrhoden

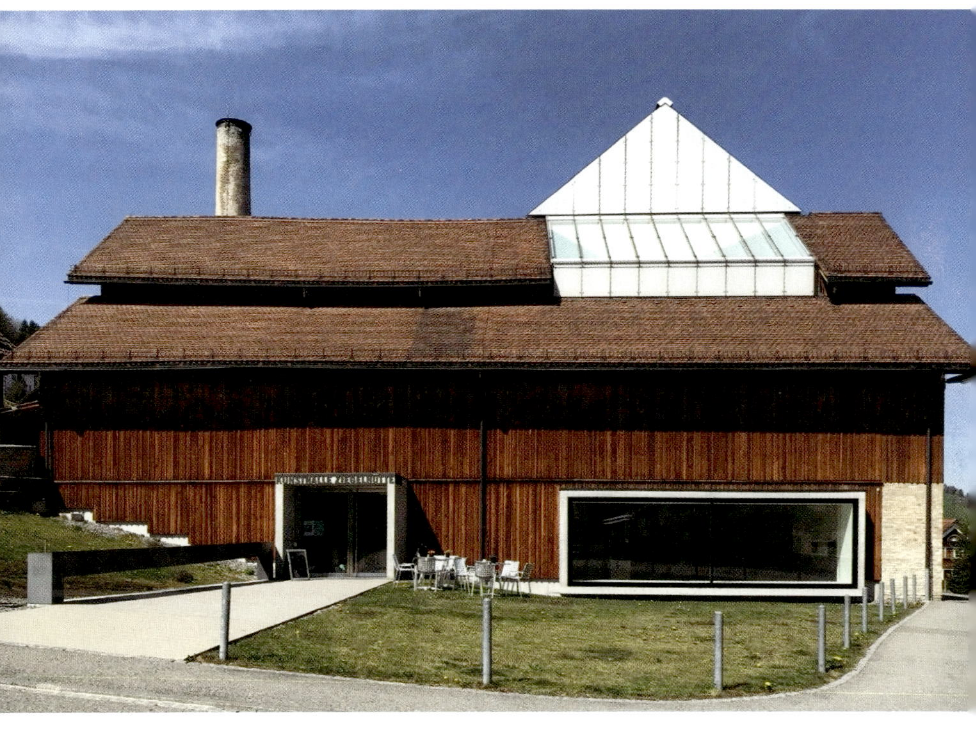

Kunsthalle Ziegelhütte
Ziegeleistr. 14
CH-9050 Appenzell
Phone: +41 71 788 18 60
info@kunsthalleziegelhuette.ch
h-gebertka.ch

Opening hours
April to October Tue–Fri 10 a.m.–noon and 2–7 p.m., Sat/Sun 11 a.m.–5 p.m. November to March Tue–Sat 2–5 p.m., Sun 11 a.m.–5 p.m. For adults, public guided tours take place on the second Sunday of the month at 2 p.m. (regular admission prices apply). Additional guided tours and workshops for children are offered. Concerts are held every first Friday of the month.
There is a small cafeteria and a shop at the Kunsthalle Ziegelhütte.

Arrival by public transportation
The Kunsthalle Ziegelbrücke is located about ten minutes on foot from Appenzell railway station on the southern outskirts of the city. The museum is signposted.

Parking
Please use the public parking spaces in the village. A good place is in the lot next to the Gringel schoolhouse, 100 m south of the Kunstmuseum, and visit both museums on foot from there.

270
Kloster Schönthal

In the middle of the Jura landscape in the canton of Basel-Landschaft, on the site of the former Benedictine monastery Schönthal, there is a sculpture park that is unique in Switzerland. The monastery and its founder, Count Adalbero of Frohburg, were first mentioned in documents in 1146. Until the monastery fell victim to the Reformation and was abolished, the Bishop of Basel was a patron. After secularization, the town experienced an eventful history. In the seventeenth century, the monastery church with its famous Romanesque west façade, which has been a historically protected building since 1967, served temporarily as a brick factory and as a woodshed until a few decades ago. In 1985, the land and buildings were acquired entirely with private funds from John Schmid, a Basel entrepreneur from the advertising industry, and carefully renovated over several years. After a second renovation phase, this special place found its new purpose as a place of cultural encounters in 2000.

During a short walk through the sculpture park, one will encounter works by Tony Cragg, Nigel Hall, Ian Hamilton Finlay, David Nash, Ulrich Rückriem, Not Vital, Steiner/Lenzlinger, and Roman Signer. Most of them are placed in open natural spaces, sometimes they are quite hidden. In 2008, Richard Long created two sculptures, which are located under the roof of a former cowshed. These fragile works are only accessible upon request or accompanied by a staff member. Otherwise, visitors are invited to move freely though Schönthal. A route map is the only orientation guide for discovering thirty-three sculptures by twenty-three international and Swiss artists across an area of around one hundred hectares. Anyone seeking to visit each work needs a few hours and sturdy shoes. In damp weather, guests can resort to robust rubber boots available in various sizes. Suspended from the outer façade of the church, they are a work of art in themselves and an extremely popular photo motif.

Collector John Schmid favors site-specific art. He invites the selected artists to stay in the monastery, finds the ideal location for the planned sculpture together with them, and accompanies its creation.

Kloster Schönthal
Langenbruck, Basel-Landschaft

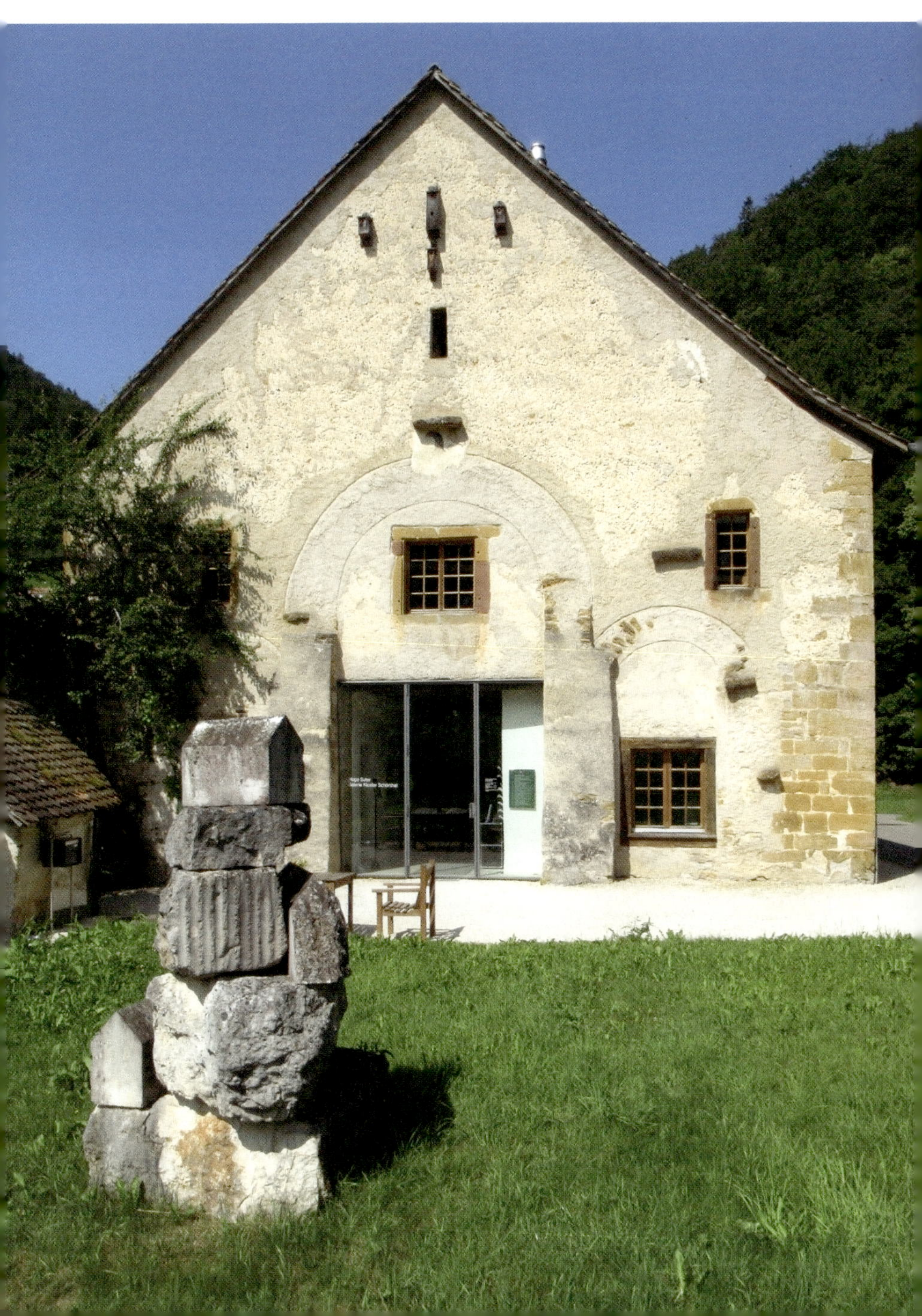

While the sculptures are permanently on view outside, changing exhibitions of contemporary art take place twice a year in the gallery Sankt Alban in the church room and the abbot's chamber in the summer months. The nonprofit foundation Sculpture at Schoenthal, founded by John Schmid in 2001, was merged with the Edith Maryon Foundation. Proceeds from the sale of objects and other income benefit new projects of the Kloster Schönthal association.

Kloster Schönthal
Schönthalstr. 158
CH-4438 Langenbruck
Phone: +41 61 7067676
mail@schoenthal.ch
schoenthal.ch

Opening hours
The sculpture park is always open to visitors. Externally guided groups and school classes must register. Guided tours can be individually arranged. Art events, concerts, and readings, which are announced on the website, also take place in the sculpture park. During the summer months, there is a small café in the monastery.

Entrance fees
Adults / Reduced / Family ticket:
CHF 10 / CHF 6 / CHF 20

Parking
The monastery has its own parking area; guests are requested to use only the marked parking spaces.

Arrival by public transportation
Coming from Basel, it takes about an hour with public transport. From Basel SBB, take the IR train in the direction of Lucerne to Liestal and change there to the regional train to Waldenburg. There, change to PostBus 94 and travel in the direction of Balsthal to the Langenbruck Dorf stop.
From the bus stop, walk only a few meters in the direction of travel along the main road and turn left into Schöntalstrasse. Follow this road for about twenty minutes (see sbb.ch for timetable information).

Restaurant tips
If you travel by car to Kloster Schönthal, you can indulge in gourmet Italian fare at the luxurious Osteria Tre in Bubendorf in the evening (badbubendorf.ch; Kantonsstr. 3; closed Sundays and Mondays). The Hotel Bad Eptingen, which has an exquisite wine list and offers rustic cuisine, is a cozy place to stay (badeptingen.ch; Läufelfingerstr. 2, 4458 Eptingen). Typical Swiss dishes are served in the lofty and secluded Restaurant Blüemlismatt, with a fantastic view of the Mittelland and Alps (bluemlismatt.ch; 4622 Egerkingen; closed Mondays and Tuesdays). Gourmets will also be delighted by the fine French cuisine of the Lampart's gourmet restaurant (lamparts.ch; Oltnerstr. 19, Hägendorf 4614; closed Sundays and Mondays).

Extra tips
After the hike, a library with art books, documentaries, and videos is open to visitors during the summer months. The former monastery can also be used as a seminar venue and for overnight stays. The property was rightly included in the Swiss Heritage Protection brochure *The Most Beautiful Hotels in Switzerland*. The John Schmid Gallery was opened in 2010 in the vicinity of the Kunstmuseum Basel (kunstmuseumbasel.ch), which is also the office and information center of Kloster Schönthal in Langenbruck (johnschmidgalerie.ch; St. Alban-Anlage 67, 4052 Basel).

Kloster Schönthal
Langenbruck, Basel-Landschaft

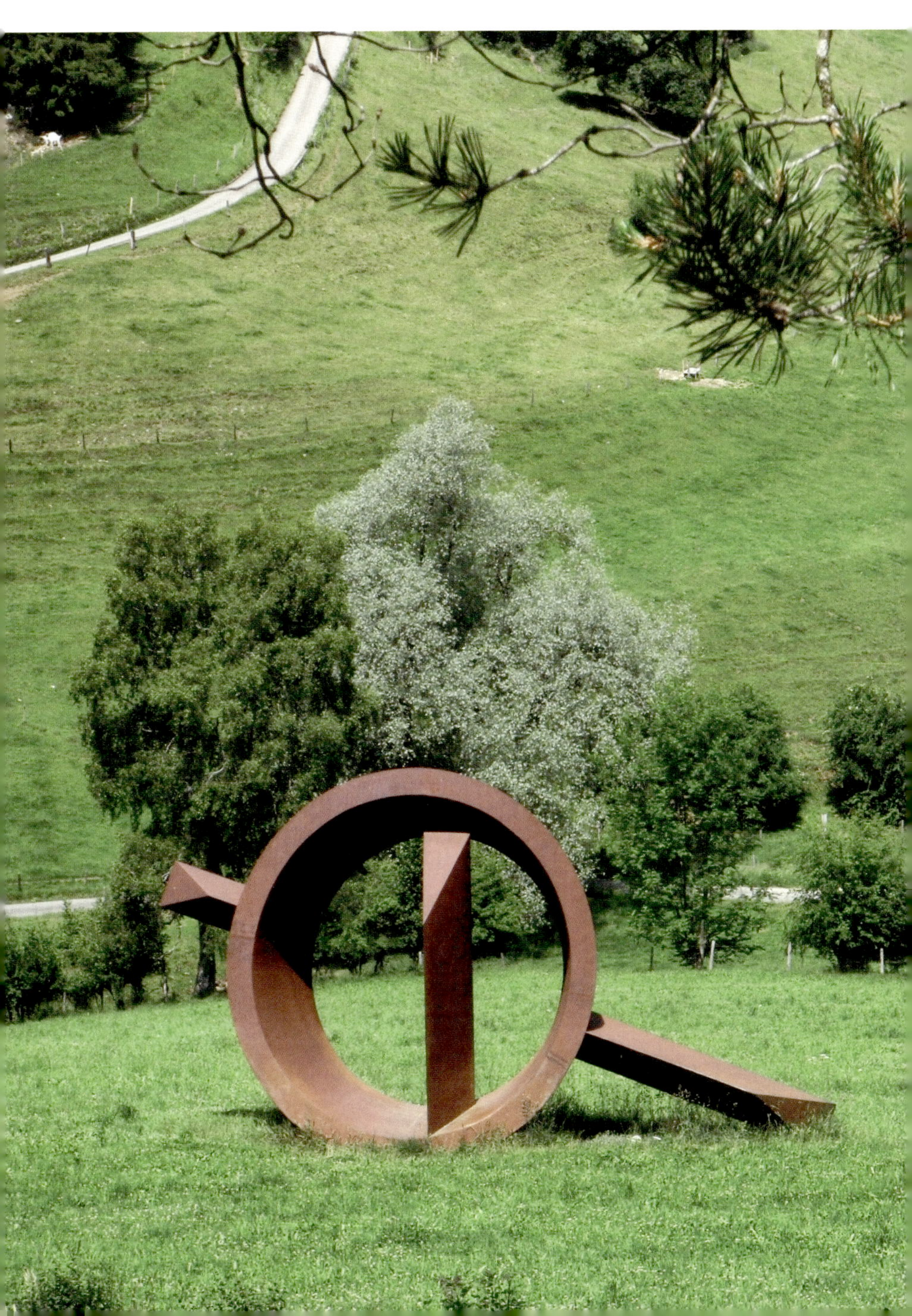

274
Fondation Beyeler

To visit the Fondation Beyeler, which opened in 1997 on the grounds of the Berower Park, you have to visit the beautifully situated outskirts of Riehen. Here, Italian architect Renzo Piano succeeded in creating a true masterpiece with the restrained, elegant building of the Fondation. Since its expansion in 2000, the building, clad in red porphyry stone from Patagonia, has had a total exhibition area of almost 3,800 m^2, with twenty-two rooms on two levels. The size of these can be changed and their tranquility and simplicity are captivating. The bright materials, natural light, and the deliberate omission of visible technical or design details achieve a unique atmosphere. The museum's construction was financed by the Fondation Beyeler, which the collector couple Hildy and Ernst Beyeler founded in 1982. Together with the Wyss Foundation, it is the sponsor of the Foundation. Following a favorable vote by the inhabitants of Riehen, the municipality made the site available for use. The canton of Basel-Stadt supports the museum financially with annual contributions.

The collection of the late Beyeler couple, which initially consisted of 230 works, grew during a period of more than fifty years parallel to their successful gallery activities. It offers a wide range of insights into classical modernism. Purchases of works by Paul Cézanne, Vincent van Gogh, and Claude Monet were made in the early years. This was followed by representative groups of works by Pablo Picasso, Joan Miró, Piet Mondrian, Wassily Kandinsky, Paul Klee, and Henri Matisse, as well as works from Pop Art and US Abstract Expressionism. Georg Baselitz, Anselm Kiefer, and Neo Rauch were also recently integrated into the collection, and today the Fondation's collection comprises of around four hundred works. The works of classical modern art are juxtaposed in several rooms with objects from tribal art from Africa, Alaska, and Oceania, often selected as exciting contrasts. The high-caliber special exhibitions, which change three times a year and occupy about one-third of the exhibition space each, either make references to current art or deepen the focus of the collection. Apart from a few monumental works, the collection is also changed three times a year.

Fondation Beyeler
Riehen, Basel-Stadt

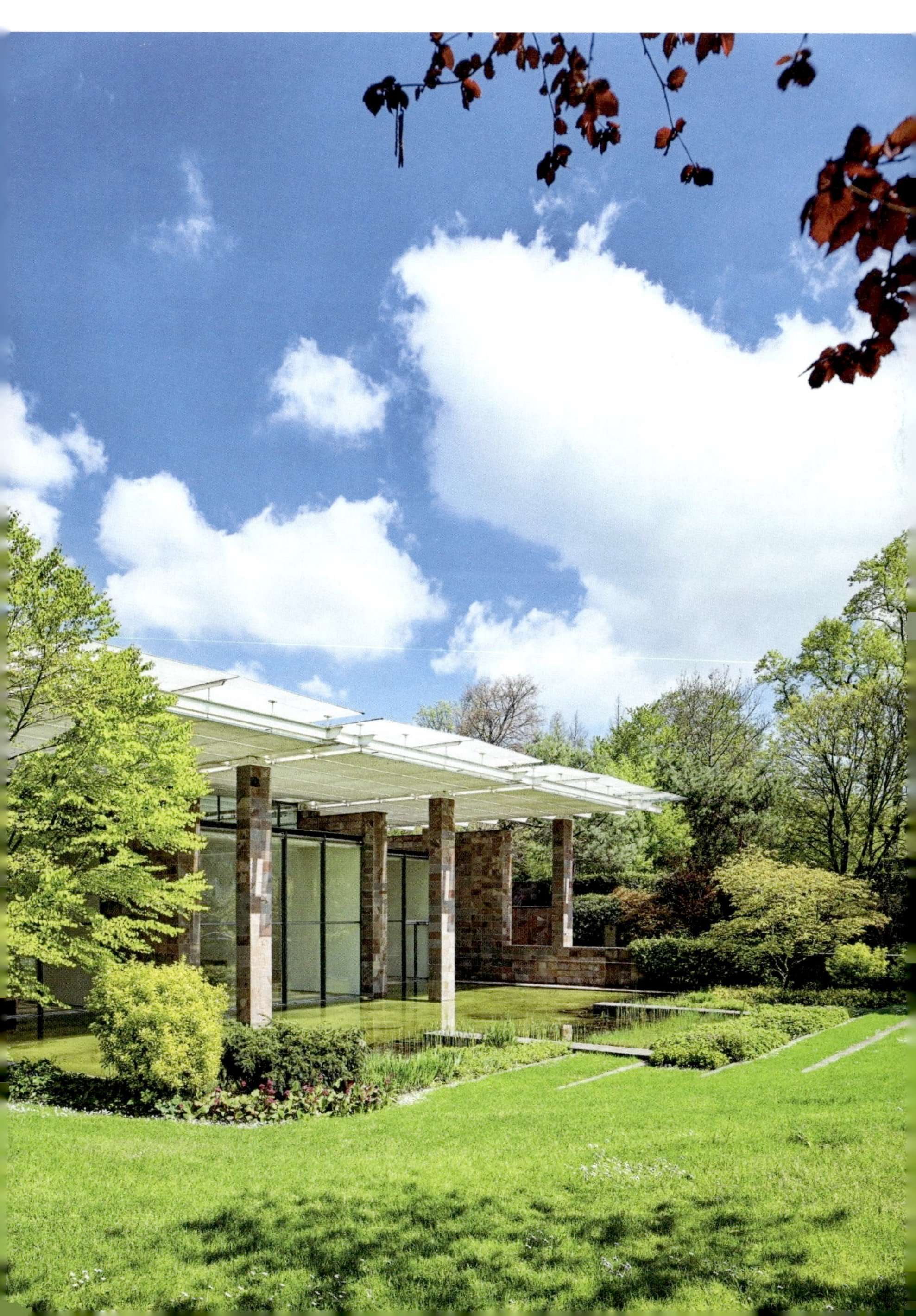

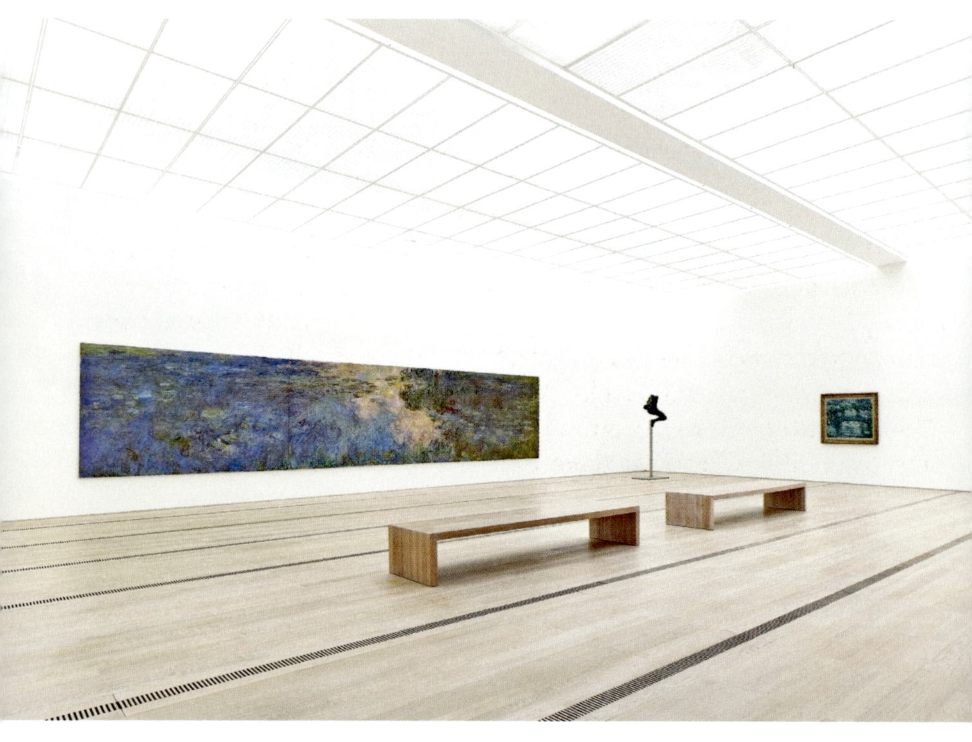

Fondation Beyeler

Baselstr. 101
CH-4125 Riehen / Basel
Phone: +41 61 6459700
info@fondationbeyeler.ch
fondationbeyeler.ch

Opening hours

Daily 10 a.m.–6 p.m.,
Wed 10 a.m.–8 p.m.
In addition to daily public guided tours (admission to the museum plus CHF 7), a diverse program of art education is offered (incl. thematic, family, and children's tours, workshops, lectures, concerts, and numerous events for school classes), which can be explored on the website.
The Berower Park Restaurant, which is attached to the Fondation, is located on the ground floor of the eighteenth-century Villa Berower.

Entrance fees

Adults / Adults from 4:30 p.m. and reduced / Students from ages 16–30 / Children up to age 15: CHF 30 / CHF 25 / CHF 25 / CHF 15 / free
The Fondation Beyeler is also part of the Museum-PASS-Musées.

Parking

It is advisable to park your car center's multistory car park.

Arrival by public transportation

Tram 6 (from the city center, Messehalle and Badischem Bahnhof) in the direction of Riehen Grenze stops directly in front of the museum at the Fondation Beyeler stop. From Basel SBB, take tram 2 and change at Badischer Bahnhof to tram 6.

Restaurant tips

Many excellent restaurants await visitors to the city of Basel.

Extra tips

The Vitra Campus with the Vitra Design Museum designed by Frank Gehry and the Vitra Schaudepot, designed by architects Herzog & de Meuron, is located on the German side in Weil am Rhein, just a few kilometers west of the Fondation Beyeler. Both exhibition buildings are worth a visit, and the architectural tours taking place on the Vitra premises are informative and entertaining (design-museum.de; Charles-Eames-Str. 2, D-79576 Weil am Rhein). The cross-border Rehberger-Weg links the Fondation Beyeler and the Vitra Campus over approx. five kilometers. Guided by 24 path markers by artist Tobias Rehberger, a diverse natural and cultural landscape can be explored (24.stopps.info). In Basel, it is possible to spend multiple days in various art museums. Particularly worth seeing is the Kunstmuseum Basel, consisting of three buildings (kunstmuseum-basel.ch; St. Alban-Graben 16 and St. Alban-Rheinweg 60), Kunst-

Fondation Beyeler
Riehen, Basel-Stadt

The Fondation Beyeler is planning an ambitious expansion. Star architect Peter Zumthor was commissioned to design an administration building and an exhibition house at the nearby Iselin-Weber-Park, recently acquired by the Fondation Beyeler. In the new Haus der Kunst, more works of art from the permanent collection will be presented on three floors with a total exhibition area of 1,500 m^2. Zumthor will create a ground-level, transparent garden pavilion for events next to the museum restaurant in Berower Park. The expansion project will be privately financed. Generous donations from the Wyss Foundation, the Daros Collection, and anonymous Basel patrons lay the foundations for its realization. Construction will begin once the financing has been fully secured and the building permits have been issued.

halle Basel (kunsthallebasel.ch; Steinenberg 7), and the Museum Tinguely (tinguely.ch; Paul Sacher-Anlage 1). In summer, a detour to the south of Basel is advantageous. In the industrial quarter, the Schaulager, designed by Herzog & de Meuron, opens its doors for a few months. Starting from the Emanuel Hoffmann Foundation, which is stored here, the Schaulager is dedicated to the handling, conservation, research, and communication of contemporary art (schaulager.org; Ruchfeldstr. 19). Close to Schaulager is the young HeK (Haus der elektronischen Künste Basel; hek.ch; Freilager-Platz 9, 4142 Münchenstein/Basel).
A trip to the canton of Basel-Landschaft to the sculpture park Kloster Schönthal (see p. 270) is also very worthwhile.

278
Kunst im Castell / Sammlung Ruedi Bechtler

In Zuoz, at one of the entrances to the Swiss National Park, visitors will find an exciting symbiosis of old hotel walls and new art. Ruedi Bechtler, Zurich artist and offspring of the Bechtler family, a family of entrepreneurs and patrons of the arts, acquired the hotel, some of which was built in 1913, as majority shareholder in 1996 together with the gallery owners Iwan and Manuela Wirth. The hotel, which has a lively history—after the First World War, the German crown prince lived here with his family and famous authors such as Stefan Zweig and Arthur Schnitzler spent the night here—last belonged to his brother-in-law. In consultation with the community, Bechtler financed the major renovation in 2004 with the construction and sale of an apartment house, which was built by the Amsterdam architectural office UN Studios on the premises of the hotel. It is part of the hotel's concept that Bechtler would make parts of his private art collection permanently available and select the location, often in close cooperation with the artists. Many works have also been created on site at art happenings or have a connection to the Engadine. He is also president of the Walter A. Bechtler Foundation, founded by his father in 1955, and is involved in the Art Public Plaiv art project. These include works such as a *Rock Bath* by Japanese artist Tadashi Kawamata, which has been in the hotel park since 1997, text works by Lawrence Weiner on the hotel's south façade, and the seven-meter *Skyspace* by James Turrell.

Inside the hotel, the art tour begins in the reception area, where installations by Thomas Hirschhorn and Carsten Höller greet visitors. On the way to the terrace and the dining rooms, the view immediately falls on Pipilotti Rist and Gabrielle Hächler's *Red Bar*, whose red bar in the form of a question mark revives a 1970s disco aura. In the Arvenstube, artist couple Steiner/Lenzlinger created a floating sculpture from found twigs, flowers, and a caiman head

Kunst im Castell / Sammlung Ruedi Bechtler
Zuoz, Grisons

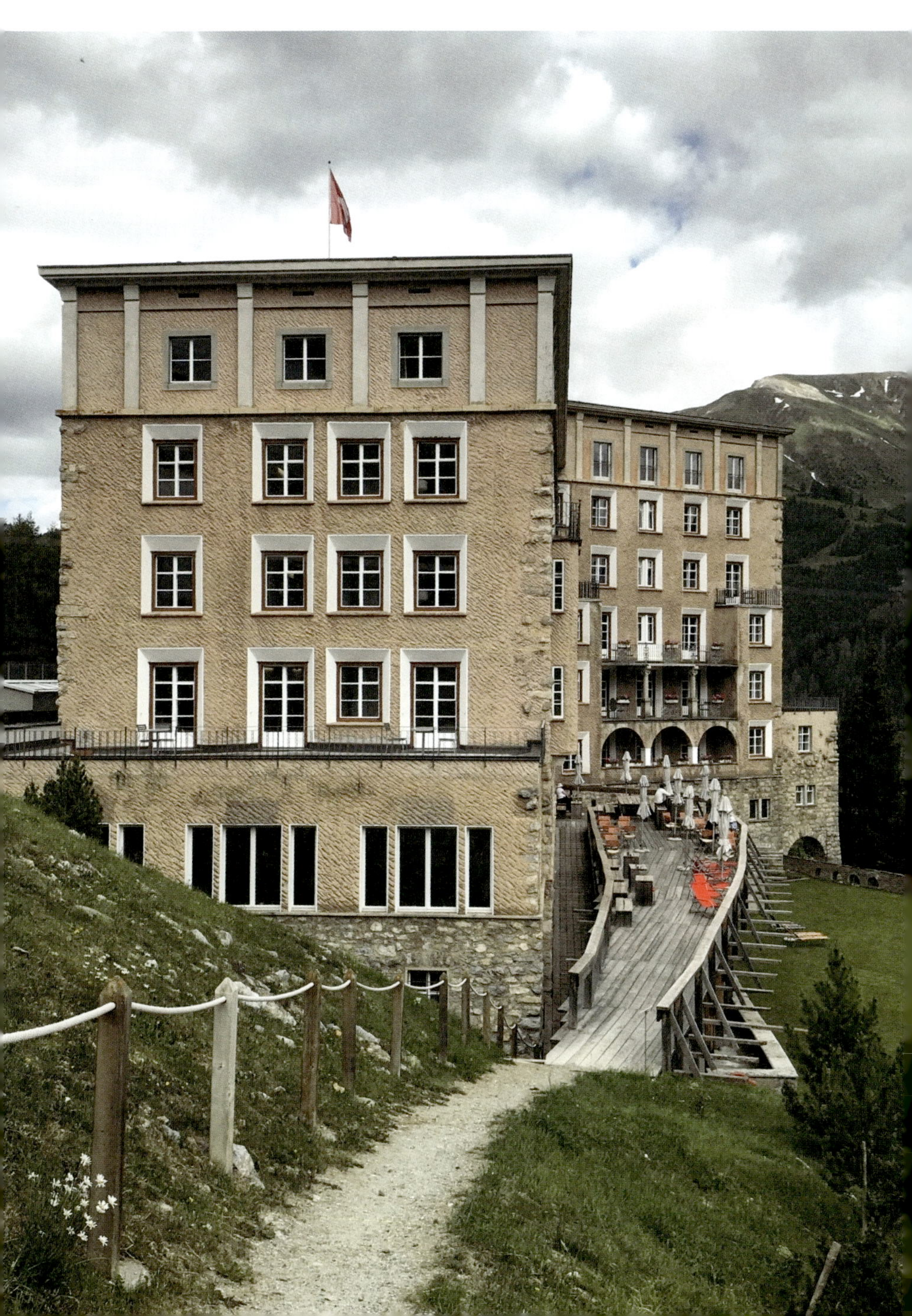

from Bechtler's grandfather. And, what at first looks like a typical terrace turns out to be a large installation by Tadashi Kawamata. The artist built it in 2004 in Zuoz following Art Basel using scrap wood. Works by artists such as Roman Signer, Fischli/Weiss, Martin Kippenberger, Wade Guyton, Mickry 3, Christine Streuli, Olafur Eliasson, Peter Regli, Gabriel Orozco, and also some works by Ruedi Bechtler himself hang in the corridors leading to the hotel rooms.

Kunst im Castell
Sammlung Ruedi Bechtler
CH-7524 Zuoz
Phone: +41 81 8515253
info@hotelcastell.ch
hotelcastell.ch/kunst-architektur/kunst-im-castell

Opening hours
There are guided tours every Thursday at 5 p.m. (one to one and a half hours) followed by a visit to the Skyspace Piz Uter by James Turrell. Registration is required. Opposite the reception area, video works by Peter Fischli, Roman Signer, and others are shown from 5 p.m. onwards. It is possible to view other artworks anytime during hotel opening hours in the winter and summer seasons. This includes a visit to Skyspace, which is particularly worth viewing at dusk.
Castell Art Weekend takes place every year in September. Seminar participants can learn more about the latest art trends, meet famous artists in person, and visit galleries in Zuoz and the surrounding area. During the season, photo days and a number of workshops for adults and children are also offered. The Studio Cinema Castell regularly shows films from all over the world (mostly Fridays and some Saturdays at 9 p.m., CHF 12 for external visitors).

Entrance fees
Free admission

Arrival by public transportation
Upon registration, visitors will be picked up at Zuoz railway station and taken to the hotel.

Restaurant tips
It is a good idea to continue the art tour with a drink in the Red Bar or a meal in the hotel's restaurant. Coffee lovers can visit Café Badilatti, Europe's highest coffee roastery, and the Caferama, the hotel's own coffee museum (cafe-badilatti.ch; Resgia District).

Extra tips
Worth a visit are Muzeum Susch (see p. 286), which only opened at the beginning of 2019, and the Alberto Giacometti Museum in Sent (p. 282). As part of the Art Public Plaiv project, the Walter A. Bechtler Foundation presents installations in and around Hotel Castell and other locations in Upper Engadine, such as Martin Kippenberger's *Transportabler U-Bahn-Eingang* (Transportable Subway Entrance, 1997) near the Zouz Golf Course (hotelcastell.ch/en/art-architecture/art-public-plaiv and bechtlerstiftung.ch).

Kunst im Castell / Sammlung Ruedi Bechtler
Zuoz, Grisons

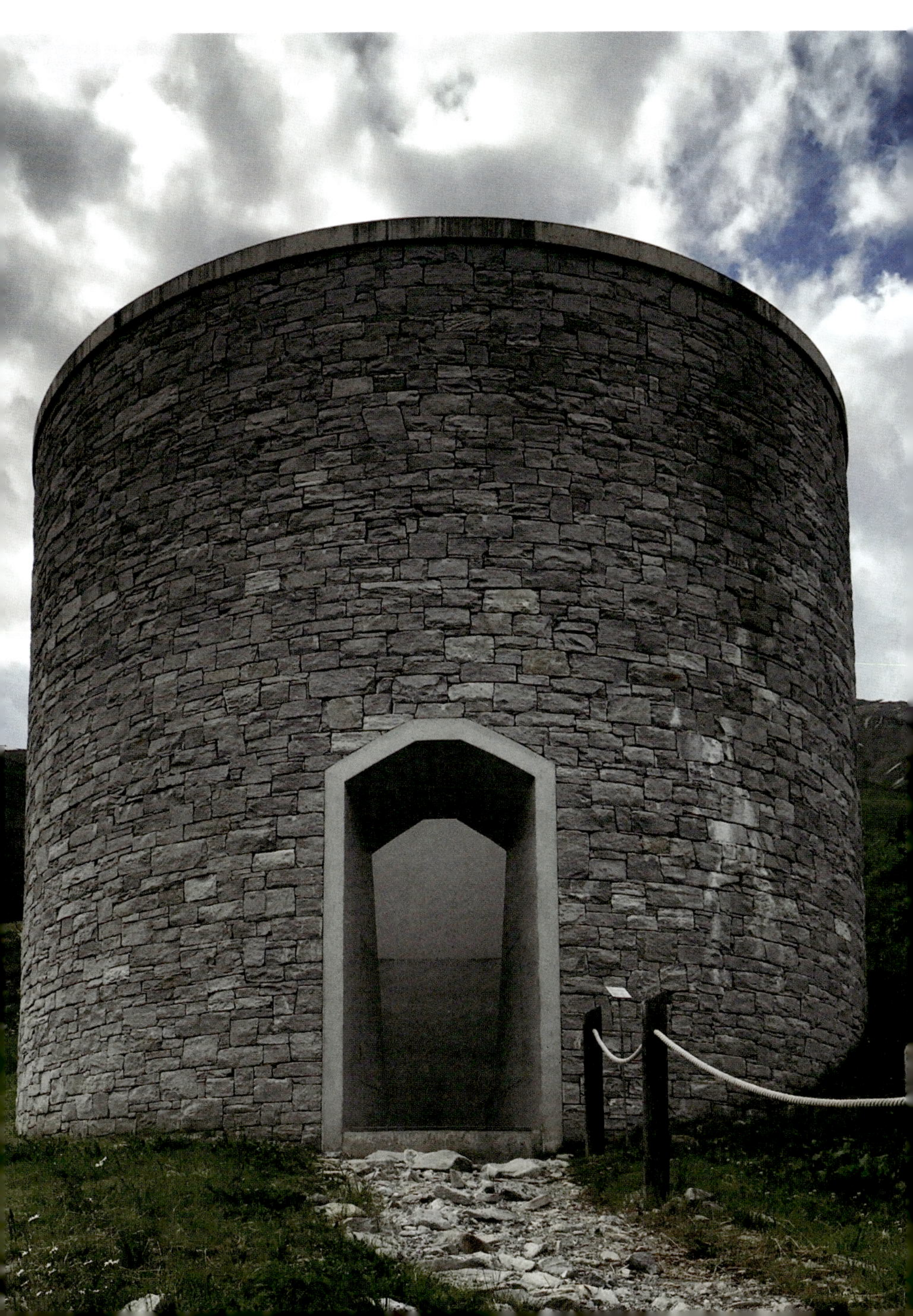

282 Alberto Giacometti Museum

In the Pensiun Aldier in the Lower Engadine village of 1,000 residents, Sent, the works of three artists are united under one roof. "Aldier" is an anagram composed of the first two letters of their first names: ALberto Giacometti, DIego Giacometti, and Ernst Scheidegger. In the entrance area are two lithographic stones by Alberto Giacometti from Mourlot, the Paris print studio, a model of a plaster bowl attributed to Giacometti, and eight bronze sculptures by Diego Giacometti, the brother and lifelong assistant of Alberto Giacometti. The restaurant and the hotel's Arvenstube are decorated with black and white photographs by Ernst Scheidegger, collotype prints by Alberto Giacometti, and his early oil painting *Maria Giovanini* (1921). The sixteen rooms include works by Alberto Giacometti, Diego Giacometti, Joan Miró, Hans Arp, Georges Braque, Eduardo Chillida, Le Corbusier, Ernst Scheidegger, Varlin, and Robert Doisneau. The heart of the hotelier Carlos Gross' collection, however, is housed in his own museum in the vaulted cellar. Here, in three rooms covering an area of around 100 m^2, the almost complete graphic works of Alberto Giacometti (1901–1966) are presented and reveal the broad spectrum of his work in stone and copper printing, 180 of which are original prints and some rare trial prints. In the middle are showcases with the complete collection—except for two copies—of all the artist's books Giacometti was involved in. The *livres d'artistes* and *livres illustrés* were created in the postwar period as collaborations between artists, writers, typographers, and publishers in small editions. The best-known publication among them is *Paris sans fin* with 150 lithographs and texts by Alberto Giacometti, which was produced posthumously in 1969 in an edition of 250 copies. The private collection comprises a total of around 300 original prints by the artist from Bregaglia.

The unusual collection is related to the eventful life of the collector. The cosmopolitan Carlos Gross, who grew up in Caracas, was interested in art during his school years and was enthusiastic about Giacometti's works at an early age. After years in Asia, he

Alberto Giacometti Museum
Sent / Unterengadin, Grisons

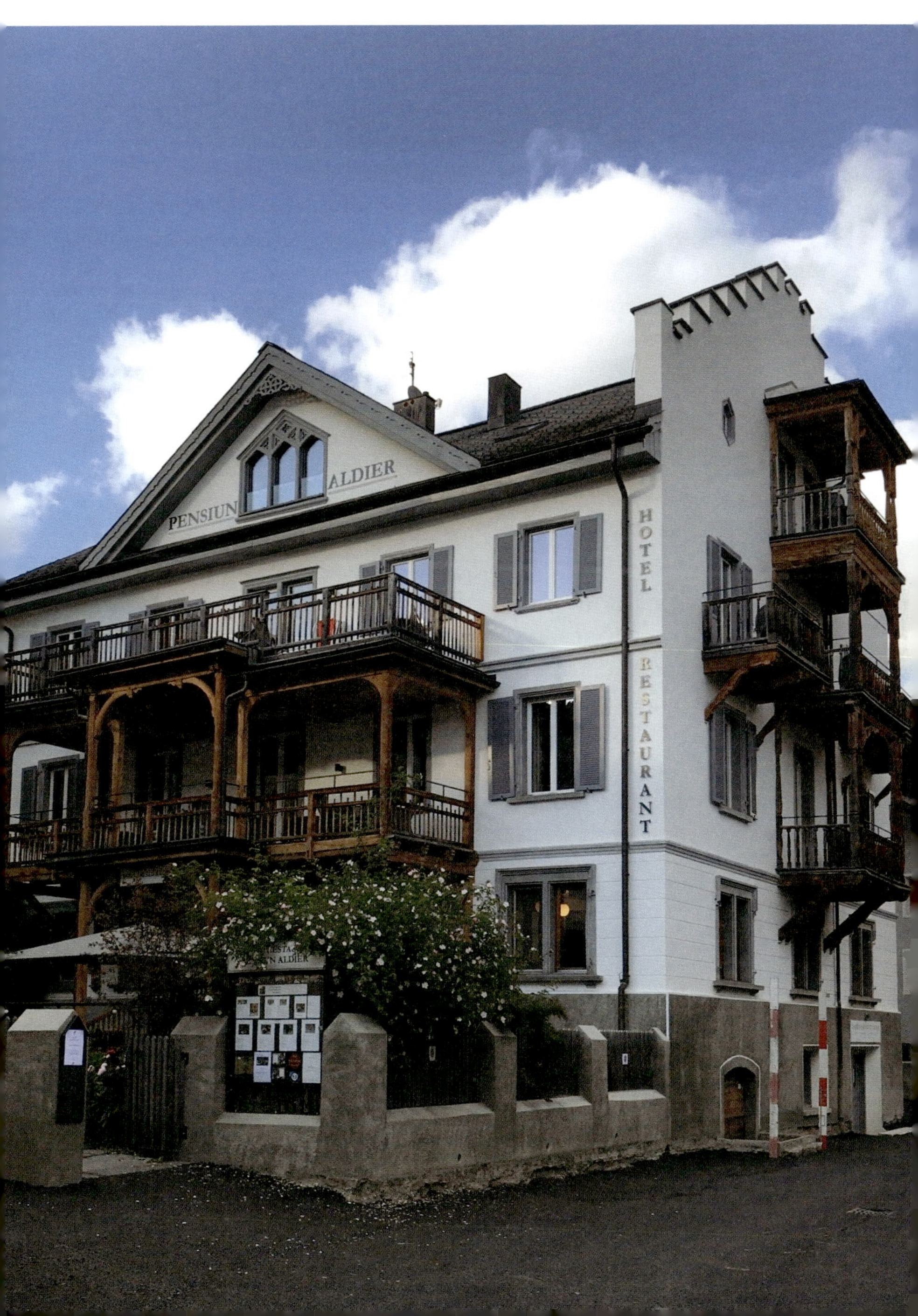

returned to Switzerland at the end of the 1970s and opened the Rosengarten Restaurant in Zurich in the mid-1980s, which is now run by his sons. At the same time, he frequently visited the nearby gallery of photographer Ernst Scheidegger to browse through his extensive collection of Giacometti prints. Scheidegger was a friend of Giacometti's for many years and documented all his artistic phases photographically and cinematically (the award-winning 1998 film *Alberto Giacometti* is permanently shown in the new wing of the Museum Berggruen in Berlin, see p. 98). The long-standing close relationship between Giacometti and Scheidegger, on the one hand, and Gross and Scheidegger, on the other, explains the extensive collection (circa eighty) of hand-signed photographs printed especially for the Gross Collection, which also show the artist's private side.

After a few years in Zurich, the Gross family moved to Piedmont in Italy at the end of the 1980s. In the mid-1990s, Carlos Gross acquired his first print by Giacometti, *Atelier au Chevalet* (1965), which was his last print, in an antiquarian bookshop. Gross began to travel more and more, became a connoisseur, and built up his collections through contacts around the world. At some point, the desire arose to combine his personal passion for art and culture with a hotel and to exhibit his collection in Giacometti's home country. In 2012, when the opportunity arose to buy a hotel in Sent that was originally built in 1865, he had it renovated in just a few months by the architect and designer Duri Vital in the style of the traditional architecture of the region.

Alberto Giacometti Museum
Sent / Unterengadin, Grisons

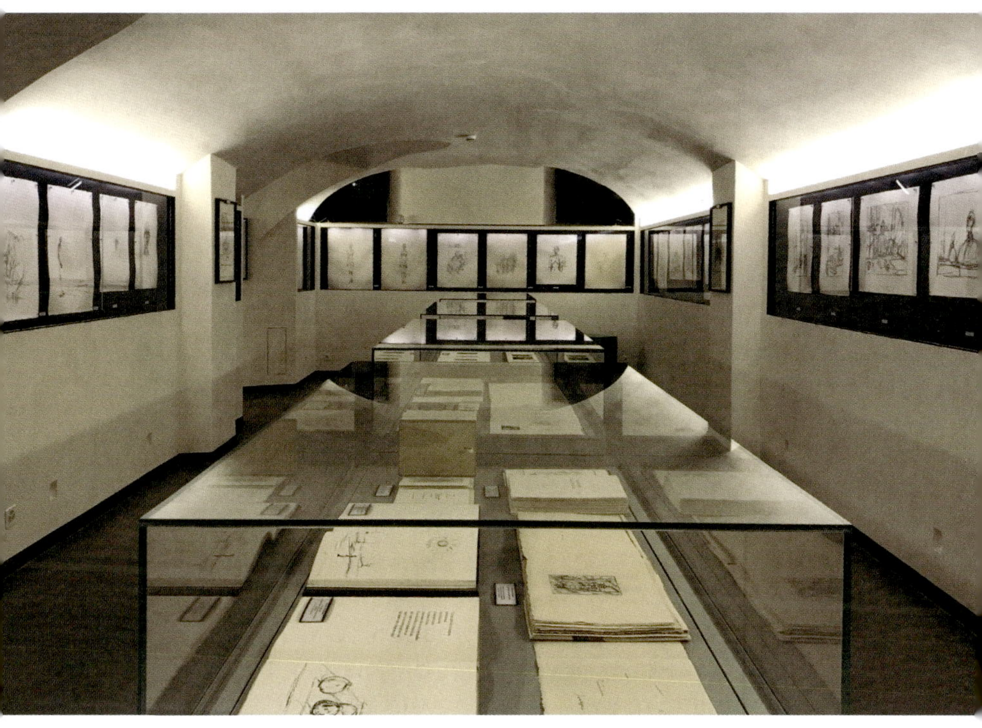

Alberto Giacometti Museum
Pensiun Aldier
Plaz 154
CH-7554 Sent
Phone: +41 81 86030000
info@aldier.ch
aldier.ch

Opening hours
During the season (mid-June to mid-October and circa December 20 to the end of March) daily noon–8 p.m.
Public guided tours are offered on Fridays at 10 a.m. by appointment. These must be booked at least 24 hours in advance. The collector often gives the tours personally. Therefore, a visit with a tour is particularly worthwhile (CHF 20 per person incl. admission). Individual guided tours at other times are also possible on request and with advance notice.

Entrance fee
CHF 10

Arrival by public transportation
From the train station Scuol-Tarasp, you can reach Sent, Platz, in about 15 minutes with the buses 923 and 925.

Parking
Parking is available throughout the town.

Restaurant tips
Local cuisine is served in the restaurant of the Pensiun Aldier. Meat lovers will be delighted by the offerings at Trais Portas, in an old Engadine house in the center of Scuol (traisportas-scuol.ch; Vi 356, Scuol 7550).

Extra tips
The sculpture park Not Dal Mot in Sent by artist Not Vital can be visited with a guided tour (sent-online.ch/attracziuns/parkin/index.html; Via Veglia Vers Scuol; June to October Friday afternoons after registration by calling +41 81 8618829). Since 2016, Not Vital has also been the owner of Tarasp Castle. A few of the circa 100 rooms can be visited daily during the season except Mondays. In 2018, Not Vital installed a version of his global project House to Watch the Sunset (schloss-tarasp.ch; Tarasp 7553) in the castle park. A very special tour of a completely different kind takes place in Ludwig Hatecke's Alpine butcher shop (Tuesdays from 6–7:30 p.m. by prior appointment at +41 81 8641175; Stradun 197, Scuol).
A visit to the Alberto Giacometti Museum can easily be combined with visits to Muzeum Susch (see p. 286) and Sammlung Ruedi Bechtler at the Hotel Castell in Zuoz (p. 278).

286 Muzeum Susch

Polish art collector and entrepreneur Grażyna Kulczyk's museum complex, which opened in January 2019 in the Lower Engadine community of 200 residents in Susch, is to become a center for artistic creativity and art mediation. Grażyna Kulczyk studied law in the 1970s in Poznań and was in contact with artists during this time; she also collected Polish film posters. During her studies, she met businessman Jan Kulczyk, to whom she was married until 2005. With the couple's financial success, their interest in art, as well as their purchasing budget, grew. Grażyna Kulczyk initially concentrated on the works of modern Polish artists. Soon, however, she expanded her sights and made the collection more international. From the very beginning, one focus was on art by women (Rosemarie Trockel, Jenny Holzer, Valie Export, Agnes Martin, Joan Mitchell, Yayoi Kusama, Geta Brătescu, and others) as well as conceptual art (including Donald Judd and Dan Flavin).

After a divorce and the division of assets, which the couple had built up together with various company shareholdings, Grażyna Kulczyk went her own successful way. In 2003, she acquired an old brewery in Poznań, which she transformed into a commercial and cultural center. Her plan to build a large private museum in Warsaw to make her collection, which had become extensive by this time, accessible to the public failed due to various obstacles.

Chance brought Grażyna Kulczyk to the Engadine Valley when she discovered its beauty during a visit with friends and she spontaneously bought an old house, where she has lived since 2009, in Lower Engadine. While driving past, Grażyna Kulczyk became aware of a dilapidated building in Susch. When she learned that a medieval monastery stood there in 1157 and that a brewery was operated there in the nineteenth century, her interest grew. In addition to the ruins, she bought three other buildings on the same street and commissioned the young architect duo Schmidlin-Voellmy to develop the Muzeum Susch project from the building complex (Kulczyk writes museum in Polish, with a "z"). Chasper Schmidlin, who grew up in the valley, and Lukas Voellmy have specialized in the restoration and reinterpretation of Engadine

Muzeum Susch
Susch, Grisons

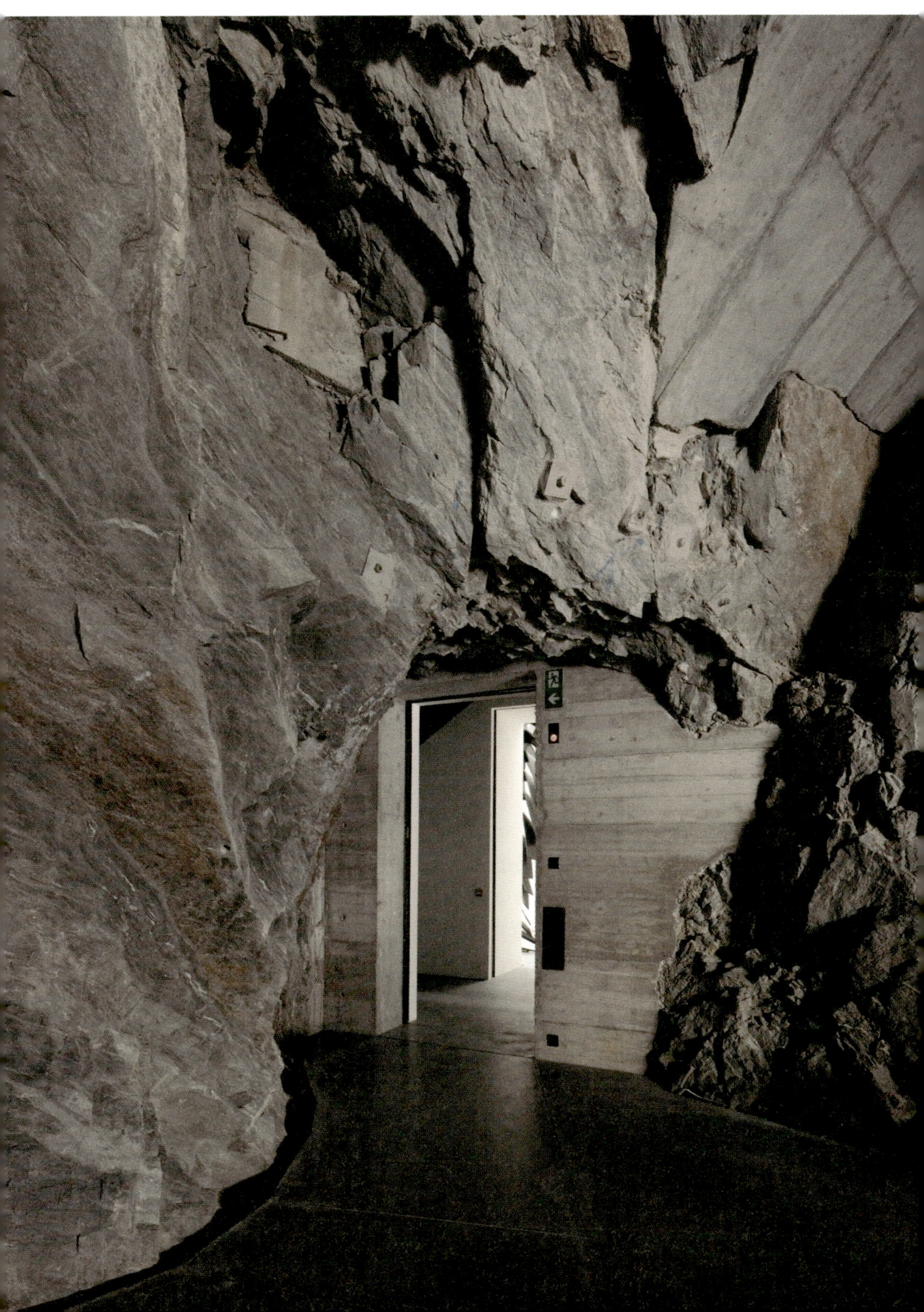

houses and the conception of art galleries. In just four years of construction, the two have succeeded in combining local tradition with international architecture. Since all the buildings were historically listed, the exhibition areas could only be extended into the interior and into the depth of the mountain. Nine thousand tons of rock were blasted out, and two cavern-like installation rooms were excavated from the mountain. On some walls, the raw rock remains, and at one point it is possible to observe the flowing spring water, formerly used for brewing beer.

The exhibition area of 1,500 m^2 extends over four floors to about twenty labyrinthine rooms. The center of the exhibition building is a whitewashed atrium which used to house the brewery's ice tower. Where cooling pipes used to lead into the brewery, there is now a huge, permanently installed steel sculpture by Monika Sosnowska. Equally impressive are a group of figures by Magdalena Abakanowicz hidden in a rock grotto and a polished steel cylinder by Mirosław Bałka which rotates in a rock cave.

Kulczyk's collection is based on the idea of drawing on history to stimulate dialogue. In addition to the numerous site-specific works of art, the museum also presents changing exhibitions twice a year, during which the works in the collection are supplemented with loans.

The Muzeum Susch is only one of five elements of the Art Stations Foundation CH, founded in 2016 in Susch. In neighboring buildings, there are artists' residences as well as space for performances and dance. The research center affiliated to the museum, in collaboration with the Institut Kunst in Basel, is dedicated to researching the role of women in art and science. Since 2017, symposia have been held annually under the title *Disputaziuns Susch* on current and future social issues, in remembrance of the fact that on New Year's day 1537/38 in the neighboring Reformed Church, Protestantism was proclaimed in a disputation in Grisons.

Muzeum Susch
Susch, Grisons

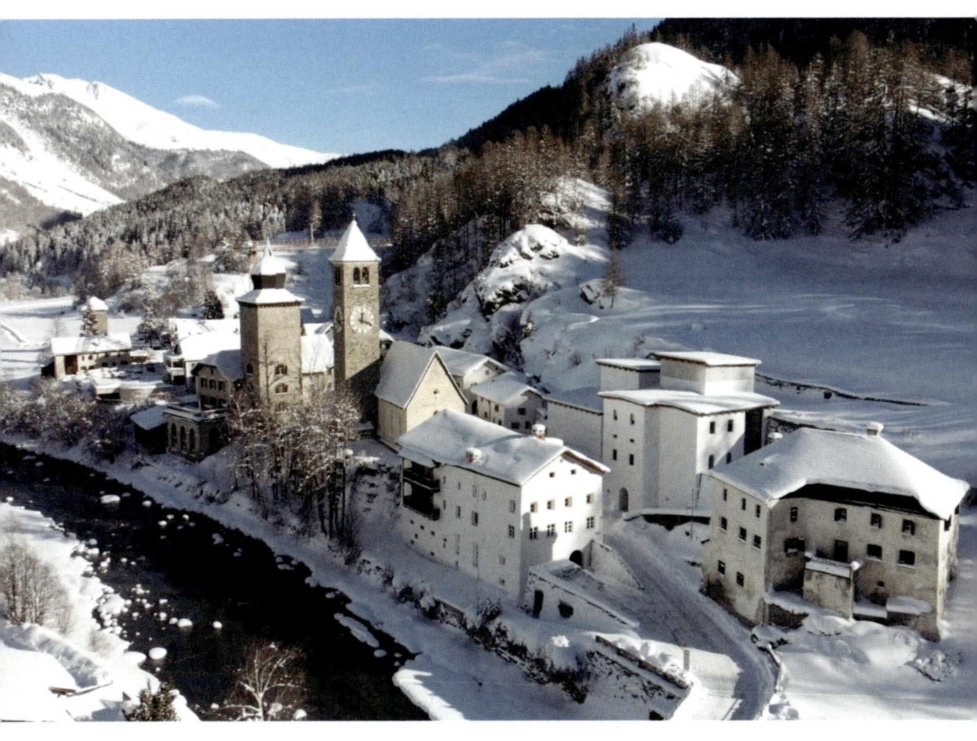

Muzeum Susch

Surpunt 78
CH-7542 Susch
Phone: +41 81 8610303
info@muzeumsusch.ch
muzeumsusch.ch

Opening hours

Thu, Fri, Sun 11 a.m.–5 p.m., Sat noon–6 p.m.
Guided tours can be booked by appointment.
Symposia, lectures, and dance events take place as part of the Art Stations Foundation CH's varied program. There is a bistro in the entrance area.

Entrance fees

Adults / Reduced / Children up to age 6: CHF 12 / CHF 6 / free

Arrival by public transportation

From Landquart, there are irregular, but direct, trains to Susch. Trains to Susch run more often via Sagliains with the Rhaetian Railway. Please note: The train only stops upon request (buttons are located in the train and on the track). Then walk along the small road Sot Chaste and cross the bridge.

Parking

The museum has a car park directly on the main road, Sot Plaz.

Restaurant tips

The Bistro Muzeum Susch specializes in regional products and dishes with weekly changing seasonal offers.
In the neighboring village of Lavin, the Giacometti pastry shop serves pear bread and the famous Bündner walnut cake (giacometti-lavin.ch; Suzöl 55, 7543 Lavin). In the same village, the Piz Linard guest house serves innovative cuisine with a regional focus, as well as coffee, cakes, and other snacks (pizlinard.ch; Plazza Gronda 2, 7543 Lavin).

Extra tips

A visit to the Ruedi Bechtler Collection at the Hotel Castell in Zuoz (see p. 278) and, a little further away, the Alberto Giacometti Museum in Sent (p. 282) are highly recommended.

290 Museum Rosengart Collection

A visit to the city of Lucerne is not only an exceptional experience for music lovers but since the opening of the Rosengart Collection in 2002 also for art connoisseurs. With works by Pablo Picasso and Paul Klee as well as twenty-three other artists such as Claude Monet, Henri Matisse, and Georges Braque, the museum has specialized in Classical Modernism and Impressionism.

In a building designed by Hermann Herter for the Swiss National Bank in 1923/24, a unique collaboration between Angela Rosengart and Basel architect Roger Diener achieved a harmonious symbiosis between the collection and the rooms. Where the National Bank's gold used to be stored as a currency reserve, secured by meter-thick reinforced concrete walls, top-class art is now presented in a unique atmosphere across an exhibition area of 1,690 m^2.

The Rosengart Collection was originally the private art collection of Siegfried Rosengart and his daughter Angela. In 1992, the latter transferred the approximately three hundred works of art to a foundation she established, to which she also contributed the funds necessary to purchase the building. In 1978, Siegfried and Angela Rosengart donated eight masterpieces by Picasso to the city of Lucerne on the occasion of its 800th anniversary, enabling the creation of the Picasso Museum, to which they later donated further contributions from their private collection. On the occasion of the opening of the Rosengart Collection, the city decided to turn over the oil paintings on permanent loan to the new museum. In 2008, the entire Picasso Museum was integrated into the Rosengart Collection, providing a complete overview of the artist's diverse late work.

The basis of the collection was secured in the 1930s and 1940s by art dealer Siegfried Rosengart through the purchase of works by Paul Cézanne, Camille Pissarro, and Auguste Renoir. After Angela Rosengart became a partner in her father's gallery in 1957, they both turned their attention to Classical Modernism. With expert knowledge and a clear eye, they collected works early on

Museum Rosengart Collection
Lucerne

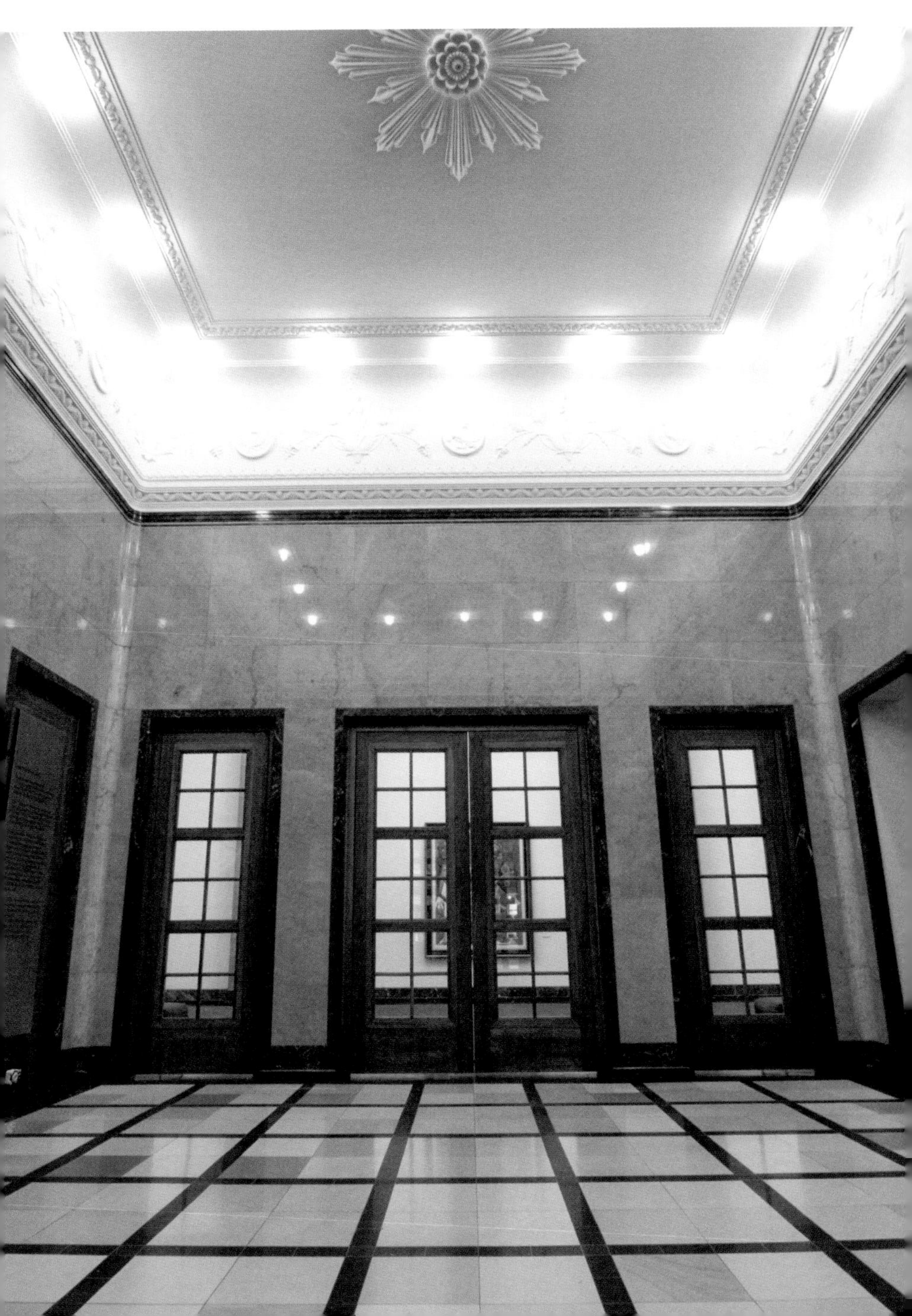

that others ignored. After the death of her father in 1985, Angela Rosengart continued collecting and selling art on her own.

Three floors were rebuilt for the exhibition of the collection, including the ground floor, which was already open to the public during the National Bank's time. It is reserved for Picasso's works, which are arranged in chronological order. Thanks to decades of friendship between the family of collectors and the artist, the latter is represented with over 130 works.

The basement houses the fantastic Klee collection, with 125 chronologically hung watercolors, drawings, and paintings from all of the artist's creative phases, including *X-chen* from 1938, which Angela Rosengart acquired at the age of sixteen.

The rooms on the second floor present various groups of works. The works of world-famous artists of Classical Modernism, Impressionism, and the late nineteenth century, such as Claude Monet, Paul Cézanne, Édouard Vuillard, Pierre Bonnard, Henri Matisse, Georges Braque, Fernand Léger, Wassily Kandinsky, Joan Miró, Marc Chagall, and others, represent a subjective selection that reflects the preference and confidence of daughter and father for high painterly quality. In addition to Picasso's drawings and graphic works, five portraits of Angela Rosengart by Picasso are exhibited here.

Museum Rosengart Collection
Lucerne

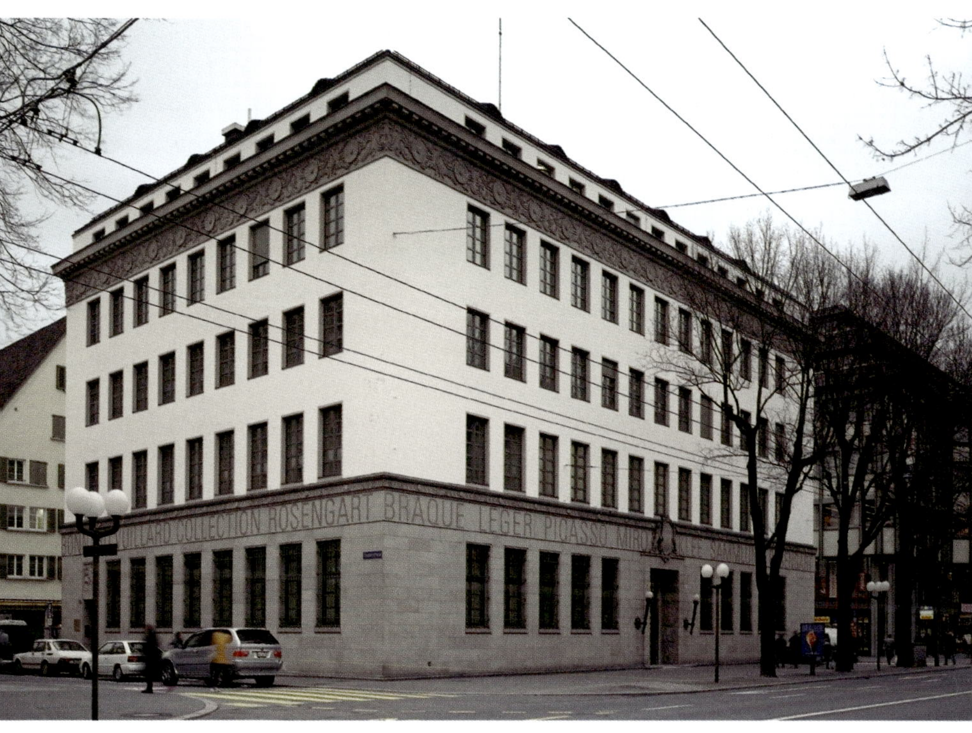

Museum Rosengart Collection

Rosengart Foundation
Pilatusstr. 10
CH-6003 Lucerne
Phone: +41 41 2201660
info@rosengart.ch
rosengart.ch

Opening hours

April to October daily 10 a.m.–6 p.m.; November to March daily 11 a.m.–5 p.m.
There are numerous guided tours and special events as well as a special children's program (children giving tours to children).

Entrance fees

Adults / Reduced / Youths and students: CHF 18 / CHF 16 / CHF 10

Parking

The best place to park is in the Luzerner Kantonalbank garage.

Arrival by public transportation

From the Lucerne railway station, it is less than five minutes on foot to the museum. Leave the station to the left, after a few meters you will reach Pilatusstrasse. Walk a few hundred meters along Pilatusstrasse. It is possible to see the collection building from the next light.

Restaurant tips

There are several excellent restaurants in Lucerne. For hearty Swiss cuisine with Rösti and Bratwurst in a traditional ambiance, the Wirtshaus Galliker is recommended (Schützenstr. 1). In the Zunfthausrestaurant Pfistern, you can also enjoy a delicious meal in a friendly atmosphere (zunfthaus-zu-pfistern.ch; Kornmarkt 4). Delicious vegan cuisine is served in the beautiful Karls Kraut (karlskraut.ch; St.-Karli-Quai 7; closed Mondays and most Sundays).

Extra tips

For those interested in architecture, it is worth making a side trip to the Lucerne Culture and Congress Centre, built by the French architect Jean Nouvel, which houses several concert and conference halls on the fifth floor as well as the Kunstmuseum Luzern. In numerous temporary exhibitions, there is a particular focus on Swiss art from the Renaissance to the present (kunstmuseum-luzern.ch; Europaplatz 1). The café, designed by Urs Lüthi, offers a magnificent view of the lake (kunstmuseumluzern.ch/cafe). The Bruchquartier (west of the railway station) is a very lively quarter with individual shops and innovative restaurants and cafés.

294 Kunst(Zeug)Haus

Housed in a former armory between the centers of Rapperswil and Jona, the Stiftung Kunst(Zeug)Haus presents Swiss contemporary art in a unique setting. In 2006, the collector couple Peter Bosshard (1942–2018) and Elisabeth Bosshard bequeathed their entire collection to the foundation. Both had become familiar with art as children in their respective homes. Peter Bosshard's grandfather, Albert Bosshard, was a lithographer and painter in Winterthur. However, Peter and Elisabeth Bosshard did not start collecting until 1970, when, after returning from a two-year stay in New York, they met artist Bernhard Schobinger, who ran a gallery in addition to his studio in Richterswil. He and his wife, Annelies Štrba, introduced the biologist and the business lawyer to the Swiss art scene. From the very beginning, it was of utmost importance for the Bossards to support artists in their work; thus, the collection is largely an expression of friendships. With the purchase of Alex Sadkowsky's *animal metaphysicum* (1969), the Bossards laid the foundation for their collection. Restricted to building it up with their actual income, the couple initially purchased mostly small-format works by young Swiss artists.

From 1985 to 1995, when they rented an essentially wall-less showroom in the former Schubiger silk weaving mill in Uznach, they added sculptures and installations by Jürg Stäuble, Stefan Gritsch, Hugo Suter, and Bernhard Schobinger to the collection. The collection's list of around five hundred artists reads to a large extent like the who's who of Swiss art over the past fifty years. Greats such as Thomas Hirschhorn, Adrian Schiess, Annelies Štrba, and Fischli/Weiss are represented with very early works, as well as works by the internationally renowned artists Meret Oppenheim, Roman Signer, and Silvia Bächli. In addition, the collection of more than 6,000 exhibits includes remarkable groups of works from all media by around thirty artists (Luigi Archetti, Rita Ernst, Marcel Gähler, Stefan Gritsch, Alexander Hahn, Alex Hanimann, Peter Z. Herzog, and Beat Zoderer, among others), from a few dozen to over a hundred works each. Peter Bosshard has also collected over 4,000 examples of robinsonade (books, but also drawings, films,

Kunst(Zeug)Haus
Rapperswil, St. Gallen

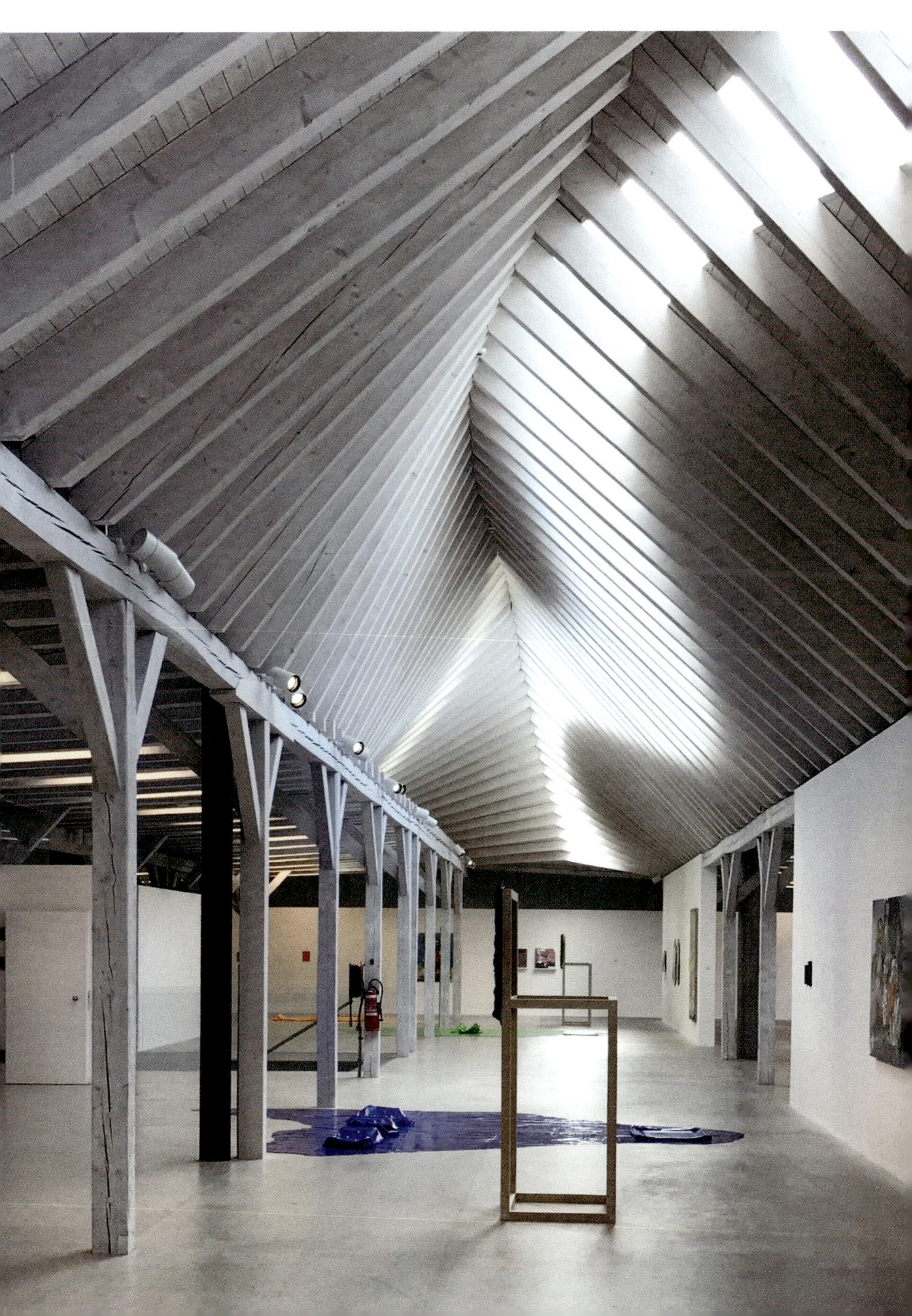

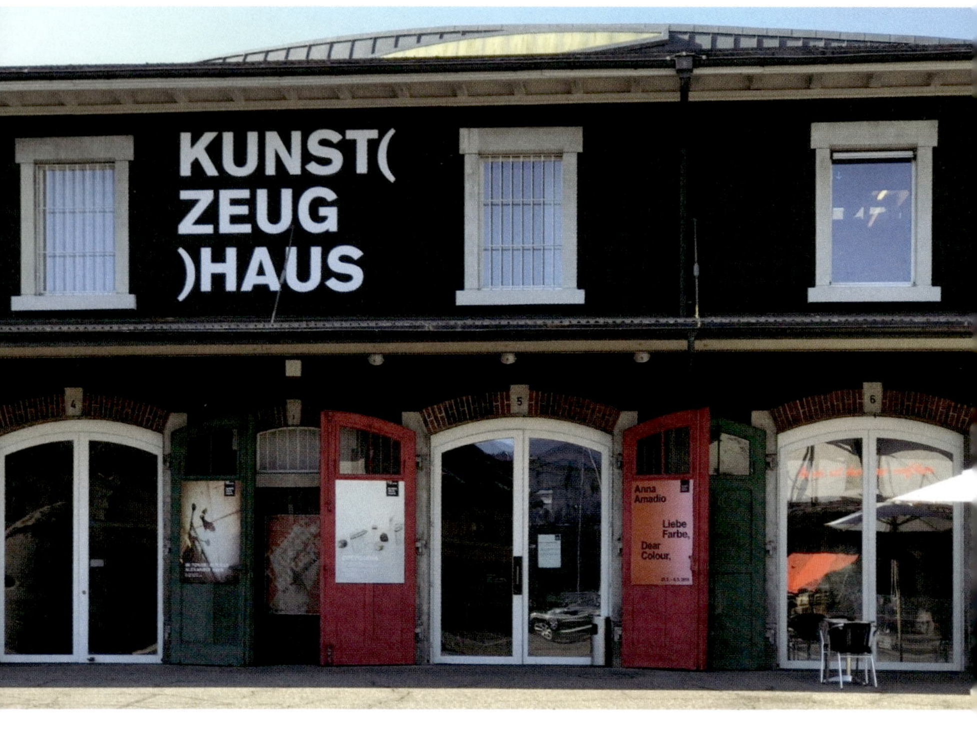

Kunst(Zeug)Haus
Schönbodenstr. 1
CH-8640 Rapperswil-Jona
Phone: +41 055 2202080
info@kunstzeughaus.ch
kunstzeughaus.ch

Opening hours
Wed–Fri 2–6 p.m.,
Sat/Sun 11 a.m.–6 p.m.
Public guided tours take place most Sundays at 11:30 a.m. There is a café and a small shop in the museum.

Entrance fees
Adults / Reduced / Family ticket / Children and adolescents (up to 16 years): CHF 10 / CHF 6 / CHF 15 / free

Arrival by public transportation
From the Rapperswil railway station, lines 622 and 995 run every half hour to the Zeughaus. If you leave the station to the right and then turn right onto Neue Jonastrasse, the museum can be reached on foot in ten minutes. Starting from the ferry terminal, it is only a few additional minutes.

Restaurant tips
Exceptional, top-class gastronomy can be found in the historical main square at the Nordic-puristically furnished Hotel Jacob (jakob-rapperswil.ch; Hauptplatz 11). Fresh waffles and coffee are served in the Café good (cafegood.ch; Marktgasse 11). The restaurant Kreuzli, run by the Stiftung Balm, is an excellent place to dine. Here, people with and without disabilities work side by side (restaurant-kreuzli.ch; Alte Jonastr. 32; only open in the afternoon and evening on weekdays).

Extra tips
A walk through the old town of Rapperswil to the thirteenth-century castle offers a good view of the lake and city. The small Liebfrauenkapelle, located between the east side of the castle and the parish church of St. Johann near the Rapperswil cemetery, is also an interesting place to visit. When the weather is fine, it is worth crossing Lake Zurich on the jetty (schweizmobil.ch/de/wanderland/routen/route-0849.html). Temporary shows from the Gebert Stiftung für Kultur* are presented in the *ALTEFABRIK exhibition space (alte-fabrik.ch; Klaus-Gebert-Str. 5).
From 2021/22 onwards, parts of the Bruno Bischofberger collection will be shown in Männedorf (southeast of Zurich). The internationally renowned Galerie Bruno Bischofberger mainly represents pop, conceptual, and minimal artists (brunobischofberger.com).

and portfolios on the history of Robinson Crusoe), one of the most important and comprehensive collections related to the eighteenth-century adventure novel.

After renting the silk weaving mill, the Bosshards also used the Braendlin spinning mill in Jona (1995–2006) as a showroom and meeting place, but soon the idea of a permanent home for the collection was born. A suitable object was found in Rapperswil with the former Zeughaus 2. In addition to the generous donation of the collection, Peter and Elisabeth Bosshard donated 500,000 Swiss francs to the foundation, which was established at the same time. This starting sum, a financial contribution from the Canton of St. Gallen and other sponsors, enabled the foundation to purchase the armory. Zurich architects Isa Stürm and Urs Wolf were entrusted with the conversion in 2006. They largely retained the character of the arsenal and only made minimal adjustments to the façades and interior of the building. The undulating arched roof connects the city centers of Rapperswil and Jona and thus symbolically marks the mediating quality of the Kunst(Zeug)Haus in the center of the city. In 2008, the year of its opening, the Kunst(Zeug)Haus was awarded the Bronze Hare architecture prize.

On the upper floor, the raised roof has created a bright area of flexible usage of approximately 1,000 m^2; four exhibitions take place here every year, which are mainly made up of loans. Since 2014, young artists have been presented here four times a year in the SEITENWAGEN series. The small treasure chamber of the Robinson Library is also located on this level. On the ground floor, excerpts from the Bosshard Collection are shown in an approximately 420 m^2 exhibition space. Within the presentation of the collection, the annual exhibition series Im Fokus illuminates a position whose works the couple had collected over many years. Both the canton of St. Gallen and the city of Rapperswil-Jona make a small financial contribution to the exhibition.

298 Fondazione Marguerite Arp

In a residential area of Solduno, it is possible to discover a small botanical paradise, wonderful works of art, and an architectural masterpiece. The estate was originally the last residence of the German-French artist Hans "Jean" Arp (1886–1966) and his second wife, Marguerite Arp-Hagenbach (1902–1994). The Fondazione Marguerite Arp-Hagenbach, Ronco dei Fiori, has been located here since 1988. Marguerite Arp-Hagenbach founded this foundation for the long-term preservation of the memories of her husband and Sophie Taeuber-Arp (1889–1943).

Thanks to her inheritance, Marguerite Hagenbach was able to collect contemporary art. After the Constructivist exhibition at the Kunsthalle Basel in 1937, she acquired two of the works exhibited there, one by Sophie Taeuber-Arp and one by László Moholy-Nagy. This was the actual beginning of the future collection, which was to develop into one of the most important private collections of international art with a focus on Constructivist and Concrete art in Switzerland. In a friendly relationship with Hans Arp and Sophie Taeuber-Arp since 1932, Marguerite Hagenbach supported the artist couple, who fled to southern France in 1940, with food parcels from Switzerland. After Sophie Taeuber-Arp tragically died of carbon monoxide poisoning at Max Bill's house in Zurich in 1943, Hans Arp plunged into a prolonged crisis. Marguerite Hagenbach assisted him both personally and financially. They undertook numerous journeys and in 1959, the year of their marriage, acquired a 4,600 m^2 plot of land in Locarno-Solduno. The property, called Ronco dei Fiori, consists of an old Ticino house, an extensive garden, and a vineyard. After conversions by the architect Fritz Bähler, the couple moved into the house in May 1960. In addition to a house designed by Sophie Taeuber-Arp in Clamart, France, and an apartment in Basel, it became their preferred place to live and work. Hans Arp set up a studio on the second floor of the house and used the studio complex of the sculptor Remo Rossi in Locarno for his sculptures. The park-like garden gradually filled with the sculptures created there.

Fondazione Marguerite Arp
Locarno-Solduno, Ticino

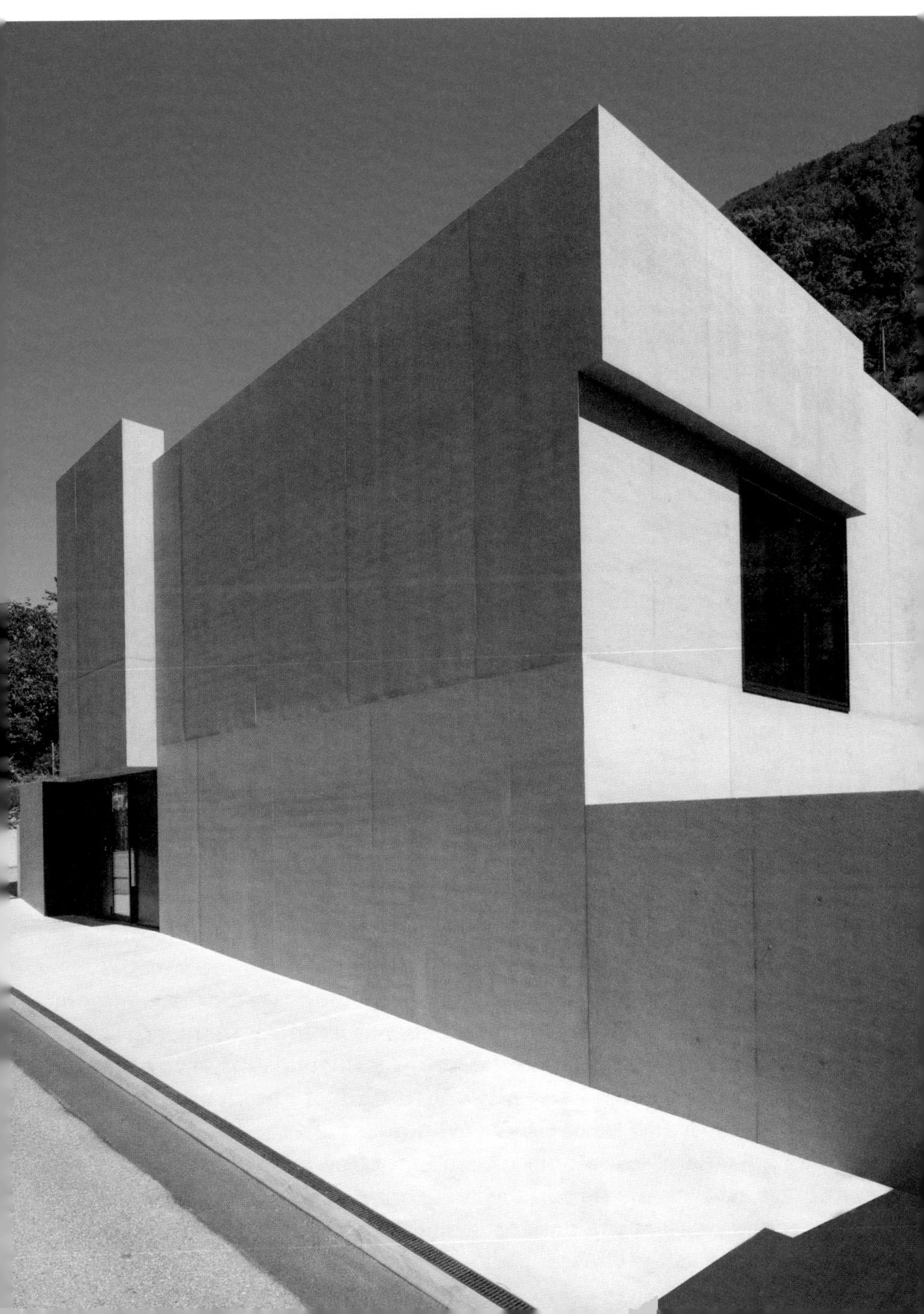

After Arp's death in 1966, Marguerite Arp-Hagenbach continued her work as a committed patron of the work of Hans Arp and Sophie Taeuber-Arp. Over the years, many generous donations to museums all over the world followed, while the collection was supplemented by purchases of works by younger artists. The Hans Arp and Sophie Taeuber-Arp Foundation was founded in 1977 in Rolandseck near Bonn, and the Fondation Arp was founded in 1979 in Clamart. In 1988, Marguerite Arp-Hagenbach transferred the remaining part of her collection and the Arp estate, the library containing around 7,000 volumes, and the property with the studio house to the Fondazione Marguerite Arp-Hagenbach, Ronco dei Fiori, founded by her.

The foundation's collection comprises approximately 1,700 inventoried works of art. By far the most significant part consists of over 750 works by Hans Arp from all creative periods. The foundation owns sixty-five works by Sophie Taeuber-Arp. Furthermore, there are works by artists such as Josef Albers, Willi Baumeister, Max Bill, Alexander Calder, Robert Delaunay, Theo van Doesburg, Marcel Duchamp, Max Ernst, Alberto Giacometti, Hannah Höch, Wassily Kandinsky, Paul Klee, Man Ray, Joan Miró, Meret Oppenheim, Francis Picabia, and Kurt Schwitters.

The Foundation cannot sell works of art in its possession, which limits its ability to adequately maintain the property and the collection and make them accessible to the public. Therefore, it is a stroke of luck that close cooperation between the Fondazione Marguerite Arp and the Liner Appenzell Foundation (now Heinrich Gebert Kulturstiftung Appenzell) has created a situation with financial leeway since 2000. Since 1965, Arp's intention to erect a kind of "gallery building" on his property in Solduno to be able to show at least part of the collection has been passed down. Almost fifty years later, in 2014, this plan became a reality thanks to the generosity of the Heinrich Gebert Kulturstiftung Appenzell and the contributions of several other institutions. Zurich architects Annette Gigon and Mike Guyer, who designed the Kunstmuseum Appenzell (see p. 264), built a compact cube of sandblasted concrete with an art depot and an exhibition space. Located on the second floor of the concrete building, the 90 m² showroom impresses with its clarity and balanced proportions. Here, annually changing exhibitions with Hans Arp and other artists from the collection are shown.

Fondazione Marguerite Arp
Via alle Vigne 46
CH-6600 Locarno-Solduno
Phone: +41 91 7512543
info@fondazionearp.ch
fondazionearp.ch

Opening hours
April–October, Sundays 2–6 p.m. The garden is open to visitors to the exhibition space on Sundays. Public tours of the exhibition take place at irregular intervals, the dates are published on the website and in the newsletter. Registration is not necessary. Private guided tours of the exhibition and the garden can also be booked outside of regular opening hours. Professionals can use the newly established library on the ground floor of the Atelierhaus by appointment.

Entrance fees
Adults / Students to age 25 / Teenagers to age 16: CHF 5 / CHF 3 / free

Arrival by public transportation
By train (FART) from Locarno station, take line 620 towards Domodossola and get off at S. Martino. From there take Via Pietro Magistra to the northwest and turn right. Take the bus line 1 from Locarno or Ascona to the Solduno bus stop. From Locarno, you can also take line 7 to the Solduno stop. From there, at the roundabout, take Via Alberto Vigizzi to the north, turn left into Via Valle Maggia and right into Via Pietro Magistra.

Parking
Public transportation is recommended. There are only a few parking spaces in front of the foundation. A few are also available at the S. Martino railway station.

Extra tips
A 1.5 km walk along the Locarno-Muralto lakeside promenade takes you past numerous Mediterranean and subtropical plant species as well as the Giardini Jean Arp, in which nine reproductions of Arp sculptures can be seen. Worth a visit is the noble house Casa Rusca, now home to the Municipal Picture Gallery (Pinacoteca Comunale Casa Rusca), where bequests from the collection of Hans Arp and Sophie Taeuber-Arp as well as other art exhibitions are presented at irregular intervals (museocasarusca.ch; Piazza S. Antonio 1). The shared grave of Hans Arp, Sophie Taeuber-Arp, and Marguerite Arp-Hagenbach is very close to the cemetery of the Church of Santa Maria in Selva (Via Valle Maggia 16F, CH-6600 Locarno). Architecture fans should definitely take a look at the Chiesa di San Giovanni Battista in Mogno near Fusio in the rear Maggia Valley. The building, designed by the Ticino star architect Mario Botta, consists of alternating layers of local Peccia marble and Vallemaggia granite. It is unique and has rightly developed into a landmark known far beyond the national borders (myswitzerland.com/de/die-bergkirche-von-mario-botta.html; Via Cantonale, 6685 Mogno).

302 Fondazione Gabriele e Anna Braglia

On the shores of Lake Maggiore, art lovers have been able to appreciate twentieth-century works of art since 2015. With the establishment of their foundation in 2014, Gabriele and Anna Braglia fulfilled their long-standing desire to preserve their art collection in its entirety for the future and to share it with an art-interested public. The initiative is supported by their sons Riccardo and Enrico. Born into an Italian collector's family, Gabriele Braglia, later a pharmaceutical entrepreneur, had an opportunity to train his eye early on. After he encountered the art scene in Milan and Pavia during his studies in the 1950s, meeting artists such as Lucio Fontana and Giuseppe Migneco in person, it was easy for him to enthuse his future wife about art as well. A passion for collecting that has now lasted for over sixty years began with the purchase of a small tempera painting by Mario Sironi in 1957, which Gabriele Braglia later gave to his wife as a Christmas gift. In the first decade, due to personal friendships and connections to the local artist milieu, the two of them focused mainly on works from the Italian Novecento and Futurism. During this period, works by artists such as Giorgio Morandi, Alberto Burri, Giuseppe Cesetti, Lucio Fontana, Amedeo Modigliani, and Gino Severini found their way into the collection. In the 1970s, interest shifted to other European art movements. The two focal points of the collection were German Expressionism with paintings by August Macke, Alexej von Jawlensky, Wassily Kandinsky, Franz Marc, Ernst Ludwig Kirchner, Emil Nolde, Lyonel Feininger, and Marianne von Werefkin, among others, as well as the work of the Yugoslavian-Italian painter Zoran Mušič. The latter is represented with sixty-eight works in the collection of over two hundred works. Thus, masters of Modern and Contemporary art such as Pablo Picasso, Max Ernst, Marc Chagall, Joan Miró, Fernando Botero, Manolo Valdés, Christo, Keith Haring, and Peter Doig have also found a home in the still growing collection.

Visitors can appreciate that Gabriele and Anna Braglia, who has passed away, have brought the same passion for furnishing

Fondazione Gabriele e Anna Braglia
Lugano, Ticino

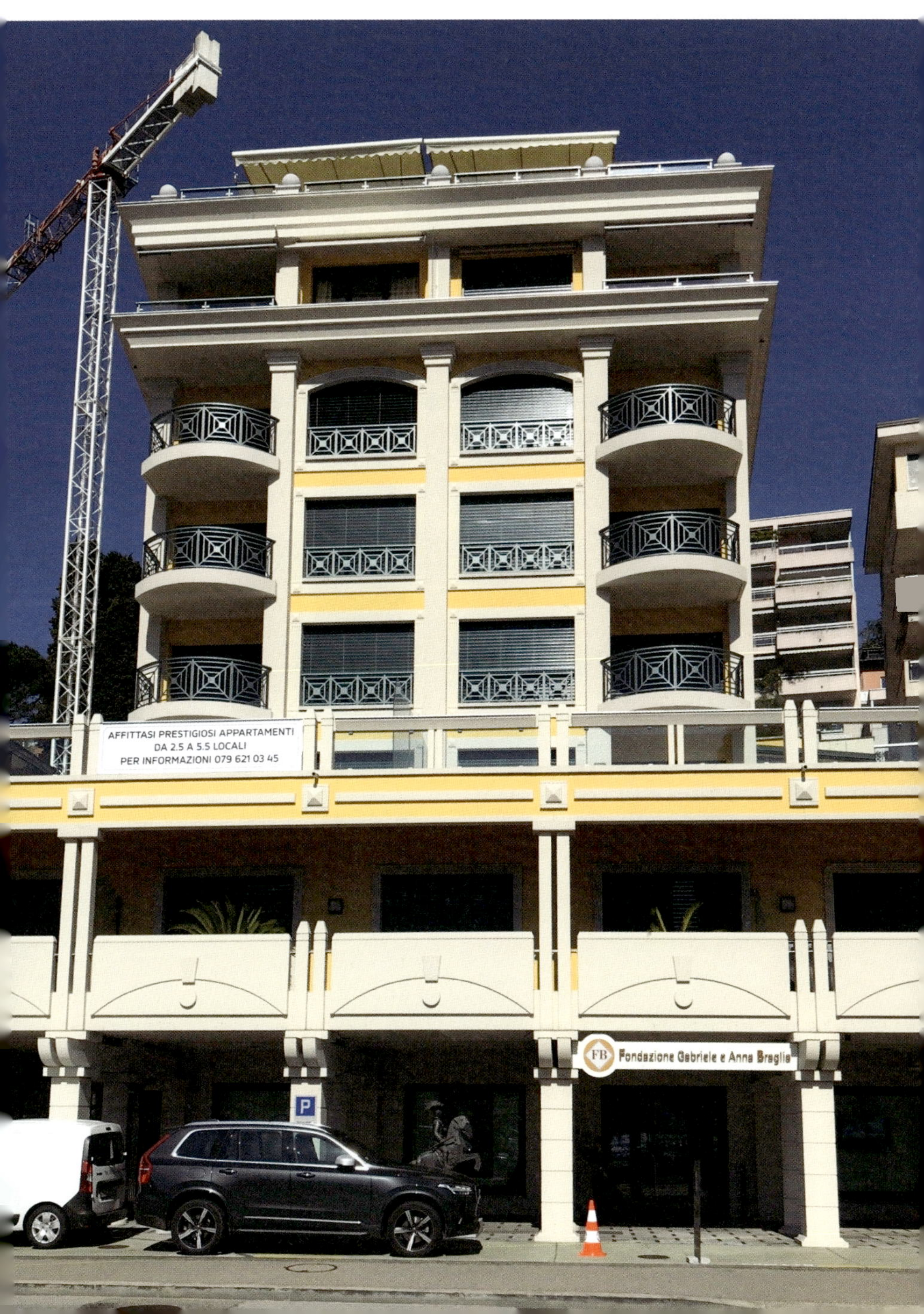

the Fondazione's exhibition spaces as they have for searching for the works of art for their collection. They commissioned Ticino architect and designer Carlo Rampazzi with the transformation of the rooms of a former bank into an exhibition area of around 500 m^2. This is spread over two levels connected by a bronze staircase designed by Rampazzi. He also designed the furniture and the sculpture cabinet in the entrance area. Despite the use of the latest technologies to preserve and present the collection, an interior has been created with exceptional craftsmanship, achieving a contemplative atmosphere and inviting art lovers to linger in the exhibition rooms and the small library. Every year, in spring and autumn, various elements of the collection are curated in relation to each other in temporary exhibitions, which is why more than one visit is recommended.

Fondazione Gabriele e Anna Braglia
Lugano, Ticino

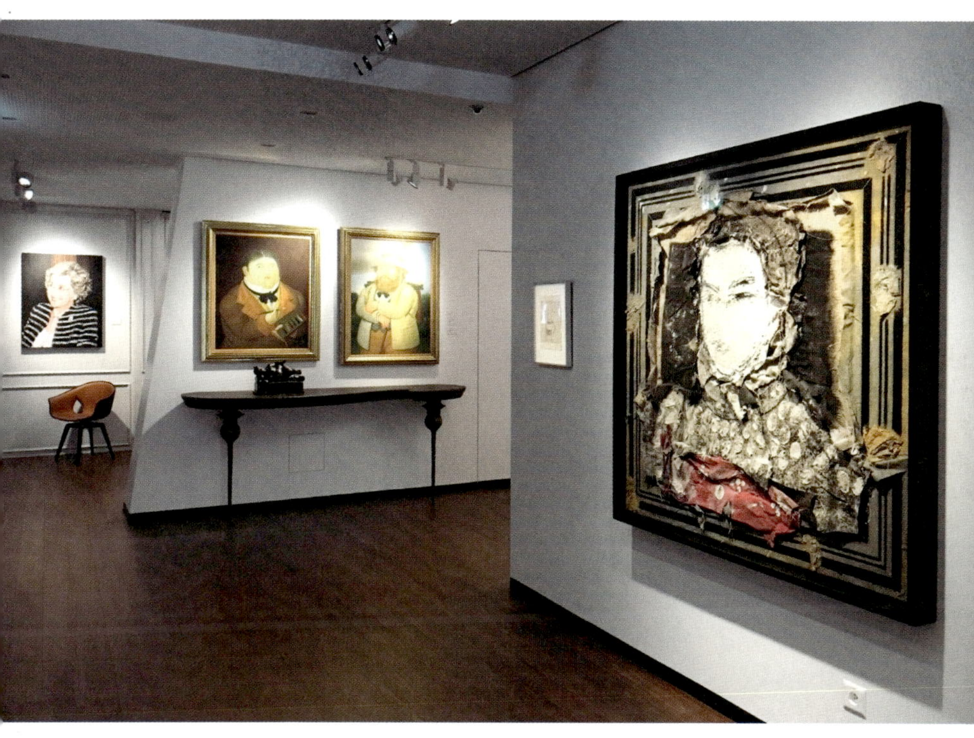

Fondazione Gabriele
e Anna Braglia
Riva Antonio Caccia 6a
CH-6900 Lugano
Phone: +41 91 9800888
info@fondazionebraglia.ch
fondazionebraglia.ch

Opening hours
March–June and end of September–December (see website for exact dates)
Thu–Sat 10 a.m.–1 p.m. / 2:30 p.m.–6:30 p.m.
Short, guided tours are available upon request on location.

Entrance fee
Free admission except for special exhibitions

Arrival by public transportation
For a visit to the Fondazione, take into account the short boat trip between Paradiso and the center. If you prefer to go by foot, walk fifteen minutes from the Lugano-Paradiso stop (S10 and S50) along Via Carona to the lake and then left along the lakeside promenade to the Fondazione. You can also start from the train station (Lugano-Stazione) (see description for Spazio -1, see p. 320).

Parking
Parking is available at the LAC cultural center and the central park (see description for Spazio -1, p. 320) and at Palazzo Mantegazza (Riva Paradiso 2).

Restaurant tips
Coffee and delicious cakes are served in the beautiful, time-honored Ristorante Grand Café Al Porto (grand-cafe-lugano.ch/de; via Pessina 3). Excellent local and international cuisine is served in the Grotto della Salute north of the station. The terrace is particularly lovely for dining (grottodella-salute.ch; Via Madonna della Salute 10). The nearby new Grotto Valletta has a hip atmosphere. The Italian-inspired kitchen is innovative and unusual despite the pizza, hamburgers, and pasta on offer (grottovalletta.com; Via dei Platani 1). The Michelin-star awarded Galleria Arté al Lago restaurant, to the east of the city, offers fine cuisine in the elegant ambiance of an art gallery (villacastagnola.com/en/gastronomy/restaurant-arté-al-lago; Viale Castagnola 31).

Extra tips
In April 2019, the Museo delle Culture (Musec) found its new home in the rooms of Villa Malpensata (mcl.lugano.ch; Riva Antonio Caccia 5). Literature fans can see a permanent exhibition about the life of Hermann Hesse in the small Hermann Hesse Montagnola Museum (hesse-montagnola.ch; Ra Cürta 2, CH-6926 Montagnola). A visit to the Spazio -1 (see p. 320) and an excursion to the Rolla Foundation (see p. 318) are highly recommended.

306 Fondazione Ghisla Art Collection

Above all, Locarno is internationally known for its annual film festival in August in the old town. Since 2014, however, more and more friends of modern and contemporary art have visited the small city center. The Fondazione Ghisla Art Collection, founded by Pierino Ghisla and his wife, Martine, the same year as the opening of the private museum, is a nonprofit foundation with the aim of presenting top-class art objects to the general public. Pierino Ghisla was born in Ticino and left Switzerland as a young man at the invitation of his Belgian uncle. In Brussels, he became a fruit and vegetable importer and met his wife, Martine. The Ghislas' almost forty years of collecting began with a fascination for a work by the French artist Georges Mathieu. After acquiring this first painting for the collection, they fell in love with an object by Christo and Jeanne-Claude. Today, the collection contains more than 250 works by many of the main representatives of Arte Povera, Pop Art, Informel, and Conceptual Art, such as Joan Miró, Lucio Fontana, Piero Manzoni, Jean Dubuffet, Fernando Botero, René Magritte, Roy Lichtenstein, Jean-Michel Basquiat, Keith Haring, Jannis Kounellis, Christian Boltanski, James Rosenquist, Cy Twombly, and Victor Vasarely. The collection is constantly expanding to include works by young, up-and-coming artists. A passion for all forms of artistic expression can also be seen in the Ghislas' open-mindedness towards architecture. After Pierino Ghisla retired and returned to Ticino, the collector couple saw potential in a 1940s office building as the future home of their foundation. In 2013, they commissioned architect Franco Moro, of MORO e MORO, to design a building that would reflect their collection. The transformation of the original building into a museum cube included the closure of all windows and the end-to-end cladding of the façade with a bright red insulating shell. Walking past a steel sculpture by Lori Hersberger on a small bridge over the moat into the extraordinary museum, one does not suspect that it is a conversion and not a new building. Pierino and Martine Ghisla

Fondazione Ghisla Art Collection
Locarno, Ticino

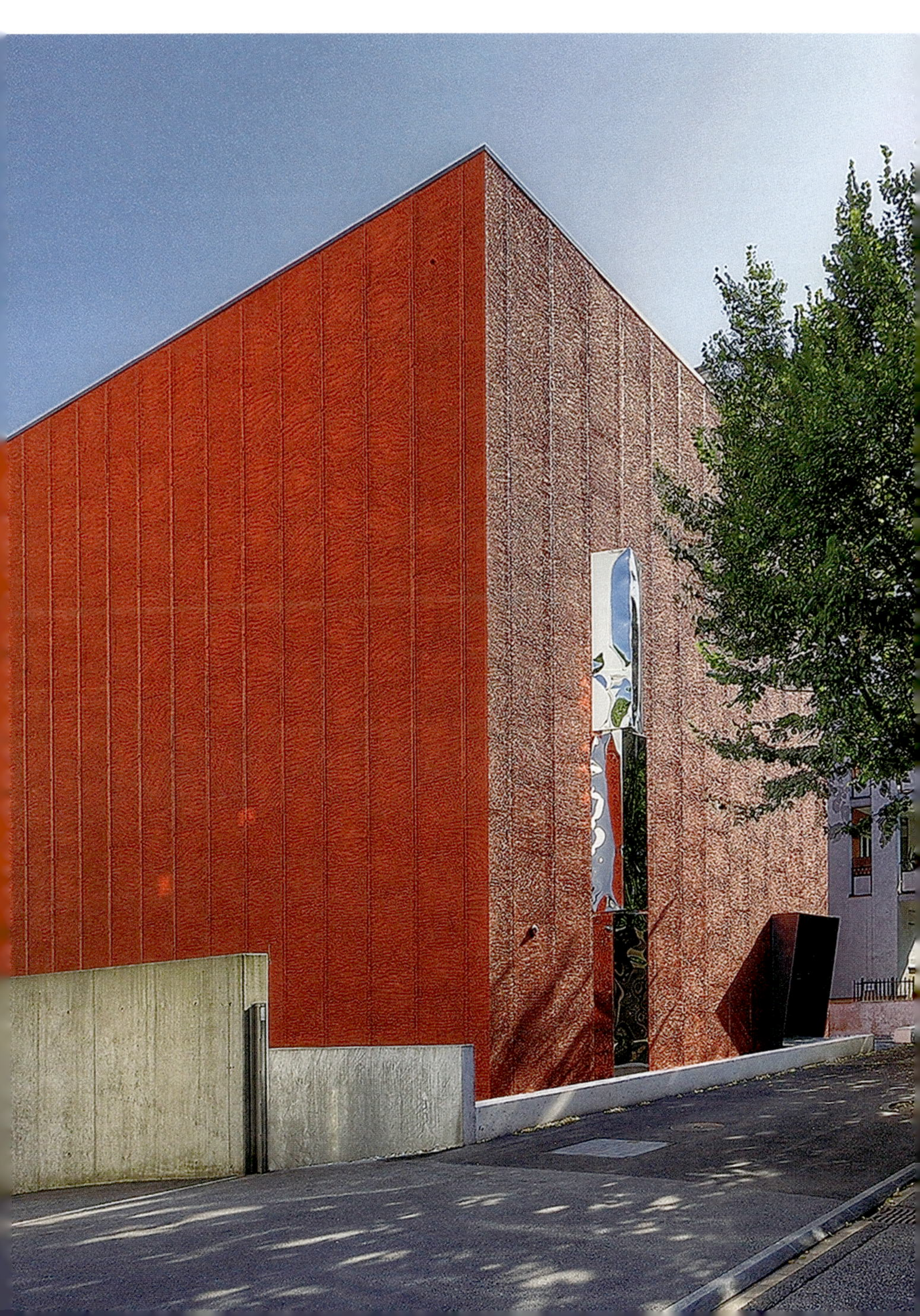

furnished the rooms as if they would receive guests there. Visitors should feel as though they are in a private house and should take the time to let the works of art have their effect on them in peace. The five approximately 370 m² rooms on the first two floors are curated exclusively with works from the museum's collection. The arrangement deliberately does not follow any strict chronology or division according to artistic trends, but rather consciously reflects the personal preferences of the collector couple. Parts of the exhibition are changed once a year and supplemented by the newest acquisitions. The three approximately 200 m² rooms on the upper floor are used for special exhibits that change twice a year.

Fondazione Ghisla Art Collection
Via Antonio Ciseri 3
CH-6600 Locarno
Phone: +41 91 7510152
info@ghisla-art.ch
ghisla-art.ch

Opening hours
Mid-March–beginning of January: Wed–Sun 1:30–6 p.m.
A wide variety of events are offered for adults and children.

Entrance fees
Adults / Pensioners / Youths (12–18 years old) and students / children: CHF 15 / CHF 13 / CHF 11 / free (including audio guide)
With the Cultural Pass Ascona-Locarno, visitors to one of the partner museums (in addition to the Fondazione Ghisla Art Collection: Pinacoteca Casa Rusca Musei comunali di Ascona, Casa Anatta Monte Verità Ascona) receive a 20% discount on admission to the other museums.

Arrival by public transportation
From the train station, it is only a five-minute walk to the Fondazione. Leave the train station south on Viale Giuseppe Cattori, turn right at the lake onto Viale Verbano, then left briefly onto Viale Francesco Balli, and then right again onto Via Antonio Ciseri.

Parking
The Centro Locarno public car park is located diagonally opposite the Fondazione.

Restaurant tips
Snacks and coffee can be enjoyed in the idyllic courtyard of the Caffè dell'Arte in the middle of the old town. There is also an art gallery and a popular boutique hotel here (caffedellarte.ch; Via Cittadella 9). In the Ristorante Vallemaggia, a social project of Pro Infirmis, delicious lunch menus with organic products from the region are offered during the week. On Thursday and Friday evenings, the chef creates a selected gourmet menu (ristorantevallemaggia.ch; Via Varenna 1). The most delicious ice cream in the region can be found in the tiny Gelateria La Dolcevita, housed in a garage (Via Vincenzo d'Alberti 4).

Extra tips
Visits to Fondazione Marguerite Arp (see p. 298), Castello San Materno in Ascona (p. 314) and Fondazione Matasci per l'Arte in Tenero and Cugnasco-Gerra (p. 310) at the same time are worthwhile.
For visitors by car, a short detour to the Fondazione Museo Mecrì on the way to the Fondazione Matasci is recommended. In the former residential building converted by Studio Inches Architettura with a minimalist extension completed in 2016, works by Aldo Crivelli (1907–1981), an archaeologist and painter from Ticino, are principally shown (mecri.ch; Via Mondacce 207, 6648 Minusio).

Fondazione Ghisla Art Collection
Locarno, Ticino

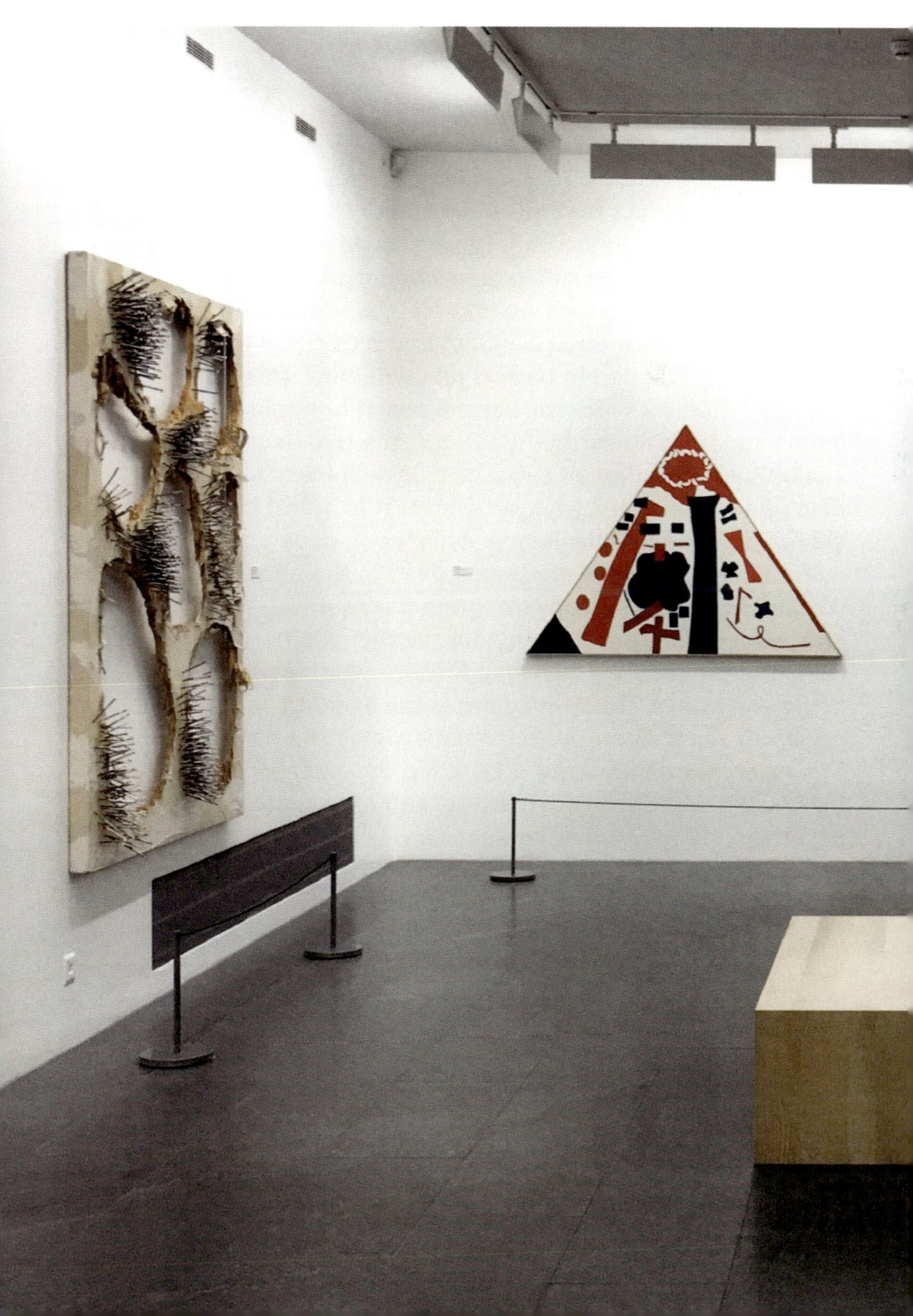

310 Fondazione Matasci per l'Arte

Matasci is well-known for local wine in Ticino. Less common, however, is the fact that the winegrower Mario Matasci has been closely associated with the art world for fifty years. It all began in 1968 with a chance conversation at an osteria in Losone. While Mario Matasci was waiting for a business partner, he was approached by painter Erwin Sauter and asked to buy a painting that he happened to be carrying with him. This work, which changed Matasci's life, still has a place of honor in the show depot's library today. After further meetings, the two decided on a first exhibition in the cleared cellar of Villa Jelmini in Tenero. Alongside managing the winery, Matasci's interest in art intensified, and the exhibition rooms in the Jelmini cellar soon developed into a small cultural center. They were then moved to the upper floors of the villa until they were finally integrated as Matasci Arte on the floor above the wine shop. Through his passion and his penchant for precision, Mario Matasci won well-known art critics as collaborators in the early days. Today, he curates the exhibitions alone and also publishes numerous art publications. Since the beginning, he has organized more than a hundred exhibitions dealing primarily with the artistic approaches of Informel and Expressionism. Matasci prefers paintings on themes such as war, expulsion, suffering, hopelessness, and death by artists from Northern Italy and Ticino such as Franco Francese, Ennio Morlotti, Alfredo Chighine, Piero Ruggeri, Gianriccardo Piccoli, Cesare Lucchini, Tino Repetto, and Edmondo Dobrzanski. Artists from German-speaking Switzerland, as well as German and international painters, including Johannes Robert Schürch, Louis Soutter, Varlin, Käthe Kollwitz, Otto Dix, Marianne Werefkin, and Zoran Mušič—whom Matasci particularly admires—are all represented in the collection, which comprises around 1,000 works. Matasci met most of the artists personally and has visited them in their studios.

Fondazione Matasci per l'Arte Tenero-Contra, Ticino

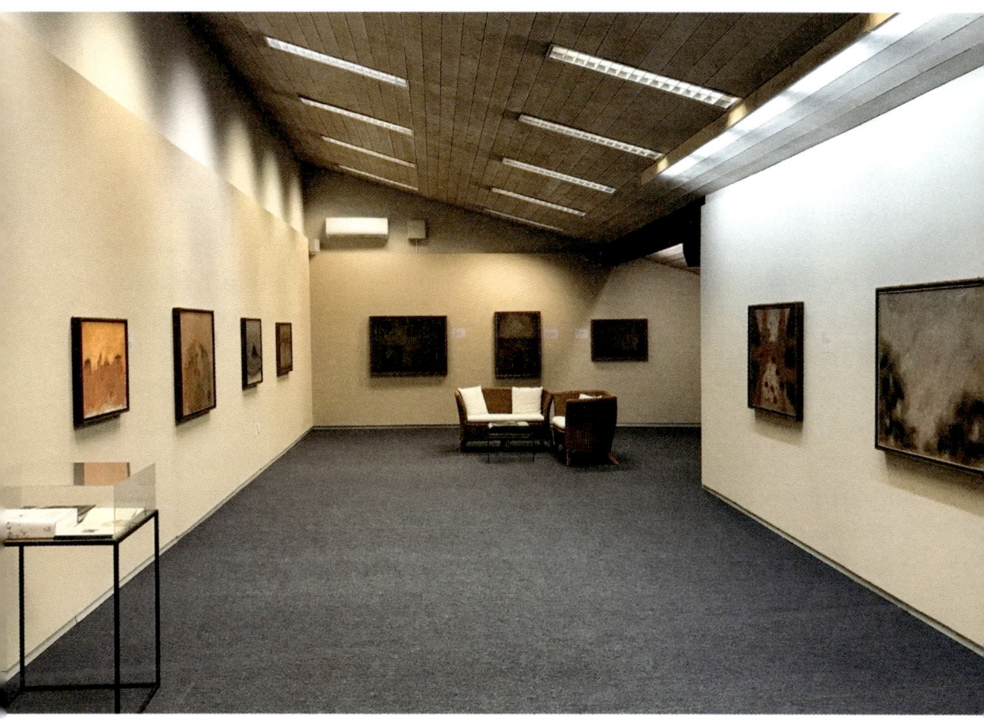

Fondazione Matasci per l'Arte
Matasci Arte
Via Verbano 6
CH-6598 Tenero
Phone: +41 78 6016024
arte@matasci.com
matasci-vini.ch/de/matasci-arte/die-kunstgalerie-in-tenero

Opening hours
Mon–Fri 9 a.m.–noon p.m./1:30 p.m.–6:30 p.m., Sat 9 a.m.–5 p.m.

Entrance fee
Free admission

Arrival by public transportation
The train station Tenero is only 200 m east of the Matasci wine shop. The S20 regularly runs from Locarno to Tenero, as does bus 1.

Restaurant tips
Ristorante Lago Maggiore is located at the entrance to the Tenero campsite and surprises with tasty Ticino and Italian dishes (risto-lagomaggiore.ch; Via Lido 2). Gran Caffè Verbano, located in Piazza Grande in Locarno, offers a variety of lunch menus as well as numerous Matasci wines (Piazza Grande 5, 6600 Locarno).

Extra tips
The Matasci winery offers a free guided tour with Merlot tasting every Friday at 4 p.m. from April to October.
On the way from Tenero to Lugano, drivers can make an excursion to Monte Tamaro. The Santa Maria degli Angeli church, designed by Mario Botta and decorated with paintings by Enzo Cucchi, can be found there. It is reached from Rivera via cable car (galinsky.com/buildings/montetamaro/; Monte Tamaro).

312 Deposito Collezione Matasci

In 2010, Mario Matasci fulfilled his wish to be able to exhibit his art collection in larger rooms to better enjoy it himself. Somewhat by chance, he was offered a commercial building in a small industrial area in Cugnasco, about 5 km from Tenero. He left the outer shell of the hall unchanged and, efficiently but easily, transformed both floors into berths and open spaces with simple walls. In this approximately 900 m^2 large showroom, the so-called Deposito, there are several seating groups, and in the background, quiet classical music plays. All of Matasci's exhibition rooms have an almost meditative atmosphere in common. Visitors are invited to linger, a library with around 10,000 art books and catalogs also invites visitors to deepen their knowledge about what they have seen. Each year, Mario Matasci curates up to four special exhibitions from the collection's holdings in sections of the Deposito. Three portraits of women by Käthe Kollwitz, Robert Schürach, and Franco Francese are among the collector's favorites and, while these and works by Jürg Brodwolf, Edmondo Dobrzanski, and Zoran Mušič are on permanent display, other rooms only change occasionally.

In 2010, Mario Matasci also founded the Fondazione Matasci per l'Arte, whose purpose is to preserve, maintain, and make the works of art in the Matasci Collection accessible to the public. With a heavy heart, he sold individual works from the collection to acquire the capital to start the foundation.

Deposito Collezione Matasci
Cugnasco-Gerra, Ticino

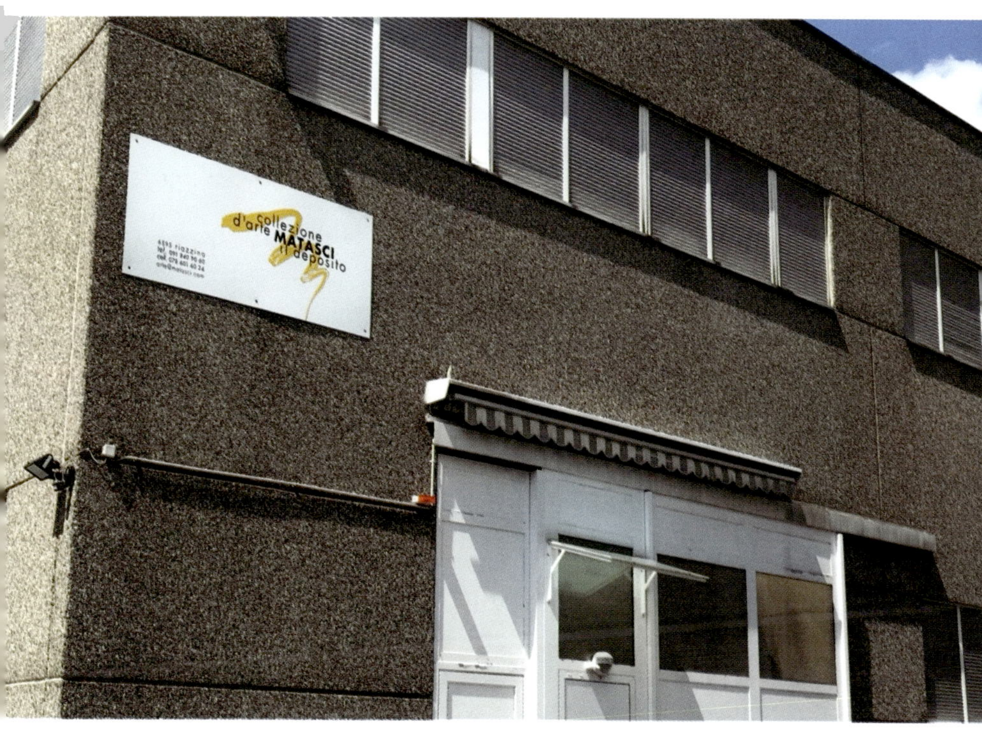

Deposito Collezione Matasci
Via Riazzino 3
CH-6516 Cugnasco-Gerra
Phone: +41 78 6016024
arte@matasci.com
matasci-vini.ch/de/matasci-arte/die-sammlung-im-deposito/

Opening hours
Sun 2–5 p.m. or after making an appointment via Phone: Once there, the collector carries out the guided tours personally.

Entrance fee
Free entrance

Arrival by car
Some navigation systems, as well as Google Maps, indicate "6595 Riazzino" as the location instead of "6516 Cugnasco-Gerra" when entering the address above. Please do not let this confuse you. Both lead to the show depot.

Arrival by public transportation
From Locarno, take bus 311 (direction Bellinzona) to the stop Riazzino, Scuole. Follow Via Cantonale for a few meters to the east and turn first left into Via Alla Cascata and then right into Via Riazzino. If you take the twenty-minute footpath, you can also take the faster and more frequent S20 from Locarno to Riazzino.

Restaurant tip
The best homemade pasta dishes in the region are served at the Osteria Locanda Brack (osteriabrack.ch; Via A. Malacarne 26, 6515 Gudo; only open in the evening, closed Tuesdays and Wednesdays).

Extra tip
If you are visiting Ticino by car via the Gotthard route, a small detour to Giornico, south of the Gotthard Tunnel, is recommended. Thirty reliefs and sculptures by sculptor Hans Josephsohn are shown here in the tiny but very worth-seeing Museo La Congiunta. Swiss architects Peter Märkli and Stefan Bellwalder designed the modern, award-winning museum building (Via Stazione Vecchia 2). The key to the museum can be obtained in the village in the Osteria Giornico (Via San Gottardo 37; 6745 Giornico).

314
Museo Castello San Materno – Fondazione per la cultura Kurt e Barbara Alten

The small Museo Castello San Materno, which is affiliated with the Museo Comunale d'Arte Moderna in Ascona, owes its existence to a public-private partnership. Located on a hill at the entrance to Ascona, the museum was opened in 2014 after careful restoration of the building and has housed the art collection of the Fondazione per la cultura Kurt e Barbara Alten since then. In a permanent exhibition on the upper floor of the Castello, on an area of 90 m^2, around sixty works by artists of the Worpswede artist colony, of German Impressionism and Expressionism such as Paula Modersohn-Becker, Otto Modersohn, Fritz Overbeck, Hans am Ende, Max Liebermann, and Lovis Corinth are on view. Also shown are works by artists from the groups Die Brücke and Der Blaue Reiter, such as Erich Heckel, Ernst Ludwig Kirchner, Hermann Max Pechstein, and Alexej von Jawlensky. Christian Rohlfs, Emil Nolde, and August Macke are represented with watercolors. On the upper floor, there is also a ceiling fresco by Andreas Jawlensky, painted by Alexej von Jawlensky's then seventeen-year-old son during a visit to his family in 1919. Since 2016, the two rooms on the ground floor have been used for a special exhibition from June to September, which is financed by the Fondazione per la cultura Kurt e Barbara Alten and is generally related to the collection. During the remaining months, a temporary exhibition organized by the municipal museum takes place here.

The eventful history of the medieval castle with its Romanesque chapel dates back to the sixth century. In 1513, the castle fell into the hands of the Swiss until, after centuries of structural decline, Frenchman Enrico de Loppinot renovated and added an extension

Museo Castello San Materno
Ascona, Ticino

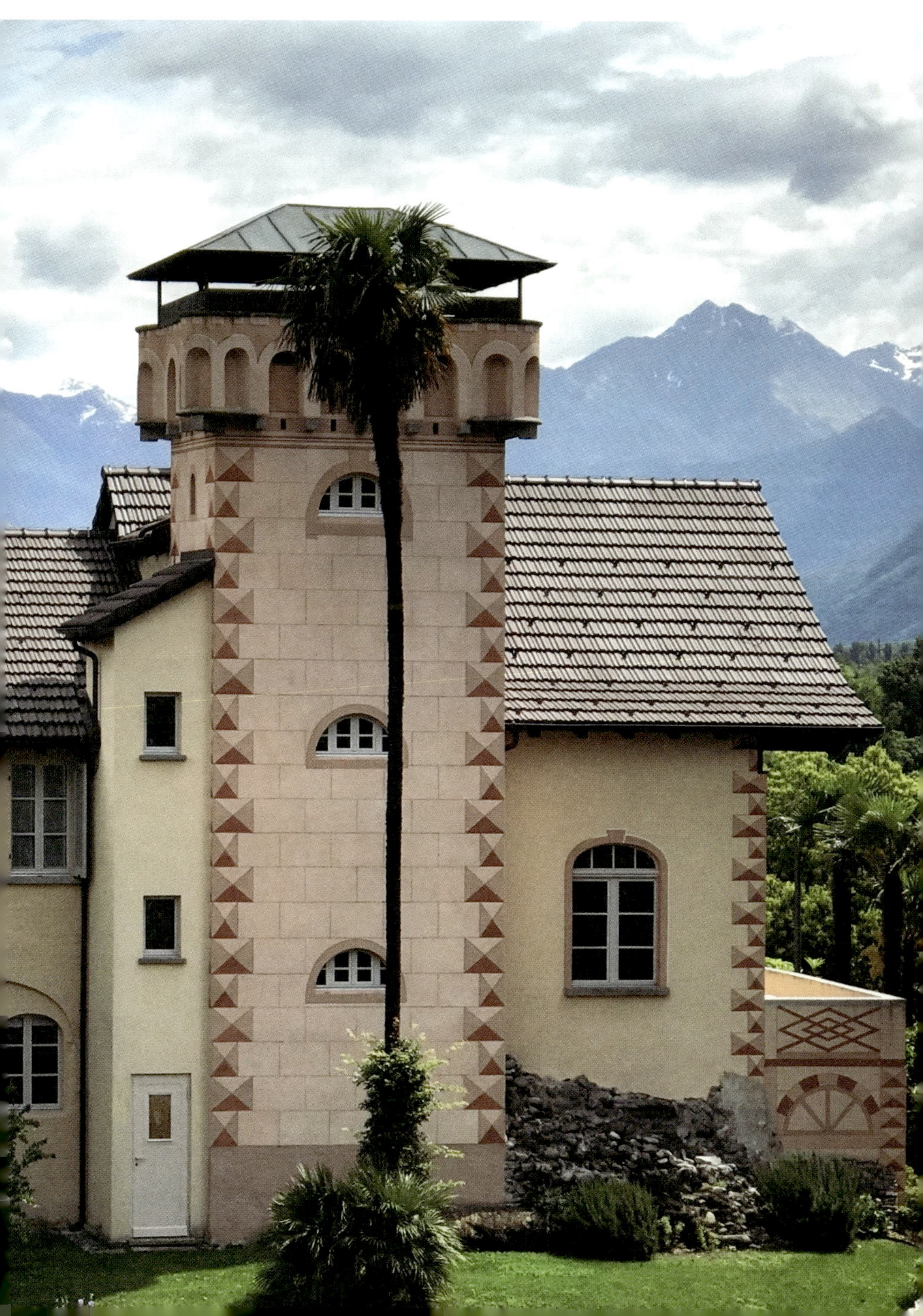

around 1850. In 1919, German silk merchant Paul Bachrach, his wife, Elvira, and his daughter Charlotte, an expressive dancer, bought the Castello and the surrounding park. From then on, it became a meeting place for writers, musicians, artists, and dancers. Christian Rohlfs discovered his enthusiasm for magnolias during his visits to the garden and later frequently depicted them in his works. In 1927, Paul Bachrach commissioned the Worpswede artist Carl Weidemeyer to design the Teatro San Materno across from the castle. The Bauhaus-style building was to be a "temple of dance" and could be used as a dance school and theater. In 1978, the theater was transferred to the municipality of Ascona. After the death of Charlotte Bara in 1987, the municipality also acquired the property and for years searched for a suitable purpose. At the same time, the Alten family was thinking about a permanent future home for their collection. Kurt Alten (1925–2009) developed the first loading ramp in 1957 as a graduate engineer. His company, Alten Gerätebau GmbH Wennigsen, grew over the years to become the European market leader in loading technology. Collecting paintings was the great passion of Kurt Alten and his wife Barbara Alten (1937–2016). Fascinated by the landscape painting of the Worpswede artists, they bought their first works during a visit to Worpswede at the end of the 1970s and also became enthusiastic about the German Impressionists and Expressionists. The collection mainly reflects, in the form of landscape painting and still lifes, artistic development in Germany from the middle of the nineteenth century to the beginning of the early twentieth century. With the acquisition of a still life by Hermann Max Pechstein and an oil painting by Gabriele Münter, the collection, first in 2002 and in a second stage in 2005, was transferred to the Fondazione per la cultura Kurt e Barbara Alten in Solothurn. Since Barbara and Kurt Alten had their second home in Switzerland, it was important to them to make the collection accessible to the public here. The purpose of the foundation is, on the one hand, to promote art and culture in the Espace Mittelland region, which is achieved by awarding an annual prize of 20,000 Swiss francs to one or two young artists. The second purpose of the foundation—the long-term loan of paintings to a museum in Switzerland—was implemented thanks to the initiative of Urs Ris, German art dealer Hubertus Melsheimer, notary and lawyer Burkhard Scherrer, founder Barbara Alten, Fondazione per la cultura Kurt e Barbara Alten, and the mayor of Ascona, Dr. Luca Pissoglio. The first talks took place in 2011, and a few years later the Museo Castello San Materno was realized.

Museo Castello San Materno – Fondazione per la cultura Kurt e Barbara Alten
Via Losone 10
CH-6612 Ascona
Phone: +41 91759 8160
museosanmaterno@ascona.ch
museoascona.ch
kulturstiftung-alten.ch

Opening hours
March–December Thu–Sat
10 a.m.–12 p.m. and 2–5 p.m., as well as Sun and some holidays, 2–4 p.m.

Entrance fees
Adults / Reduced / Adolescents up to age 18: CHF 7 / CHF 5 / free
Combination ticket incl. admission to the Museo Comunale d'Arte Moderna: Adults / Reduced: CHF 12 / CHF 8

Arrival by public transportation
From the Locarno railway station, take the bus 1 to Ascona and get off at San Materno. From there, walk a few meters northeast along Viale Monte Verità and turn left into Via Losone.

Parking
Opposite the cemetery, there is a public car park (Via Buonamano 69).

Restaurant tips
The Ristorante Grotto Broggini is famous for its grilled chicken (ristoranti-ff.ch; Via S. Materno 18, 6616 Losone). The Ristorante Elisabetta serves innovative dishes (pensione-elisabetta.com/Restaurant_&_Terrasse_en; Via Livurcio 50, 6622 Ronco sopra Ascona). Italian cuisine can be enjoyed on the terrace of the Ristorante Albergo Ronco (hotel-ronco.ch/en/restaurant; Piazza della Madonna 1, 6622 Ronco sopra Ascona). Wood-oven pizza and other Italian dishes are available at the Ristorante Pizzeria del Centro (ristorantedelcentro.ch; Via Livurcio 4, 6622 Ronco sopra Ascona).

Extra tips
The municipal museum Museo Comunale d'Arte Moderna is located in the pedestrian area of Ascona (museoascona.ch; Via Borgo 34). A trip to Monte Verità, whose location attracted anarchists, free-living vegetarians, artists, writers, dancers, and philosophers already in the beginning of the twentieth century, is highly recommended. The German-Swiss banker and patron of the arts Eduard Freiherr von der Heydt had a Bauhaus-style hotel built by Emil Fahrenkamp on Monte Verità in 1929. Traces of the various residents of the area are present everywhere. There is also a hotel, a restaurant, and a Japanese teahouse. A visit to Casa Anatta with an exhibition on the history of Monte Verità, curated by Harald Szeemann, (monteverita.org; Strada Collina 84, 6612 Ascona) is particularly impressive.
Highly recommended is a visit to the Fondazione Marguerite Arp (see p. 298) and the Ghisla Art Collection in Locarno (p. 306) at the same time, as well as the Fondazione Matasci per l'Arte in Tenero and Cugnasco-Gerra (pp. 310, 312).

318
Rolla Foundation

Since 2010, friends of photography have been enjoying trips to the village of Bruzella in the Valle di Muggio—because in 2008 Rosella and Philip Rolla reached an agreement with the municipality to leave the vacant rooms of the former kindergarten on the upper floor of the community hall to them as exhibition rooms for the next thirty years. After a renovation financed by the Rolla Foundation, the bright exhibition rooms, which are approximately 100 m^2 in size, are now used for monographic or themed photography exhibitions that change twice a year. Although the Rollas were initially interested in Minimalist art, they wanted to give photography enthusiasts access to important works by Robert Adams, Josef Sudek, Albert Renger-Patzsch, Bernd and Hilla Becher and Christof Klute, Thomas Struth, Hiroshi Sugimoto, and Vincenzo Castella. Philip Rolla's personal history and professional career explain his particular preference for German and American architectural and industrial photography: born in 1938 near San Francisco into an Italian family, he completed his studies in engineering and economics at Santa Clara University. From an early age, Philip Rolla was fascinated by the aesthetics and technology of racing boats and cars. In the early 1960s, he moved to Turin and then to Ticino. Here, he found the perfect place to establish his ship propeller company. He also believes that he owes his ideas for his propellers' functional design to his enthusiasm for Conceptual and Minimal art.

Rolla Foundation
Bruzella, Ticino

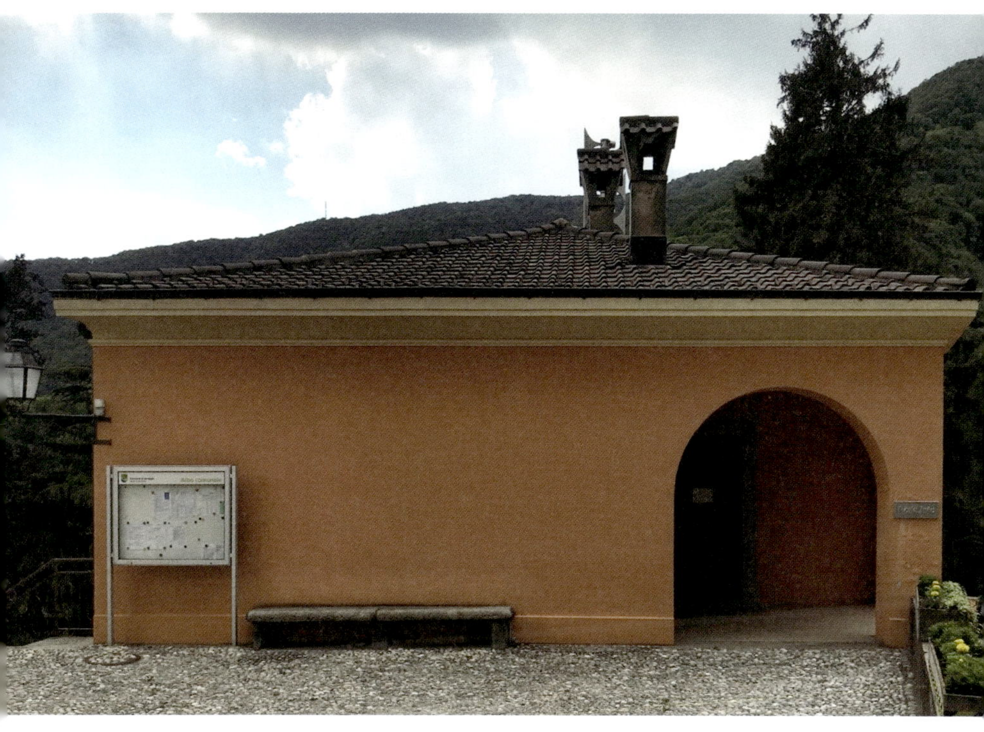

Rolla Foundation
Strada Végia
CH-6837 Bruzella
Phone: +41 77 4740549
e.brunati@rolla.info,
rosella@rolla.info
rolla.info

Opening hours
Every second Sunday of the month, 2–6 p.m. during the exhibition and by appointment (by telephone or email).

Entrance fees
Free admission

Arrival by car
Some navigation systems have difficulties locating the road. It helps to enter "Via Municipio 5." Google Maps only recognizes the road if you enter "Fondazione Rolla."

Arrival by public transportation
From Mendrisio station, take bus 513 to Morbio Superiore, Posta. There change to bus 515 and get off at Bruzella, Paese.

Parking
There are several parking spaces near the building.

Restaurant tips
Regional specialties are offered at Grotto del Mulino (grottomulino.com; Via ai Crotti 2, 6834 Morbio Inferiore). Lombard cuisine is served on the Italian side of the border at Gatto Nero (Via Sant'Elia, 21059 Viggiù, Italy; +39 0332 488482).

Extra tips
From Bruzella, it is possible to reach the famous contemporary collection of Count Giuseppe Panza di Biumo in the Villa Menafoglio Litta Panza in Italy by car in about one hour (fondoambiente.it/villa-e-collezione-panza-de; Piazza Litta 1, 21100 I-Varese). On the way to Italy, you can make a detour to the Museo Vincenzo Vela. In addition to a sculpture collection by Vincenzo Vela (1820–1891), the residential house and museum renovated by Mario Botta is home to the estate of sculptor Lorenzo Vela and painter Spartaco Vela, a pinacotheca of nineteen-century-Lombard and Piedmontese artists, as well as one of the oldest private collections of photographs in Switzerland (museo-vela.ch; Largo Vincenzo Vela 5, 6853 Ligornetto).

320 Spazio -1 / Collezione Giancarlo e Danna Olgiati

The Spazio -1 exhibition space, in the basement of Central Park and opposite the LAC Cultural Centre, is a joint project of the city of Lugano, the Olgiati collector couple various other sponsors, and a charitable foundation. The owner of the former parking garage turned it over to the city within the framework of a foundation on the condition that it be used for cultural purposes. After Giancarlo and Danna Olgiati agreed with the city fathers to make parts of their collection available to the public as a showroom in the MASI, which has been housed in LAC since 2015, Ticino architect Ivano Gianola, who also designed the LAC, was commissioned with carrying out the conversion. He realized a spatial concept in which the 1,200 m^2 floor can be flexibly subdivided with variable partition walls to create more spacious areas or more intimate bunks, depending on the exhibition. The result was a perfect platform for the continually growing collection of over five hundred works, including European movements such as Futurism, Spazialismo, Nouveau Réalisme, and Arte Povera. It includes paintings, sculptures, drawings, photographs, and installations by Yves Klein, Marisa Merz, Lucio Fontana, Piero Manzoni, Alighiero Boetti, Giovanni Anselmo, Jannis Kounellis, Michelangelo Pistoletto, Luciano Fabro, Arman, Antony Gormley, Jimmie Durham, Wolfgang Tillmans, and Tauba Auerbach. The continually changing collection was established in the early 1960s, when Giancarlo Olgiati, then a young lawyer, began to purchase art. In 1985, he found his life and collecting partner with the gallerist of the Galleria Fonte d'Abisso in Milan. As an expert on Futurism, Danna integrated it into the collection, making the Futurism room the only area that remains permanently on display. Since its opening in 2012, all other rooms have been rehung once a year. The aim is to use the collection's changing installations to constantly re-examine the connections between historical and contemporary works through

Spazio -1 / Collezione Giancarlo e Danna Olgiati
Lugano, Ticino

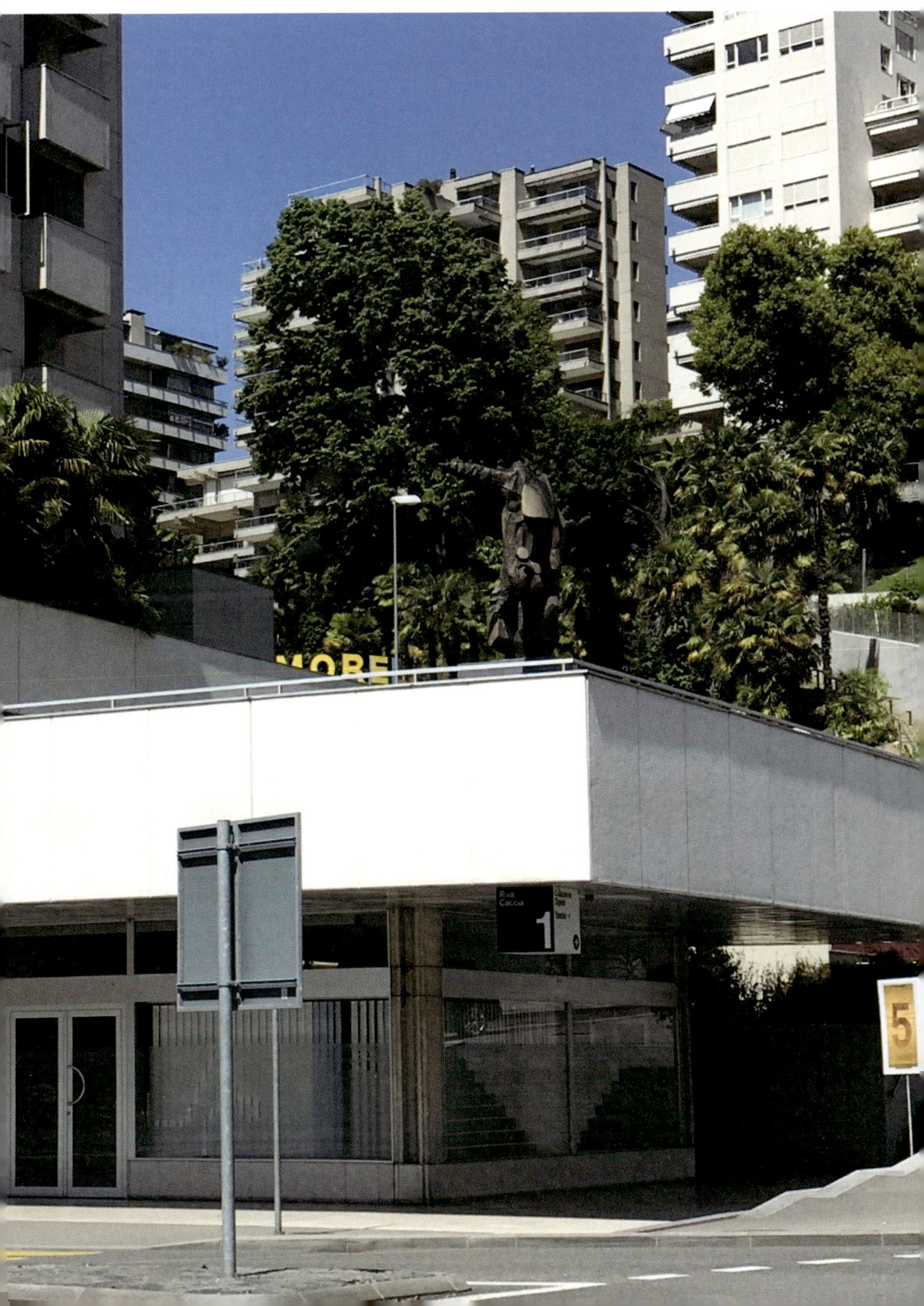

other correspondences. By supplementing the exhibitions with new additions to the collection, the aim is to clarify what collectors understand by "collection in progress."

The cultural center and Spazio -1 see themselves as a cultural crossroad between Northern and Southern Europe with the declared aim of linking the two regions.

Spazio -1 / Collezione Giancarlo e Danna Olgiati
Riva Antonio Caccia 1
CH-6900 Lugano
Phone: +41 91 9214632
info.menouno@lugano.ch
collezioneolgiati.ch

Opening hours
Mid-September to early January and April to June Fri–Sun 11 a.m.–6 p.m.
Free guided tour on Sundays at 3 p.m., no registration required.

Entrance fees
Free admission

Arrival by public transportation
Leave Lugano Stazione to the right and follow Via Clemente Maraini in a southern direction. After turning left onto Via Giuseppe Motta, you will see steep stairs leading to the lake. At the northwest end of the lake, turn right towards Riva Vincenzo Vela and follow the road to the roundabout. The entrance to Spazio -1 is a little hidden on the opposite side of the roundabout, directly at the corner of the large building.

Parking
The car park of the LAC Cultural Centre is opposite Spazio -1.

Restaurant tips
Excellent wines and a selection of dishes are offered at Bottegone del Vino (Via Massimiliano Magatti 3). There is excellent dining at La Cucina di Alice overlooking the lake (lacucinadialice.ch; Riva Vincenzo Vela 4).

Extra tips
The new art and culture center, LAC Lugano Arte e Cultura, designed by Ivano Gianola, with a theater and concert hall, is the new home of the Museo d'Arte della Svizzera Italiana (MASI) (luganolac.ch; Piazza Bernardino Luini 6). Right next to LAC is the church of Santa Maria degli Angioli. It houses a representation of the passion and crucifixion of Jesus by Italian artist Bernardino Luini (1480–1532), a pupil of Leonardo. The work is considered to be the most famous Renaissance fresco in Switzerland. Open Gallery – Arte Urbana Lugano (AUL) takes place twice a year. Galleries, museums, and art spaces open their doors free of charge on two Saturdays between 3–8 p.m. (opengallerylugano.ch).
A simultaneous visit to the Fondazione Gabriele e Anna Braglia (see p. 302) and an excursion to the Rolla Foundation (see p. 318) is highly recommended.

Spazio -1 / Collezione Giancarlo e Danna Olgiati
Lugano, Ticino

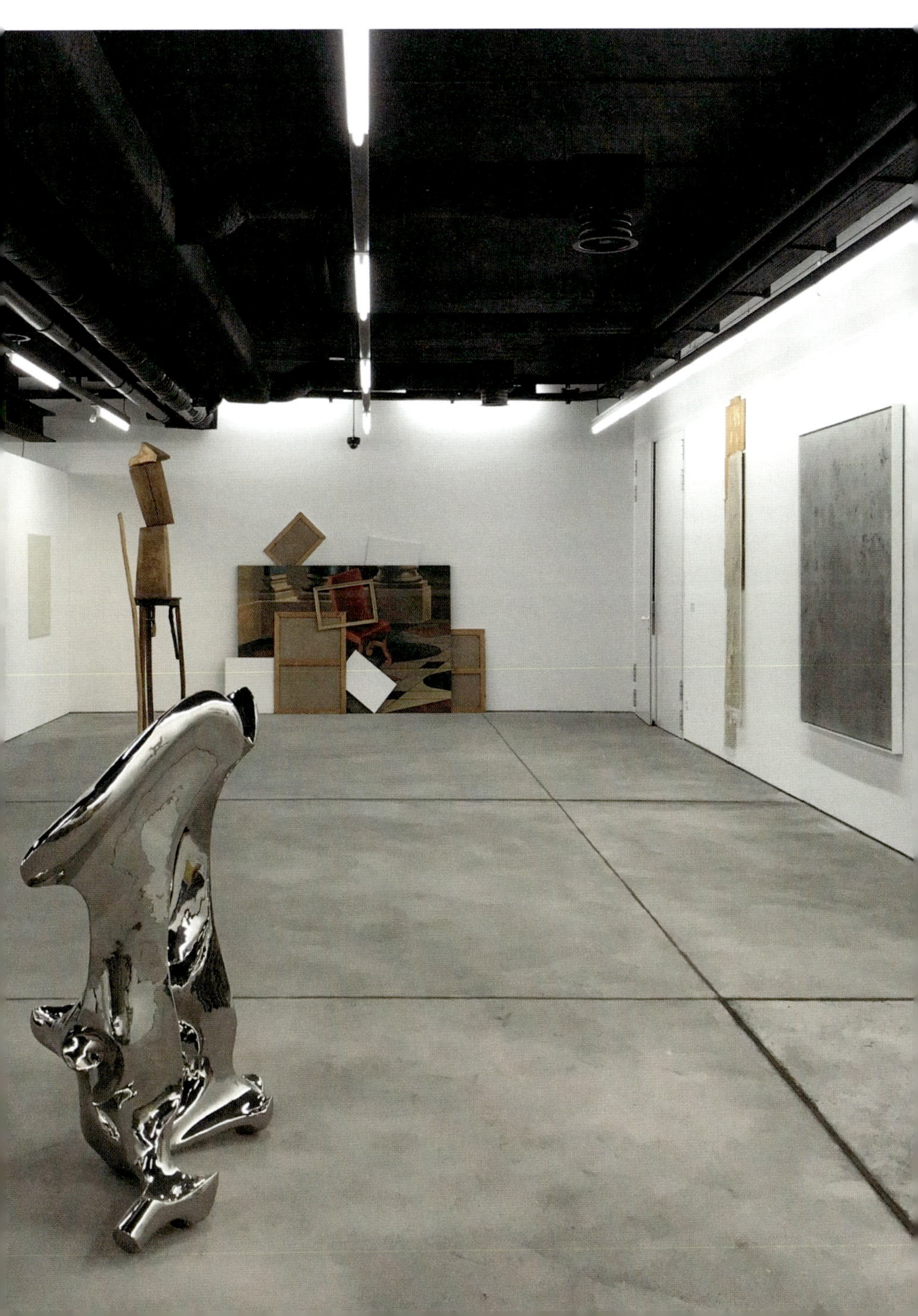

324 Fondation Pierre Gianadda

Situated in the southwest of Switzerland in the Valais Alps, the town of Martigny owes its place on the international art and culture calendar to the engineer, contractor, journalist, artist, and much-honored art patron Léonard Gianadda. In 1976, he discovered the remains of a Gallo-Roman temple—the oldest of its kind in Switzerland—on a plot of land on which he wanted to build an apartment building. A few months later, his younger brother Pierre died as a result of a plane crash. Léonard Gianadda decided to establish a cultural foundation in his honor. Above the temple's excavation site, he erected a self-designed and -financed concrete building as a future cultural center. It was inaugurated on November 19, 1978, the same day Pierre Gianadda would have celebrated his fortieth birthday. This new building houses two permanent exhibitions on two levels: the Gallo-Roman Museum, which is centered on the early history of the town, and a unique collection of vintage cars built between 1897 and 1939. The central, open room in the basement of the main building is used for more extensive exhibitions and classical concerts. Every year, two to three comprehensive, theme-related temporary exhibits are shown here. These are mainly curated with loans from museums and private collections.

Another highlight is the permanent sculpture exhibition in the gardens of the Fondation. Between Gallo-Roman relics and small ponds, visitors can see more than forty objects by Joan Miró, Auguste Rodin, Niki de Saint Phalle, Jean Arp, Henry Moore, Alexander Calder, Constantin Brancusi, and other twentieth-century sculptors. The majority of the sculptures were purchased by the Fondation with financial means from Léonard Gianadda. Companies or private collectors donated individual works of art, for example, the reconstructed mosaic pavilion by Marc Chagall, which Georges Kostelitz donated to the Fondation in 2003.

At the edge of the park, there is another larger building, the Vieil Arsenal, where the permanent exhibition *Leonardo da Vinci, the*

Fondation Pierre Gianadda
Martigny, Valais

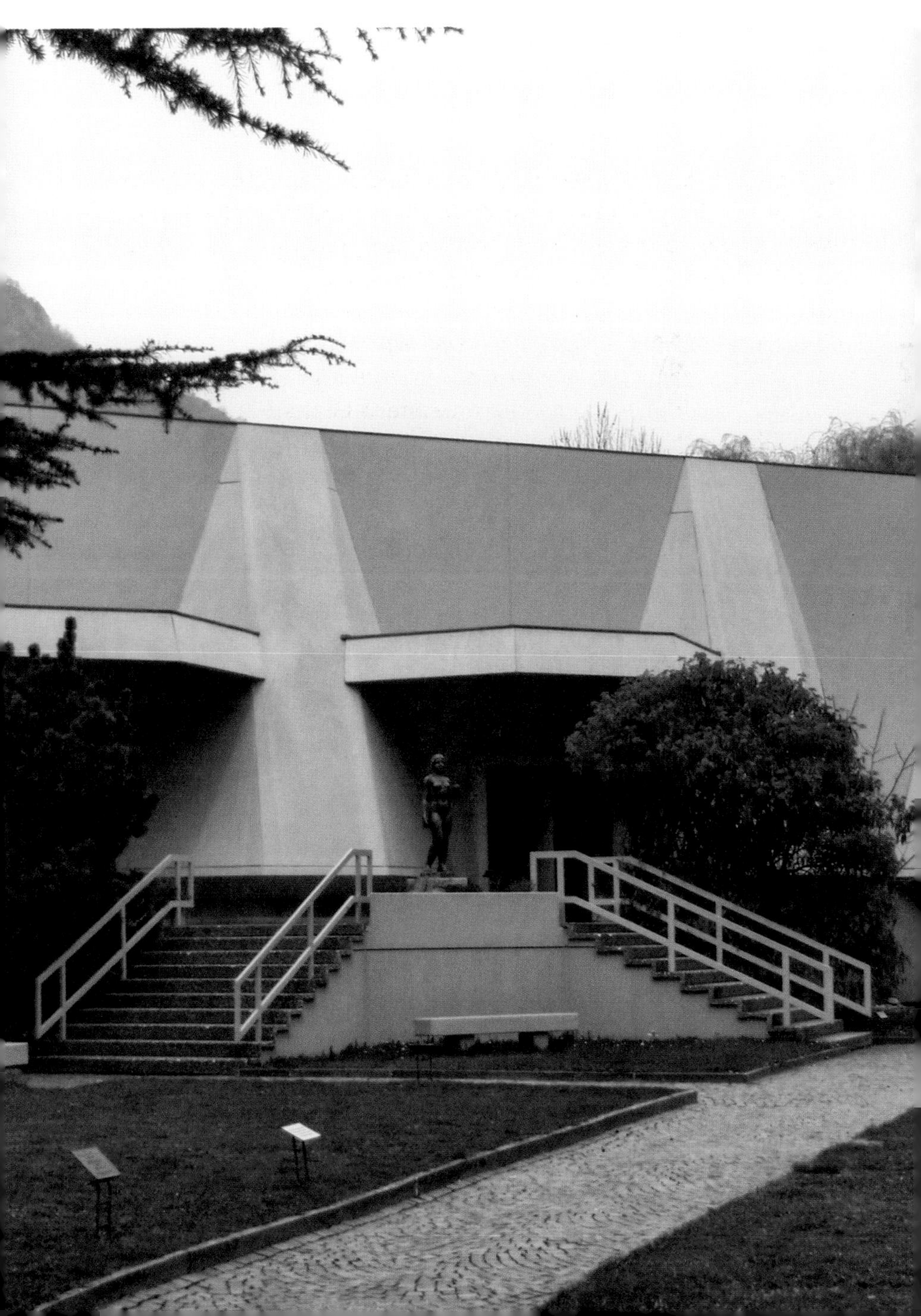

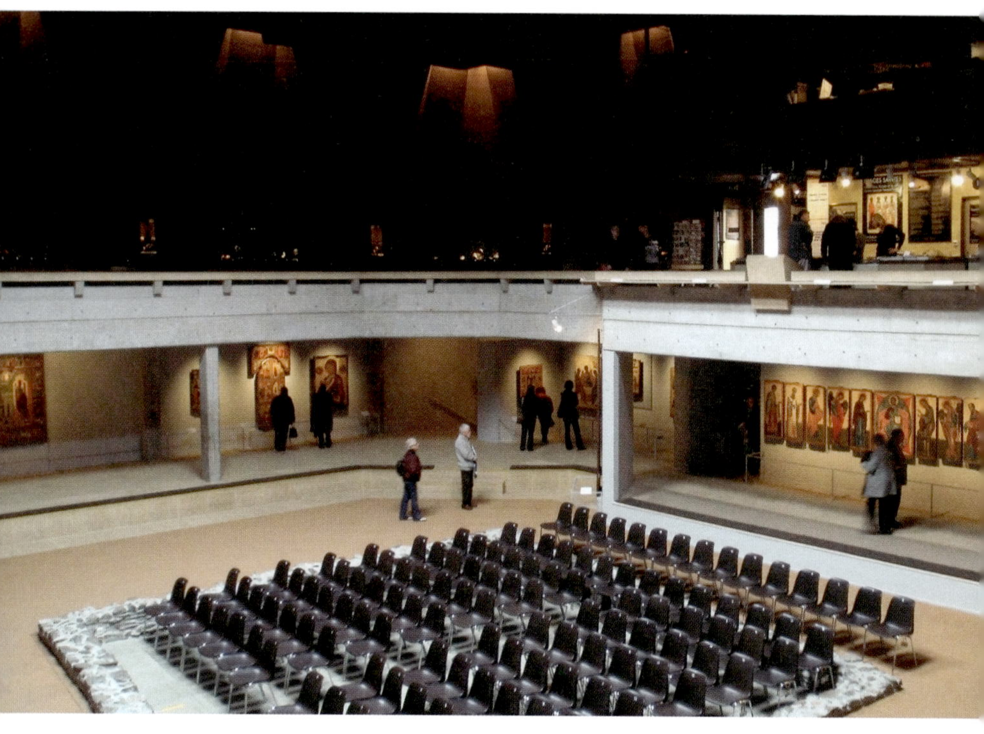

Fondation Pierre Gianadda
Pierre Gianadda Foundation
Rue du Forum 59
CH-1920 Martigny
Phone: +41 27 7223978
info@gianadda.ch
gianadda.ch

Opening hours
November to June daily 10 a.m.–6 p.m.; June to November daily 9 a.m.–7 p.m.
In good weather, the sculpture park is open in July and August from 7 to 10 p.m. and can be visited free of charge during these times. Almost every Wednesday at 8 p.m., guided tours or lectures are offered in French. Private tours can also be booked in other languages. Classical concerts with world-famous artists such as Cecilia Bartoli, Maurizio Pollini, and Martha Argerich also take place every month. Reservations can be made by telephone or in writing. The current program is on the website. From March to November, drinks and snacks are offered in a pavilion in the park. There is a bookshop with art books, exhibition catalogs, postcards, and souvenirs on the ground floor of the foundation.

Entrance fees
Adults / Seniors / Children and students / Family ticket: CHF 15–18 / CHF 13.50–16 / CHF 8.50–10 / CHF 33.50–40

Parking
There is a parking lot next to the foundation.

Arrival by public transportation
After arriving at the Martigny Central Station, take the 201 bus to the Fondation Gianadda stop (see sbb.ch, the destination is "Martigny, Fondation Gianadda"). From the bus stop, cross to Rue Pré-Borvey, which leads directly to the Fondation.

Restaurant tips
The beautiful Place Centrale has numerous cafés and restaurants offering excellent Valais specialties. During the summer months, it is possible to sit outside while relishing the north Italian atmosphere. Visitors with a penchant for cozy cellar vaults will enjoy the eighteenth-century mill in the Caveau du Moulin Semblanet. Here you will find delicious varieties of fondue and other regional specialties (moulinsemblanet.ch; Rue des Moulins 11; closed Mondays and Tuesdays). The family-run Restaurant le Bourg-Ville has a beautiful terrace. Lamb lovers in particular will enjoy the menu (bourg-ville.ch; Avenue du Grand-St-Bernard 40a; closed Mondays). Gourmets will be delighted by the innovative cuisine of the modern Restaurants Les Touristes (touristes-martigny.ch; closed Sundays and Mondays). The Gelateria Patella offers deli-

Inventor, is shown every year from March to November. More than a hundred facsimiles and mobile models made especially for the exhibition illustrate the creative power of this genius. There is also an exhibition on the life and career of Léonard Gianadda.

On the walkway in front of the entrance area of the main building, a “Walk of Fame” has been created, similar to the Californian model. Here, handprints or footprints, in some cases also signatures of famous artists and musicians, are immortalized on plates on the path. The cityscape has also been artistically enriched: the Fondation and the Gianadda couple have provided Martigny with numerous sculptures for outdoor spaces.

cious ice creams (gelateriapatella.ch; Avenue de la Gare 3).

Extra tips
An archaeological tour makes it easier to experience the Gallo-Roman artifacts in the Martigny region; the impressive amphitheater should not be missed. A free brochure about the collection, as well as numerous sights and the contemporary sculptures scattered throughout the city, can be found in the entrance area of the Fondation. The hiking trail over the terraced vineyards of Martigny takes about two hours from the town center to the Château de la Bâtiaz and the village of Plan-Cerisier. The walk is a chance to get to know wine growers, wine cellar owners, and wine shops in Martigny and the surrounding area. A good overview of the region can be found on the website of the tourist office (martigny.com).

328 Oskar Reinhart Collection "Am Römerholz"

Only a few art collections in the twentieth century were built with such determination and vision as that of Oskar Reinhart (1885–1965). Even before he began to acquire paintings on a large scale, the future collection was clearly defined as a "musée imaginaire." Julius Meier-Graefe's books were groundbreaking, as was his 1906 visit to the Centennial Exhibition of German Art in Berlin's Nationalgalerie from 1775 to 1875. Reinhart's ambition was to acquire only the most important masterpieces, even if he had to wait decades to purchase an object. He never intended to compile a complete overview of art history; rather, he concentrated on certain phases of the work of artists who particularly impressed him.

The foundation for Oskar Reinhart's interest in art was laid in his family home, which was characterized by art and the arts. His father, Theodor Reinhart, headed the Volkart Brothers empire, a wholesale company for goods such as cotton and coffee that was active on every continent. In addition to his commercial activities, he was a paternal advisor and confidant to numerous artists and an influential member of the Kunstverein Winterthur. Thus, Oskar Reinhart enjoyed the privilege of growing up among young Swiss and German artists. During his training abroad and after joining the family business, he spent all his free time in museums and art galleries. At the age of thirty-nine, he was able to realize his dream and withdraw from the company to dedicate himself to collecting and promoting art. In 1924, Reinhart acquired the stately location "Am Römerholz," situated in an elevated position on the edge of the forest of Winterthur, as a residential domicile. The Geneva architect Maurice Turrettini originally built the villa between 1915 and 1918 for the industrialist Jakob Heinrich Ziegler-Sulzer. The simple design of the building and, in part, the interior echoes the architecture of the Italian Renaissance. After acquiring the property, Oskar Reinhart commissioned Turrettini to add a three-part

Oskar Reinhart Collection “Am Römerholz”
Winterthur, Zurich

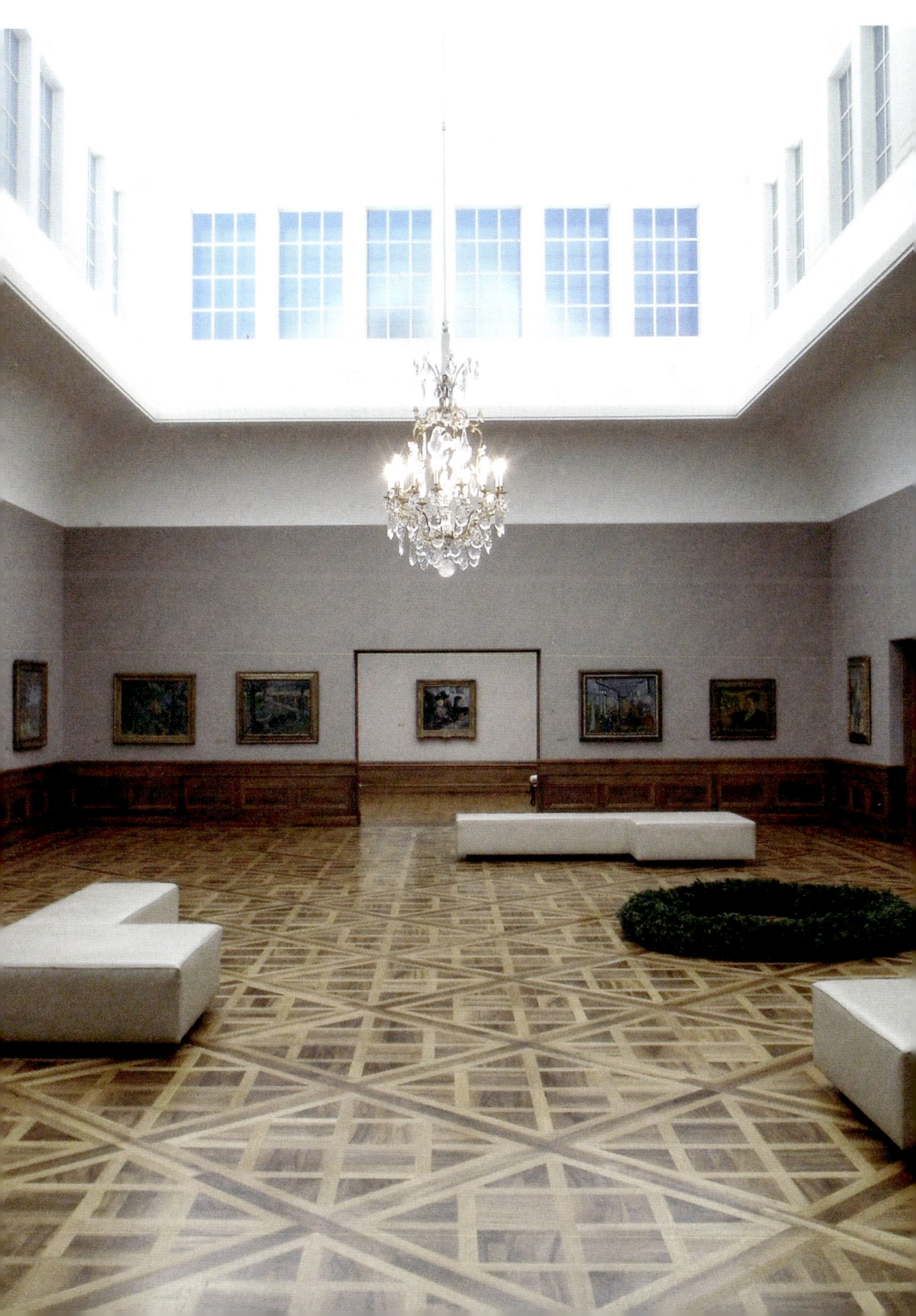

painting gallery in which deliberately omitted historical reminders to avoid impairing the effect of the works of art. The painting gallery was opened to the public with a separate entrance during Oskar Reinhart's lifetime. Reinhart lived in this Winterthur domicile, surrounded by his beloved works, until his death in 1965.

True to his maxim of serving the general public with his art collection, as early as 1940 he ordered a donation of his works by German, Swiss, and Austrian artists from the eighteenth to twentieth centuries to the city of Winterthur. In the 1930s, he came up with the idea of redesigning the premises of the former grammar school, built by Leonhard Zeugheer between 1838 and 1842, to meet the needs of an art collection. In 1951, the Oskar Reinhart Foundation, later the Oskar Reinhart Museum am Stadtgarten, and since 2018 the Kunst Museum Winterthur / Reinhart am Stadtgarten, was opened in the city center.

With his death, Oskar Reinhart bequeathed the remaining holdings in the villa, a selection of Old Master paintings, and works of French painting and sculpture, together with the land, of the Swiss Confederation. Today, this collection of some two hundred works is the only federal collection of paintings. The paintings of the Old Masters (Hans Holbein the Younger, Lucas Cranach the Elder, Peter Paul Rubens, El Greco, and Francisco de Goya, among others) are a juxtaposition to the central part of the collection, French nineteenth-century painting. Oskar Reinhart was fascinated by the artistic quality of works from Nicolas Poussin, Honoré Daumier, and Gustave Courbet to the late Impressionists Vincent van Gogh and Paul Cézanne.

The Villa "Am Römerholz" was first opened to the public in 1970 after a fundamental change to the original architecture. Between 1996 and 1998, however, Zurich architect duo Annette Gigon and Mike Guyer were able to restore the elements destroyed during the first conversion and thus restore the original character of the residential building. The architects created three new rooms in the wing between the villa and the painting gallery. The last renovation, under the direction of P&B Partner Architekten in 2009/10, was to update the technology and redesign of the café and administration rooms. Thus, as intended by the founder, the collection of paintings is now presented in its original surroundings, both in the former residential building and in the gallery extension. Following the collector’s high design standards, the works are not arranged in strict chronological order but enter into a dialogue with each other across epochs and styles, which makes a visit particularly exciting. Since 2005, the museum has also shown individual works from the collection in small exhibitions at intervals of one to two years in an art-historical context with other works.

Oskar Reinhart Collection
“Am Römerholz”
Haldenstr. 95
CH-8400 Winterthur
Phone: +41 58 4667740
sor@bak.admin.ch
roemerholz.ch

Opening hours
Tue–Sun 10 a.m.–5 p.m.,
Wed 10 a.m.–8 p.m.
Free thematic tours take place every two weeks on Wednesdays at 6:30 p.m.; free guided tours of the collection every Sunday at 11:30 a.m. There are also special tours for children and cultural events on themes directly related to the collection or temporary exhibitions.

Entrance fees
Adults / Reduced / Children up to age 16 and Wednesdays from 5 p.m.: CHF 15 / CHF 12 / free of charge

Parking
Parking is available on Haldenstrasse and Eichwaldstrasse, 50 m behind the museum entrance.

Arrival by public transportation
The museum bus runs hourly from the SBB railway station, sector G, from 9:45 a.m. to 4:45 p.m. to the museum and returns hourly from Römerholz from 10 a.m. to 5 p.m. From the railway station, you can also take bus 10 in the direction of Oberwinterthur to the Haldengut stop. From here, walk in the direction of the roundabout, cross it, and walk uphill for about ten minutes (for timetable information, see also stadtbus.winterthur.ch). From the main station, a footpath along the tracks via Lindstrasse and Haldenstrasse (stairs to the Haldengut intersection) leads to Römerholz in approx. twenty minutes uphill.

Restaurant tips
There are numerous cafés and restaurants in the old town. Close to the collection, the modern Trois Tilleuls restaurant in the Lindberg private clinic offers creative regional and international specialties (trois-tilleuls.ch; Schickstr. 11).

Extra tips
The extensive works of Swiss, German, and Austrian art (especially early Romanticism and Realism) from the former Oskar Reinhart Collection are still on permanent display at the Kunst Museum Winterthur / Reinhart am Stadtgarten (kmw.ch/museum/portrait-reinhart-am-stadtgarten; Stadthausstr. 6). It is also a good idea to visit the Kunst Museum Winterthur / Beim Stadthaus in the immediate vicinity (kmw.ch/museum/portrait-beim-stadthaus; Museumstr. 52), as well as the Villa Flora, which also belongs to the museums’ network and will presumably be reopened after restoration in 2022 (kmw.ch/museum/portrait-villaflora; villa-flora.ch; Tösstalstr. 44).

Colophon

Editor
Skadi Heckmüller

Concept
Skadi Heckmüller, DISTANZ Verlag

Design
Bureau Mathias Beyer

Texts
Skadi Heckmüller

Translation
Alicia Reuter

Copy Editing
DISTANZ Verlag

Proof Reading
Steve Wilder

Production Management
DISTANZ Verlag

Printing and Binding
Livonia Print, Riga

Artists of the depicted works and photo credits
Unless mentioned otherwise, the image rights are held by the respective collections and/or photographers.

p. 9 Gerhard Richter, Günther Förg, Museum Frieder Burda, photo: Skadi Heckmüller; p. 11 Benar Venet, Museum Frieder Burda, Photo: Skadi Heckmüller; p. 13 Lori Hersberger © Kunstraum Alexander Bürkle, photo: Bernhard Strauss; p. 15 Max Schmitz, Bernhard Luginbühl, Domnick Collection, photo: Skadi Heckmüller; p. 17 Stadtregal Tag © Sammlung FER Collection, photo: Fotodesign Buhl, Neu Ulm; p. 19 Donald Judd, Dan Flavin, Giulio Paolini, Keith Haring, Carl Andre, Sol LeWitt © Sammlung FER Collection, photo: Jan Windzus, Berlin; p. 21 © Froehlich Collection, Stuttgart, photo: Frank Burgemeister, Pfullingen; p. 23 Gerhard Richter, "Abstraktes Bild", 1982 © Froehlich Collection, Stuttgart, photo: Josh von Staudach; p. 25 Exterior view Fürstlich Fürstenbergische Sammlungen © Fürstenberg Zeitgenössisch, photo: Kathrin Gralla; p. 27 © KUNSTRAUM GRÄSSLIN / museum restaurant Kippys, photo: Wolfgang Günzel; p. 29 Gratianusstiftung, photo: Skadi Heckmüller; p. 31 Museum Villa Haiss, photo: Skadi Heckmüller; p. 33 Lluis Cera, Museum Villa Haiss, photo: Skadi Heckmüller; p. 35 Museum für aktuelle Kunst / Sammlung Hurrle Durbach, photo: Skadi Heckmüller; p. 37 Dieter Krieg, Museum für aktuelle Kunst / Sammlung Hurrle Durbach, photo: Skadi Heckmüller; p. 39 KUNSTWERK / Sammlung Klein, photo: Skadi Heckmüller; p. 43 Exterior view kunsthalle messmer © messmer foundation, photo: D. Schille; p. 45 Morat-Institut für Kunst und Kunstwissenschaft, photo: Michael Jensch; p. 47 Herbert Maier, Morat-Institut für Kunst und Kunstwissenschaft, photo: Bernhard Strauss; p. 49 Exhibition view "Selinka Classics", Kunstmuseum Ravensburg, Pierre Alechinsky © VG Bild-Kunst, Bonn 2019, Karel Appel © Karel Appel Foundation/© VG Bild-Kunst, Bonn 2019, photo: Wynrich Zlomke; p. 51 Kunstmuseum Ravensburg, photo: Roland Halbe © Kunstmuseum Ravensburg; p. 53 Museum Ritter © Museum Ritter, photo: Achim Mende; p. 54 Exhibition view with works by Imi Knoebel © Museum Ritter, photo: Gerhard Sauer; p. 57 SCHAUWERK Sindelfingen, photo: Frank Klein; p. 58 Exhibition view with works by Klaus Heider, Thomas Ruff, Roland Fischer and Carsten Meier, SCHAUWERK Sindelfingen, photo: Frank Kleinbach; p. 61 Keith Haring, Kunsthalle Weishaupt, photo: Skadi Heckmüller; p. 63 Bill Woodrow, Richard Deacon, Würth Collection, photo: Skadi Heckmüller; p. 65 Kunsthalle Würth, photo: Skadi Heckmüller; p. 67 Anselm Kiefer, Museum Würth, photo: Skadi Heckmüller; p. 69 Schloss Bönnigheim, southern side © Zander Collection, photo: Frank Kleinbach, Stuttgart; p. 71 Exterior view Museum Brandhorst, photo: Haydar Koyupinar © Museum Brandhorst; p. 72 Interior view "Rosensaal" by Cy Twombly, photo: Haydar Koyupinar, Bayerische Staatsgemäldesammlungen, Munich © Museum Brandhorst; p. 75 Buchheim Museum, photo: Skadi Heckmüller; p. 79 Walter De Maria, Blinky Palermo, DASMAXIMUM KunstGegenwart, photo: Skadi Heckmüller; p. 81 DASMAXIMUM KunstGegenwart, photo: Skadi Heckmüller; p. 83 Sammlung Goetz, architects: © Herzog & de Meuron, Basel, Courtesy Sammlung Goetz, Munich, photo: Franz Wimmer, Munich; S. 85 Sammlung Goetz, architects: © Herzog & de Meuron, Basel, Courtesy Sammlung Goetz, Munich, photo: Franz Wimmer, Munich; p. 87 Günther Förg © Metropol Kunstraum, photo: Johannes von Mallinckrodt; pp. 88/89 Günther Förg © Metropol Kunstraum, photo: Johannes von Mallinckrodt; p. 91 Alexander Tutsek-Stiftung, photo: Skadi Heckmüller; p. 93 Jonathan Meese, Thomas Westphal, Helge Leiberg, KUNSTMUSEUM WALTER, photo: Skadi Heckmüller; p. 95 The Walther Collection, photo: Skadi Heckmüller; p. 99 Thomas Schütte, Museum Berggruen, photo: Skadi Heckmüller; p. 101 Pablo Picasso, Museum Berggruen, photo: Skadi Heckmüller; p. 103 © Boros Collection; p. 105 Avery K. Singer, "Untitled", 2015 and "Topos", 2014 © Boros Collection; p. 107 Museum Frieder Burda / Salon Berlin, photo: Skadi Heckmüller; p. 109 Georg Baselitz, Flavio de Marco, Museum Frieder Burda / Salon Berlin, photo: Skadi Heckmüller; p. 111 Exhibition view "In Wonderland – A Birthday Exhibition for Timo Miettinen", 2015/16 © Salon Dahlman / Miettinen Collection, photo: Nick Ash; p. 113 Maurice Lemaître, Isidore Isou, EAM Collection, photo: Skadi Heckmüller; p. 115 Installation view of The Feuerle Collection, Khmer Deities from 10th to 13th century with Chinese Platform, Han Dynasty, China, 2nd century BC – 2nd century AD, photo: def image © The Feuerle Collection; p. 117 The Feuerle Collection, photo: def image © The Feuerle Collection; p. 119 Fluentum, photo: Skadi Heckmüller; p. 120 Guido van der Werve, Fluentum, photo: Skadi Heckmüller; p. 123 Nikolaus Eberstaller "HONEY – Home Made Money", Series Kraskόw I, 2011, offset print, 59,4 × 42 cm and "HONEY MONEY" (Bode-Edition), 2016, Giclée prints, 30 × 40 cm © Sammlung Haupt, photo: Sammlung Haupt/Hermann Büchner, Berlin; p. 125 Lawrence Weiner, "MILK AND HONEY TAKEN FAR FAR AWAY...", 1994/96; Teresa Murak, "Rasenskulptur", 1996, Courtesy Sammlung Hoffmann, Berlin; S. 127 Hermann Nitsch, "Das Orgien Mysterien Theater, 6-Tage-Spiel 3.–9.8.1998 Prinzdorf an der Zaya", 1998, DVD; "Kreuzwegstation", 1961, blood and dispersion paint on jute; "Aktionsrelikt (Aktionsmalerei) der 80. Aktion Prinzendorf 1984 (Großes 3 Tage-Spiel)", 1984, oil on paper on canvas; "Das O.M. Theater", 1973, velvet case with printed and overpainted papers and photographs; "das orgien mysterien theater I–IV", 1975, four books with b/w-photographs, collages, prints etc. in red slipcase, Courtesy Sammlung Hoffmann, Berlin, photo: studioschuurman; p. 129 Kienzle Art Foundation © Kienzle Art Foundation; p. 131 me Collectors Room Berlin / Olbricht Foundation, photo: Daisy Loewl; p. 133 Wunderkammer Olbricht © me Collectors Room Berlin / Olbricht Foundation, photo: Bernd Borchardt; p. 135 Dietrich Oltmanns, Collection Regard, photo: Skadi Heckmüller; p. 137 Sammlung Scharf-Gerstenberg, photo: Skadi Heckmüller; p. 139 Henri Laurens, Jean Dubuffet, Michel Nedjar, Gerhard Altenbourg, Sammlung Scharf-Gerstenberg, photo: Skadi Heckmüller; p. 141 Exterior view JULIA STOSCHEK COLLECTION, Berlin, photo: JULIA STOSCHEK COLLECTION; pp. 142/43 JULIA STOSCHEK COLLECTION, Berlin, photo: Robert Hamacher; p. 145 Courtesy Tchoban Foundation, © Photo: Martin Krebes; p. 147 Installation view "VISIONEN DER WELTARCHITEKTUR. ILLUSTRATIONEN ZU VORLESUNGEN VON SIR JOHN SOANE AN DER ROYAL ACADEMY OF ARTS", Courtesy Tchoban Foundation, © photo: Michaela Schöpke; p. 149 Wolfgang Mattheuer, Museum Barberini, photo: Skadi Heckmüller; pp. 152/153 Martin Kippenberger, Neo Rauch, Museum Barberini, photo: Skadi Heckmüller; p. 155 Simon English, Richard Artschwager, Ena Swansea, © Falckenberg Collection, photo: Egbert Haneke; p. 157 Santiago Sierra, Hellen Almeida, Craigie Horsfield, Gabriel Orozco, © Falckenberg Collection, photo: Egbert Haneke; p. 159 Ewert Hilgemann, Museum Modern Art, photo: Skadi Heckmüller; p. 161 KUNSTHAUS TAUNUSSTEIN, © photo: Christine Haas; p. 163 Thomas Demand, Schloss Kummerow, photo: Skadi Heckmüller; p. 165 Schloss Kummerow, photo: Skadi Heckmüller; p. 167 Till Richter Museum – Schloss Buggenhagen, photo: Skadi Heckmüller; p. 169 Sculpture Park Wesenberg & Künstler Bei Wu, photo: Skadi Heckmüller; p. 170 Shona Nunan, Sculpture Park Wesenberg & Künstler Bei Wu, photo: Skadi Heckmüller; p. 173 Hall Art Foundation / Schloss Derneburg Museum, Derneburg, photo: derneburg.de; p. 175 Installation view, Hermann Nitsch, Hall Art Foundation / Schloss Derneburg Museum, Derneburg, © Hall Art Foundation, photo: Heinrich Hecht; p. 177 Exterior view © Kunstmuseum Celle with Sammlung Robert Simon, photo: Peter Gauditz; p. 179 Lienhard von Monkiewitsch, Ben Willikens, Otto Piene, Hartmut Neumann, Douglas Swan © Kunstmuseum Celle with Sammlung Robert Simon, photo: Pauline Fabry; p. 181 Museum DKM, Jai Young Park "Der Ort der Bilder", 1995–2000, © Stiftung DKM; p. 183 © Draiflessen Collection, Mettingen, photo: Henning Rogge; p. 184 © Draiflessen Collection, Mettingen, photo: Draiflessen Collection; p. 187 Langen Foundation, photo: Skadi Heckmüller; p. 189 Richard Deacon, exhibition view, "On the Other Side", Langen Foundation, photo: Skadi Heckmüller; p. 191 Museum Insel Hombroich, Photo: Tomas Riehle © Stiftung Insel Hombroich; p. 195 Kunsträume der Michael Horbach Stiftung, photo: Skadi Heckmüller; p. 196 Beat Presser, Kunsträume der Michael Horbach Stiftung, photo: Skadi Heckmüller; p. 199 Alicja Kwade, KAT_A, photo: Skadi Heckmüller; p. 201 Katharina Grosse, KAT_A, photo: Skadi Heckmüller; p. 203 Interior view Sou Fujimoto, "Garden Gallery", 2011, Skulpturenpark Köln © Stiftung Skulpturenpark Köln, 2019, photo: Axel Schneider, Frankfurt a.M.; S. 205 Museum Wilhelm Morgner, Foundation Conceptual Art with SCHROTH COLLECTION, © photo: Gero Sliwa; S. 207 Frank Gerritz, Mike Meiré, Foundation Conceptual Art with SCHROTH COLLECTION; S. 209 MKM Museum Küppersmühle, silo platform on the extension building by Herzog & de Meuron (simulation) © Herzog & de Meuron; S. 211 MKM Museum Küppersmühle with the extension building by Herzog & de Meuron (simulation) © Herzog & de Meuron; p. 213 Tea Mäkipää (with Halldór Úlfarsson), Museum Schloss Moyland, photo: Skadi Heckmüller; p. 217 Philara Collection, photo: Skadi Heckmüller; p. 221 Exterior view, JULIA STOSCHEK COLLECTION Düsseldorf, © photo: Ulrich Schwarz, Berlin; p. 223 Installation view JULIA STOSCHEK COLLECTION Düsseldorf, Ed Atkins & Simon Thompson, "Sky News Live", 2016, Courtesy of the artists, photo: Simon Vogel, Cologne; p. 225 Tony Cragg, Skulpturenpark Waldfrieden, photo: Skadi Heckmüller; p. 226 Skulpturenpark Waldfrieden, photo: Skadi Heckmüller; p. 229 Gereon Krebber, Felix Droese, Kunstraum am Limes / Zeitgenössische Kunst, photo: Skadi Heckmüller; p. 231 Tomás Saraceno and Katrin Heichel © the artists & G2 Kunsthalle Leipzig; p. 232 Exterior view G2 Kunsthalle © G2 Kunsthalle Leipzig, Photo: G2 Kunsthalle Leipzig / Hildebrand Collection; p. 235 Kunstsammlungen Chemnitz – Museum Gunzenhauser, photo: PUNCTUM/Bertram Kober; p. 236 Willi Baumeister © VG Bild-Kunst, Bonn 2019, Emil Schumacher © VG Bild-Kunst, Bonn, 2019, Ernst Wilhelm Nay © VG Bild-Kunst, Bonn 2019, Kunstsammlungen Chemnitz – Museum Gunzenhauser, photo: Lásló Tóth;

p. 239 Gerisch Sculpture Park, photo: Skadi Heckmüller; p. 241 Magdalena Abakanowicz, Rupprecht Matthies, Gerisch Sculpture Park, photo: Skadi Heckmüller; p. 243 Museum Kunst der Westküste, photo: Skadi Heckmüller; p. 245 Rune Guneriussen, Peter Balke, Hans Fredrik Gude, Johannes Duntze, Georg Anton Rasmussen, Friedrich Thöming, Museum Kunst der Westküste, photo: Skadi Heckmüller; p. 249 Museum Liaunig, photo: Skadi Heckmüller; p. 251 Manfred Wakolbinger, Thomas Stimm, Herbert Albrecht © Museum Liaunig, Photo: Museum Liaunig; p. 253 Museum Angerlehner, photo: Skadi Heckmüller; p. 254 Xenia Hausner, Museum Angerlehner, photo: Skadi Heckmüller; p. 257 Kunst im Rohnerhaus, photo: Skadi Heckmüller; pp. 262/263 Museum Langmatt, photo: Skadi Heckmüller; p. 265 Kunstmuseum Appenzell, © Hans Arp, © photo: Urs Baumann, Gais; p. 267 Kunstmuseum Appenzell, photo: Skadi Heckmüller; p. 269 Kunsthalle Ziegelhütte, photo: Skadi Heckmüller; p. 271 Tony Cragg, Kloster Schönthal, photo: Skadi Heckmüller; p. 273 Nigel Hall, Kloster Schönthal, photo: Skadi Heckmüller; p. 275 Fondation Beyeler, photo: Mark Niedermann; p. 276 Fondation Beyeler, photo: Mark Niedermann; p. 279 Tadashi Kawamata, Kunst im Castell / Sammlung Ruedi Bechtler, photo: Skadi Heckmüller; p. 281 James Turrell, Kunst im Castell / Sammlung Ruedi Bechtler, photo: Skadi Heckmüller; p. 283 Alberto Giacometti Museum / Pensiun Aldier, photo: Skadi Heckmüller; p. 285 Alberto Giacometti, Alberto Giacometti Museum / Pensiun Aldier, photo: Skadi Heckmüller; p. 287 © Studio Stefano Graziani, Courtesy Muzeum Susch, Art Stations Foundation CH; p. 289 © Claudio Von Planta, Courtesy Muzeum Susch, Art Stations Foundation CH; p. 291 Museum Sammlung Rosengart Luzern, photo: Réne Limacher; p. 293 Museum Sammlung Rosengart Luzern; p. 295 Kunst(Zeug)Haus, photo: Skadi Heckmüller; p. 296 Anna Amadio, Kunst(Zeug)Haus, photo: Skadi Heckmüller; p. 299 Fondazione Marguerite Arp, photo: Roberto Pellegrini; p. 303 Fondazione Gabriele e Anna Braglia, photo: Skadi Heckmüller; p. 305 Manolo Valdés, Fernando Botero, Enrico Ghinato, Fondazione Gabriele e Anna Braglia, photo: Skadi Heckmüller; p. 307 Courtesy Fondazione Ghisla Art Collection, © Zoe Moro; p. 309 Günther Uecker, Shirley Jaffe, Fondazione Ghisla Art Collection, photo: Skadi Heckmüller; p. 311 Zoran Mušič, Fondazione Matasci per l'Arte, photo: Skadi Heckmüller; p. 313 Deposito Collezione Matasci, photo: Skadi Heckmüller; p. 315 Museo Castello San Materno – Fondazione per la cultura Kurt e Barbara Alten, photo: Skadi Heckmüller; p. 319 Rolla Foundation, photo: Skadi Heckmüller; p. 321 Spazio -1 / Collezione Giancarlo e Danna Olgiati, photo: Skadi Heckmüller; p. 323 Wade Guyton, Danh Võ, Tim Rollins & K.O.S., Giulio Paolini, Massimo Bartolini, Christo, Jimmie Durham, Not Vital, Spazio -1 / Collezione Giancarlo e Danna Olgiati, Photo: Skadi Heckmüller; pp. 325/326 Fondation Pierre Gianadda, photo: Skadi Heckmüller; p. 329 Sammlung Oskar Reinhart „Am Römerholz", photo: Skadi Heckmüller

Distribution
edel Germany GmbH
www.edel.com
international-books@edel.com

ISBN 978-3-95476-286-6
Printed in Europe

Published by
DISTANZ Verlag
www.distanz.de